Using History, Making British Policy

Also by Peter J. Beck

BRITISH DOCUMENTS ON FOREIGN AFFAIRS. Reports and Papers From the Foreign Office Confidential Prints: The League of Nations 1918–1941, vols 1–10

SCORING FOR BRITAIN: International Football and International Politics, 1900–1939

THE FALKLAND ISLANDS AS AN INTERNATIONAL PROBLEM

THE INTERNATIONAL POLITICS OF ANTARCTICA

Using History, Making British Policy

The Treasury and the Foreign Office, 1950–76

Peter J. Beck
Kingston University

palgrave
macmillan

© Peter J. Beck 2006

All rights reserved. No reproduction, copy or transmission of this publication may be made without written permission.

No paragraph of this publication may be reproduced, copied or transmitted save with written permission or in accordance with the provisions of the Copyright, Designs and Patents Act 1988, or under the terms of any licence permitting limited copying issued by the Copyright Licensing Agency, 90 Tottenham Court Road, London W1T 4LP.

Any person who does any unauthorised act in relation to this publication may be liable to criminal prosecution and civil claims for damages.

The author has asserted his right to be identified as the author of this work in accordance with the Copyright, Designs and Patents Act 1988.

First published 2006 by
PALGRAVE MACMILLAN
Houndmills, Basingstoke, Hampshire RG21 6XS and
175 Fifth Avenue, New York, N.Y. 10010
Companies and representatives throughout the world

PALGRAVE MACMILLAN is the global academic imprint of the Palgrave Macmillan division of St. Martin's Press, LLC and of Palgrave Macmillan Ltd. Macmillan® is a registered trademark in the United States, United Kingdom and other countries. Palgrave is a registered trademark in the European Union and other countries.

ISBN-13: 978–1–4039–4706–2 hardback
ISBN-10: 1–4039–4706–6 hardback

This book is printed on paper suitable for recycling and made from fully managed and sustained forest sources.

A catalogue record for this book is available from the British Library.

Library of Congress Cataloging-in-Publication Data
Beck, Peter (Peter J.)
 Using history, making British policy : the Treasury and the Foreign Office, 1950–76 / by Peter J. Beck.
  p. cm.
 ISBN 1–4039–4706–6
 1. Great Britain—Politics and government—1945– 2. Great Britain Treasury—History—20th century. 3. Great Britain—Economic policy—1945–1964. 4. Great Britain—Economic policy—1964–1979. 5. Great Britain. Foreign and Commonwealth Office—History—20th century. 6. Great Britain—Foreign relations—1945– 7. History—Philosophy. I. Title.
 DA589.7.B433 2006
 327.41009′045—dc22   2006042324

10 9 8 7 6 5 4 3 2 1
15 14 13 12 11 10 09 08 07 06

Printed and bound in Great Britain by
Antony Rowe Ltd, Chippenham and Eastbourne

Contents

List of Tables and Boxes	vii
Preface	viii
Acknowledgements	x
List of Abbreviations	xi

Part I	**Introduction: Using History in Britain**	**1**
1	British Policymakers and History	3
2	Using Official Histories and Public Records to Present Britain's Past to a Global Audience	22
Part II	**Using History in the Treasury**	**51**
3	The Treasury Becomes 'Very Historically Minded', 1957–60	53
4	Pushing Ahead with "Funding Experience", 1960–62	72
5	The Public Enterprises Division (PE) as a Case Study, 1962–65	92
6	The 'New Stage' in the Treasury's Historical Work, 1965–68	118
7	Retuning the Treasury's Historical Activities after Fulton, 1968–70	143
8	Moving Towards the Closure of the Treasury Historical Section, 1971–76	161
9	Using History in the Treasury	170
Part III	**Using History in the Foreign Office**	**191**
10	The Foreign Office's 1962 Abadan History	193
11	Using Butler's Abadan History to Reappraise British Foreign Policy	211
12	Using History in the Foreign Office	229

Part IV Conclusion   239

13 Making British Policy, Using and Ignoring History   241

Appendix: Treasury Historical Memoranda   252
Notes   253
Select Bibliography   292
Index   301

List of Tables and Boxes

Tables

6.1	The Treasury's historians in the mid-1960s	123
6.2	Managing history in the Treasury, 1965–70	124
6.3	Treasury histories awaiting divisional clearance, February 1968	129
7.1	History, policy and prescription charges	147

Boxes

1.1	John Tosh's rationale for studying history	6
9.1	The Treasury's "funding experience" outputs	171
9.2	Policymaking stages studied by Treasury histories	175
10.1	The lessons of Butler's history	203

Preface

This book draws upon my longstanding research interest in history and government dating back to the late 1970s when I began studying Anglo-Argentine relations. This particular project began when I came across a file on Rohan Butler's 1962 Abadan history while working upon another topic. As my first-ever publication, an article in the *Journal of Contemporary History* (1974), centred upon an earlier Anglo-Iranian dispute, I read on. In 2004 research on Butler's history provided the subject matter for my keynote lecture delivered to BISA's British International History Group conference. Subsequently, this lecture was developed into an article for publication in the *Historical Journal* (2006). While preparing the lecture, I consulted Treasury files by way of providing a footnote on the broader context. However, it soon became clear that the Treasury's historical activities warranted far more than a mere footnote. The resulting project has been supported by the Arts and Humanities Research Council's Study Leave scheme and the History Research Group at Kingston University.

Apart from enhancing our knowledge and understanding about the role of history in the British policymaking process, this monograph offers informed insights regarding the nature and purpose of history, with particular reference to longstanding debates about our ability to learn from history. Reportedly, Samuel Taylor Coleridge asserted that 'If men could learn from history, what lessons it might teach us! But passion and party blind our eyes, and the light which experience gives us is a lantern on the stern, which shines only on the waves behind us!'. This book illuminates one British attempt to direct the light on the bow.

Invaluable oral and written testimony was provided by former Treasury officials: James Collier, Sir David Hancock, Guy Hartcup and Sir Douglas Wass. Treasury staff enabled access to files closed under the 30-Year Rule. My research has benefited from the assistance and constructive advice of Gillian Bennett, John Dickie, Sally Falk, Christopher Hill, Wm. Roger Louis, Steve Marsh, Zara Steiner, D.J. Thorpe and Chris Wrigley. George Peden and Michael Lee deserve special praise for providing speedy informed commentaries on the whole manuscript. Likewise, the library staff at Kingston University, most notably Lyn Porteous and the interloans staff, proved extremely helpful. As ever, my family provided a supportive home environment.

Peter J. Beck
Kingston University

Acknowledgements

I am grateful to the following for permission to quote from private papers: Lady Avon (Lord Avon); Rory J. Brocklebank (Sir W.K. Hancock); Churchill Archives Centre (Lord Strang); Rt. Hon. Charles Clarke (Sir Richard Clarke); A.J. Collier (A.J. Collier); Sir David Hancock (Sir David Hancock); LSE Archives (Hugh Dalton); the Museum of the History of Science, Oxford (Margaret Gowing); and Professor Ann Oakley on behalf of Richard Titmuss's literary estate. The photographs on the book cover are used by permission of the BP Archive, University of Warwick. British government records are Crown copyright. Every effort has been made to contact copyright-holders. If any copyright has been inadvertently infringed, the author will acknowledge copyright in any future publication. Material used in Chapters 10–12 is based in part upon an article, entitled 'The lessons of Abadan and Suez for British foreign policymakers in the 1960s', scheduled to appear in June 2006 in the *Historical Journal*, vol. 49(2), published by the Cambridge University Press.

List of Abbreviations

ACPR	Advisory Council on Public Records
AIOC	Anglo-Iranian Oil Company
BEA	British European Airways
BOAC	British Overseas Airways Corporation
BP	British Petroleum Co. Ltd.
CIA	Central Intelligence Agency
CSD	Civil Service Department
DBFP	*Documents on British Foreign Policy*
DEA	Department of Economic Affairs
EEC	European Economic Community
FCO	Foreign and Commonwealth Office
MAFF	Ministry of Agriculture, Fisheries and Food
MHLG	Ministry of Housing and Local Government
MI6	British Military Intelligence Section 6
MP	Member of British Parliament
MPNI	Ministry of Pensions and National Insurance
NRDC	National Research and Development Council
PRO	Public Record Office (now The National Archives)
PUS	Permanent Under Secretary of State
SSRC	Social Science Research Council (now the ESRC)
TCSDHC	Treasury and Civil Service Department Historical Committee
THC	Treasury Historical Committee
THM	Treasury Historical Memoranda
THS	Treasury Historical Section
TNA	The National Archives, Kew
UKAEA	United Kingdom Atomic Energy Authority

Treasury divisions

AT	Agriculture, Towns and Transport
DM	Defence Policy and Materiel
FC2	Finance-Coordination
F(EC)	Finance (Exchange Control)
GE	General Expenditure
HF	Home Finance

xii List of Abbreviations

HOPS	Home and Overseas Planning Staff
IF	Imperial and Foreign
NRI & NRII	National Resources I and II
OC	Overseas Coordination
OF	Overseas Finance
PE	Public Enterprises
SS	Social Services

Part I

Introduction: Using History in Britain

1
British Policymakers and History

Reporting Margaret Gowing's 1978 Rede Lecture for *The Times*, Peter Hennessy headlined her strong attack upon British policymakers for 'neglecting history'.[1] Despite reflecting primarily upon her role as the official historian of atomic energy in Britain, Gowing, Professor in the History of Science at the University of Oxford, used her prestigious Cambridge lecture to complain about history's marginal role in the British policymaking process.

> But why, if the status and usefulness of historical knowledge *are* high, is there so little of it in central and local government? Since the machinery of government is reorganised so often and ministers, civil servants and policies are so ephemeral, surely a collective memory is required? Surely government needs to understand the complex roots of policies and problems? Surely analysis of past experience should be fed back into the system? ... who can do this except historians?[2]

Gowing's critique raised serious questions about public policy in Britain, with particular reference to history's contribution, if any, to the formulation and conduct of government policy.[3] Asserting that 'historians are just as necessary as economists to government', was Gowing right to complain that 'no one listens to them'? Was history largely irrelevant to policymakers dealing with everyday issues? How far was history, particularly the so-called "lessons of history", treated as an actual policy input by ministers and officials responsible for making and carrying out public policy? Or were historical analogies used merely for rhetorical effect? Did policymakers merely learn from the mistakes of the past how to make new ones in the present? Were those failing to remember the past condemned to repeat it? Or was misremembering the past as dangerous as ignoring the historical dimension? Was past experience, as recorded by history, difficult, if not impossible, to integrate into the policymaking process?

Within this context, this book seeks to illuminate these issues by investigating the way in which British policymakers viewed and used history as a tool for making and conducting policy. The focus will be placed upon the period between 1957 and 1976 when Whitehall offers invaluable case studies enhancing our knowledge and understanding of the use, or more frequently the non-use, of history by administrators and policymakers.

Academia and public policy

Inevitably, debates about the use of history by governments for some current purpose focus attention upon the perceived gap existing between the two worlds of academia and public policy. Pressing the case for the history profession to move on from merely addressing its own members, Jeremy Black presented a cogent rationale for bridging this gulf:

> My starting point is the view that there are essentially two types of history – history as questions and history as answers – and that many academics tend to focus on the former and underplay the role of the latter, despite the fact that it is particularly important to the public use of history. Instead, I wish to emphasize that history is important for the uses to which it is put outside the academy as well as in it.[4]

History's contemporary media visibility – this has been highlighted by the popularity of television histories featuring Niall Ferguson, Simon Schama and David Starkey, among others – has reinvigorated longstanding debates about the extent to which historians can, or should, provide 'a usable past' reaching out to an audience outside academia.[5] Certainly, recent conferences have ranged beyond the usual scholarly topics to cover 'History and the media' (December 2002), 'What can historians contribute to public debate?' (November 2003), 'International public history: people and their pasts' (September 2005), 'The influence of history in public life' (October 2005) and 'History and the public' (February 2006). Postgraduate degrees have been launched in 'Public History', such as by Ruskin College, Oxford.

A research centre on the public understanding of the past is being created at the University of York. A 'History and Policy' website is edited by members of Cambridge's history faculty in collaboration with the University of London's Centres for Contemporary British History and History in Public Health. Regretting that 'contemporary policy debate has too often displayed little or no genuine historical knowledge and, at best, a radically foreshortened historical perspective', the 'History and Policy' project seeks to encourage policymakers and advisers to treat historical knowledge, perspectives and interpretations with a new respect when formulating and applying policy.[6]

The usable past

In this manner, historians, standing as they do at the crossroads between the university and the wider world, are beginning to re-engage with the public by way of using history to provide a collective memory, set contemporary matters in historical perspective, and draw out the lessons of history.[7] Whether or not this role can be undertaken without losing scholarly integrity remains questionable. Indeed, there exists a strong undercurrent of inertia, even resistance, encouraging historians to ignore the dread mantle of relevance and – to quote the late Geoffrey Elton – 'set their faces against the necessarily ignorant demands of "society"... for immediate applicability'.[8] Dead and gone, "the past" should be viewed, it is argued, as fundamentally different from "the present". From this viewpoint, the otherness of the past, alongside the uniqueness of events and the ever-changing historical context, qualifies the prospects of providing policymakers with the answers demanded by Black.

By contrast, others adopt a more functional approach by championing the concept of a 'usable past' linking, even subordinating, historical writing to present-day objectives.[9] Significantly, three categories in Tosh's fourfold rationale for studying history (Box 1.1) – his use of the word 'rationale', implying use, is equally revealing – treat history very much as a means to an end.[10] Of course, "functional histories" raise serious questions about how far the purpose affects both methodology and the nature of the outcomes, even prompting debate about the extent to which the final product merits the descriptor of "history". In particular, "use" is often interpreted as really meaning "abuse" in terms of resulting in accounts more reminiscent of propaganda than sound historical scholarship.[11]

6 *Introduction: Using History in Britain*

Box 1.1   John Tosh's rationale for studying history

(a) to discover what happened in the past;
(b) to identify the patterns of historical development;
(c) to serve some current purpose;
(d) to draw insights and lessons from the historical record.

Paradoxically, "functional history", though invariably dismissed as academically suspect, has a much longer history than the allegedly purist variant ushered in by von Ranke over a century ago. As Donald Cameron Watt reminded us, 'The role of history was traditionally to justify the rulers and to glorify the heroes and the politically victorious.'[12] Just as Thucydides' *History of the Peloponnesian War* pushed a range of political messages explaining Athens' defeat, so Machiavelli's *The Prince* (1513) drew upon history to provide a practical manual of statecraft, even presenting historical knowledge as one way of gaining and retaining power:

> As for mental exercise, a ruler should read historical works, especially for the light they shed on the actions of eminent men: to find out how they waged war, to discover the reasons for their victories and defeats, in order to avoid reverses and achieve conquests; and above all, to imitate some eminent man, who himself set out to imitate some predecessor of his who was considered worthy of praise and glory, always taking his deeds and actions as a model for himself.[13]

Furthermore, the fact that "history" is produced by historians means that – to quote Lamont – 'we should look to it for contributions to debate rather than for the transmission of certainties'.[14] Notwithstanding the predictability and objectivity implied by the descriptor "lessons of history" or the claims of those stressing history's links with the social sciences, the insights offered by historical scholarship lack the scientific precision required to provide "answers" in the form of either firm predictions or unequivocal generalizations. Just as historians present different, even conflicting, versions of the past so they provide varying, often contrasting, answers to most questions. Indeed, there exists a kind of double jeopardy, given the way in which the subjective nature of any history, even a comprehensive account based upon sound historical methodology, is compounded by the fact that any lessons are rarely obvious, and prove largely a matter for conjecture upon the part of the history's readers.[15] Postmodernist uncertainties have merely complicated the problem.

Using history to understand today's society

At some stage or another, most historians have addressed questions surrounding history's role in society, or at least been forced to take a position thereupon.[16] For example, lecturing in 1984 at the University of California, Davis, about 'What can history tell us about contemporary society?', Eric Hobsbawm presented historians as uniquely qualified to provide society with an informed and accurate historical perspective on today's world, and particularly a critical explanation of the nature and origins of present-day policies. For Hobsbawm, historians possessed responsibility for society's 'memory bank of experience', and hence for guiding a world in which people constantly interpret their past experience in time perspective: 'We cannot help learning from it, for that is what *experience* means'.[17] A related task is that of protecting society from the damaging effects of mythologies and propaganda masquerading as "history".[18]

Of course, Hobsbawm's Marxist credentials mean that some will question his personal take upon the past. For William Palmer, Hobsbawm is one of the 'greatest of the English synthesizers' facilitating an informed understanding about the contemporary world.[19] By contrast, Andrew Roberts advised 'anyone wishing to remind themselves of the sort of rot so many lefties were spouting' for much of the twentieth century to read Hobsbawm's histories.[20] Notwithstanding such controversies, Hobsbawm provides a good example of the way in which historical reference points frame any historian's reflections upon the contemporary world. Thus, in 2004, when reviewing recent events in Afghanistan and Iraq in the broader historical context, he concluded that there seemed 'scant chance of success' of reinforcing world order by spreading democracy to those countries: 'The campaign to spread democracy will not succeed. The 20th century demonstrated that states could not simply remake the world or abbreviate historical transformations.'[21]

From Munich to Suez and beyond

At the same time, as Hobsbawm has warned elsewhere, learning from history is risky: 'We may learn the wrong things – and plainly we often do.'[22] Looking back from 1984, Hobsbawm illustrated this risk to his audience at Davis by observing how 'most politicians in the past forty years read the international danger of war in terms of the 1930s – a replay of Hitler, Munich and the rest'.[23] Appeasement, such as practised by Neville Chamberlain at the 1938 Munich Conference, was presented as having failed to prevent war. Even worse, it was criticized for bringing war nearer. Learning from Munich stressed the need henceforth to be strong in order to negotiate from strength as well as to be capable of resisting, not appeasing, an aggressor, who might be another Hitler with unlimited ambitions and immune to rational negotiation.[24]

Perhaps the most vivid and controversial use of the Munich analogy in Britain occurred in 1956, when Egypt's nationalization of the Suez Canal Company led Anthony Eden (prime minister, 1955–57) to interpret President Nasser as another dangerous unappeasable dictator in the Hitler/Mussolini mould. Certainly, Eden was a great believer in the value of drawing upon past experience; indeed, in many respects the 1956 Suez Affair, though having an unwelcome outcome as far as he was concerned, merely strengthened his belief about the dangers of ignoring the past.[25] Looking back in 1961 on what he saw as the misguided approach adopted by the American government in 1956, Eden – he was soon to become Lord Avon – opined that 'the only rule of history is that mankind never learns'.[26] During the late 1950s and after, his publications, correspondence and speeches recorded his undiminished faith in the utility of learning from history; thus, speaking as 'an elder statesman' at Boston in April 1965, he referred to the mistakes of the 1930s when asserting that 'the past is only useful if we will learn from those mistakes and not commit them again'.[27]

Revealingly, Eden, who had resigned as Chamberlain's Foreign Secretary in February 1938, deliberately chose 'Full Circle' as the title for the first volume of his memoirs (1960) to stress the present-day relevance and use of the past: 'The lessons of the 'thirties and their application to the 'fifties... are the themes of my memoirs.'[28]

> It is important to reduce the stature of the megalomaniacal dictator at an early stage.... Some say that Nasser is no Hitler or Mussolini... I am not so sure. He has followed Hitler's pattern... Egypt's strategic position increases the threat to others from any aggressive militant dictatorship there.[29]

During the late 1930s, appeasement led to world war: 'As my colleagues and I surveyed the scene in these autumn months of 1956, we were determined that the like should not come again.'[30] Furthermore, a paper-thin temperament made Eden determined to respond forcefully to backbench critics in his own party, who had depicted him when Foreign Secretary (1951–55) as an appeaser for negotiating the Suez Canal Base Agreement (19 October 1954) providing for eventual British withdrawal from the Canal Zone.[31] Reportedly, even Winston Churchill, the prime minister (1951–55), 'was in a rage against A.E. [Eden], speaking of "appeasement" and saying he never knew before that Munich was situated on the Nile'.[32]

In the event, in 1956 British military intervention, albeit undertaken with France, failed to achieve the projected objectives. The Suez Canal Company remained nationalized, Nasser remained in power, the Anglo-American relationship reached a nadir, French irritation did little to help subsequent British efforts to enter the Common Market, and Eden was forced to resign. Moreover, the resulting crisis, presented frequently as a seminal moment in Britain's history, proved – to quote Kipling's phrase used by Anthony Nutting to title the memoir justifying his resignation as Eden's Minister of State at the Foreign Office – 'no end of a lesson'.[33] For John Young, the episode revealed further evidence of 'Britain's lack of economic strength and reliance on the US': 'What Suez did show was Britain's inability to wield large-scale military power, even in cooperation with its ally of 1914 and 1939, France.'[34] Perhaps, it is easy to overstate Suez's impact – for David Carlton, its impact was more symbolic than seminal – and to draw too many lessons from one event, but it is difficult to deny the way in which the episode's perceived lessons fuelled declinist narratives and dominated discussions about Britain's current and future role in the world.[35] Moreover, Suez's omnipresent place in contemporary political vocabulary, frequently complementing the use of Munich, reflects the fact that for many the episode remains still a sensitive issue. As Peter Hennessy conceded several decades afterwards, 'I still suffer emotional spasms (disturbingly conflicting ones) when the word "Suez" is mentioned.'[36]

The 1982 Falklands War provided yet another example of the appeasement analogy at work in Britain. Margaret Thatcher (prime minister, 1979–90), whose uncompromising stance towards the Soviet Union had earned her the sobriquet of the 'iron lady', viewed the Argentine invasion of the Falkland Islands, at least in part, through the lens of Munich. Subsequently, she confessed to being impressed by 'a wonderful letter from Laurens van der Post, who pointed out that there was one principle, more important even than sovereignty, at stake in the dispute: "To appease aggression and evil is to connive at greater aggression and evil later on"... Of course, he was entirely right.'[37] Likewise, an official government publication, entitled *The Falkland Islands. The Facts* (1982), made a strong appeal to the past when reassuring those in search of guidance: 'History provides many examples where the international community's failure to take action on such acts by aggressive powers led to much graver crises later.'[38]

Nor has the Munich analogy lost its political power, as evidenced by the way in which it figures regularly still in the *public rhetoric* of British politicians and opinion-makers justifying strong action against a perceived contemporary threat. Speaking at Chicago in 1999, Tony Blair (prime minister, 1997–) warned against appeasing Slobodan Milosevic, the Serb leader, over Kosovo: 'We cannot let the evil of ethnic cleansing stand . . . We have learned twice before in this century that appeasement does not work. If we let an evil dictator range unchallenged, we will have to spill infinitely more blood and treasure to stop him later.'[39] Two years later, this theme was developed by Jack Straw, the Foreign Secretary (2001–), when addressing Parliament after the 9/11 terrorist attack on the USA:

> In considering the approach we now take, we would do well this week to draw lessons from the experience of the 1930s. Our predecessors then were so desperate to avoid further military action that they made a huge, if understandable, mistake. . . . It was not until too late that our predecessors realised that the aggressors . . . did not accept the norms and decencies that the rest of us took for granted. We all know the consequences of what followed.[40]

Speaking at the Labour Party Conference a few weeks later, Straw reminded delegates about the lessons of history:

> In our history we have been here before. In the 30s, there were those, from both main parties, who argued that war in any circumstances was to be avoided. But theirs was a fundamental mistake. For they believed that the fascists could be reasoned with – that they were subject to the same standards of human decency as the rest of us. They were not. . . . In the same way today, if we believe that those who planned, organised and perpetrated the attacks in New York, Washington and Pittsburgh can be dealt with by negotiation and reason, we wholly delude ourselves.[41]

Inevitably, descriptors based upon events during the late 1930s helped frame the bitter controversies surrounding the 2003 Iraq War in a manner demonstrating the continued ability of "appeasement" and "Munich" to polarize contemporary debate as well as to cloud rational argument with highly charged emotions. For example, the late Robin Cook, who resigned as Leader of the House of Commons in March 2003 in protest at British policy, complained in his diary about the way in which 'several papers tag me as "an appeaser"'.[42] The quotation marks reaffirmed the historical reference. The episode established also the enduring force of the Suez analogue. Believing that 'Tony ought to worry about parallels with Suez', Cook frequently warned Blair about the political risks of undertaking military action upon an allegedly flimsy pretext *à la* 1956; thus, following one informal exchange in September 2002, Cook parted company with Blair by saying, 'All I ask is that every morning you remember what happened to Anthony Eden.'[43]

British policymakers and history

As indicated by this chapter's opening paragraph, Margaret Gowing (1921–98) was to the fore among historians in taking a close and enduring interest in debates about history's relevance and value to public policy in a fast-moving world. Her career, spanning both academia and government, enabled her to speak with authority on the theory and practice of the history–policy linkage.[44] Nor was she content merely to use lectures for articulating the value of history in supporting the everyday work of government. Soon after delivering the 1978 Rede lecture, she reminded Sir Douglas Wass, the Permanent Secretary at the Treasury, of her key point: 'As my Rede lecture at Cambridge this year emphasised, I believe that the Government's attitude to history is important.'[45] In fact, the Treasury had received already extracts covering the key themes developed in a lecture whose public visibility and impact was enhanced through Hennessy's report for *The Times*.[46]

Following graduation from the London School of Economics in 1941 with a first in Economic History, Gowing worked as an assistant principal in the civil service (1941–45), based in the Ministry of Supply and the Board of Trade, before joining the Cabinet Office's Historical Section in 1945. Here she worked for over a decade on the Second World War civil histories supporting the editorial responsibilities of Professor W. Keith Hancock and jointly authoring two volumes. For a historian like Gowing, working on the official histories provided an incomparable opportunity for studying at first hand, from the inside, the government machine in operation at every level up to and including the Cabinet as well as for securing oral testimony from a wide range of policymakers.[47]

Subsequently, the scaling down of the official histories' project during the mid-1950s led to Gowing's secondment to the Treasury, where her pioneering historical work in support of its everyday activities provided the foundation for what became the Treasury Historical Section (THS). More importantly, in December 1957 this historical experiment inspired Sir Norman Brook, the Cabinet Secretary (1947–62) and Joint Permanent Secretary of the Treasury and Head of the Civil Service (1956–62), to launch a policy initiative exhorting all Whitehall departments to follow the Treasury's lead in using history more systematically in their everyday work. In-depth case studies illustrating the proposal's implementation, and non-implementation, form the central subject matter of this book.

In 1959 Gowing became archivist/historian at the United Kingdom Atomic Energy Authority (UKAEA), where she wrote Britain's official nuclear history, 'a serious historical work written for publication and aimed primarily at the intelligent layman'.[48] For many readers, her meticulously researched volumes covering the making and execution of British nuclear policy showed that official histories were capable of combining high academic standards with readability.[49] Like her internal Treasury histories, the published atomic energy histories went beyond providing a mere narrative to draw out the key lessons from past experience: the serious problems posed by the sheer magnitude of the task, the government's obsession with secrecy, the lack of any coherent body of strategic thinking, and the problematic Anglo-American relationship on atomic energy matters. Furthermore, as indicated in the next chapter, the UKAEA project proved influential in encouraging the British government to commission official histories covering the post-1945 peacetime period.

Gowing's role as the UKAEA's historian-cum-archivist both reflected and reinforced her longstanding interest in the whole question of public records, particularly their contribution to effective administration and good history. Service on two major official enquiries on public records (the Grigg Committee, 1952–54; the Wilson Committee, 1978–81) was complemented by membership of the Lord Chancellor's Advisory Council on Public Records (1974–82). In 1969 she even applied for the post of Keeper of Public Records. By this time, however, Gowing, though remaining the UKAEA's official historian (1959–93), had moved into academia to become Reader in Contemporary History at the University of Kent (1966–72) before taking up the newly created chair in the history of science at the University of Oxford (1973–86), where she was instrumental in establishing the Contemporary Scientific Archives Centre.

As a result, when using the Rede lecture to criticize the repeated failure of British governments to use history in the formulation and conduct of policy, Gowing, though describing herself as 'a concerned outsider', was able to draw upon extensive practical experience of both academia and government.[50] Indeed, she exploited her official contacts to elicit the statistical data used to reinforce her message. Regretting the apparent 'lack of historical depth in administration' – for her, the THS's recent closure in 1976 merely strengthened the argument – Gowing described British policymakers as 'impervious to the usefulness of history': 'historical knowledge, it seems, is not a necessity, but a luxury. It is not a living thing to them, an approach to be included in the assessment of a problem. The day before yesterday is dead indeed.'[51] Central government, she complained, employed nearly 18,000 scientists and engineers and some 900 social scientists, but only 'a mere handful of historians'. Nor was history included in courses run by the Civil Service College. Likewise, government expenditure on scientific and social scientific research totalling *circa* £1200m and £21m respectively contrasted with less than an estimated one million pounds on historical research. Drawing unfavourable comparisons with the flourishing state of history in both the universities and the world of publishing as well as with the USA, Gowing pressed the subject's utility and cheapness: 'History should be an essential part of government.'[52]

Significantly, Gowing had discussed the draft text of her Rede lecture with both academics, like Hugh Trevor-Roper, and government officials, most notably Sir Ian Bancroft, a former Treasury colleague and now Head of the Home Civil Service (1978–81).[53] For Bancroft, her critique seemed 'less than fair':

> Civil servants in my experience are meticulous recorders, use and draw great benefit from the records of their predecessors, and in policy formulation are most conscientious in looking back before they look forward. Indeed, as *you* know, it is a standard criticism of civil servants that they are 'hidebound by precedent'.[54]

Gowing welcomed his response, but stood her ground:

> There is surely a great difference between a regard for precedents and careful historical analysis of policy or administration. I feel real temerity in disagreeing with you on how the civil service works. However I did not make the remarks in my lecture lightly. In my 33 years as an official historian, working on thousands of recent files

in many government departments (plus a few years as an assistant principal), I have found that the recording even of high policy has often been inadequate and that when the record exists, subsequent policy formation has often taken no account of it or has misunderstood it. This is partly because of frequent staff changes or because crisis action is required. Many civil servants, as well as other official historians, have agreed with me. Indeed, 20 years ago, this belief prompted Norman Brook's historical initiative, which I mentioned in my lecture.[55]

Nor did things improve during the next five years or so, as highlighted in May 1983, when Gowing reiterated her misgivings in evidence given to the House of Commons Education, Science and Arts Committee's enquiry on public records. For Gowing, public records were essential for sound and efficient government administration: 'they are the collective memory of the government and are essential for policy evaluation and to avoid "reinvention of the wheel" at frequent intervals'.[56] Reportedly, she complained, only a very limited amount of reference to past records was undertaken by government departments for current administrative purposes.

Professor Gowing: I think it is unfortunate that the British public service has been so unhistorically minded and has done very little evaluation of past policies, dropped policies and so on.... I think that the 're-invention of the wheel' point which I referred to in my memorandum is very important; a subject, such as wages policy is brought in, is dropped, and then somebody suddenly says, 'Why don't we have a wages policy?' – and everybody starts from scratch thinking how we should do it without thinking of going back over the enormous amount of information which exists on the question.
Chairman, Christopher Price: So it has been your experience while you have had contact with Government that Governments in the past have not used public records for policy formation?
Professor Gowing: Very little.[57]

Even so, as Gowing realized, it was one thing to espouse the theoretical benefits of Treasury histories. It was an entirely different matter to ensure their incorporation into the government machine. In this vein, Gowing liked to look back to the late 1950s to recall her experience of acting as the Treasury's history 'guinea pig' responsible for using departmental records for 'the writing of historical studies not for publication but as aids to administration'.[58] Indeed, she preferred to describe these studies as 'policy evaluations', not straight history, by way of emphasizing their functional character codifying and evaluating past experience in an accessible user-friendly format for current administrative purposes.

What can history offer policymakers?

Of course, there remained still the fundamental problem of ensuring that policymakers actually read, let alone used, relevant histories when formulating and conducting policy. Preoccupied with today's world and the immediate future, ministers and officials have always found it difficult to draw history into the policymaking process.

The resulting gulf between using history in theory and practice has proved an enduring focus for study, most notably across the Atlantic by Ernest May and Richard Neustadt. Drawing upon their experience of teaching policymakers at Harvard's Kennedy School of Government 'about how to *use* experience, whether remote or recent, in the process of deciding what to do today about the prospect for tomorrow', they pointed to the key problem: 'They're too busy. Can't read what they get now. They'll glance at papers in the limousine, thumb them while someone is talking, or just wing it. If you do get their attention, you can't keep it. They will have to catch a plane or go to a press conference.'[59]

In any case, policymakers rarely know exactly what they expect of history. Clearly, the last thing required in a crisis situation is a lengthy history, however well researched and authoritative, as reaffirmed by Lord Strang, the Permanent Under Secretary of State (PUS) at the Foreign Office between 1949 and 1953:

> Decisions on foreign policy have often to be taken at short notice on incomplete information and with not much time for thought. Ministers are very busy and harassed men. They cannot – or most of them cannot – bear to read long and elaborate disquisitions. Their orders to their advisers are almost invariably: 'Do please try to keep it short.'[60]

Nor, given their penchant for drawing analogies between past and present, do policymakers want to be told that such a practice is fundamentally unhistorical. What they really want is to be given an appropriate historical quote or example to employ for rhetorical effect in a forthcoming speech, a brief response to a query about some past event, or to have complex matters concerning, say, background, context or analogues, simply and clearly explained, but – to quote Zara Steiner – 'without the qualifications that are almost the hallmark of our profession'.[61] Analogies, enabling the current situation to be presented straightforwardly in shorthand form as like some previous occasion, have proved attractive for this very reason. But, like statistics, analogies can be, and often are, used and abused. Just as what seems an appropriate precedent may be squeezed to fit the situation in order to put a familiar face on something uncertain, even strange, so the 'bothersome analogues' might be conveniently dodged.[62] Nor might account be taken of the fact that current circumstances were no longer conducive to an analogy's application.

Within this context, the historian's task is to encourage, hopefully to educate and train, policymakers not only to use history but also to use it better, such as in terms of applying historical analogies in a manner designed to assist, not mislead, them. Detached from day-to-day official responsibilities, historians are also well equipped, it is argued, to challenge traditional mindsets by prompting thinking about alternative ways forward within and outside the box, most notably thinking the unthinkable.[63] Moreover, they can teach policymakers to place actors and complex events in the continuum of time, since 'an understanding of the past helps with the placing of the present situation and casts light on probable outcomes'.[64] For John Lewis Gaddis, policymakers can only benefit from the way in which history enables them to look backwards when confronted by a challenging present and an uncertain future.

> History can serve something of the function a rear-view mirror does in an automobile. One would not want to drive down the road with eyes glued to the mirror because sooner or later one would wind up in the ditch. But the mirror is useful in determining where one has been; it is even more helpful in revealing who, or what, is coming up from behind, a consideration of some importance in what is still a competitive international environment.[65]

In a fast-moving, uncertain and often dangerous world, Gaddis's 'rear-view mirror' example epitomizes history's ability to expand in a systematic and informed manner the immediate experience of policymakers by making them aware of long-term patterns, like the ever-changing power balance, the risks of over-commitment, or the intimate correlation between power and economic performance. It recalls also an assertion attributed to Mark Twain to the effect that 'History doesn't repeat itself; at best it rhymes'.

The research focus

Generally speaking, public policy in Britain has been characterized as having a somewhat erratic, often detached, relationship with professional expertise, most notably that offered by historians. For Jose Harris, this resulted in part from the 'extreme haphazardness and uncertainty' of policymakers' access to expert advice and information alongside the persistence of traditional currents of thought and ways of doing things during a period of rapidly expanding state activity.[66] Whitehall's historian, Peter Hennessy, highlighted the relatively unsystematic, even amateur, nature of staff development and training for policymakers in post-1945 Britain:

> But self-confident and experienced and sometimes highly decorated though they were, the postwar Whitehall intake had much to learn quickly as Mr Attlee's engine-room pushed forward the boundaries of state activity. They learned on the job. The Civil Service College was some twenty-five years away and its precursor, the Centre for Administrative Studies, nearly twenty. The learning process was Whitehall's equivalent of the school of hard knocks, as the lessons of politics, internal and external, were brought home to the young men.[67]

As detailed in the next chapter, in 1957 Brook, when Cabinet Secretary and Head of the Civil Service, presented "funding experience" through history as one way of improving the machinery of government, and hence in effect short-circuiting reliance on 'the school of hard knocks' and learning 'on the job'. Histories funding *recent experience* came to be seen as possessing a clear relevance to public policy, as recognized by Jean Nunn of the Cabinet Office: 'we ought to be learning from our experience and to be using this experience for the training of the new generation of civil servants and the sociologists and others working in related fields outside'.[68]

Focusing upon Brook's 1957 policy initiative, this book investigates the resulting use, and non-use, of history by administrators and policymakers. Themes illuminated include:

- the value and limitations of historical awareness and knowledge, most notably the so-called lessons of history, as a tool when making, conducting and implementing British policy in a rapidly changing world. Close attention will be devoted to the extent to which history represented the real driver of policy, or merely fulfilled a rhetorical

purpose in terms of acting as a mobilizing device in support of a policy adopted without a meaningful historical input;
- the practical value of historical activities in supporting the work of administrators and policymakers, given the rapid turnover of ministers, the regular movement of officials within and between departments, and frequent departmental restructuring;
- the specific nature of history's contribution, most notably in providing a collective departmental memory, enabling a sense of historical perspective, and offering an analytical tool helping to define situations and possibilities for policymakers;
- the receptivity of policymakers to historical inputs based upon the concept of learning from experience;
- and the role of historical expertise in government, including the problems faced by those working as historians therein.

The broader significance of this project is accentuated by the fact that the period between 1957 and 1976 was a time when the position of Britain both domestically and internationally was under intensive scrutiny and debate. Concern about Britain's perceived decline as a great power – these perceptions were encouraged by such developments as the growing predominance of the USA and the Soviet Union as the Cold War superpowers in a bipolar world, the 1956 Suez debacle, the end of empire, the parlous state of the British economy, and repeated balance of payments problems – prompted an active and wide-ranging discussion about both the methods and goals of British policy by way of checking and managing, if not reversing, declinist trends. There resulted also a focus upon ways of rationalizing and enhancing the performance of the machinery of government such as through the introduction of planning (for example, the Foreign Office's Planning Section or the National Economic Development Council) and think tanks, like the Central Policy Review Staff, or the greater use of expertise as part of a broader 'Administrative Revolution'.[69]

Research will concentrate on case studies based upon the Cabinet Office, Foreign Office and Treasury. Traditionally, the military, which is invariably accused of re-fighting previous wars, have been the principal users of history for a current purpose, such as for formulating military plans or officer training.[70] However, the Service departments do not figure prominently in this study, partly because of lack of space and partly because of their relative lack of response to Brook's 1957 policy initiative. For the defence departments, their post-1945 preference was to write about past wars for the sake of the historical record rather than as a policy resource, even to the extent that the historical sections complained that – to quote the Head of the Naval Historical Branch – 'the "proper" work of the historians was being interrupted by the volume of day-to-day questions coming in'.[71]

During the period of study, the Cabinet Office emerged to 'become *the* central department of government'.[72] Even so, at one stage during the mid-1960s its Historical Section was threatened with closure until survival was ensured by the commencement of the peacetime official histories series. Notwithstanding the Cabinet Office's growing role at the centre of government, Treasury officials still saw their department as 'the main central department' exercising considerable power and influence throughout Whitehall.[73] Moreover, its longstanding preoccupation with good housekeeping through control of government revenue and expenditure had been extended to embrace responsibility for managing and guiding the whole economy in order to maintain British power and influence; secure full employment, price stability and a sound balance of payments; and promote increased prosperity.[74] The Treasury was responsible also for the overall management and efficiency of the civil service. Important developments framing its transformation included the Plowden Report on the control of public expenditure (1961), radical internal reorganization (1962, 1975), the transfer of economic planning work to the Department of Economic Affairs (DEA) between 1964 and 1969, the Fulton Report (1968), and the subsequent hiving off of functions to the newly formed Civil Service Department (CSD). Likewise, the Foreign Office, confronted by the search for an alternative British role in Europe and the wider world as well as the enhanced importance of international economic issues, was subjected to the Plowden (1963) and Duncan (1969) reports as well as to restructuring, such as in 1968 through the merger with the Commonwealth Relations Office to form the Foreign and Commonwealth Office (FCO).

Conclusion

The intellectual justification for using history in government has proved the subject of numerous publications.[75] These studies highlight the escalating level of interest in history and public policy upon the part of historians and political scientists, particularly those based in the USA, as well as their strong focus upon international relations and war as compared to domestic policy.

Despite the enduring penchant of British politicians and journalists for articulating the lessons of history, there have been fewer analyses of the way in which history has been used – and not used or misused – by British policymakers when reaching, implementing and justifying decisions. However, the recent launch of the *History and Policy* website reflects an emerging British interest in studying history and policy on a broad front. Peter Nailor's *Learning from Precedent in Whitehall* (1991) offered a brief overview of Whitehall practice when exhorting departments to make more use of history, but focused principally upon the late 1980s and early 1990s, not the period covered by this book.[76] Nor did it study the Treasury. Hence, there exists a major gap on both past and recent aspects of the Treasury's historical work, especially as the standard histories of the Treasury published by Edward Bridges, Richard Chapman, George Peden and Henry Roseveare, among others, make occasional use of some internal Treasury histories as sources, but fail to cover this actual activity.[77] Despite focusing upon the impact of policy learning upon the Treasury and British economic policy in the 1960s, Hugh Pemberton glosses over the role of history as a tool when illuminating the underlying 'process of policy feedback, network growth and idea transmission'.[78] As a journalist taking a close interest in the Whitehall machine at work during the 1970s, Hennessy offered contemporary reflections on the contribution of the Treasury's 'excellent historical section', quite apart from regretting its closure in 1976.[79] Furthermore, in June 1978, he wrote to Wass requesting the release of 23 Treasury histories closed under the 30-Year Rule: 'the studies prepared by the Treasury Historical Section since 1945... would be of great interest to myself, the readership of The Times, and sections of the public at large, not to mention the country's economic historians'.[80]

Using history in public policy is central also to discussions about the nature of history, its present-day relevance and society's historical literacy, as considered in a general way by, say, Richard Evans, Arthur Marwick or John Tosh. Moreover, historical reference points, like "Munich" and "Suez", still figure prominently in the present-day political vocabulary of politicians and journalists when initiating, advocating, supporting or justifying policy. The 2003 Iraq War highlighted the manner in which public figures and media commentators exploit the past in an ahistorical manner to make, or rather press, the case for some present-day political purpose: 'history served as a box from which words and images could be pulled for citation'.[81] Even so, as ever, it proved difficult to decide whether or not history, though having a rhetorical impact, exerted any influence upon the actual policy-making process. For John Tusa, an informed observer reviewing the

British scene some 25 years on from Gowing's Rede lecture, little had changed:

> Why do we seem to be reluctant to learn from the past, to prefer this unhistorical indulgence in speculation about the future? The most persistent indulgers in prospective presentation are Whitehall's spin doctors. They weave a perfect world in the future where targets once set are met, where... prediction of the future is preferable to the history of the past.... It also reflects a belief that by trying to conjure up a reality of things that will happen, this supersedes the brutal actuality of the past where the best laid plans, five year plans, key deliverable, predicted outcomes turn into dust and disappointment.[82]

And yet, as Tusa argued, histories provide useful road maps for policy-makers confronted by the challenges posed by the contemporary world and an uncertain future. Indeed, *the outlines of an answer*, as opposed to *the* answer, to today's problems 'are far more likely to lie in historical examination of the past rather than wholly unfounded speculation about the future'.

2
Using Official Histories and Public Records to Present Britain's Past to a Global Audience

In October 1957 a lengthy Cabinet Office minute, entitled 'The Historical Sense in Departments and so forth', reflected the emerging debate within Whitehall about the role of history in government.[1] Written by Burke Trend, the deputy secretary to the Cabinet (1956–59), this minute fed into ongoing exchanges between ministers and senior officials about future policy concerning a range of history-related issues:

- public records, most notably the length of the closed period as well as access to and citation of closed documents by former ministers and officials when writing their memoirs;
- the future of official histories, including the proposal to move on from the Second World War to the post-1945 period;
- the case for departments to publish edited collections of documents along the lines of the Foreign Office's *Documents on British Foreign Policy* (*DBFP*);
- the fate of the Cabinet Office's Historical Section, which held responsibility for official histories and related matters; and
- history's policymaking potential within the governmental machine in terms of using confidential internal histories to support a department's everyday work.

These topics, albeit not generally treated as of high political priority, frequently raised sensitive issues requiring discussion and decisions at the highest level of government, that is by the prime minister, the Lord Chancellor, individual ministers as well as the Cabinet as a whole. 'Historical Research' proved a regular agenda item at the annual Permanent Secretaries Conferences held at Sunningdale. Nor was debate about history and public policy confined to Whitehall, as demonstrated by media coverage of the historical profession's emergence as an active pressure group pushing for action.[2] In turn, the resulting measures – these frame this book's case studies – included two Public Records Acts (1958, 1967) specifying closure periods of 50 and then 30 years; the gradual, albeit reluctant, adoption of a more relaxed attitude towards the use and citation of closed official documents in the memoirs published by former ministers and officials; the introduction of peacetime official histories and an edited collection of India Office documents; the retention of the Cabinet Office's Historical Section to manage the new peacetime histories, among other activities; the creation of a Treasury Historical Section designed to make history an input to the departmental policymaking process; and the Foreign Office's use of a pilot project to test history's utility in its everyday work by way of supplementing the department's active historical publications policy.

The 1960s proved also a period of rapid expansion in higher education as well as in the study of contemporary history on the part of historians, international relations specialists, political scientists, economists and sociologists, among others.[3] Moreover, the emerging focus upon recent history impacted upon government policy, as indicated by the escalating pressure exerted by historians and others for the adoption of a more liberal approach towards the closure period for public records and official historical publications. Also, an expanding higher education sector, alongside enhanced employment opportunities for historians in academia, was seen within Whitehall as impacting adversely upon the recruitment of official historians. Thus, employment as an official historian often came to be viewed somewhat unfairly as merely – to quote Jeffrey Grey – 'a consolation prize for the worthy but dull'.[4] Certainly, the perceived problem of getting good academic historians to accept commissions proved a factor influencing official thinking upon the subject, especially regarding the question of publishing official histories.[5]

Brook's 1957 "funding experience" initiative

As the civil series of the Second World War official histories drew to a close, in December 1957 Sir Norman Brook, the Cabinet Secretary, Joint Permanent Secretary to the Treasury and Head of the Home Civil Service, issued a policy initiative setting out alternative approaches for using history in the machinery of government.[6] In particular, he was anxious to retain, at least in a 'more modest' manner, the fundamental principle underlying the wartime official histories, that is 'to fund experience for

Government use'. Pressing the case for Whitehall to 'do much more' to record its post-1945 experience, he sounded out departments about whether this 'very successful' experiment held 'any practical lessons for the future'. Were official histories worthy of continuation? If so, was publication of post-1945 topics politically feasible? Or were the options limited, given the way in which party political considerations seemed likely to limit, even rule out, publication? Would any post-1945 official histories be restricted to departmental use only?

Brook's desire to preserve, even to develop, the functional use of history by policymakers led him to encourage departments to move on from the mere noting of precedents and the occasional writing of histories to a more systematic strategy for recording past practice and experience as 'an aid to current administration'. Concluding that publication of peacetime histories was politically impossible, he urged Whitehall to commission 'departmental histories' providing a 'consecutive narrative' focused upon either 'particular episodes of policy or administration which have been of particular significance in a Department's work' or recurring 'stock situations which vary in their incidentals but essentially raise the same difficulties'. In effect, Brook saw the resulting confidential internal histories as providing policymakers and administrators with what one Treasury official described subsequently as 'the tools of their trade'.[7] Over time, *internal* histories promised to provide policymakers with a permanent stock of experience to be drawn upon as required, thereby correcting Whitehall's existing failure to monitor systematically the outcome of past policy decisions:

> They would enable the administrator to see his current problems in the perspective of the original decisions and of the modifications subsequently made, both in policy and in administrative practice. Moreover, they would provide a useful means of checking the validity of assumptions which were made at the outset. It is a feature of our administrative system that we make many forecasts but few retrospects. More post-mortems would be salutary – not, of course, for the purpose of attributing praise or blame but of analysing how forecasts and judgments originally made have stood the test of time.[8]

The fact that such histories were destined for confidential official use only, *not* for publication, meant that political sensitivity was no longer a constraint.

Background to Brook's proposal

Brook's thinking about the use of history in government, though guided by lengthy personal experience and ongoing historical work in the Treasury, was moulded in part by recent reports written by Sir Edward Bridges and Professor Sir W. Keith Hancock in April 1955 and January 1957 respectively, Trend's October 1957 minute on 'The Historical Sense in Departments', and the ongoing review of the official histories undertaken by the House of Commons Select Committee on Estimates.

Bridges' advocacy of official history

Keith Hancock credited Edward Bridges, the Cabinet Secretary (1938–46), Permanent Secretary of the Treasury and Head of the Home Civil Service (1945–56), with prime responsibility for both commissioning the Second World War civil series – they were his 'brain child' – and coining the descriptor "funding experience".[9]

Looking back in 1955 to the Second World War, Bridges recalled how the lack of any civil histories covering the First World War rendered it difficult to discuss 'promptly and authoritatively' what had been done in the past to tackle similar wartime questions. As a result, in 1941 it had been deemed advantageous 'on broad national grounds' to have available 'an *impartial account* [author's emphasis] of something to which the nation devotes so much blood and treasure' with a view to 'bottling the experience for our own future use' by politicians, officials and soldiers.[10] Thus, there occurred, even before the conflict ended, the commissioning of an extensive series of official histories intended to provide – to quote Trend – 'the records by professional historians of the great crises in this country's existence'.[11] From this perspective, the Second World War's total nature meant that it was 'right' to commission official histories recording government policy and procedures on civil and medical as well as the more usual military topics.

The civil, medical and military series were edited by Professor Keith Hancock, Sir Arthur S. MacNalty and Professor James Butler respectively.[12] There was also a separate diplomatic history of the war written by Llewellyn Woodward. The civil series covered the history of administrative, economic and social topics rather than that of individual departments. Produced under the overall editorship of Keith Hancock with Gowing's assistance, individual volumes were written by authors employed by the Cabinet Office's Historical Section. Contributors, who included William Ashworth, Betty Behrens, W.N. Medlicott,

Michael Postan and Richard Titmuss, received varying degrees of official support, including privileged access to classified public records, funding and research assistance. Their research benefited also from authoritative oral testimony provided by officials and politicians involved in the actual events under discussion as well as from departmental feedback on draft manuscripts.[13]

The decision to commission a series of Second World War histories, taken in 1941 in the midst of a major conflict making tremendous demands upon the nation's resources and manpower, reflected the British government's belief in the *potential utility* of official history in 'funding experience for government use' in the event of another war. For Gowing, it represented 'a vote of confidence in the importance of history'.[14] From experience, policymakers came to realize from their use of histories written on the First World War as well as discovering what had *not* been recorded about the civil dimension of that war, that such histories were capable of providing informed practical guidance. For these reasons, official histories had to be 'critical', as asserted by Keith Hancock in the preface to *British War Economy* (1949): 'To have told a "success story" – even when the success had been in the end resplendent – would have been futile and dangerous; the main processes of trial and error had to be revealed.'[15] Thus, Christopher Savage informed readers that his volume on *Inland Transport* (1957) sought to do far more than provide a mere historical narrative. Rather his history was designed to reveal the process of trial and error 'during which many of the most important lessons of wartime transport policy were learned'.[16]

Nor would future attempts to learn from the wartime past be helped, Bridges argued, by the vast extent of wartime documentary records, their dispersed character across government, and the temporary character of many Second World War departments. For Bridges, official histories, drawing upon documentary sources *and* oral testimony, 'had to be done contemporaneously or not at all'.

Keith Hancock's report on the civil series

Succeeding Bridges upon his retirement in 1956, Brook gave considerable thought to ways of applying his message, whose impact was soon reinforced by receipt of Keith Hancock's report on the civil histories series.[17] The report, dated January 1957, gave readers a measured and generally positive view of the series' historical merits and – more importantly for Brook – actual value in "funding experience" for the government's current use. Within Whitehall, official histories were presented, *at least on paper*, as a historical resource fulfilling a reference role for policymakers.[18] Significantly, when asked to comment upon draft official histories, most departments commented positively about their perceived value. Drawing upon her lengthy experience of producing histories for 'a wary audience within Whitehall', Gowing recalled that 'many departments found the detailed analysis and cool conspectus of their problems and policies valuable for current purposes'.[19] In part, such praise reflected the success of Keith Hancock's editorial policy based upon the assumption that prioritizing government failures rather than successes would prove 'more instructive' for readers.[20] Furthermore, such historical expertise was cheap. Reportedly, between 1941 and 1956 expenditure upon the civil histories project amounted to *circa* £250,000, that is a mere annual cost of £830 per Whitehall department![21]

What caught Brook's eye in Keith Hancock's report was the outline of the wide range of extra activities undertaken by official historians during both the Second World War and the post-1945 periods. Thus, their practical contribution went far beyond responsibility for the published histories to embrace – to quote Keith Hancock – 'a number of useful services for administrators', most notably writing histories for confidential internal use taking advantage of their status as repositories of specialist historical knowledge.[22] Histories cited as being 'used a good deal by departments' included Postan's historical memoranda for the Ministry of Supply and internal histories written by Sir John Shuckburgh and W.N. Medlicott to provide 'a useful record of wartime activities' for the Colonial Office and the Ministry of Economic Warfare respectively. Reportedly, Postan's history of the tank problem, commissioned by the Ministry of Production, figured prominently in the drafting of a White Paper on Tank Production. Medlicott's internal history was printed as a Cabinet Paper, while Joel Hurstfield's study of 'Conservation and Substitution of Raw Materials' fed into Anglo-American exchanges.

Initially, the Second World War official histories, like the *ad hoc* historical projects mentioned above, were prepared for confidential government use only, not for publication, but once the war ended policy reasons led the government to accept the case for publication, and hence to target an external audience *outside of Whitehall*. As a result, in July 1946 Hancock instructed his authors that 'the publication of those Civil Histories which attain the necessary quality has now been approved in principle'.[23] Quite apart from offering posterity a record of major historical events in their own right, official histories came to be presented increasingly as providing history's 'first word' on the past, thereby helping to 'smooth the paths of the scholar' through the unprecedented mass of wartime documentation and responding to historians's demands for histories of the recent past.[24] In turn, the objective of enhancing public knowledge and understanding was accompanied by the perceived need to 'show the flag' (Keith Hancock), that is to present an authoritative version of Britain's role in winning the war to both domestic and foreign audiences in order to complement, even correct, existing histories.[25] As Keith Hancock stressed in the preface to *British War Economy* (1949), the histories were a 'United Kingdom series.... Official history must follow (it may be hoped not too slavishly) the paths of national sovereignty'.[26]

Admittedly, sales were modest but, like any specialist history, the target audience outside Whitehall was limited largely to academia in terms of responding to demands for histories of the recent past as well as to a limited section of the general public defined to cover 'the grade of reader attracted by, say, *The Economist*'.[27] Unsurprisingly, Keith Hancock expressed pleasure that the latter had reviewed every volume. For Trend, the North American audience was a priority, as evidenced by his belief that the British Information Service in New York should do more to exploit that market.[28]

Keith Hancock on official history

Keith Hancock used his report also to offer an informed commentary upon history and government in the light of debates, especially critiques, prompted by the official histories project. However, what follows below will draw also upon the subsequent publications and correspondence used to reflect his thinking upon the subject.

For many historians, the descriptor "official history" proved a contradiction in terms of being more akin to "propaganda" presenting carefully packaged and sanitized government versions of the past rather than "history" conforming to the accepted standards of historical scholarship.[29] In effect, official histories were seen as giving British governments 'a useful way of managing the past, offering a judicious mixture of concessions and control'.[30] Perhaps, the most influential contemporary critique in Britain emanated from Cambridge's Sir Herbert Butterfield, who warned readers about the missing dimension of official histories: 'I do not personally believe that there is a government in Europe which wants the public to know the truth.'[31]

Notwithstanding such attacks, Keith Hancock pressed the view that official histories, at least those published in Britain, were 'independent histories' produced within an official framework. Official historians, though employed and managed by the Cabinet Office's Historical Section, were selected by and largely responsible to the series editor, who was a historian like Keith Hancock. Moreover, the so-called British case was in reality the informed interpretation of an expert academic historian based upon research supported by the government and enabled by privileged access to closed official records and oral testimony from those involved in the actual events.[32] Thus, individual volumes carried a brief inscription stating that 'the authors of the Civil Histories have been given free access to official documents. They and the editor are alone responsible for the statements made and the views expressed.' Brook defined the official position as follows:

> While there is an obligation on authors to avoid personal bias or perverse interpretation, responsibility for the printed work rests in the last resort on them and on the Editor of the Official Histories. The resulting histories make no claim to infallibility. They should represent the best work that the official historian is capable of doing, and it is his professional duty to give an exact and truthful picture of events.[33]

Throughout their projects, official historians were able to call upon the help and advice of the departments immediately concerned, with initial plans, interim drafts and the final manuscript being submitted for comment. Unsurprisingly, authors took departmental comment and criticism in varying ways. For example, Richard Sayers welcomed Treasury praise for his interim drafts on *Financial Policy* (1956), but was – to quote Keith Hancock – 'almost frothing at the mouth' following receipt of one Treasury critique.[34] For Richard Titmuss, interminable delays in feedback proved extremely frustrating: 'my mood is one of rebellion'.[35]

Departmental feedback, though often used to correct and improve the text, did raise occasional difficulties regarding content, even resulting in editorial concerns about the use of departmental screening for censorship purposes. In general, individual historians possessed relative freedom over the text subject to adherence to the convention of ministerial responsibility, the non-disclosure of Cabinet records, including ministerial disagreements, and the need to avoid damage to current policy interests. But privileged access to departmental files did not necessarily permit publication of the information contained therein. Acting in consultation with the Cabinet Secretary, Keith Hancock developed 'a drill' designed to defend individual historians against unreasonable departmental pressure, thereby reconciling the public interest with the series' historical integrity.[36] Participating 'in scores' of such discussions, Keith Hancock asserted that the key priority 'was not to achieve diplomatic compromises, but upon every issue to get as close as possible to the historical truth'; thus, his preparedness, if necessary, to withhold problem volumes from publication rather than to emasculate them.[37]

Generally speaking, Keith Hancock found that such a 'drill' proved effective in persuading government departments to play the rules of 'our historical game'.[38] Even so, he came close to resignation at times, most notably over the volumes written by Postan and Titmuss.[39] If nothing else, the 'drill' ensured the Cabinet Office's support against any critics. For example, when the chiefs of staff tried to block Postan's volume on *British War Production* (1952) on the grounds of revealing too much about Britain's war-making capacity, both Bridges and Brook proved influential in securing prime ministerial approval for the book's publication against 'those whippersnappers'.[40] Once again, the fact that such issues reached Attlee and then Churchill established the perceived political significance of official histories.[41]

For Keith Hancock, the need to conform to sound historical methodology, albeit a natural consequence of his professional training and academic vision of the official histories series, was reinforced by an awareness that in time academic historians, among others, would gain access to public records: 'The official historians of this generation have consciously submitted their work to the professional verdict of the future.'[42] For this reason, it was stipulated that the documents used in writing any volume should be stamped to ensure preservation for subsequent use by historians and others upon the expiration of the closed period.[43] Even so, the usual concerns about official secrecy meant that the published British wartime official histories, unlike many overseas counterparts, did not list sources. Fully referenced versions were produced, but were reserved for confidential official use within relevant departments.

Furthermore, the academic and public credibility of official histories required the editor to be an outside academic, not a government insider, even if, as Keith Hancock himself was only too aware, this raised the enduring personal difficulty of balancing editorial work with his university duties at Oxford and then London. Life, he frequently complained, was 'too crowded'.[44] To some extent, his burden was alleviated by the editorial assistance of Gowing, whose collaboration in writing the *British War Economy* (1949) represented a 'definite piece of good fortune': 'it would have been quite impossible for W.K.H. to have finished the job without the succour of M.G.'[45] Individual official historians faced similar pressures. Pointing to the frequent delays resulting from the problems experienced by, say, Behrens and Savage in balancing academic and official obligations, Keith Hancock advised that contributors should take leave of absence from their respective universities or go part-time for the duration of the project. Reviewing the qualities required of authors, he identified the occasional failure alongside some surprising successes:

> The work requires not only high intellectual ability but certain gifts of character. It demands a devotion that must amount to fanaticism if the historian is not to falter amidst the mountains of documents and if he is to forgo other more tempting jobs in order to see the job through.[46]

For Keith Hancock, the civil service itself yielded few suitable candidates in spite of the reputed prominence of history graduates among its entrants: 'on the whole experience showed that the qualities of the good administrator and the good historian are rarely synonymous'. As discussed below, officials often saw things differently.

Keith Hancock's legacy

Naturally, Keith Hancock liked to publicize the series' qualities, most notably its historical credibility, through descriptive phrases – these included 'competent and honest history' and 'critical history' – familiar to academia.[47] Conceding the occasional 'pedestrian' effort, Keith Hancock claimed that most volumes made 'distinguished contributions' to historical knowledge and understanding, as evidenced by the favourable response in both American and British academic circles.[48] As Gowing pointed out, specific volumes attracted high praise; thus, Titmuss' *Problems of Social Policy* (1950) became a standard text on the Welfare State. More importantly, she claimed that the *British* official war histories 'dispelled the understandable suspicions of the dubious alliance of "official" with "history"'.[49] For Gowing, Keith Hancock's contribution was crucial: 'It was largely due to Keith's efforts that the whole concept of official history ceased to represent the prostitution of the profession and became rather an important contribution to understanding in an age when Government policy bulks so large.'[50]

According to Brook, the official histories possessed another legacy. Writing to Keith Hancock in February 1958 – by this time Keith Hancock had returned to Australia, where he presented himself as editing from a distance at the Australian National University the remaining 'few stragglers' in the civil series – Brook admitted that the report had impacted heavily upon his thinking.[51]

> After studying your own Report on the Civil Series of the Official Histories, I considered whether there was any way in which the technique that the Historians had successfully worked out could be applied in peacetime. Reluctantly, I decided that this was impracticable, if only because histories of peacetime administration would founder on the rocks of Party political controversy. Nevertheless I was anxious to encourage Departments to do something more to fund their experience and decided therefore on a more modest approach.[52]

As outlined earlier, Brook's 'modest approach', inspired by Keith Hancock's outline of the proven utility of the histories written for internal departmental use by official historians as part of their duties, sought to continue the official histories project into the post-1945 years, while discounting for the time being the possibility of publication.

Trend on Whitehall's 'historical sense'

Recognizing its broader relevance, Brook circulated Keith Hancock's report throughout Whitehall together with a covering note describing the series as a 'substantial achievement', as validated by the generally positive reception accorded in academia, the media and official circles.[53] In turn, supportive departmental feedback, in conjunction with discussions held with Margaret Gowing and staff representing the Public Record Office, among others, encouraged the Cabinet Office to give serious thought to what Burke Trend described as 'The Historical Sense in Departments'.[54]

Appreciating their potential value to policymakers, Trend used his minute to propose commissioning peacetime official histories of 'particular episodes of administration' – possible topics included the post-war development of the Health Service, civil aviation policy and economic controls – enabling 'current problems to be considered in a better historical perspective'. For Trend, such histories would prove of 'considerable administrative value (not least by illustrating the errors of the past) but would also be of considerable historical significance as a record of the way in which major policies have been translated into administrative action'. Unlike volumes covering the two World Wars, the histories would have to be produced, he advised, for confidential official use only, not for publication, given their reliance upon closed files and coverage of politically contentious topics. For this reason, Trend doubted whether historians working in academia would be attracted by such commissions; in fact, unlike Keith Hancock, he suggested that the work could easily be undertaken by an experienced administrator with an interest in historical research.

Cabinet Office thinking was informed, indeed driven forward, by positive reports about ongoing historical work in the Treasury, where Gowing was giving substance to the concept of "funding experience". After reading draft versions of her initial histories, Trend was impressed by the way in which detailed historical narratives based upon departmental records yielded informative accounts and useful lessons supportive of the Treasury's current activities. For example, he saw Gowing's study (1957) of 'the deplorable history' of the Festival Gardens project as providing 'an awful warning against any future attempts to repeat this particular blend of public and private enterprise'.[55] Building upon this foundation, Trend sounded out the rationale for making more use of history in government by harnessing 'the technique that the Historians have worked out in the last ten years or so' for the official histories as well as the Treasury's internal histories? Should history, he asked, be made a formal input to the actual policymaking process in the interests of greater efficiency and economy?

More importantly, Trend's minute linked the proposed adoption of a more systematic approach towards writing internal histories with the ongoing debate conducted about future government policy towards public records in the wake of the 1954 Grigg Report. Regardless of official reservations about the prospects of publishing peacetime volumes, Trend pointed to the way in which official histories offered one way of making accessible the content of closed public records, thereby helping to counter or deflect demands from historians and others for improved access. In 1958 the Public Records Act established a 50-Year closure period, while requiring departments, among other public bodies, to adopt more methodical procedures for processing (and preserving) records of 'real historical value'. In fact, the UKAEA's obligations under this legislation led in 1959 to Gowing's appointment as its archivist/historian. But, as indicated below, the act failed to stop the pressure from historians for further concessions.

Parliament casts a 'chilled eye' upon official histories

Although Brook claimed not to take its critique too seriously, another factor impacting upon the Cabinet Office's review of history and public policy was the 'chilled eye' cast upon official histories by the parliamentary Select Committee on Estimates.[56] Certainly, its report, published on 22 November 1957, established that official history was far from unproblematic, as evidenced by the manner in which media coverage of the costs and publication delays touched upon the alleged use of official histories to distort the past through 'calculated inaccuracy' and concealment of sources.[57]

Of course, the overall cost, averaging about £100,000 per annum between 1949 and 1956, was – to quote the *Glasgow Herald* – 'a relatively trifling sum' in the context of total government expenditure, but this failed to prevent "Cassandra", the leading columnist in the best-selling *Daily Mirror*, from complaining about 'the more than a tidy sum to record the horrors of world wars': 'As with the task on [painting] the Forth Bridge, so with the writing of Official Histories of the Wars. It goes on for ever and the pen men never run out of words – or wars'.[58] Regarding delays, the report drew attention to delayed First World War histories, such as on East Africa, as well as the abandonment of a single-volume popular history of the Second World War at sea due to the author's lack of progress over a seven-year period.[59] Exploiting contemporary anxieties about a nuclear holocaust, "Cassandra" reflected that 'these leisurely historians will have a much shorter task when it comes to describing the next world war. Just a bang and a whimper!'.[60] Likewise, the fact that forty years on some First World War volumes had yet to appear led the *Glasgow Herald* to assert that 'the audience had long ceased to care whether it got the end of the story or not. To formal history it preferred Mr Sheriff [sic] and Mr Remarque and felt that the poets were, on the whole, the better historians.'[61]

The Treasury's example

Nor were Brook's proposals, as circulated in December 1957, mere theoretical speculation. As Joint Permanent Secretary of the Treasury, he had followed closely the recent growth in the department's historical activities centred upon the studies written by Margaret Gowing, an experienced official historian. Gowing, whose Treasury historical work is elaborated in the next chapter, was on secondment to the Treasury following the scaling down of her editorial responsibilities for the Second World War official histories civil series. In fact, the satisfactory results of this historical experiment, in conjunction with positive feedback from consultations upon the subject with several departmental permanent secretaries, led Brook to support not only the continuation of this work by the Treasury but also its extension throughout Whitehall. Individual government departments, albeit given discretion to decide whether or not to act upon the proposal, were urged to draw up a long-term "funding experience" programme as well as to keep the Cabinet Office's Historical Section apprised of progress, with special reference to practical impacts upon policy and administrative practice. Acknowledging departmental concerns about costs and staffing, Brook hinted at the possibility of limited financial support as well as the prudence of using retired staff, but anticipated that in the long term the resulting simplification and speeding up of administration through using history would save the department's time and, more importantly, money! For Brook, "funding experience" represented a fundamental element in his desire to make the machinery of government more efficient and cost-effective: 'If we can save time we shall save money.'[62]

Departmental responses

Confirming history's minimal role in the current everyday activities of Whitehall, responses to Brook's proposals indicated that considerable scope existed for individual departments either to introduce a limited amount of "funding experience" work or to improve upon existing efforts. Reportedly, replies fell into four main categories.[63] First, the service departments claimed to possess already well-established historical sections responsible for the publication of official military histories, covering the two World Wars as well as more specific departmental projects, like the War Office's annual historical summaries embodied in 'The Novel'.[64] Secondly, the 'Executive' departments, like the Inland Revenue, Customs, General Post Office, Ministry of Pensions and National Insurance (MPNI), and the Ministry of Works, claimed to have in place already systems for recording precedents, but saw little scope for historical narratives of the type proposed by Brook. Thirdly, the 'Overseas' departments undertook already 'a good deal of recording and summarising in the ordinary course of business', but agreed that more could be done, and done better, with more staff. In the event, as elaborated in Chapters 10–12, the Foreign Office made one of the more positive practical responses. Finally, other departments, like the Ministry of Power, conceded the scope for action, but planned to do little in the near future.[65]

As Brook anticipated, staffing was often presented as a major constraint. Indeed, for the Ministry of Health, staff shortages warranted deferment of any action. By contrast, the Ministry of Housing and

Local Government (MHLG) advanced the 'ingenious idea' of borrowing Gowing from the Treasury to progress its plans![66] Both the Ministry of Transport and the MPNI saw retired senior staff, or those nearing retirement, as offering a possible solution. There were also influential sceptics, like Sir Edward Playfair, the PUS at the War Office (1956–60), whose reservations might seem surprising in the light of the longstanding historical work of the service departments. According to Playfair, ever-changing circumstances diminished history's value as a policy input, since lessons could never be learnt or, if they could, they were so generalized as merely to cover the obvious.[67]

However, Brook was far from discouraged by such reservations. On the contrary, impressed by the proven utility of Gowing's initial histories, he advocated an enhanced "funding experience" effort throughout Whitehall. Over time, he anticipated that the Treasury's example would help to counter the force of Playfair-type critiques by throwing light upon the practical support "funding experience" activities could offer policymakers.

The historians's campaign on public records

When succeeding Brook as Cabinet Secretary at the close of 1962, Trend recognized that hitherto Whitehall's response to the "funding experience" initiative had proved relatively disappointing, even if, as indicated in Chapters 3–12, the Board of Trade, Foreign Office and Treasury had made a start. Several issues appertaining to history and public policy required his early attention.[68] Perhaps the key question still awaiting action concerned the future of the official histories and, by implication, that of the Cabinet Office's Historical Section. As Trend warned Sir Alec Douglas-Home, the prime minister (1963–64), 'unless we become involved in another major war, the Section will have lost its original *raison d'être*'.[69]

Another ongoing issue, attracting considerable visibility, was the question of public records. The 1958 Public Records Act failed to prevent renewed demands for yet a further relaxation of the closed period. In many respects, the issue was 'brought to the boil' by the parliamentary and media controversy surrounding Sir Anthony Eden's privileged access to closed documents covering the 1956 Suez Crisis when writing *Full Circle* (1960).[70] In turn, the growing flood of memoirs penned by former ministers and officials came to be perceived as undermining the case for maintaining a rule, traditionally justified by the need to protect the convention of collective ministerial responsibility and the confidentiality of exchanges between ministers and officials. Moreover, despite critiques of the blinkered world of officialdom, Cabinet Office staff were beginning to acknowledge the emerging academic interest in 'contemporary history' as well as the manner in which the accessibility of public records impacted upon academic research and teaching.[71]

Drafting a minute to guide Trend's thinking, Michael Cary followed Brook in conceding the problem, but concluded that the case for writing peacetime official histories contemporaneously, possibly even for publication, was perhaps stronger.

> From the point of view of our responsibility to posterity it seems to me that by turning a first class historian on to recent events with full access to official records it would be possible to produce, when the time comes, a far more valuable contribution to knowledge than if we merely allow the records to accumulate all over the place and release them in fifty years time.[72]

In particular, authors would benefit from the use of oral testimony furnished by the principal actors therein.

> An historian working on recent material will be able to fill in gaps, explain discrepancies and produce a continuity of thought and narrative which may be literally impossible in fifty years time when so many of the characters in the drama will have disappeared.

Inevitably, their coverage of controversial topics based upon confidential sources raised questions about their suitability for publication, but in the meantime any peacetime histories remained available for internal use. Nor could Cary avoid recognizing the way in which future policy towards official histories linked up with the increasingly active debate about public records. Publishing official histories offered a potentially useful instrument for 'policing the past' across a range of history-related topics, while offering one way of deflecting the mounting pressure being exerted by historians, among others, for improved access to public records.[73]

The Cabinet Office monitored closely the emerging campaign conducted by the historical profession for improved access to public records. Indeed, in December 1963, when meeting an Oxford–Cambridge–London group of leading British 'recent historians' – they included Alan Bullock (Oxford), Francis H. Hinsley (Cambridge), Michael Howard (London), Herbert G. Nicholas (Oxford) and

Donald C. Watt (LSE) – Cary was left in no doubt about their determination to bring about change.[74] One argument striking a chord among Cabinet Office staff was the stress upon the national interest, that is the need to present the British case on international, especially colonial, issues covered unsympathetically, if not negatively, by existing histories. Unsurprisingly, in 1961 the publication of the official history on the bomber offensive against Germany had been welcomed as offering a fresh British perspective upon a highly controversial subject.[75] Officials worried also about the unfavourable comparisons drawn with 'the tempo of American official publication', most notably by H.G. Nicholas' article in *The Times*, following the State Department's adoption of a 30-Year rule and President Kennedy's recent stress upon expediting the coverage of the *Foreign Relations of the United States* series of diplomatic documents: 'It is the policy of this Administration to unfold the historical record as fast and as fully as is consistent with national security and with friendly relations with foreign nations.'[76]

By contrast, in Britain, as reaffirmed in 1963 by Ian Bancroft, 'official policy is still solidly for the 50 year rule'.[77] Or, at least, this was the line pronounced in public. Both Harold Macmillan (prime minister, 1957–63) and then Douglas-Home opposed any early modification of the closed period when answering parliamentary questions on the subject.[78] Indeed, Macmillan, pointing to the prudence of giving the new rule a fair trial, even asserted that there was no demand for any change![79] Soon afterwards, Douglas-Home echoed his predecessor's intransigence, while admitting his personal inclination to tighten up, not relax, the rule.[80]

Despite appearing unmoved by the 'new offensive' launched by historians in his advice to Macmillan and Douglas-Home, Trend pointed to the escalating pressure exerted by historians through the press, meetings, lectures and the Advisory Council on Public Records (ACPR) when arguing the case for investigating strategies for 'appeasing our own disgruntled historians'.[81] As a result, he secured prime ministerial permission to initiate inter-departmental exchanges conducted under the aegis of the Cabinet Office in order to examine alternative ways forward *within the parameters of the 1958 Public Records Act*.

Linking public records with official histories

Drawing upon Cary's advisory minute and the arguments made by historians, Trend acknowledged the prudence of taking certain steps to ensure that the British case was adequately represented in 'the increasingly competitive business of international historiography'.[82] For Trend, it was adjudged essential 'to defend our own reputations' against the partial, frequently biased, accounts published in other governments' official histories and the memoirs of foreign politicians: 'there is clearly a danger that the British side of the story may go by default'.

One option was to commission academic historians to write official histories providing 'authoritative narratives of major episodes' during the post-1945 period: 'The justification for this type of history was... that after 50 years some official records might have been lost and the leading actors would either be dead or too old to be consulted.'[83] However, the fact that such volumes were likely to be 'more controversial than the official histories of the two world wars', alongside their reliance upon closed public records, was viewed as ruling out publication until the files upon which they were based were opened up under the 50-Year Rule. Alternatively, departments might be encouraged to emulate the Foreign Office's published series of *DBFP*.[84]

Meanwhile, undeterred by the negative position assumed in public by the Macmillan and Douglas-Home governments, the historians maintained, even escalated, the momentum and visibility of their campaign, as highlighted in July 1964 by Butterfield's presentation to the ACPR and Nicholas' lecture at the Anglo-American Conference in London.[85] Significantly, Gowing, who was then working at the UKAEA, sent the Cabinet Office the full text of Nicholas' lecture. There seemed – to quote Clifton Child, the Foreign Office's Director of Research and Head of the Library, after reading yet another article by Watt – 'a lot of sting' in their demands.[86]

Moving to a 30-Year Rule and peacetime official histories

In many respects, the parameters of debate were transformed in October 1964, when a change of government coincided with the conclusion of the ACPR's review of public records culminating in its recommendation to the Lord Chancellor for a reduction of the closed period to 40 years.[87] Certainly, the ACPR's change of stance informed the advice submitted in January 1965 by Trend to Douglas-Home's successor, Harold Wilson (prime minister, 1964–70).[88]

In retrospect, the advent of the Labour Government appears decisive in taking things forward on several fronts, since Wilson proved predisposed towards fresh thinking upon the whole subject as well as prepared to gloss over official reservations about the early amendment of the 1958 legislation.[89] Trend advised Wilson that official peacetime histories, written by academic historians commissioned by the Cabinet Office's Historical Section enjoying unrestricted access to records, offered one way of responding to and containing the historians's pressure for improved access to public records. Naturally, decisions about the choice of topic as well as publication would rest with the government of the day acting through a cross-party committee:

> This course would have the advantage of *keeping the whole process under official control* [author's emphasis] but ensuring that, at the same time, that *objective studies* [author's emphasis] of suitable historical episodes could be prepared while the principal participants in the events concerned were still alive.[90]

To some extent, the need for the government to make a decision about Gowing's UKAEA atomic energy history – the completion of her volume on the wartime period meant that the UKAEA was now seeking permission for coverage of the post-1945 years – strengthened the case for positive action. Indeed, Trend saw the eventual publication of Gowing's post-1945 volume as timely in terms of giving greater prominence to the often overlooked British scientific and technical contribution to the development of atomic energy, thereby correcting existing American accounts.

When discussing policy options with Lord Gardiner, the Lord Chancellor, and Trend on 30 April 1965, Wilson displayed a relatively relaxed attitude towards both official histories and public records.[91] Indeed, the two ministers, pointing to the political benefits of publicly presenting the British case through peacetime official histories, assumed the likelihood of publication in spite of their use of records subject to the 50-Year Rule:

> There were strong arguments for the more frequent commissioning of such histories in order to present the British case more effectively; other Governments often released documents and accounts of recent events which gave only a partial picture of the events they purported to describe. *Official histories were, however, a special case because their content and scope was entirely within the control of the Government of the day and due care could be exercised to ensure that national or individual interests were not harmed by their publication* [author's emphasis].[92]

Nor did Wilson follow official advice in interpreting peacetime official histories *as an alternative* strategy to the adoption of a more liberal approach regarding access to public records. On the contrary, he inclined towards a more radical position than that assumed by the ACPR, let alone officials.[93] Indeed, W. McIndoe, the head of the Cabinet Office's Historical Section, criticized the way in which Wilson's preparedness to offer 'a sop to historians' led him to disregard official advice about treating peacetime histories as an alternative, not a supplement, to the new closure rule.[94] As a result, on 5 August 1965, when approving in principle the adoption of a 30-Year Rule for public records, the Cabinet accepted as part of one overall decision the case for introducing peacetime official histories:

> On occasion the Government of the day might judge it to be in the public interest that a history of relatively recent events should be undertaken while the written records could still be supplemented by reference to the personal recollections of public men who had taken part in the events in question. For this purpose, the range of the Official Histories, which had so far been confined to the two world wars, might be extended to include selected periods or episodes of peacetime history, on the understanding that the publication of works of this kind would need to be suspended for a time which would normally be at least equivalent to the 30-year closed period.[95]

Thus, notwithstanding the tone of the exchanges between the prime minister and Lord Chancellor, publication still remained problematic in November 1965, when the Cabinet's decision was submitted for approval by Edward Heath and Jo Grimond, the leaders of the two Opposition parties.[96] In fact, on 9 March 1966, when announcing the government's proposed introduction of a 30-Year Rule – in 1967 this led to a new Public Records Act – and a series of peacetime official histories providing 'comprehensive and authoritative narratives' on 'important' fields of government activity since 1945, Wilson warned Parliament that individual histories would not necessarily be released for publication 'before the expiry of the "closed" period'.[97] The Cabinet also supported in principle the publication of edited collections of documents. Like the *DBFP*, any documentary collections must focus upon the historical development and execution of policy, but exclude 'the internal records of discussions by which policy was formulated'.

There was another complication. Despite appearing to represent merely a chronological continuation of the Second World War series, peacetime official histories raised an important *political issue*, as stated by the Cabinet Office: 'The reason why they have in the past always been confined to the military operations in major wars is mainly the fact that these are the periods when controversial issues of domestic politics have been in abeyance.'[98] For this reason, as Wilson informed Parliament on 10 August 1966, responsibility for approving topics for inclusion in the new series would be assigned to a cross-party standing group of privy counsellors.[99] In brief, the latter would make their decisions from a shortlist of topics compiled by an interdepartmental Committee on Official Histories of Peacetime Events, which was instructed to ensure that individual volumes set out 'the British case' and were vetted for not only 'usefulness' but also the avoidance of 'matters of acute controversy' possessing party political and foreign policy implications. Finally, overall responsibility for the new series was assigned to the Cabinet Office's Historical Section, thereby safeguarding its future.[100]

The Foreign Office and history

Responding on 10 August 1966 to a specific parliamentary question from Edward Heath, the Leader of the Opposition, Wilson recognized the Foreign Office's special position regarding historical publications when excluding it from the new centralized procedure directed by the Cabinet Office's Historical Section.[101] Naturally, this concession was welcomed by the Foreign Office, whose reservations about having to operate through 'cumbersome' interdepartmental machinery were compounded by resentment about the threatened loss of its traditional autonomy over historical publications.[102]

Despite participating in the interdepartmental committee on Second World War official histories, the Foreign Office had largely gone its own way on historical publications, as evidenced by its distinctive focus upon the *DBFP* and the fact that Woodward's diplomatic history of the Second World War was not treated formally as part of the published official histories series.[103] Lacking a specific history section, during the early 1940s, the Foreign Office gave the tasks of editing the diplomatic documents and writing the wartime diplomatic history to Llewellyn Woodward, who was on secondment from Oxford University. Writing in 1944, Woodward contrasted the Foreign Office's minimalism with the more 'exhibitionist' position adopted towards history by the Service departments and Cabinet Office through their large history sections.[104]

Like other departments, the Foreign Office saw the 1967 Public Records Act as giving rise to serious policy and logistical problems given the 'major exercise' of clearing 20 years of files by 1968 to ensure public access under the new 30-Year Rule.[105] More seriously, the proposed change was interpreted as threatening to undermine the market for the *DBFP*, the cornerstone of its historical publications programme. Nor did the Foreign Office welcome the concept of peacetime official histories. On the contrary, the department – to quote Clifton Child – regarded the prospect as an 'absolute nightmare' given the manner in which published official accounts of past international events risked causing 'great harm' to British interests by giving serious offence to other governments and political leaders.[106] For this reason, Woodward's five-volume diplomatic wartime history, though completed one decade earlier, had yet to be cleared for publication, except in an abridged, expurgated version published in 1962. Likewise, Michael Foot's *SOE in France, 1940–1944* (1966), albeit helping to reaffirm Britain's role in wartime resistance, soon established the ability of official histories to exert unwelcome, even embarrassing, political and legal problems.[107]

In September 1966, Rohan Butler, the Foreign Secretary's historical adviser and Woodward's successor as senior editor of the *DBFP*, discussed recent developments with McIndoe, the head of the Cabinet Office's Historical Section.[108] Having warned McIndoe about the Foreign Office's 'special difficulties' in publishing official histories, Butler reaffirmed its future focus upon the *DBFP*, with priority attached towards accelerating the pace of publication of the existing series, improving the coverage of the late 1920s through an additional series (1A), and contemplating moving onto the post-1945 period.[109] One month later, when the interdepartmental committee met to progress the peacetime histories project as well as to consider the potential of the *DBFP* model for emulation elsewhere in Whitehall, Paul Gore-Booth, the Foreign Office's PUS, confirmed his department's prioritization of the *DBFP*.[110] Although the Foreign Office did not rule out commissioning further histories funding past experience for *confidential internal use*, published peacetime official histories would be treated as 'very exceptional'.[111]

Commissioning the first peacetime official histories

Following clearance from relevant departmental ministers, in April 1968, Wilson personally approved the initial seven-topic shortlist of peacetime histories submitted by the interdepartmental committee.[112] Prime ministerial endorsement cleared the way for the cross-party standing group – its initial membership comprised Douglas-Home (Conservative), Patrick Gordon Walker (Labour), a former Foreign Secretary (1964–65), and Lord Ogmore (Liberal) – to finalize the selection process and agree a publication schedule.[113] As a result, on 18 December 1969, Wilson announced the commissioning of three histories – *Colonial Development, 1945–1964*, *Environmental Planning* and *Nationalisation: An Analytical Account, 1945–1960* – to inaugurate the new series.[114] Once again, Wilson highlighted the link between official histories and public records by taking the opportunity to announce plans for expediting the release of official records relating to the whole Second World War period.

Significantly, when approving the shortlist, Wilson queried the absence of Indian independence, given the topic's perceived public and international interest as well as his anxiety to record for posterity the Attlee government's major achievements.[115] Seemingly, he had forgotten that in 1967 Professor P.N. Mansergh had already been appointed to edit published volumes of India Office documents covering the transfer of power to India and Pakistan.[116] Perhaps the major gap was the 1956 Suez Crisis, particularly given the repeated demands of Labour MPs for an official history thereupon. Adopting a somewhat different stance when in power to that assumed by him when in opposition, Wilson followed his Conservative predecessors in refusing repeated requests emanating principally from his own backbenchers.[117] Soon after becoming prime minister, Wilson's reply to a parliamentary question provided a framework for dealing with further questions on this topic:

> Official histories deal primarily with the strategy and tactics of military operations in major wars. Students of military history would have nothing to learn from any official history of these military operations, except what to avoid. On the wider question of the responsibility for the initiation of the operations, common humanity would suggest we should not further embarrass the right Hon. Gentlemen opposite.[118]

Subsequently, Wilson maintained this line, as highlighted in June 1967, when the ongoing Middle East crisis – on the same day, George Brown, the Foreign Secretary, pressed the urgent need for an effective ceasefire in the Arab–Israeli War – reinforced the case for inaction:

> I do not think that it is appropriate at this moment, when we have these very great difficulties, to enter into certain questions which are relevant from 1956 to the present situation or to enlarge on the difficulties which 1956 caused in the Middle East and for Britain in the handling of this crisis at this time. There will be a time to say all that later.[119]

As a result, 'the House might well feel that it would be unwise for the Government to commission a work of this kind at the present time, when all our efforts should be directed towards reducing the tensions in the Middle East'. For Wilson, enough had been written about Suez already by leading participants like Eden and Nutting: 'we saw no need for an official history because so many distinguished persons concerned with that episode have since turned Queen's evidence.' Of course, the reality was that there was no prospect of an official history on Suez gaining cross-party support – MPs had no need to be apprised of this point – but the episode reaffirmed the problems of including politically sensitive international topics in the official histories series.[120]

Rather than having a group of permanent historians based in the Cabinet Office, 'historians of merit and repute', adjudged capable of combining the project with their academic duties, were commissioned for each topic.[121] By this stage, the Cabinet Office assumed publication, especially as the series was rationalized increasingly by a desire to assuage the apparent 'hunger' of historians for material on the recent period.[122] Publication was viewed also as a key precondition for securing the services of good historians.

Official history and government

Whether or not Second World War official histories represented a form of institutionalized learning feeding into the policymaking process is uncertain. Indeed, it is questionable how far most wartime official histories, even the fully referenced copies held within Whitehall departments for internal use, possessed a peacetime utility. Anecdotal evidence suggests that officials referred to wartime official histories in the civil series only occasionally, if at all, during the course of their everyday activities. As Denys Hay, the co-author of the official history on the *Design and Development of Weapons* (1964), observed, the lack of another world war largely undermined their intended relevance: 'It is much to be doubted whether solutions found for any emergency are much use ten or twenty years later.'[123]

Despite being presented and justified as potentially relevant to public policy, official histories were treated in practice as of 'restricted importance and utility'.[124] Official histories remained on the shelf or – as Woodward complained about the five-volume draft of his unpublished diplomatic history – in a dusty cupboard.[125] Whether or not the peacetime official histories would fare any better as policy inputs remained questionable, especially as their projected publication established that the target audience was located largely outside of Whitehall. Thus, their functional role centred principally upon the policy benefits of presenting 'the British case' to a wider domestic and external audience confronted increasingly by rival histories. In this vein, in 1971, Trend pressed Heath (prime minister, 1970–74) to approve a series of official histories on intelligence intended in part to correct the perceived distortions of the historical record resulting from recent revelations in the memoirs of Kim Philby (*My Silent War*, 1968), among others.[126]

Meanwhile, the official peacetime histories, albeit lacking the drive, scale and unified editorial framework of the Second World War histories, moved ahead.[127] The initial studies – Norman Chester's *The Nationalization of British Industry, 1945–1951* and J.B. Cullingworth and G.E. Cherry's first two volumes on *Environmental Planning, 1939–1969* – did not appear until 1975. Gowing's two-volume *Independence and Deterrence: Britain and Atomic Energy, 1945–1952* was eventually cleared for publication in 1974.[128] One often overlooked product of the 'new situation' arising from the introduction of the 30-Year Rule and the subsequent decision (December 1969) to release all Second World War files in January 1972 was the Cabinet Office's agreement to reprint out-of-print official histories of the Second World War, including the referenced versions hitherto reserved for confidential official use.[129]

Conclusion

During the 1950s and 1960s, a series of seemingly separate issues touching upon history and public policy became increasingly interlinked, at least in the minds of policymakers, who took things forward on several fronts at the same time. Moreover, these issues – they included official histories, internal histories, access to public records, and the future of the Cabinet Office's Historical Section – became the subject of public debate, even parliamentary and media controversy, thereby acquiring political significance. Within Whitehall, there occurred also upon the part of both ministers and officials a kind of 'learning curve' regarding the use and management of official history and public records.[130]

Regardless of the way in which this book foregrounds history's role in government, history-related topics are frequently dismissed as marginal political issues to be glossed over, even totally ignored, by most histories. But, as mentioned above, this should not be equated with political insignificance. On the contrary, as Trend reminded prime minister

Wilson in January 1965, 'many of the points involved are highly political', and – to quote Hunt, Trend's successor – 'as an act of public policy' required action at the highest level of government as well as cross-party consensus.[131] Likewise, when discussing the 30-Year Rule's implications for the Foreign Office with Sir John Nicholls, a Deputy Under Secretary, and Rohan Butler, Michael Stewart (Foreign Secretary, 1965–66) pointed to the tendency of such seemingly minor questions to prove most politically complicated and difficult.[132] In practice, these topics, whether concerning official histories, histories written for confidential departmental use, or public records, raised substantial political, constitutional and legal issues appertaining to, say, domestic and foreign policy interests, the convention of collective ministerial responsibility, official secrecy, and the confidentiality of exchanges between ministers and officials. Furthermore, they impacted upon the way in which the past actions of British governments, departments, ministers and officials were presented at the bar of history at home and abroad. The lengthy delays in the publication of Woodward's five-volume wartime diplomatic history, alongside the refusal by successive governments to commission an official history of the Suez Crisis, reflected the perceived power of history to damage present-day British policy interests.

In many respects, the 30-Year Rule marked a significant opening up of what was viewed as a relatively closed system of government noted for its fierce defence of official secrecy. Even so, as asserted by a former head of the prime minister's policy unit, the closed period still presented serious obstacles to historians and others seeking access to documents for the purpose of making balanced and informed assessments of the performance of British governments: 'The Official Secrets Act and the Thirty Year Rule, by hiding peacetime fiascos as though they were military disasters, protect Ministers and officials from embarrassment. They also ensure that there is no learning curve.'[133] Indeed, looking back from 1977, David Henderson – like Gowing, he had moved between academia and government – argued that 'most organisations, in Britain as well as elsewhere, are less interested in learning from their mistakes than in concealing them'.[134] For Henderson, official secrecy, the 30-Year rule and civil service anonymity ensured an emphasis upon process and competence rather than the quality of advice, that is a system accepting 'the unimportance of being right'.[135]

Even so, departments were not prevented from using records closed to academic historians, among others, to learn from past experience in the way proposed by Brook in 1957. In the event, as Gowing lamented,

Brook's proposal for using history to record and evaluate experience, having been inspired in part by her work therein as well as by the additional internal histories produced for departments by official historians, 'took root in only one department, the Treasury'.[136] As a result, the Treasury offered the best example of this process of moving on from wartime official histories – to quote Elsie Abbot, the Treasury's Establishment Officer – 'which tend to be read once and never looked at again' to a more focused format for codifying the departmental memory.[137] By 1969, when the Wilson government commissioned the first peacetime histories, the Treasury had already been using internal histories to fund past experience for over a decade. Even then, the Treasury experienced considerable difficulty in drawing history formally into the policymaking process, as evidenced by the ups and downs charted in Chapters 3–9 and the THS's eventual closure in 1976. In many respects, the fact of closure recognized the fundamental problem of actually using history in government – typically, the linkage worked better in theory than practice – just as the whole episode highlighted also the difficulty of sharing the fruits of the Treasury's past experience throughout Whitehall.

For historians, official histories offered one way of enhancing historical knowledge and understanding about topics for which the public records were closed.[138] Despite the government's screening procedures, British official histories came to be valued as a major historical source, especially upon the part of the growing number of historians, international relations, politics and public administration specialists studying the history of the recent period. Such developments provided also alternative ways of linking historians working in academia with government. For example, in 1974, Michael Lee, Reader in Politics at Birkbeck College and a member of the SSRC's Social Sciences and Government Committee with experience of a Treasury secondment between 1967 and 1969, formed an administrative history study group, whose membership included Ogilvy-Webb, a Treasury historian figuring prominently in subsequent chapters, and representatives of the Public Record Office (PRO).[139] Furthermore, the official histories project gave academic historians and social scientists, like Gowing, first-hand experience of working within government, while confronting them with the fundamental dilemma faced by such historians, that is the tensions arising on the one hand from membership of their professional guild and on the other hand their status as temporary civil servants writing functional histories subject to the Official Secrets Act and departmental laundering procedures.[140] As Keith Hancock admitted, all experienced a serious conflict of loyalties: 'as a craftsman I must follow the practice of my guild but as an official I must obey the instructions of my superiors'.[141] Subsequent chapters establish that similar conflicts were to face those involved in writing internal histories within Whitehall departments.

Part II
Using History in the Treasury

3
The Treasury Becomes 'Very Historically Minded', 1957–60

The Wilson government's revision of the closed period for public records led the Treasury, like other Whitehall departments, to prepare for the earlier opening up of its archives in accordance with the 1967 Public Records Act. More importantly, the proposed introduction of the peacetime official histories series, in conjunction with the forthcoming start of work by the new interdepartmental Committee on Official Histories of Peacetime Events, prompted an urgent re-think of existing lines of policy in the light of what had been achieved already.

During the late 1950s and early 1960s, the Treasury had become increasingly active writing up 'administrative' histories of past departmental policy and procedures showing 'administrators in action' with a view to supporting, streamlining and enhancing present-day and future work.[1] As Ian Bancroft, the Deputy Establishment Officer, claimed, 'we are having a drive on what is now called by the fashionable phrase "funding experience"'.[2] Indeed, the Treasury, having partly inspired Brook's 1957 policy initiative, led Whitehall in giving effect to his proposals by funding past experience, as represented in departmental files and oral testimony provided by participants, through a range of historical outputs produced for confidential internal use only, *not for publication*.

Moreover, the recent creation of both the Treasury Historical Committee (THC) and the THS in 1965 represented yet another attempt to integrate "funding experience" activities more effectively into the department's everyday work. Soon afterwards, the expanding range of internal histories led Abbot, the Establishment Officer, to remind Sir William Armstrong and Sir Laurence Helsby, the Joint Permanent Secretaries, that 'on this I think we have done rather well'.[3] In turn, the resulting primacy attached to using history for internal purposes led Abbot, the Treasury's representative, to inform the interdepartmental official committee of the conditional nature of her department's participation in new projects. Any additional commitments, such as those arising from the new peacetime official histories, must not be undertaken at the expense of ongoing historical activities: 'the writing of official histories should not interfere with nor slow down the work of "funding experience" for the immediate advantage of Treasury divisions'.[4]

In fact, the Treasury's use of history to fund past experience for departmental purposes was – to quote James Collier, the Deputy Establishment Officer – 'quite a different matter' from producing official histories for publication targeted primarily at an external audience.[5] Writing in April 1964, Collier articulated clearly and concisely the perceived role of history in furnishing a departmental memory supportive of the Treasury's present-day work:

> The Treasury are becoming very historically minded these days and a great deal of emphasis is put on writing up descriptions of various episodes of recent and fairly recent Treasury activities, and of tracing Treasury policy through a series of episodes. *This is only in small part for historical reasons; its main purpose is to give divisional officers a brief picture of the problems which have affected their predecessors and the ways in which they have tackled them, their successes and perhaps even their failures. These pieces are not meant to be post mortems, however; their purpose is strictly to be helpful* [author's emphasis]. There is so much activity (and... the documentation of the Treasury's activities has not always been perfect!) and it really is very difficult for a divisional officer to know everything that has gone before him, either in his own immediate responsibilities, or even more so, in other spheres of Treasury activity which might help him in his present problems.... Although... these papers have historical interest *their purpose is to give the divisional officer, and particularly the divisional officer who comes newly to the work, a quick and accurate conspectus of all that has gone before him* [author's emphasis].[6]

At least, this was the theory. Whether or not these principles fed through into the administrative process and actually impacted upon departmental practice in the way intended remains questionable, especially as the Treasury's successive re-launches of the "funding experience" initiative indicated the enduring problem of persuading divisions to use the resulting histories in their day-to-day work.

Gowing's early Treasury histories

As mentioned in previous chapters, the Treasury's experimental historical activities were instrumental in inspiring Brook's policy initiative launched in December 1957. Earlier that year, when looking back upon the serious challenge posed by recent events, Sir Alexander Johnston, a Third Secretary, had advised Brook that it would 'greatly assist' the 'Supply side' of the Treasury's work 'if we had a record in convenient form of what has been done in disasters of one kind or another'.[7] The government's difficulties in dealing with such events as the 1953 East Coast Floods – for the Treasury, the offer to match voluntary subscriptions pound-for-pound proved 'very embarrassing' financially – were very much in his mind. More recently, in 1956, when refugees proved a major preoccupation, he recalled how 'it would have been of great value to us in handling the Hungarian and Egyptian problems if we had had in fairly concise form an account of the lessons of the East Coast floods'.

For Johnston, there seemed considerable merit in commissioning for future reference a history drawing out the lessons of the East Coast floods, alongside 'any relevant earlier cases', and then doing the same for the 1956 refugee problems. As a result, in any future crisis policymakers would benefit from an ability to draw immediately upon such case studies for informed guidance upon the requisite administrative and financial checks on public expenditure, the exercise of official control over the use of funds raised by voluntary bodies, and the Exchequer's liability upon the exhaustion of voluntary contributions. Johnston pointed also to the case for commissioning a history of the 1951 Festival Gardens project, which represented a black spot in the departmental memory: 'we need note of lessons to be learned from Festival Gardens, where we lost a lot of money'.[8]

> The Treasury had some sobering experiences in connection with the running of Festival Gardens, Limited, but that experience is now buried in a large bundle of files. If another case came along, there is a danger that we should fall into the same pitfalls because of the difficulty, amid current problems, of delving into these old files and extracting what is of value.

For Brook, Johnston's proposal, originating out of a genuine practical need to use history, linked in well with ongoing developments about the role of history in government, as outlined in Chapter 2. Readily agreeing, he placed Margaret Gowing, whose work on the

Second World War official histories had now largely finished and was already working in the Treasury, under Johnston's supervision.[9] In March 1957, Johnston explored possible ways forward with Gowing, who was currently writing a history of monetary policy covering the past five years for the Treasury's Economic Section and HF (Home Finance) division for submission to the Radcliffe Committee.[10] Following this meeting, the Treasury commissioned Gowing to write histories of both the Festival Gardens project and Acts of God.[11] As requested, Gowing worked quickly, and completed the two memoranda by early November 1957, when she moved on to a history of exchequer aid to colonies.

Brook and Johnston were impressed by Gowing's speed of work, especially as she was undertaking other Treasury assignments at the same time; for example, in September 1957 she completed a history for the Economic Section covering the government and nationalised industries' loan operations between 1951 and 1957.[12] More importantly, both officials, praising the memoranda as 'documents of *long-term use* [author's emphasis] which Treasury officials will wish to keep by them', approved the extra costs of printing 150 copies with cardboard covers for circulation within the Treasury down to the level of Assistant Secretary.[13] In this manner, Gowing inaugurated what became known as the Treasury Historical Memoranda (THM) series. Moreover, the memoranda's perceived applied value reinforced Brook's determination to do something more to draw "history", defined as codifying the fruits of past experience hitherto buried in the files, more formally into the policymaking process; thus, within weeks of reading Gowing's draft memoranda he launched the "funding experience" initiative encouraging other Whitehall departments to emulate the Treasury model.

Gowing's Treasury histories

Gowing's first THM, entitled *The Treasury and Acts of God*, provided a history of government financial assistance in response to natural disasters.[14] Drawing upon brief narrative accounts of seven post-1945 Acts of God, including floods at Salford (October 1946), Lynton and Lynmouth (August 1952), the East Coast (January–February 1953) and Moray-Nairn (July–August 1956), Gowing's 12-page history used the case studies to identify 'some useful lessons on policy' concerning government responses and their financial consequences.[15]

According to Gowing, the late 1940s witnessed a significant change of course by government as compared to the pre-1939 period when 'less was expected of the Government'.[16] As happened at Louth in 1920, compensation was handled previously through charitable relief funds, *not* state assistance:

> It is clear that the austere doctrine of non-interference by the Government in the consequences of Acts of God – as pronounced in the case of the Salford floods – is dead. The doctrine pronounced at the time of the Border floods in 1948 – that the Government only helps with national disasters – has also been superseded. The question now is rather when should the Government give help?[17]

Pointing to the haphazard and inconsistent nature of past responses as well as to the difficulties experienced in dealing with losses, Gowing recorded key points for future reference, including the initial official tendency to exaggerate the extent of damage; the consequent oversubscription of relief funds; the open-ended fiscal commitment arising from the mistaken promise to match voluntary contributions pound-for-pound; the importance of Treasury control over expenditure from relief funds, including clarity about their use to prevent political storms over compensation; and the need to avoid government assistance becoming interpreted as a substitute for property under-insurance.[18] Gowing warned that providing government assistance through several channels risked duplicating effort and 'spending more money than is needed'.[19] In this vein, she pressed the merits of the USA's National Distress Fund, while describing Treasury objections – these centred upon its preference for pragmatic rather than generalized responses – as 'exaggerated'. Nor were existing administrative arrangements adequate, since no department possessed primary responsibility for coordinating emergency relief. For Gowing, the MHLG seemed the most obvious candidate. Finally, she mentioned the prudence of conducting post-mortems into future government responses to natural disasters by way of keeping the THM up to date.

Gowing's second THM, also dated November 1957, focused upon what Trend described as 'the deplorable history of the Festival Gardens' project set up as part of the 1951 Festival of Britain.[20] Indeed, he anticipated that, when finished, Gowing's study 'should serve as an awful warning against any future attempts to repeat this particular blend of public and private enterprise'. On the surface, the Festival of Britain was a brilliant success, a box-office triumph, a massive boost to national morale amidst post-war austerity, and a bold statement of Britishness.[21] Thus, Gowing recorded that the Festival Pleasure Gardens, attracting over eight million people, proved such a popular success that they were kept open for an extra year, that is 1952–53. However, despite drawing far more than the estimated number of visitors, within Treasury circles the project came to be viewed as a 'sorry story', as demonstrated by the fact that the conclusion to Gowing's history of this 'whole miserable business' was headed 'Why did things go so badly wrong?'.[22]

As the nine-page THM demonstrated, repeated delays meant that the Festival Gardens opened one month later than scheduled. More seriously, accounting miscalculations, including the escalating costs arising from the choice of a cost-plus rather than fixed price contract, contributed to high losses. Nor were things helped by lax financial controls: 'no one bothered very much. *In my view* [author's italics] this error was fundamental and provides one of the main lessons for future experience.'[23] For Gowing, the episode offered the Treasury several lessons to take forward into the future:

> Treasury officials have said that the Festival Gardens were an object lesson in what happens when financial control is deliberately forsworn. I think this opinion conceals some confusion of thought which was partly responsible for the trouble... at the beginning a great deal of time and thought was spent in ensuring that there was a close control through a tight Loan Agreement. Having established the control, however, nobody bothered to exercise it effectively or, as far as the Treasury was concerned, to see that it was being exercised. On any similar occasions I suggest that the Treasury and other Departments concerned should be absolutely clear in their minds about the degree of control they are trying to exercise.[24]

To some extent, the problem was compounded by the fact that departmental responsibility was 'badly blurred', at least until 1952–53, when the Ministry of Works was given the lead role.[25] Even then, the Treasury could not stand aside, as stated in the THM's concluding paragraph.

> On any occasion when responsibility for a company is not absolutely clear cut, the Treasury should itself make sure that it is laid down in writing from the outset exactly who is expected to do what. If there is a sponsoring department it is not, of course, the Treasury's job to supervise the company but the Treasury should satisfy itself from time to time that the duties of supervision are being properly fulfilled.

Formalizing historical work

Following the completion of these two THMs, Gowing moved on to her next project, a history of exchequer aid to colonies for the Imperial and Foreign division (IF). Meanwhile, the Treasury had been devoting serious thought to future policy towards such historical activities. In August 1957, Peter Vinter, an Under Secretary, minuted Sir Robert Hall, the Director of the Treasury's Economic Section (1947–61) and Economic Adviser to the Government (1953–61), about initiating a series of Treasury histories improving upon 'Last Year's Bradshaw' to supplement the Treasury's understandable preoccupation with present-day issues and future developments.[26] The perceived practical utility of Gowing's history of monetary policy, written for submission to the Radcliffe Committee, was clearly prominent in Vinter's thinking: 'It must have been borne upon a good many people in Whitehall at one time or another that it is extraordinarily hard to get quickly – and quickness is usually the real need – an adequate account of (a) what happened in the recent past, and (b) how events compared with what was supposed to happen, i.e. did policies work out and if not why not?'. Normally, the first type of question was usually 'the easier kind to answer' from available material.

> But (b) is rarely easy, and yet it is something we very much need since *policy is usually as much rooted in the past (about which we could know more if we were organised to do so) as it is concerned with the future* [author's emphasis], about which we can only guess and have strong hunches. The paper in the Radcliffe series 'Monetary Policy and the Control of Economic Conditions: a Note on Recent Experience' shows, I suggest, how valuable this kind of work can be.

For Vinter, the present moment seemed 'opportune' for 'a kind of continuing economic history', recording what actually happened over, say, a five-year period ending some 18 months from the present. The ideal person, preferably attached to the Economic Section, required historical sense and judgement allied to expertise in economics.[27] By October 1957, Vinter had secured agreement in principle from his superiors for a proposal designed in effect to regularize Gowing's ongoing historical work. Both Sir Robert Hall and Richard Clarke, Third Secretary and head of HOPS (Home and Overseas Planning Staff), welcomed what seemed 'a good idea' worthy of implementation.[28] Even so, as Clarke reminded Vinter, there was also an urgent need for the Treasury to get departmental records, the basic historical resource, into 'better shape' for easy access before allocating staffing and other resources to historical work.[29] In the event, Abbot 'sat' on Vinter's proposal for a month or so, given her awareness of the fact that Brook himself was thinking along similar lines and preparing what became his "funding experience" initiative.[30]

In any case, Gowing was fully occupied for the time being on exchequer aid to colonies. Discussions were taking place also about her personal position in the light of the temporary nature of her Treasury posting, the imminent termination of her civil histories assignment based upon the Cabinet Office, and talk about interdepartmental history projects based upon the Cabinet Office under Gowing's overall supervision.[31] Johnston's anxiety to retain her services led him to suggest Gowing's permanent transfer to the Treasury, where there existed for the 'foreseeable future' suitable opportunities writing histories designed to draw lessons from 'difficult Treasury cases in the past'.[32]

Responding to Brook's initiative

In May 1958, G. Bell, the Deputy Establishment Officer, circulated Treasury divisional heads with details of Brook's "funding experience" proposal.[33] The notice was supported by an outline of the Treasury's historical activities to date, copies of Gowing's first two THMs, future plans and a request for divisions to propose further topics adjudged useful to their work for inclusion in Gowing's programme or writing up within divisions. Unsurprisingly, contrasting interests, alongside differing workloads, meant that individual divisions responded with varying degrees of enthusiasm. Rates of response also proved variable; indeed, in July several divisions were sent reminders about their failure to reply. Even so, a further reminder was required to elicit a response from the Home Finance division.[34] The decision to chase up non-respondents reflected the belief that even a nil return was preferable to non-submission in the sense that it led divisions to give at least some thought to the subject.[35] Reviewing initial responses in June 1958, Bell believed that Gowing could be kept busy for a 'considerable time' on worthwhile projects.[36]

However, by this time the future progress of the Treasury's historical experiment seemed threatened by indications that Gowing herself was far from happy with her conditions of work.[37] Reportedly, a perceived sense of isolation from both Treasury officials and the outside world led Gowing to feel – to quote from Johnston's report to Brook – 'very lonely and isolated' and complain 'that the Treasury has not been friendly towards her'. Progress upon the history of colonial aid had been seriously hampered by the way in which the 'quite shocking' pressures of everyday work meant that divisional officials found little time to assist her work. For Johnston, the episode emphasized the need for the Treasury 'to take more trouble over people who prepare historical memoranda. It is not enough to give them the papers and expect them to handle the matter for weeks on end in complete solitude.' Possibly another division – Clarke's HOPS was floated as one possibility – might provide a friendlier environment. Even worse, Gowing's complaints were compounded by resentment about the restricted circulation of her historical memoranda. Despite sympathizing with Gowing's natural desire as a historian for meaningful dialogue with other researchers, like D.N. Chester, Johnston reiterated that the distribution of THMs outside the Treasury was ruled out by the confidential nature of sources and the need for memoranda to cover topics in a 'frank' manner. Nor was the situation helped by Gowing's enduring anxieties about her lack of established status as a civil servant, and especially her pension arrangements.

Brook was sufficiently worried about the position to see Gowing within days of receiving Johnston's report about her uncongenial working environment, since this impacted adversely upon the quality and pace of her historical work.[38] Gowing informed him about the problem of trying to work with officials, who displayed little or no interest in what she was doing and proved reluctant either to respond to queries or to comment upon drafts. For Brook, reports of Gowing's grievances struck a chord, since a recent letter from Keith Hancock had mentioned the 'loneliness' of official historians working for government.[39] Believing that Gowing's 'work would be better done, and more useful' if she was drawn more effectively into the Treasury's everyday work, Brook sounded out various options, while pressing the prudence of launching a 'missionary effort' to remind divisional heads about the benefits of "funding experience" activities, including the fact that more would be achieved through the interest and collaboration of their staff.

Clarke's enthusiastic support for "funding experience"

When reviewing Gowing's position, Brook contemplated her re-assignment to Clarke's HOPS. Like Vinter, Clarke emerged as an influential high-level supporter favouring the introduction of a historical dimension into the everyday work of the Treasury.[40] Undoubtedly, "funding experience" represented one of the 'new constructive developments' pressed by Clarke during this period.[41] Guided by exchanges with HOPS's staff, Clarke apprised Brook about his strong belief in the value of the 'systematic "funding of experience"' of significant episodes of administration and policy. Indeed, this proposal seemed 'tailor-made for us', given the 'novel and experimental ... greatly changed' and 'episodic' nature of HOPS's activities: 'It is important to get these episodes properly recorded and indexed, so that when new problems come up, we can search for pointers.'[42]

For the time being, Clarke prioritized "seeded files" – frequently he used "selected files" as his preferred descriptor – comprising leading documents on topics marked by a senior official as having 'potential future interest'. In time, he anticipated that HOPS would possess a policy resource 'invaluable when the same or similar problems recur': 'it would help a lot. It would help newcomers to find their feet. And it would help us to tackle new jobs.' Over time, "seeded files" would become, he anticipated, a routine and invaluable part of the day-to-day work of the section, not a burdensome add-on. Clarke specified that "seeded files" should include papers showing how a project started – this was 'very important' – and finished – 'even more so' – as well as principal intermediate points, together with minutes of chief meetings, decisive analyses, correspondence and memoranda, and submissions to ministers. Finally, there should be added a brief overall narrative of the topic plus a retrospective comment written by a senior official. For lesser topics justifying only a short file, he advised against abstracting the principal papers. Rather the file itself would be treated as a "seeded file". Clarke conceded that progress depended upon future workloads, but everyday pressures rendered it unlikely that more than 12 such files would be produced in any one year.

Despite attaching lower priority to histories on the lines of Gowing's THMs, Clarke acknowledged the value of having at 'our fingertips' in-depth studies of past experience on specific subjects – he cited investment control since 1945 and the methods employed by government since 1945 to prioritize defence and housing – by way of preparation for a possible change of government. Regarding bids for inclusion in Gowing's future programme, Clarke opined that their diffuse nature meant that such histories would be 'better done by an administrator than by a historian'.[43] Sections of Clarke's early draft replies, albeit omitted from the final version sent to Brook, are worth citing by way of revealing his thinking about the merits of an incremental historical strategy beginning with "seeded files".[44] Despite conceding that 'there would almost certainly be useful lessons to be learned' from histories upon, say, German support costs negotiations, Clarke saw no reason to write such histories 'until we had established our system of "seeding" the results of current work, and had built our bank of "seeded files" for the most important projects of recent years'. In any case, the difficulty of fitting such historical activities into 'our flow', alongside the likely need for additional staffing, encouraged him to dismiss extended histories as 'premature'.

Welcoming his generally positive tone, Brook began a regular exchange of views with Clarke about the funding of experience.[45] Despite admitting that "seeded files" provided 'a useful practical record for use on future comparable problems', Brook pressed the case for more extensive 'historical work' undertaken by staff not engaged in everyday tasks. In addition, he claimed that Gowing's training as an economic historian, alongside her substantial experience on the official war histories, meant that she was well equipped to work on demanding HOPS's subjects.

Gowing's departure for the UKAEA

The MHLG was to the fore among other Whitehall departments anxious to respond positively to Brook's "funding experience" initiative, but lacked, or so it claimed, suitable staff. Subsequently, the Treasury complained about being 'harassed' by correspondence and phone calls from the MHLG which saw Gowing as the ideal person to build upon her study on the 1953 East Coast Floods.[46] The Treasury proved unforthcoming, partly because Gowing's scheduled commitments for IF stretched at least to the end of the year and partly because she claimed to have 'had enough of floods' and hence little inclination to rehash the same material from a slightly different departmental perspective.[47] Notwithstanding recent complaints about her working conditions, Gowing proved reluctant to move to another department following Brook's reassurances and indications of Clarke's support. Clearly, at a time when senior officials had been taken aback by the strength of her grievances, Abbot deemed it important to heed Gowing's personal preferences: 'Sir Norman Brook is anxious that we should do all we can to make her feel "wanted" '.[48] Following an exchange of ideas with Gowing, Clarke concluded that she promised to be 'v. useful to us', even suggesting that HOPS was capable of keeping her occupied indefinitely.[49]

Undeterred by previous Treasury stonewalling, in November 1958 the MHLG renewed its request to borrow Gowing. Yet again, the Treasury gave a negative response.[50] Then, a mere two months later, the Treasury learned that Gowing had applied for the post of historian/archivist at the UKAEA.[51] For Gowing, the post promised not only greater scope and interest but also the opportunity for publication ruled out by the confidential nature of her work at the Treasury. More personal reasons, arising from longstanding worries about her status as a temporary civil servant lacking established status and a pension, compounded her desire to move: 'The Historical Section was never intended to be, and never has been, a career for anyone.'[52] Brook pressed her to stay, but conceded that, though able to offer extra remuneration, he was unable to arrange established status and inclusion in the civil service's pension scheme.[53] Gowing's UKAEA job application was successful, and hence she gave notice of leaving the Treasury in June 1959.[54] As a result, when the MHLG next repeated its request to borrow Gowing, the Treasury's usual rejection was accompanied by an admission that this time she was no longer available for its own future work, let alone that of other departments. Having recently predicted that Gowing would have a 'fairly long sojourn' in the Treasury, Nicholls was forced to admit to the MHLG that 'now we are in much the same position as yourselves – and so far we have given no thought where to turn ourselves'.[55]

Gowing's final project

When moving to the UKAEA in June 1959, Gowing was still in the process of completing the history of exchequer aid to colonies approaching independence. Codifying the 'general principles' influencing British policymakers would, it was anticipated, support the everyday work of the IF Division, and provide 'newcomers to IF with fairly comprehensive accounts of previous history'.[56] In fact, the specific need to record the divisional memory on the topic led Gowing to make the history 'very much longer' than planned in order to include case studies illustrating the general principles.

In the event, progress was hindered by a series of practical difficulties, which delayed completion and hampered full and up-to-date coverage of individual colonies and topics. Problems in accessing files still in 'constant use' were compounded by the constant struggle to secure responses to factual queries and timely feedback from officials on interim drafts. For instance, Colonel William Russell-Edmunds confessed his 'decidedly red face' for taking so long to review sections covering Malta and colonial defence costs.[57] In turn, the failure of both IF and the Colonial Office to meet requests for data left Gowing reliant upon 'tentative' guesstimates. By the time of her switch to the UKAEA, Gowing had scaled down initial plans for a comprehensive history of the subject: 'This is not now possible so I have simply collected together the various studies that were to form part of a coherent whole.'[58] As a result, upon her departure the history comprised little more than a series of separate case studies – these included British Guiana, Malaysia, Malta and the West Indies – prefaced with a draft introductory note seeking to identify the general principles governing exchequer aid, or rather the lack thereof. According to Gowing, policy developed in a piecemeal manner, thereby causing disparity of treatment. For Gowing, the Treasury's prime objective, itself 'a legacy of the past', was the desire to avoid imposing large burdens on British taxpayers, even if the cost, amounting to *circa* £40–50 million per year, represented an 'insignificant' proportion of overall government expenditure.[59]

When leaving the Treasury, Gowing indicated that, excepting the usual final editorial work prior to printing, only a few gaps and queries had still to be covered alongside some updating of the text.[60] Responsibility for completing the history was placed upon Shirley Littler, an Assistant Principal, who assumed that only minor editorial work was required prior to printing, especially as divisional staff had been actively involved throughout the production process. Indeed, Littler herself had written notes to 'lead' Gowing on British Guiana and Cyprus, and commented upon interim drafts.[61] In the event, her expectations were foiled. Littler soon realized that 'quite a lot of work' remained to be done, such as upon 'Colonial Development and Welfare'.[62] The section on colonial defence costs had yet to be revised in the light of Russell-Edmunds' tardy comments, while the whole text, which currently went only as far as mid-1958, required updating until the start of the 1959–60 fiscal year.

As a result, within days of Gowing's departure, serious questions were raised by officials whether the history should be terminated, even binned. The resulting episode proved of interest in illuminating the contrasting agendas of historians and officials. In particular, it cast serious doubt upon the receptiveness of Treasury officials, especially staff below the higher levels, towards the everyday relevance and value of "funding experience" work, even outcomes resulting from their active involvement. Nor were things helped by the fact that by June 1959 the history had lost its initial perceived policy utility. When commissioned in late 1957, the history was intended to guide officials formulating colonial development policy for the 1958 policy review. As Peck, the head of the Imperial and Foreign division, complained in 1959, 'the memoranda were not available in time and the policy has now been settled'.[63] To some extent, the divisional emphasis upon the need for speed to meet a specific current purpose can be seen as conflicting with the historian's adoption of a more measured approach to recording past experience. In the event, as mentioned above, most delays were beyond Gowing's control. Even so, Peck and Littler, recalling Gowing's problems working for their division, were inclined to treat the history's shortcomings as in part a function of her perceived lack of empathy for IF work, and hence to view her as an unsympathetic and inexpert outsider parachuted into the division. Revealingly, Peck marked the following part of Littler's minute:

> I know that Mrs Gowing found it difficult to establish an easy working contact with I.F. and I doubt whether she ever quite got the 'feel' of I.F. work and its relationship to wider aspects of H.M.G.'s policies e.g. balance of payments and so on. . . . I think it essential that before the question of printing is decided (or indeed before any major tidying up is started) someone in I.F. should read all the papers through to see how far you are happy with the general picture they present.[64]

Although IF officials articulated reservations about specific case studies, their strongest criticism was targeted at Gowing's introductory note. Written of necessity towards the close of the project, this section had not yet been submitted for comment by officials. Initial reactions were far from encouraging, as evidenced by Peck's sharp critique about the 'very detailed' text sprinkled throughout with what he saw as unacceptable value judgements rather than informed critical assessments:

> I would find it very hard to agree that the introductory section should be printed since it seems to present the Treasury, and indeed successive Governments, in a rather odd light. This is because it seems to me to suffer from a number of serious omissions and also a lack of balance. . . . The document would have to be fundamentally recast if it were to be in a form which I could personally endorse.[65]

Problems areas were neither marked nor specified, but the following examples taken from Gowing's draft were likely to incur Peck's wrath.

> It would be a mistake to see this effort [i.e. the UK's aid to colonies as under-developed countries] as governed by some general strategy of

developing the Colonies. There has not been any radical re-thinking about the total sums that the United Kingdom should make available, nor of the profitable ways of spending United Kingdom Government money in the Colonies. The administration of Exchequer aid does not seem to have been related to the vast amount of discussion and thought that goes on in the world at large about the problems of developing under-developed territories. Rather policies have been formulated piecemeal.... The Treasury tries to exact as much control [that is over aid given to colonies] as the political circumstances of any particular Colony will allow. This may be realistic but it is doubtful whether it is logical.[66]

Nor had Gowing covered all policy considerations. For Peck, 'serious omissions' included the failure to take account of the constraints exerted by Britain's physical capacity and balance of payments difficulties; the fact that exchequer aid was treated as part of a properly integrated development programme for individual territories, not an *ad hoc* initiative; and the need to view economic aid within the political and strategic context.

Peck and Littler considered three options: first, completing the project for printing by remedying perceived deficiencies, that is filling the gaps, updating the text, 're-writing' the value judgements, and improving the introduction; secondly, printing the papers without any new work, excepting the omission of the introduction and other disputed points; and thirdly, retaining the papers as they stood in the division as a 'useful historical summary'. One key constraint resulted from the fact that neither official claimed to have the time, let alone the inclination, for the 'formidable task' of preparing the history for printing as a THM; thus, Littler complained that 'I am nearly always busy in this office.... Research on additional points, or re-writing of the earlier bits must inevitably compete with my own work.'[67] Unsurprisingly, in the end the decision was taken to retain the history in its current state for divisional use, as and when required, and not to waste further time upon what Nicholls described as a 'slightly abortive' memorandum.[68]

Interestingly, some 19 years later Gowing returned to enquire about the fate of her history, given its omission from a list of THMs published in *The Times* in the wake of Hennessy's efforts to secure their release under Lord Croham's 1976 open government initiative.[69] Having been led by Johnston to believe that the history would be printed as a THM, in 1978 Gowing raised the issue with Sir Douglas Wass, the Treasury's Permanent Secretary.[70] The latter confirmed that the draft history, albeit made available in 1971 to David J. Morgan by way of background for his official peacetime history on *Colonial Development* (1980), had never been finalized for printing as a THM.[71] Gowing was left to speculate about the reasons for the Treasury's failure to complete the project.

> I remember hearing that some of the Treasury Civil Servants involved at the time with colonial affairs did not agree with my analysis, but it was always intended that these historical memoranda should be good critical history and not some anodyne, and therefore pretty useless, 'agreed version'. Thus I believe Colonel Russell Edmonds (*sic*) did not like certain things I wrote which were critical of some of his arguments on the files, but this would be no reason for withholding the memoranda from the series.[72]

Nor did Wass accept Gowing's subsequent offer to complete the history for printing.

Conclusion

Regardless of official reservations regarding the utility of her unfinished history on colonial aid, Gowing's departure left a large gap in the Treasury's future plans, given the manner in which she had given practical effect to Brook's "funding experience" aspirations: 'I was engaged at the personal request of Sir Norman Brook, in experimental work on historical administration studies for departmental use.'[73] Her two THMs were specifically drafted to offer policymakers a useful and accessible reference tool illuminating past policy, with special emphasis placed upon the nature and development of events, the critical analysis of the principal problems, and the identification of lessons for future action. Each history, embodying the fruits of informed and close study based upon substantial Treasury documentation, reflected the product of a historical research process difficult, indeed impossible, for officials to undertake properly in a fast-moving situation, especially in times of crisis. Even so, Gowing reminded readers of the dangers of generalizing from the particular, and hence the need to appreciate that 'some of these [i.e. shortcomings] may seem peculiar to the circumstances' of the specific project.[74]

In addition, Gowing's histories, written for confidential internal use and not for publication, helped establish also a sharp differentiation between the Treasury's approach to history and the official histories project, as noted by Ogilvy-Webb:

> Because publication of the results was precluded (completed studies are circulated strictly within the confines of Whitehall and given a stringent security classification), academics on the whole were unlikely to find it appealing. Despite this major disadvantage by comparison with the Cabinet Office scheme, however, the Treasury one has the compensation that it permits of a considerably more penetrating approach. By virtue of being known to be non-disclosable outside Government circles, the Treasury studies are able to be more rounded and a good deal more forthright in their conclusions.[75]

The saga centred upon Gowing's colonial aid history provided an early indication of the varying, frequently conflicting, agendas of historians and officials working in the Treasury. Despite Gowing's presentation of her Treasury histories 'as "policy evaluation" rather than straight history', officials often viewed them as excessively academic and lengthy, even somewhat abstruse.[76] In this vein, her complaints about feeling isolated within the Treasury, in conjunction with the strong reservations articulated by officials about the perceived merits of this history, foreshadowed what was to become a serious gulf dividing Treasury historians and officials. Notwithstanding the high level of commitment to "funding experience" on the part of senior staff like Brook, Clarke, Johnston and Vinter, officials working within divisions often proved less supportive, partly because of a fundamental lack of conviction about the theoretical and practical merits of "funding experience". As Littler minuted, from the divisional point of view, 'the object is to produce papers which are useful to I.F. and of general interest to the Treasury'.[77] By implication, the division's decision to shelve Gowing's draft history reflected its view that it was not adjudged to meet this criterion.

Gowing's initial THMs were read in both draft and printed formats by senior officials, most notably Brook, Clarke and Trend, as evidenced by the way in which they inspired the 1957 "funding experience" initiative. Whether or not these initial histories were actually read more generally across the Treasury by officials, let alone impacted upon their thinking and everyday actions, remains more questionable. Anecdotal evidence exists establishing their enduring value in preserving a departmental memory and providing knowledge as a basis for action or inaction. Indeed, even Littler acknowledged that she had 'learnt a lot' about the history of exchequer aid from reading Gowing's interim drafts.[78] In 1962 Clarke, when informing Brook of his support for THMs, admitted that Gowing's Acts of God history had proved 'very useful'.[79] Reportedly, the Public Income/Outlay division also derived 'considerable advantage' from this history.[80] Likewise, in December 1971, Douglas Henley, a Deputy Secretary, recalled the way in which Gowing's THM on the Festival Pleasure Gardens reminded Treasury officials that the episode, far from being the 'idyllic interlude' suggested by the title, represented 'in fact a sad story of financial mismanagement'.[81]

By contrast, in February 1978, that is shortly before delivering the Rede lecture mentioned in Chapter 1, Gowing received discouraging feedback about her THMs. Following criticism of the government's inaction regarding recent floods, she had contacted Chris France, the Treasury's Establishment Officer, to enquire whether her 1957 THM on Acts of God had been consulted and 'been of use to anyone' dealing with what the press described as the worst floods on the East coast since 1953.[82] Pointing to the way in which a copy was produced quickly for him on demand as well as its inclusion in a list of THMs circulated in 1977 to divisional heads encouraging their use 'to reduce the amount of research which might otherwise be required in dealing with unusual cases', France reassured Gowing that her THM was 'certainly not lost to view'.[83]

> Nevertheless, it seems that your own memorandum was not used in considering the question of possible relief for those who suffered from the recent floods. I understand that the Treasury was consulted by the Department of the Environment, but the fact is that public expenditure issues (and local authority finance) are handled very differently from what was the case in 1957, and the Treasury tends to stand back from detailed issues considerably more than it did in those days.

Disappointed by news that her THM was presented as of limited 'administrative use', Gowing's interest in the history–public policy linkage led her to pursue the matter in order to ascertain 'whether this was because it was useless or because no-one knew it existed'.[84] France's reply was revealing, most notably highlighting the impact of a changing organizational framework over time, the way in which the need for urgent action discouraged the expenditure of time and effort on using history to fund 'collective experience', and the limited shelf life of any THM.

What happened over the recent floods was that the Department of the Environment, having to move quickly, got in touch with the Treasury and quoted a fairly recent precedent for emergency support to local authorities. The Treasury accepted the precedent as a sound one, and the support was provided accordingly. So no-one consulted your memorandum (as I said in my earlier letter) but that does not mean that it was (or is) 'useless', which is a strong word. What happened here was that the collective experience had developed, so to speak, and that Whitehall had only to cast its mind back a few years to find something that was helpful. Now that the major spending departments are so much more closely involved in the overall control of public expenditure (through the Public Expenditure Survey Committee) than they once were, the Treasury can usually rely on them to propose the sensible way round a problem. But that does not mean that the day will never come when the Treasury has to go back to first principles to find the solution in a particular case.[85]

Nor were things helped by the fact that Gowing's THM only covered the period until 1957 and had never been updated; thus, in 1978 policymakers using her THM would have found a lengthy 20-year gap in historical coverage of Treasury practice.

Impressed with Gowing's 'splendid work' on both the official histories and the THMs, Brook had sought in vain to retain her services as a Treasury historian.[86] Inevitably, her departure raised serious question marks about what would happen next to the Treasury's historical activities? Like Gowing's history of exchequer aid, would they become 'slightly abortive', particularly given the lack of enthusiasm shown by divisional staff for such histories? As Clarke informed Brook shortly after Gowing's resignation, hitherto the Treasury had 'hardly scratched the surface' in terms of writing and using history.[87] Subsequent chapters establish that neither Gowing's departure nor the shelving of her exchequer aid history deflected the Treasury's "funding experience" ambitions. During the early 1960s, Brook, strongly supported by Clarke and Vinter, proved instrumental in pushing ahead with the Treasury's historical work. Gowing's legacy lived on.

4
Pushing Ahead with "Funding Experience", 1960–62

In the short term, Gowing's move to the UKAEA in June 1959 was seen as posing a serious threat to the future of the Treasury's historical work in general and the THM series in particular. In the event, the continued support of leading officials for "funding experience" activities ensured that the early 1960s saw further progress in terms of the amount and variety of historical work undertaken within the Treasury. Ongoing projects, conducted within divisions through "seeded files" and divisional notes, were of course unaffected.

During the late 1950s, Richard "Otto" Clarke, the Third Secretary responsible for HOPS, emerged as a prominent and influential enthusiast for policy-related historical work. When reviewing HOPS's progress with Brook soon after Gowing's departure, Clarke pressed his belief that there was scope for the Treasury as a whole to do far more by way of implementing the 1957 "funding experience" initiative.[1] Hitherto, progress had proved patchy across the whole department, even if Clarke was able to report that his divisions, that is the Overseas Coordination Division (OC), National Resources Divisions I (NRI) and II (NRII), had made a good start in spite of having to rely wholly upon their own staff. Soon afterwards, Clarke arranged the transfer of A.K. (James) Ogilvy-Webb, a Treasury Principal, from administrative work with a view to the production of THM-type histories for HOPS.

In November 1962, Clarke's promotion to become Second Secretary (1962–66) – this was seen as equivalent in rank to the PUS of other departments – in charge of the Public Sector Group reflected his growing prominence in the Treasury, as highlighted by the way in which the 1961 Plowden Report was imbued with his thinking about the case for a more strategic approach viewing public sector expenditure within the national economic context. As a Treasury colleague observed, 'These were seemingly simple ideas but new and indeed revolutionary in their implications.'[2] Subsequently, Clarke proved instrumental in putting these proposals into practice through PESC, the inter-departmental Public Expenditure Survey Committee responsible for the control and management of public expenditure.[3]

Clarke's incremental strategy towards historical work

At first, HOPS's historical work concentrated upon "seeded files" containing selected leading papers on topics adjudged to be of 'practical use for current work' and future reference.[4] Topics covered included the European Nuclear Energy Agency, nationalized industries, and the history of German support costs negotiations. Reportedly, these initial efforts referencing the division's 'accumulated experience' were 'warmly welcomed' by HOPS's staff as worthwhile, even 'indispensable', given their mobility across the Treasury: 'The advantage of having this kind of material organised *in usable form* [author's emphasis] is so great that *the preparation of seeded files is really a prerequisite for any major review of policy*' [author's emphasis].[5] The practice enabled busy officials not only to avoid 'carting round piles of bulky files' but also to find the crucial papers – 'the needles... in the haystacks' – more easily and quickly.[6] For example, some 80 Overseas Coordination division files dealing with the Free Trade Area negotiations between January 1956 and November 1958 had been processed to make a mere ten "seeded files". A covering commentary was in draft form, awaiting divisional feedback, and a historical narrative was planned to help users.

For Clarke, the seeding process had to be done currently: 'the man who has been occupied on the work is the best qualified to do it. Tackling a big retrospective job from scratch is formidable.' His own personal experience was used to make the point:

> Mr Figgures and I have both had a pretty long and intimate experience of European economic cooperation, so that when we returned to this field in autumn 1955 we brought a good deal of capital with us. But if a few months later, when we had to do a radical reappraisal of our European economic policies, we had needed to learn from the records, we should have found it extremely difficult to do so.[7]

At the same time, Clarke acknowledged the way in which the lack of historical perspective hindered the selection of both topics worth seeding and key documents for inclusion within "seeded files": 'it is never certain which will emerge as the significant papers and incidents'. Despite HOPS's concentration upon "seeded files", one divisional note – such notes provided brief histories of specific topics – of the 1958–59 Reflation Exercises in Public Investment was under preparation with a view to guiding staff when discussing policy later in the year. Pressure of work, in conjunction with serious understaffing, meant that far less had been achieved than anticipated, but historical work would be continued as and when time and the opportunity arose.

Reading Clarke's July 1959 review of HOPS's historical work on his return from overseas, Brook welcomed its positive tone, while endorsing comments about the utility of "seeded files" in terms of enhancing the accessibility of key documents for busy policymakers.[8] Despite acknowledging the constraints on progress, Brook reminded Clarke that 'staffing, like politics, is the art of the practicable'. By implication, it remained still as difficult for the Treasury to predict the outcome of its historical plans as to forecast the future course of the British economy!

Reviewing divisional bids

Although divisional heads had been invited in May 1958 to propose topics adjudged useful for their work for either inclusion in Gowing's programme or writing up within their respective divisions, some time elapsed before the matter was progressed.[9] It was not until September 1959 that P. Nicholls, the Deputy Establishment Officer, reviewed divisional bids for 'writing up useful histories of important episodes for precedents'.[10] Admittedly, a certain amount of pressure, reinforced by reminders, had been exerted on divisions to submit bids, but the number and extensive range of proposals was deemed encouraging in spite of the nil returns from several divisions, including Establishments (General), Establishments (Manning), Establishments (Professional) and Governmental and Allied Services. The Overseas Finance Division (OF) submitted the highest number of proposals, that is 10 topics, which included the 1949 devaluation, the government as a shareholder in commercial companies, and convertibility. By contrast, as Nicholls specifically recorded, there was no bid from the Imperial and Foreign division, which had shelved Gowing's final history on exchequer aid.

At the same time, resource constraints meant that few projects could be commissioned. Nor were things helped by Gowing's recent departure. As Nicholls minuted, proposals had been solicited 'in the days when we had somebody specifically employed on the job'. Continuing uncertainty about whether or not Gowing would be replaced imposed a serious check upon the Treasury's plans for further THMs because of her central role in initiating and pushing ahead this series. For the time being, divisions would have to rely largely upon their own resources, thereby slowing down the overall pace and range of work across the Treasury.

The Treasury history of wages policy, 1945–60

When reviewing the bids, Nicholls saw the moment as opportune to raise questions about the Treasury's "funding experience" strategy, with special reference to the type of output. Whereas Gowing's work had focused principally on THMs, HOPS prioritized "seeded files".

> There is a good deal of thought still to be given to whether there is a distinction between the original idea of composing Treasury Historical Memoranda and the sort of work on what Mr. Clarke calls 'seeding' files, which may be an end in itself without the actual writing up of the episode which the distilled collection of papers contains.[11]

Presented in this manner, the two approaches appeared very different, whereas in reality, as Clarke himself admitted, they proved complementary. Thus, "seeded files" were not only often accompanied by brief historical narratives of the events covered therein but also viewed as providing *in time* an essential foundation for writing more substantial THM-type histories.

Indeed, during the early 1960s, Clarke's divisions, though continuing to build up their stock of "seeded files", moved onto the next stage, that is the production of more extensive histories of selected past episodes.[12] Even so, within HOPS NRII, though active in seeding files to support its work when drafting annual reviews of public expenditure and investment, proved an exception, since its work was deemed to offer little scope for such histories.[13] HOPS's initial large-scale history, commenced in summer 1960, comprised an extensive study for NRI on 'The Government and Wages' since 1945. For Clarke, a history of post-war wages policy – this topic was selected in preference to alternative proposals like economic planning or the control of public investment – was timely: 'The existing policies seemed to have come to a dead end: the alternatives did not command ready confidence. It was thought that it might be useful to bring to bear the experience of the previous fifteen years.'[14] Throughout, Clarke stressed the history's functional purpose in "funding experience" to provide 'a permanent record within the Treasury... ready for whatever use may be required', most notably identifying the principal 'lessons to be learned' about wages policy.[15] From this perspective, he saw the history as both 'very relevant' to the Treasury's current preoccupations and potentially 'extremely useful' in the future 'if and when the Government begins to develop an active wages policy, for it would provide just the right kind of "funding of experience" for those who have to work on this problem'. At the same time, Clarke saw the project as having a broader role within Whitehall by offering a practical example of the value of using history, as evidenced by his proposal to circulate the printed history to a wider audience outside the Treasury.

The history of wages policy

The task of writing the history was assigned to Ogilvy-Webb, who took some 18 months bringing the project to completion. Despite being allowed access to Treasury files and relevant Cabinet papers, he was not permitted to consult the files of other departments, like the Ministry of Labour. Clarke maintained a close watch over Ogilvy-Webb throughout the whole project, monitoring progress and exerting pressure to ensure the history's utility and expedite completion. Reviewing the project in February 1961, Clarke decided that coverage of the period 1945–51 was 'progressing well' and authorized Ogilvy-Webb to move on to the post-1951 period with a termination date of *circa* 1958.[16] Eventually the end point was extended until July 1960, that is when Selwyn Lloyd became Chancellor of the Exchequer. Subsequently, the excessive length of the draft history – the three volumes totalled over 100,000 words – led Clarke to commission a shorter version for limited circulation within and outside the Treasury as a THM.

Clarke's editorial role, drawing on his journalistic experience and drafting skills, involved heavy use of the blue pencil on early drafts to make the text user-friendly, such as by removing excessive factual detail and moderating Ogilvy-Webb's tendency to express himself 'in a style that might give offence to some readers'.[17] Clarke favoured a 'neutral' style designed to 'remove any risk that a reader coming to the subject for the first time might form an impression of prejudice and thus question the historical objectivity of the narrative. This is essential in all official history, but particularly so in this controversial and politically sensitive subject.'[18] For Ogilvy-Webb, this was easier said than done: 'summarisation forces one into interpretation'.[19] As a result, throughout the project drafts required a good deal of editing by Clarke, who also ruled out the naming of civil servants: 'one must avoid giving any impression of trying to hold a post mortem on what any particular individuals had said at any particular time'.[20]

By the closing months of 1961, Clarke opined that Ogilvy-Webb's 'book' stood up reasonably well as 'a record': 'My own impression is that you have got most of the relevant facts included, but the real difficulty is that in a very "general" subject of this kind a great deal of important discussion takes place on occasions which are not recorded on "wages" files.'[21] As a result, before finalizing the long and short versions of the history, Clarke instructed Ogilvy-Webb to solicit the views of senior officials, like Alec Cairncross, the Economic Adviser, Bryan Hopkin, the Deputy Economic Adviser, Sir Robert Hall, E. Maude, a Under Secretary, and Vinter, previously involved in wages policy to check whether the history represented 'a sound record'.[22] Following Matthew Stevenson's advice, feedback was solicited also from the Ministry of Labour.[23] In the event, Laurence Helsby, its Permanent Secretary, pointed out that his department's view of past events was somewhat different, but asked for no alterations.[24] However, his response is worth quoting in the light of Helsby's forthcoming move to become Joint Permanent Secretary of the Treasury acting as the line manager for its historical activities. In brief, Helsby accepted that 'the writer carried out his instructions to be objective', but saw the history as 'a Treasury document' with a pronounced 'Treasury slant':

> The narrative on wages policy... does deal with matters on which the Treasury and Ministry of Labour have often disagreed. We could, I think, also disagree about the way in which these differences are sometimes presented in the narrative. In fact, if we were to produce our own account of wages policy in the post war years it might have a rather different complexion, at some points at least. But any attempt to produce an agreed document would be a lengthy process and I do not think that there is anything in the present paper to embarrass us, bearing in mind that it could not be shown to more than a limited circle of senior officials. In the circumstances I do not want to propose any alterations.

Helsby commented critically also about the history's perceived utility:

> It is not easy to assess the usefulness of the exercise in relation to present problems. The narrative is naturally a highly condensed account of a complex series of events. In the nature of the case it could

not give a full assessment of the background against which views were formed and decisions taken. It is arguable that in any case the circumstances surrounding incomes policy have changed so greatly in the last year that past experience, even when fully understood, is of limited value as a guide to the future.

On 30 November 1961, Ogilvy-Webb requested Clarke's approval of the final revised versions of both the three-volume *The Government and Wages, 1945–1960* and the shorter 14,000-word THM.[25] Despite extensive research, Ogilvy-Webb admitted the history's limitations, including the possible need to develop specific aspects:

I have worked without the files of other Departments and without the benefit of the views of most of those who have taken part. To make the work really useful it therefore needs, I suggest, to be subjected to frank and detailed criticism from as many as possible of those who know about the subject. I shall be happy to meet criticism, but in the process I may have to do some further odd pieces of research.[26]

As a result, Ogilvy-Webb used the preliminary section of the three-volume history to outline the principal problems hindering his research.[27] Treasury papers were incomplete. The subject matter was both vast, embracing a wide range of economic activity, and intensely 'political' in the sense that ministers often expressed views other than their purely departmental interests. Furthermore, policymakers, he asserted, were frequently handicapped by the lack of theoretical knowledge about an economy experiencing full employment. In this vein, Ogilvy-Webb placed his historical narrative alongside existing secondary studies written by 'outsiders', like Benjamin C. Roberts (*National Wages Policy in War and Peace*: 1958) and Hugh Clegg and Rex Adams (*The Employers Challenge: A Study of the National Shipbuilding and Engineering Disputes of 1957*: 1957): 'all these books seem almost to suggest that... official and ministerial efforts were doomed at the start by the general economic circumstances and by doctrines from which there was no escape... I have continued to assume, however, that Ministers and officials had some freedom of choice'.[28]

The whole project, representing a kind of historical apprenticeship supervised by Clarke, had proved an invaluable learning experience for Ogilvy-Webb: 'I have got to the point where I can perhaps take a view of the process of trying to write this sort of history. I have personally found it extremely rewarding and indeed fascinating.' Drawing upon lengthy administrative experience dating back to the Second World War, Ogilvy-Webb acknowledged the functional value of funding past experience:

> I have always felt that the relatively short period during which officers normally hold particular posts in divisions makes it difficult for them to carry out a continuous policy, because of their lack of background knowledge. In the case of Treasury Supply Divisions I am pretty certain that outside Departments trade on this knowledge. I have therefore felt that this kind of work is well worthwhile.

He added that 'I can only hope that my readers will feel the same.'

Certainly, Clarke was one such reader. In fact, his fundamental belief in the value of "funding experience" meant that he saw this historical narrative as far more than a departmental reference resource on wages policy. For Clarke, the outcome offered Whitehall an excellent example of the case for using history to learn from past experience. Hence, his decision not only to instruct Ogilvy-Webb to prepare a shorter THM version for wider circulation but also to write a foreword by way of articulating both the merits of such histories in preserving a departmental memory and the key lessons about wages policy. Repeatedly, when reading Ogilvy-Webb's history, Clarke had a feeling of *déjà vu*:

> The purpose of having a narrative prepared was to throw light on the present problem; and this has proved well worthwhile. One gets a powerful impression throughout the narrative of *'having been there before'* – *situations, reactions, ideas, decisions. It is indeed rather sobering to see how many times the ground has been traversed* [author's emphasis].[29]

Within this context, Clarke apprised readers of the manner in which the history's identification of 'recurrent themes' yielded useful *general lessons* for policymakers. Referring to the reliance placed upon the reconstruction of the National Joint Advisory Council (1946) and the Council on Prices, Productivity and Incomes (1957) and to their lack of impact upon the wage problem, he concluded that 'throughout the period, one gets the impression of excessive reliance upon machinery, as distinct from Government policy':

> One striking illustration has been the propensity, on each occasion of crisis, to seek a solution in the creation of new organisations which

would solve the problem without the need for any specific Government policy, and to form hopes, which in retrospect have appeared to have been quite extravagant, about the contribution which the new organizations would make to the problem.

The history's 'conclusions', Clarke observed, drew attention to a series of shortcomings on the part of successive governments regardless of political complexion, including an incomplete appreciation of relevant underlying economic theory, a consistent tendency to underrate the fundamental difficulties of finding a solution to the wages problem, and the repeated failure to improve public understanding of the key issues.[30] At the same time, Clarke, though presenting the history as 'a useful contribution to our deliberations' about future policymaking, followed Ogilvy-Webb in acknowledging the THM's limitations consequent upon its Treasury slant and limited research base: 'there may be some lack of balance for this reason: but the attempt to do this on a complete "official history" scale would have taken so much longer that it would have destroyed much of the practical value of the work'.[31] Paradoxically, Clarke used the foreword to praise Ogilvy-Webb's historical objectivity while simultaneously warning readers about his championing of a 'positive wage policy'! He acknowledged also the need to interpret any lessons within the ever-changing context:

> This has been in a sense the history of an era and we are now moving into new territory. As Sir Frank Lee [Joint Permanent Secretary] has said 'it will never be the same again', and some of the themes of the narrative are unlikely to re-appear. It would seem unlikely, for example, that there will remain a substantial body of Whitehall opinion that... the Government 'does not need a wage policy'.... The experience of the past may have some relevance to the development of policy in the future and to the methods by which Whitehall deals with the task.[32]

In July 1962 copies of the three-volume version bound with stiff covers, accompanied by a covering note from Clarke, were sent to each Treasury division involved in wages policy as a reference work for use by 'present incumbents' and 'required reading' for newcomers.[33] NRI was required to update the narrative each year, thereby preserving the history's reference value and preventing it from becoming a dead document. In fact, access for reference purposes was strictly confined to officials; thus, Clarke ruled that 'it is not proper to show the material to

Ministers' because of the use of papers covering more than one government. Classified as 'secret', the three volumes were to be 'kept under lock and key'. Nor could they be circulated outside the Treasury. As Clarke minuted, the volumes were treated as of 'purely domestic interest' for 'reference and record': 'these are for Treasury eyes alone – they inevitably contain material that it would be tactless (to say the least) and irrelevant to circulate elsewhere'.[34] A few selected senior individuals, like William Armstrong, a Third Secretary, also received a copy. The shorter history represented a heavily abridged version edited by Ogilvy-Webb to omit anything adjudged likely to be regarded as 'tendentious by the most sensitive reader'.[35] Prefaced by Clarke's foreword, the shorter history was printed as a 34-page THM for circulation to Treasury divisions as well as to the Permanent Secretaries Group on Wages. Like most THMs, it was subject to the usual secrecy restrictions, including the ban on ministerial access.

Clarke looks back on an invaluable learning experience

For Clarke, 'getting the history written has been an interesting operation in itself'.[36] The whole episode had proved an invaluable learning exercise illuminating the pros and cons of actually "funding experience" as well as guiding his thinking about 'the next steps that might usefully be taken to build on this experience'. In part, the positive tone of his comments reflected the fact that Clarke had performed a prominent and active role throughout the project in terms of regularly spending time and trouble to offer Ogilvy-Webb encouragement, guidance and support in initiating the project, reading and commenting promptly and constructively upon interim drafts, and finalizing the text. Unsurprisingly, in April 1962 he took pleasure in sending Brook a copy of the shorter history by way of informing him about the completion of the 'most ambitious project' yet undertaken within his section in response to the 1957 "funding experience" initiative.[37] Reporting the positive reception given to the history upon the part of senior staff, like Abbot, Sir Frank Lee, the Joint Permanent Secretary, Maude, Stevenson and Vinter, Clarke observed that the history had proved already of actual value in his section's recent work.[38]

Writing privately to the Joint Permanent Secretaries, Clarke recorded the history's value for policymakers: 'I think the history on a big subject is the most valuable for policy formation in uncharted territories, such as "wages" have been and "planning" is.'[39] Although the history had already proved its utility, even in draft form, Clarke admitted that it would have been even more useful if it had become available earlier, but 'we did have it in time to enable Mr. Stevenson and myself to derive considerable use from it during the policy discussions last autumn'.[40] In any case, as Maude remarked when reading Ogilvy-Webb's history, 'the wages problem is always with us'.[41] Certainly, Clarke saw the history as contributing to the more systematic handling of wages policy in future:

> All of us in Whitehall are ill-informed about these wage problems (other than civil service wage problems); and we need to build up an expertise now that incomes policy is a recognised part of Government activity; and I would put these narratives and post-mortems pretty high in developing it.[42]

Such histories, though treated as 'a little intimidating' by some readers, filled 'a real need' by furnishing 'indispensable background' formerly scattered across a wide range of files, offering a 'real starting point for the next developments', outlining analogous cases, and providing a corrective 'to avoid misleading posterity'.[43] As such, they promised to benefit many divisions and 'a lot of people (many of whom often feel out of their depth)'.

Within this context, Clarke codified for Brook and other senior officials some early lessons about using history. Ideally, 'the work needs to be done contemporarily', since this enabled the history's writer to secure both oral testimony and informed feedback on the draft text from those actually involved in the events under discussion.[44] Historical work, though not necessitating in his view a professional historian, was best undertaken by full-time staff undistracted by everyday administration, since it required genuine research, 'not dissimilar, for example, to that involved in the preparation of the wartime official histories': 'When one has found a suitable man, it is worth keeping him – Mr Ogilvy-Webb reckons that he will be able to work faster next time, now that he knows the ropes.'[45] Clarke praised Ogilvy-Webb in terms of doing the research, identifying the facts, processing the material, and communicating the results in an appropriate format. At the same time, Clarke's praise for the 'valuable and productive' nature of Ogilvy-Webb's work was tempered by concern about the downside. Certainly, the 18-month production period was well in excess of the time span originally envisaged by Clarke, who suspected Ogilvy-Webb at times of unnecessarily chasing the facts in pursuit of additional areas of enquiry. In brief, whereas Clarke wanted "funding experience" activities targeted at deadlines relevant to the 'man at the desk', Ogilvy-Webb seemed at times to be acting too much like an academic historian. Furthermore, the resulting need for close supervision – this was required to expedite completion and ensure a sharp focus upon the topic – proved an additional chore for an already busy senior official.

Even so, Clarke's reservations did not prevent him from formulating plans for further 'historical work'; indeed, HOPS, he claimed, could keep Ogilvy-Webb occupied indefinitely.[46] At the same time, he stressed the need for Ogilvy-Webb to be placed under 'sympathetic but firm direction' based upon a strict timetable, an agreed programme of work, and clearly defined projects capable of completion within six to nine months.[47] Close supervision by senior staff, albeit essential to ensure that historical work 'will be useful for the Department's needs', was required also to reassure 'the historian that his work *is* important to the Department': 'it can be frustrating for the historian (and unproductive) if he is treated as an enclave outside the run of office business'. Clearly, this observation, though prompted largely by the experience of monitoring Ogilvy-Webb's work, was influenced also by memories of Gowing's sense of isolation within the Treasury.[48]

In many respects, Clarke saw Ogilvy-Webb as not only taking on Gowing's mantle but also moving the Treasury on from the relatively circumscribed projects covered in her THMs to 'big general subjects' promising a larger return from historical research:

> One would like to see many more of these done (the particular one mentioned ['The Treasury and Acts of God'] has been very useful). But a very large number of these must be done before the historical work can be said to be making any real impact on the Department's work, and I am firmly of the opinion that we can get a much larger Departmental return for a year's historical research on a big subject of general policy than on a number of small individual subjects. (This is of course on the assumption that the researcher is capable of tackling the general policy subject, which does call for wider knowledge and experience.)[49]

Notwithstanding his 'strong opinion' in favour of 'a forward movement throughout the Department', Clarke conceded that for the time being staffing and other constraints compelled a more limited approach across the Treasury as a whole. Meanwhile, Abbot approved Clarke's proposal to retain Ogilvy-Webb for historical research for a further year in order to write a THM-type history of planning as well as to help out with seeding files.[50] Although the case was presented principally in terms of the benefits of "funding experience", Clarke stressed also the fact that Ogilvy-Webb's contribution as a Treasury historian was in marked contrast to 'his poor performance over a considerable period of years' as an administrator:

> My impression is that this historical work has given him a sense of purpose and accomplishment which he has failed to find in his normal work as a Principal for many years past... this is the way for the public service to get the best value out of Mr. Ogilvy-Webb's abilities.

History and the Overseas Finance Division

One of the more positive divisional responses to Bell's 1958 Office Notice about "funding experience" came from the Overseas Finance divisions (OF).[51] Even so, M.E. Johnston, the head of OFT3 therein, employed the opportunity to raise questions about both staffing and the wisdom of writing histories from a specifically Treasury point of view, since much of the division's work covered international 'episodes', like the 1951 Abadan crisis or the nationalization of the Suez Canal Company in 1956, involving collaboration with the Foreign Office, among other departments:

> It would falsify the story to record it only in its economic aspects, and to assume that this was the extent of Treasury interest in practice. I would therefore regard these episodes as belonging to the history of this country's foreign policy and not to that of the Treasury.[52]

At the same time, he acknowledged the serious challenge posed by such projects, since it proved 'difficult to draw a line between a survey of past policies and a criticism of present policies. Nonetheless, I think such a study... would be very useful.'

During the next year or so, 'the intervals from more pressing work' allowed OF to make limited progress in writing histories focused upon the government's relationship with commercial companies, beginning with J.E. Lucas's history of the *Relationship between H.M.G. and B.P.* [British Petroleum].[53] This 32-page historical narrative, based upon Treasury files, was largely factual; but, as Lucas, a principal, observed, his focus upon what happened reflected the history's functional role: 'I have aimed at including within one Note all the information which can have any bearing on the subject... I think this Note... should save a great deal of reference in the future to files.'[54] This reference role constrained the history's scope: 'I did not think that it was appropriate in a Note of this kind, which was intended to be largely factual, to attempt to reach any final conclusions on a matter which is of very considerable political importance.' Lucas' minimal attempt to draw out general conclusions was qualified by the insertion of a section considering the case for and against any change in the current relationship. Certainly, Ronald Symons, the head of OFG, agreed that the exercise was 'well worth doing':

> It will be a very useful 'tool of trade' for those currently dealing with problems in this field. With that aim in view it quotes extensively from original documents which otherwise we should have to continue to hunt for and consult out of a large mass of files.... From the Division's point of view it is just what was wanted.[55]

However, the history was not included in the THM series. Indeed, it was deemed unsuitable for wider circulation outside the OF division because of the highly confidential nature of exchanges between the Treasury and BP, including financially sensitive information. In any case, the note, drafted deliberately in a style specifically suitable for OF use, was adjudged to contain 'much more detail than people outside the Division will need, or care to spare time in reading'.

In March 1960 Lucas completed another history for OF. Confronted by an extremely 'complicated' subject, that is the government's working relations with the oil companies on exchange control, his prime objective had been to provide a sound divisional reference source codifying past experience for the purposes of current and future administration.[56] For A.W. Taylor, an Under Secretary, recent changes – these included the unification of non-resident sterling (1958) and moves towards the liberalization of trade (1959) – rendered the history extremely timely: 'an era in the relationships between the oil companies and the Departments has now been closed, and we can look back on it with fresh memories, but with some detachment'. For the record, Taylor minuted that Lucas' history demonstrated that the success of exchange controls in saving dollars derived largely from the goodwill and mutual confidence existing between the oil companies on the one hand and the Treasury and the Bank of England on the other. Like its predecessor, this specialist history received only a limited circulation within the division for the purposes of recording experience for reference and other purposes.

Using the expertise of retired staff

Inevitably, the THM series suffered from a certain loss of momentum after Gowing's departure.[57] Only one more THM appeared during the next three years, that is in January 1960 when THM 3 on Civil Service Superannuation was printed. Produced for the Establishments (Superannuation) division, this project followed Brook's advice by drawing upon the expertise of retired staff, that is R.C. Sugars, formerly Assistant Secretary of the Superannuation Division (1949–53).[58] In fact, this 83-page 'history' was more a chronological listing of relevant legislation than a historical narrative. For Gowing, who saw a draft copy, it proved 'very unsatisfactory as a piece of analytical history'.[59]

The Overseas Finance Division also followed Brook's advice about using recently retired staff in order to both harness their specialist knowledge and expertise and overcome staffing constraints; thus, it commissioned Sir Hugh Ellis-Rees to write a history of the 1947 Convertibility Crisis. In turn, the resulting 66-page history, printed in December 1962 as THM 4, was even considered as the basis for a peacetime official history of overseas finance. Drawing largely upon his former roles as Assistant Secretary of OF (1943–48) and Permanent British delegate to the Organization for European Economic Cooperation (OEEC), Ellis-Rees used the history to record his 'recollections of some of the problems confronting us in the Treasury in the post-war years, and, in particular, those connected with the convertibility crisis of 1947': 'Much of the detail, long ago forgotten, I have recalled by reading the relevant papers... I have also included incidents of which there is no record that I can trace.'[60]

Seeking to provide readers with a clear picture of 'the most important event in our economic experience between the end of the war and the Marshall Plan', Ellis-Rees prioritized a narrative approach. Even so, his history was sprinkled with revealing assessments based upon the opportunity to revisit not only the past but also 'the knowledge that we have long since gained in the hard school of practical experience'.[61] For Ellis-Rees, the post-1945 'struggle' to build confidence in Britain's determination to maintain sterling's value was 'too much for us'.[62] Nor were things helped by the USA's attitude, as reflected in the 1945 Washington monetary agreement: 'What strikes me today as difficult to understand is the apparent indifference to the world economic situation... their lack of appreciation of the extent to which the European economy had been dislocated and how little recovery had been possible.'[63]

Despite recognizing the shortcomings of counterfactual history, Ellis-Rees drew out of his narrative a series of concluding reflections suggesting how 'the critical situation' might have been alleviated, if not avoided.

> Given the fact that we had to make the attempt to comply with the Washington Agreement, it is doubtful whether we could have brought about a different result however we tackled the task: it was out of joint with the times and the forces we had to contend with were too strong. But we might have eased the critical situation if we had (a) taken drastic measures in March 1947 to reduce overseas spending, instead of six months later; (b) delayed committing ourselves to the extension of the new facilities to the European Governments until much later; and (c) made a more determined effort to obtain the assent of the holders of sterling to maintain a higher level of balances. Such measures might have helped us to make a more orderly and longer retreat and to have retained more confidence than we did in our fight for solvency; they might have enabled us to last out until the Marshall Plan came to the forefront, though this is perhaps carrying speculation too far.[64]

He recorded also the impact exerted by the convertibility crisis upon policymakers' mindsets in the years which followed:

> At least we can say that our experiences during the convertibility crisis of 1947 made such an impression that we were able to resist temptations, in the years which followed, to offer the convertibility of sterling until we were strong enough to do so with the assurance of success.

The fact that Brook's "funding experience" initiative originated partly out of discussions centred upon the future of the official histories project imparts interest to the way in which the OF's historical work prompted speculation about the case for an official history focused upon its post-war activities. Thus, in March 1961 Clarke, who had already raised with Brook in 1958 the possibility of an official history funding experience on post-war international economic policy, proposed using Ellis-Rees' recently completed THM as the basis for a peacetime official history of overseas finance between 1945 and 1952: 'There should be an official history for just the same reasons as there is an official history of the war.'[65] Responding to Brook's fears that peacetime histories might provoke party political controversy, Clarke minuted that 'the subject matter is not unduly party-political; and many of the main protagonists are dead; there is background that is relevant to an understanding of much that goes on now'.

However, Derek Mitchell, when asked to advise Sir Denis Rickett, the Second Secretary, doubted the proposal's merits, even moving on to question the fundamental utility of "funding experience" by recalling the reported scepticism of Sir Edward Playfair, among others, regarding Brook's original proposal.[66] Mitchell, an Assistant Secretary, wondered how far a published official history would meet Brook's objectives: 'Experience so far with departmental historical memoranda brings out quite clearly that to be of practical value to administrators the studies have to be completely candid about the mistakes that were made.' The Treasury was no exception to the reluctance of Whitehall departments to publicize past failures, as evidenced by the hesitation about showing, even on a private and personal basis, Gowing's 1957 Festival Gardens THM to Sir David Milne (Scottish Office) in order to demonstrate how the Treasury was giving effect to Brook's initiative.[67] Following Brook, Mitchell believed that any Treasury peacetime official history of postwar overseas finance would have to be heavily sanitized before being shown to other departments, let alone published by the government. Debatable decisions were taken and mistakes made by, or in the name of, ministers. Admittedly, some ministers were now dead, but the fact that others remained alive raised the serious risk of public controversy. Nor could the Bank of England's participation be taken for granted in a project requiring its active cooperation. Quoting Keith Hancock's report on the official histories, Mitchell doubted also whether a good academic historian would be willing to take on the assignment, given the uncertainties about publication.

Conclusion

Notwithstanding the Treasury's sustained encouragement, even pressure, for all divisions to do something, the concept of "funding experience" made varying impacts across the department. Whereas HOPS, like the Overseas Finance division, moved ahead relatively fast, most divisions made little or no headway in terms of introducing a historical dimension into their everyday work. Thus, the example of HOPS, benefiting from Clarke's enthusiastic espousal of the concept and consequent switch of Ogilvy-Webb to historical work, was far from typical. Inaction, rooted in a deep-rooted scepticism about the present-day relevance of history reinforced by the pressures of everyday work, was much more common. Rationalizing the Social Services division's poor track record to date, J. Hansford pointed to the low priority attached to historical activities:

> There is so much current work which cannot be left that one tends to forget about historical reviews which are not germane to a particular problem under consideration. And even then, when reading up old files, one tends to register the points relevant to the particular problem and to ignore the rest.[68]

Nor, in Hansford's view, did his division's 'chaotic' filing system enable easy access to relevant files for historical activities in spite of the fact that the latter were often rationalized in terms of enabling busy officials to find relevant information more quickly. By contrast, Clarke, complaining that 'life is too short' and the relevant files voluminous and scattered, liked to claim that Treasury 'history fills a real need which the filing system cannot do'.[69]

Hansford's mention of his division's lack of spare capacity established the fact that staffing remained an enduring constraint upon historical work, which suffered more than other activities from what Mitchell described as the Treasury's full, 'even over-full', employment.[70] Few divisions felt able to resource the funding of experience, let alone to accelerate the current slow rate of progress, from current staffing levels, especially given their difficulty in balancing the rival demands made upon staff. Contrary to Brook's hopes, present-day tasks and "funding experience" activities had yet to become regarded as complementary rather than mutually exclusive. In any case, the 'fundable' potential of activities varied across the department, as shown by the manner in which specialized divisions, like Organisation and Methods, sought exemption from the whole exercise on the grounds that the nature of their work rendered it difficult to find suitable historical subjects.[71] Writing THM-type histories placed a substantial burden upon divisions because of the time required by the author to identify and refer to relevant files, check the facts, collect oral testimony, secure comment and feedback upon initial, interim and final drafts, and write up the narrative. Forced to rely largely upon their own resources, most divisions adopted a less ambitious course centred upon divisional notes and "seeded files" rather than THMs. Even then, the quality, and hence the utility, of "seeded files" was seen as dependent upon the status of the officials responsible for their production. From experience, Clarke indicated that files produced by senior staff were frequently impressive in their quality, whereas junior officials seemed incapable of doing little more than 'put the old paper in clean jackets'.[72] Naturally, such senior staff encountered even greater difficulty in finding time for such tasks.

Although few divisions derived little direct benefit from her attachment to the Treasury, Gowing's departure left a serious gap regarding access to specialist historians with the time, inclination, historical skills and subject knowledge to write THMs.[73] In the event, Ogilvy-Webb, a Treasury principal switched from an administrative role, emerged as a replacement historian; but, like Gowing, his contribution was confined to only a small section of the department. His initial project, supported by Clarke, resulted in a 'valuable and productive' THM, which provided the basis for his continued employment on history-related work and the subsequent formation of the THS in 1965.[74] From this perspective, Ogilvy-Webb's first THM represented – to quote from a 1977 internal history – 'a significant milestone in the development of history writing within the Treasury'.[75] Another interesting trend concerned the THMs written by recently retired senior officials, like Ellis-Rees and Sugars. Apart from helping to overcome staffing constraints, such histories drew upon the expertise of officials invited to recollect in tranquillity their accumulated knowledge and experience, that is the type of insights failing to find their way into official documentation.

Whatever the doubts articulated by divisional staff, "funding experience" continued to enjoy the support of the Treasury's senior staff. Following his reading of Ogilvy-Webb's THM on wages policy, Lee, the Joint Permanent Secretary, saw it as reflecting well on Brook's initiative: 'I am sure that the exercise is in itself a striking justification of the action taken by Sir Norman Brook to secure more 'funding of experience' in Whitehall by means of historical narratives of this kind.'[76] Naturally, Brook himself retained a close interest in his department's progress in implementing the "funding experience" initiative, and was encouraged by the fact that Clarke, one of the Treasury's rising stars, emerged as an enthusiastic and influential supporter commissioning and resourcing historical activities. As Nicholls observed in 1959, 'Mr. Clarke's divisions are really in a class by themselves, partly because he has already grasped the nettle.'[77] Moreover, Clarke sought to spread the word to an often sceptical audience within and outside the Treasury, as highlighted by his use of the foreword of the 1962 THM on wages policy circulated to Treasury divisions and several PUSs outside the Treasury:

> An important point that emerges from a perusal of the narrative is the strong tendency for the same arguments and actions to recur at frequent intervals without the officials concerned being apparently fully aware of what had gone before. For this reason and because the current development of Government policy can best be understood in the light of the events of the last 15 years it has been decided to print and circulate the short narrative for use in Departments generally.[78]

In fact, divisional reservations about their relevance to day-to-day administration, alongside a consequent reluctance to resource such low priority activities, prompted an emerging focus upon the practical application of the Treasury's historical outputs. Within the Treasury, the actual utility of "funding experience" could never be taken for granted.

5
The Public Enterprises Division (PE) as a Case Study, 1962–65

During the early 1960s, the annual Permanent Secretaries Conferences, held at the Civil Defence Staff College, Sunningdale, regularly reviewed the progress made by Whitehall departments in implementing the "funding experience" initiative launched by Brook in 1957 to improve the operational efficiency of government.[1] The fact that a topic entitled 'Historical Memoranda' was deemed worthy of placement on the agenda of such an august official gathering was perhaps more significant than the resulting discussion. Even so, background papers tabled for each session provided selective evidence of what had been achieved, or rather not achieved, to date across Whitehall.

For example, in October 1961 the Permanent Secretaries Conference was informed that since 1958 the Board of Trade had undertaken a limited amount of "funding experience", that is writing histories of episodes adjudged significant for policy and administrative reasons.[2] Although the programme had been scaled down in May 1960, histories would continue to be written 'whenever there is something of lasting value to record' – one example was Russell Bretherton's 'Development of Policy about the Common Market, 1955/57, with special reference to the Board of Trade' – and made accessible to those 'who may have occasion to use them'. Likewise, the Admiralty reported the modest response of its Naval Conditions and Welfare Branch, which had begun recording past practice on such personnel questions as terminal leave and requests for transfer to another service. In this manner, "funding experience" enhanced the branch's 'ability to check *quickly* whether something or other has been allowed or refused in the past; and to quote *the facts* of a previous case in order to throw light on a new case. . . . We cannot do our job efficiently unless we are able to answer questions of that kind – and answer them without a long delay.'[3] "Funding experience" was seen as enabling staff to avoid going 'round the same policy buoy again and again'. One year later, the 1962 Permanent Secretaries Conference was informed about a Ministry of Transport history of salaries for the new Transport Commission.

Despite such regular updates, it proved difficult to disguise the fact that most government departments were doing little or nothing apart from taking measures to improve existing procedures for recording precedents. Indeed, the apparent lack of activity elsewhere in Whitehall tended to magnify the extent of the Treasury's limited achievements to date. Moreover, background papers distributed at Sunningdale established that the conflicting views held in the Treasury about the perceived utility of history to the everyday work of government were replicated through Whitehall. Thus, whereas Burke Trend, who was soon to succeed Brook as Cabinet Secretary, was quoted as praising the utility of the Ministry of Transport's history, Sir James Dunnett, the PUS (1959–62) responsible for commissioning the study, found the resulting history rather too detailed to be of practical value.[4] From this perspective, perhaps the Admiralty paper, circulated at the 1961 Permanent Secretaries Conference, identified the key factor affecting the present-day use of history: 'No system, however good, is enough by itself. It is your attitude to the problem of continuity that matters.'[5]

Reviewing the Treasury's progress to date

The radical organizational overhaul of the Treasury, announced in July 1962 and implemented the following November, was based largely upon a modernizing blueprint drawn up by Clarke and William Armstrong in the wake of the 1958 Report of the Select Committee on Estimates on Treasury Control of Expenditure and the 1961 Plowden Report.[6] Reforms, motivated principally by a desire to ensure the more effective performance of the Treasury's economic planning and management roles, were accompanied by personnel changes, with Armstrong and Helsby (also became Head of Home Civil Service) replacing Lee and Brook as Joint Permanent Secretaries. Quite apart from its more obvious impacts upon the structuring and functions of divisions and the movement of staff and tasks across the department, reorganization prompted a re-think about the Treasury's historical activities in the light of experience to date.

In the short term, restructuring accentuated the everyday pressures of work, thereby reinforcing the ongoing reluctance to devote precious time and resources to reading and writing about past experience.

At the same time, the radical overhaul led many officials to appreciate the merits of historical work in preserving departmental and/or divisional memories for the purposes of everyday reference, and particularly for inducting and guiding staff moving to a different division and confronted by a mass of unfamiliar files covering a new sphere of activity. As Abbot informed Armstrong, reorganization prompted both the seeding of files and writing of divisional notes to guide divisions taking over new responsibilities; for example, she pointed to the Social Services division's note on university pay.[7] In this vein, following his transfer to Treasury Officers of Accounts, L.J. Taylor was soon made aware that 'one is left... with recourse only to such precedents as can be produced either from one's technical knowledge or from various registers maintained by the clerks'.[8] Even so, he admitted that normally current preoccupations restricted the amount of time available to read up past files in order to fill such gaps. From experience, Taylor appreciated the difficulty of integrating such activities into a busy division's normal workload. Nor was he optimistic about making much headway in the near future, unless extra staff were allocated to such work:

> All of which does little more than recognise the problem, without suggesting any real way of tackling it! I see little hope of making much progress with our present staff which... seems barely able to cope with the volume of current work flowing in to the division.

Nor was "funding experience" work unaffected by the critical review conducted of the Treasury's activities and procedures during the early 1960s by way of background to the restructuring exercise. Henceforth, the Treasury decided to monitor the future momentum of its historical work through regular reviews conducted by the Establishment Officer's Branch to 'force divisions to keep an eye on this matter'.[9] In turn, the resulting need to respond to annual requests for information compelled divisions to monitor what had been done to date, or more frequently not done, as well as to formulate some sort of view about "funding experience" by way of explaining their respective returns.

In August 1962 the impending departmental reorganization, alongside a desire to use "funding experience" to ease the process of transition, led Abbot 'to take stock' of the current position.[10] The resulting note, albeit intended largely to secure information, allowed her the opportunity to remind divisional heads about 'the importance which is attached to the funding of experience by the preparation of Treasury historical memoranda and in other ways'. Responses were requested on a series of points:

progress to date in the varying types of "funding experience"; future plans, including proposed topics adjudged worthy of coverage in the light of the forthcoming departmental reorganization; and staff available for historical work. Then, in December 1962 Abbot used divisional returns to update the Joint Permanent Secretaries about the satisfactory progress and changing pattern of the Treasury's historical work.

> The magnificent folder called Treasury Historical Memoranda Vol. 1 which was distributed some five years ago is still pretty empty. But this does not reflect inactivity. The fact is that by a sort of natural process of evolution we have rather turned away from writing post mortems and cautionary tales *(which tend to be read once and never looked at again)* [author's emphasis] to producing more useful day to day tools of trade such as 'seeded files' and divisional notes on important topics. And on this quite a lot has been done.... All in all, I think we can be moderately satisfied with progress on this front.[11]

On 14 January 1963 Armstrong and Helsby, the Joint Permanent Secretaries, together with the Second and Third Secretaries, met to review Abbot's report. Expressing pleasure about progress to date, the meeting instructed Abbot to report back to divisions and to liaise with divisional heads about their respective forward programmes.[12]

Soon afterwards, Abbot reported back to divisions. The relatively positive tone of her feedback, when viewed against the variable record of progress across the whole department outlined in the previous chapter, was revealing in terms of indicating the way in which the support of senior staff for "funding experience" led them to view the survey results through rose-tinted spectacles. Thus, Abbot's report informed divisional heads that much had been achieved: 'Divisions have been doing quite a lot in the field of funding experience – more than had been realised.' However, recently divisions had found it 'more useful' to concentrate upon divisional notes and "seeded files" rather than THM-type histories.[13] Despite proving 'very valuable for major topics', THMs made substantial demands upon staff time and resources, while there remained continuing anxieties about their limited use, the lack of a central index building upon the Central Registry's alphabetical listing of titles, and the consequent impossibility of knowing what was already available. Of course, even "seeded files" proved problematic, since 'experience has shown' that the selection of leading papers could 'only be done by fairly high-grade staff', that is at principal level and above.[14]

Looking ahead in the light of the recent restructuring exercise, Abbot pointed to the need for the introduction of a more systematic Treasury-wide approach towards "funding experience". Henceforth, individual divisions would be required to submit annual returns, including future plans extending over a period of two to three years taking account of their recently revised functions and responsibilities. Noteworthy was her emphasis upon history's functional purpose:

> The ultimate objective would be for each Division to have a set of notes and seeded files which will be of direct use as working tools in handling current or future problems. When assembled, these summaries of the facts and of the administrative techniques applied to analogous situations in the past should point the way towards a more systematic approach both to the fundamentals and to the details of Treasury administration.[15]

In this manner, the Treasury's reorganization was used to refocus and reinvigorate the utility of such work, which was seen as supporting both everyday activities and the induction of staff moving across divisions. Even so, no real effort was made to enhance the resourcing of such work. Despite recognizing that staffing remained a 'crucial' determinant upon progress, Abbot warned that there existed 'no early signs of easing'; thus, divisions were expected still to rely principally upon their own resources.

Typically, replies, though requested by 30 April 1963, arrived slowly and frequently late. As a result, it was not until the close of the year that the Establishment Officer's Branch completed an informed analysis of returns for submission to the Joint Permanent Secretaries for action.[16] Notwithstanding the usual wide variations in performance across divisions because of differing work loads, staffing resources, and levels of commitment to historical projects, the overall situation was deemed 'encouraging'. Most work in progress at the time of the 1962 survey had been completed and a start made on the forward two-year programmes. Nor were nil returns viewed as indicating disinterest. For example, despite appearing inactive in the previous survey, the Accounts Branch's return, dated May 1963, recorded the completion of three divisional notes providing histories of Civil List pensions, the day-to-day management of the Exchequer, and travelling expenses.[17] Further histories were in preparation, such as on the collection of fines due to the Crown, or planned.

The THM on economic planning

Economic planning, one of Clarke's initial shortlisted topics, fell by the wayside until Autumn 1962, when it was taken up by Ogilvy-Webb upon the completion of the THM on wages policy. It was anticipated that a history of planning, covering the period 1945–51, would be followed by others covering the post-1951 period. Clarke, who was now Second Secretary in charge of the Public Sector Group, saw the history as not only fulfilling a perceived need but also taking advantage of Ogilvy-Webb's availability to progress 'big general projects'.

Clarke began by directing Ogilvy-Webb to focus initially upon two elements, the control of public investment and long-term planning: 'Both of these are highly topical and valuable, and involve many Divisions; and I would hope to see them well forward by the end of the year. (We could use both very usefully right now.)'[18] As before, Clarke, who had played a leading part in drafting the actual 1948–52 Plan, performed an active role throughout the project. Commenting on draft chapters, frequently at length, he pressed Ogilvy-Webb to adopt a stronger narrative line 'so that people can see what was said and thought', suggested additional sources – these included the official history on the *British War Economy* – and complained about the excessive length of drafts.[19] Clarke was particularly critical of 'tactless' phrasing as well as Ogilvy-Webb's somewhat subjective, frequently polemical, style.[20] In fact, the latter aspect proved a central focus for another reader, Douglas Allen, the head of the National Economy Group, who raised what was to become a key focus, the perceived need to emphasize that Treasury histories did not necessarily represent the department's collective view.[21] By way of response, Ogilvy-Webb rationalized his subjective approach in terms of the apparent consensus existing about planning at the time: 'thus, I have been *forced*, in order to make the story mean anything, to become a protagonist myself'.[22] Pointing also to an excessive reliance upon 'after-knowledge', Clarke urged Ogilvy-Webb to avoid appearing 'too wise after the event' regarding, say, Britain and Europe. Perhaps, he conceded, Britain should have 'gone into Europe' in 1948 by way of forcing a customs union and integration, but then continental Europe was 'pretty chaotic': 'We felt we could just scrape through with the Cripps "Dunkirk" spirit, provided we weren't held back by Europe.'[23]

By the close of 1963, Ogilvy-Webb had revised the draft chapters in accordance with Clarke's instructions. Redrafting was employed also to tone down the subjective element, even if, as noted by Clarke's foreword, the final history still offered a clear point of view. Drastic editing resulted also in a much shorter version of the original 120,000-word manuscript. As Rawlinson, an Assistant Secretary, reminded Ogilvy-Webb, 'if it is to be operationally influential, the bulk must somehow be reduced'.[24] Nevertheless, the resulting history still amounted to 94 pages when printed as a THM in April 1964. The fact that planning impacted upon most divisions – the National Economic Development Council ("Neddy") was created in 1961 – resulted in the THM's relatively extensive circulation within the Treasury, even extending in certain divisions beyond Assistant Secretaries to include principals.[25] Once again, for reasons outlined by Clarke in the foreword, that is the coverage of previous governments, the history could not be shown to ministers.[26] Following consultations with Helsby, Clarke's initial plans for wide circulation outside the Treasury were scaled down to include only Trend, Sir Richard Powell, PUS at the Board of Trade, and Sir James Dunnett, PUS at the Ministry of Labour.[27] Significantly, C. Keeling, who had repeatedly requested the use of THMs for training purposes, was among those deleted from the circulation list.[28]

As happened with previous THMs, even interim drafts were welcomed by readers as not only useful contributions to the historical record but also operational resources 'for those who are today concerned with planning matters', even allowing for the fact that there existed a 'good deal of difference between what is being done today, especially in connection with NEDC, and the events of 15 years ago'.[29] In particular, Ogilvy-Webb drew attention to the problem of definition. Thus, lacking a clear meaning, the concept of "economic planning", as practised by the 1945–51 Attlee governments, was capable of covering firstly, the 'coordination' of previously unrelated decisions regarding, say, shortages, secondly, 'government intervention' to secure such aims as "full employment" and "fair shares", and thirdly, merely 'looking ahead'.[30] In the event, 'looking ahead' proved extremely limited in both scope and time: 'long-term economic planning does not seem to have looked ahead beyond the next slump or boom'. In theory, "planning" might have been used between 1945 and 1951 to help Britain's transition from war to peace, whereas in practice, Ogilvy-Webb concluded, the government failed to use "planning" to promote post-war economic growth, changes in economic structures and attitudes, or balance of payments equilibrium. Nor did the gradual relaxation of controls prevent economic planning becoming popularly associated with restrictions, rather than enterprise: 'In reality, the great framework of control acted to preserve the existing structure and organization of industry, though at the cost of hampering it.'

Nothing positive had been done to encourage the efficient and penalise the obsolete and inefficient. Investment was kept low, by modern standards, in the interests of consumption and was not effectively discriminatory. Manufacturers were protected from competition, workers from unemployment, consumers from price inflation and everyone from reality.

Following the precedent of Ogilvy-Webb's previous THM, Clarke contributed a three-page foreword with a view to highlighting this history's actual utility alongside the merits of "funding experience" in general. However, he began by acknowledging the problems experienced by Ogilvy-Webb in dealing with such a wide-ranging topic; indeed, it had proved difficult to avoid making it a history of economic policy during the late 1940s.[31] Nor was it easy to integrate a diverse range of concepts, predictions, actions and appraisals into a coherent narrative allowing readers to evaluate critically policy decisions in the light of subsequent successes or failures. Like any historian, Ogilvy-Webb had to tread a fine line:

> A *critique* may therefore be a better description than a *narrative*. Mr. Ogilvy-Webb, as it will be seen, has a very definite point of view, and most readers will sometimes agree and sometimes disagree with him. But the selection and description of the facts and documents has been entirely objective.

Several points in the history struck Clarke as possessing 'some relevance to present problems and preoccupations', even if his repeated use of the qualifier 'some' indicated an awareness of the need for caution when drawing analogies between past and present. Nevertheless, he emphasized the 'repeated feeling' experienced by policymakers when reading such histories of 'having been there before':

> The problems of 'planning' in 1961–63 are seen clearly in embryo in 1945–51. How to make a plan; how to distinguish and link together what we want to happen and what we expect to happen; the relevance of the plan, when made, to the decisions of real life; how the makers of the plan should be related to the Governmental machine.

In addition, during a period when Britain was seeking to join the Common Market, the THM threw 'some light' on initial British thinking about Europe. In this vein, the history showed that Britain failed to take the lead upon European cooperation during the late 1940s because policymakers saw a continental link as a potential source of weakness, not strength, liable to impede Britain's post-war recovery.

Clarke reminded readers of the way in which the mindsets of post-1945 policymakers were moulded by memories of the unemployment, depression and social dislocation prevalent between the wars. Thus, the emphasis placed upon both stability and import-saving in the 1948–52 Plan was understandable in the broader historical context, even if this strategy merely made things worse by discouraging economic modernization and sapping Britain's competitive power and export potential. Nor, as Clarke noted, did government policy foster economic growth:

> To those with heavy responsibilities through the period, Mr. Ogilvy-Webb may appear somewhat less than just, for he tends to give more weight to the inadequacies of the time than to its achievements. But it may well be that the better growth performance of most of the European countries and Japan in the 1950's had its roots in the changes of social and industrial structure which were enforced upon them in their dire experience of the 1940's.[32]

In addition, Clarke pointed to the way in which Ogilvy-Webb's case studies touched upon a paradox characteristic of both the late 1940s and the early 1960s, when government planning focused upon the private sector and failed to treat the nationalized industries as economic entities for planning purposes. Finally, Clarke introduced a sense of perspective for readers moving on from his foreword to Ogilvy-Webb's history.

> But the truth may well be that at that time the concept of 'long-term planning' had not reached a stage of political preparation or technical effectiveness to enable it to play a larger role than it did in fact play. In the crushing pressure of the time, and the rapidly changing world situation, moreover, there was always a very real question of how far it was sensible to divert resources to 'long-term planning' and away from the immediate problems.[33]

The Public Enterprises Division moves ahead

Prompted in part by Abbot's recent reminder about the need for an annual return on "funding experience", in June 1963 Vinter, the head of the Public Enterprises (PE) division, called for a divisional meeting to review progress and future plans. Barbara Granger-Taylor, who had been recruited recently as a temporary principal to help build up a historical background to PE's various activities, was invited to attend.[34]

Vinter began by outlining the division's activities to date in the sphere of "seeded files" and divisional notes. Granger-Taylor, he reported, had been working on a large scale history of aircraft purchasing by British airline corporations since the Second World War, a topic which has been 'of importance for years and is likely to become a burning one again'. Reviewing the varying formats, Vinter pointed also to his preferred approach. THMs took longer to produce, but were more useful than either "seeded files" – these failed to indicate what happened – or divisional notes, which proved 'less thorough and complete than a proper narrative'.

> It seems to me that ultimately narrative is probably more useful than anything else because once the heavy job of bringing past events up-to-date has been done, it can then be kept up-to-date year by year with comparatively little effort. The snag is of course the large amount of work involved in the initial task.

Vinter reminded staff that "funding experience" was 'especially important' for PE because of its responsibility for the nationalized industries. Indeed, its ability to monitor their relative performance was partly dependent upon the possession of such histories: 'it can hardly be done at all in the absence of the mobilised facts and a long memory'. For Vinter, histories represented an invaluable tool – what he described as 'some artificial contrivance' – drawing together the fruits of past experience for divisional use.

> Indeed, because we are so few and departments of the industries are so numerous this is one of the few advantages we have in dealing with them – apart of course from the conduct of the purse. In both these tasks we can only really do our job effectively if our memories are long, and since we shift around at intervals of two to five years we need some artificial contrivance to ensure that our memories are as long or longer than our opposite numbers.

Working within the framework defined by Vinter, on 6 June 1963 a PE divisional meeting agreed a programme designed to ensure that, subject to the pressures of everyday work, 'past experience is more readily available in future to both us and to our successors than it often has been in the past'.[35] Although Granger-Taylor's presence enabled progress on

THM-type histories, the principal focus would be placed upon divisional notes and "seeded files". In addition, it was agreed to circulate a list of available historical outputs to all divisional staff in order to encourage their everyday use.

Following the PE staff meeting, Vinter reviewed ways for his 'hard-pressed division' to progress the agreed programme, given history's 'undoubted' utility and the fact that such work was best undertaken when fresh in the minds of staff. Obviously, current business 'has got to be despatched', but, like Brook and Clarke, Vinter anticipated that the eventual availability of a wider range of "seeded files" and divisional notes would support the work of busy staff as well as save them time. Staff were urged to keep these points in mind when attempting to reconcile conflicting pressures upon their time and work load. Vinter conceded that THM-type histories represented a 'different proposition', but fortunately for the time being his division was able to call upon the full-time services of Granger-Taylor.

Generally speaking, during the next year or so, PE, acting under Vinter's supportive guidance and benefiting also from Granger-Taylor's attachment (1963–66), made sound progress in implementing its plans.[36] Indeed, annual returns submitted to the Establishment Officer's Branch confirmed that it was responsible for by far the largest "funding experience" output. By 1965 it claimed two THMs, twenty-eight divisional notes, eight "seeded files", and one research paper entitled 'A survey of the arguments advanced in favour of nationalisation from about 1890 up to 1964'.[37] In addition, the principal responsible for producing the annual investment review for each nationalized industry was required to draft a short divisional note recording briefly the lessons learned and points of difficulty to be taken into account in the following year. Unsurprisingly, in May 1965 John Hunt, Vinter's successor as head of PE, informed the Establishment Officer's Branch that the division was reasonably well provided for in terms of staffing, and hence had no need to bid for extra resources to undertake its historical plans.[38]

Granger-Taylor's aircraft purchasing THM

Public Enterprises Division confined Granger-Taylor's work to major historical projects partly because it seemed the most productive use of her time and partly because "seeded files" and shorter histories embodied in divisional notes were viewed as best undertaken by the responsible principals.[39]

In 1963 recent controversies centred upon the costs of the VC10 aircraft proved instrumental in PE's decision to commission her to write a history of aircraft purchasing.[40] Like Clarke, Vinter kept a close eye upon historical work in his sphere of responsibility; thus, he offered Granger-Taylor constant encouragement to build upon her 'splendid start', read and commented upon interim drafts, pressed for clearer presentation, and pointed to aspects in need of elaboration.[41] Interim and final drafts were passed on for comment to other officials, including Clarke and Douglas Henley, as well as to the Defence Policy and Materiel (DM) division. As ever, the process of consulting another division was dogged by delays; for instance, despite being asked in July 1964 for comments on the final draft, DM had still not replied by the end of October.[42]

As a result, it was not until early 1965 that Granger Taylor, working under Vinter's guidance, began to finalize her text and to draw out the key conclusions from this history.[43] Perhaps the most striking lesson revealed by her history was the problematic relationship between British aircraft manufacturers and corporations. Rather than demonstrating to the wider world the achievements of the British aircraft industry, British European Airways (BEA) and British Overseas Airways Corporation (BOAC) were handicapped repeatedly by delays in deliveries, design shortcomings, operational inefficiencies and serious aircraft failures, most notably the three De Havilland Comet crashes (1953–54). Nor were the aircraft corporations blameless, given the manner in which they specified aircraft unsuitable for an export market captured increasingly by American manufacturers. Further problems arose from the Treasury's failure to exert close supervision of fiscal questions as well as its tendency to assume that the aircraft corporations knew best: 'The only aspect the Corporations really understand better than everybody else is the operating economies of their routes.'

Upon completion, printing was delayed because of a serious controversy centred upon the history's circulation. When reading drafts, the subject matter led several senior officials to propose that, as happened with the THM on wages policy, a copy should be sent to the PUS of the relevant Whitehall department, that is to Sir Richard Way of the Ministry of Aviation, as well as to David Henderson, his Economic Adviser, in connection with his work for the Plowden Committee's study of the aircraft industry. For Vinter, who did not want the Ministry of Aviation to know about the history's existence, let alone its content, the proposal raised a serious question of principle. Describing the study as a 'one-sided' Treasury history of a controversial political topic written for confidential departmental use upon the basis of Treasury files covering more than one government, Vinter feared 'something going wrong' through external circulation.[44] There was also an understandable reluctance to reveal details about either the Treasury's shortcomings or its strategy when dealing with other departments.[45] However, several colleagues, including Cairncross, Clarke, Henley and Hunt, failed to see a problem.[46] Clarke accepted the need to be 'very careful' on certain sections, but justified the exception: 'in this case the history is an important tool for getting the right decision'.[47] In many respects, Clarke's relatively outgoing stance followed on naturally from sentiments expressed the previous December when delivering his Stamp Memorial Lecture: 'Only by coming together and by exchanging papers can the Departments learn from each other's experience.... It is worth spending some resources of time and organisation to disseminate the lessons quickly throughout Whitehall.'[48] For Cairncross, Granger-Taylor's history drew together 'exactly the kind of analysis of the past that is helpful to an Economic Adviser'.[49] Indeed, any restriction raised serious questions about the Treasury's purpose in funding past experience: 'It seems to me natural to ask what purpose the document has been prepared.' Nor did those consulted fear any risk of a leak from Henderson, a former Treasury colleague.[50]

In the end, the question was submitted to Helsby, the responsible Joint Permanent Secretary. Having read the text, he saw no reason why the history should not be shown to Way and Henderson, subject to certain exclusions, most notably the section outlining the Treasury's methods of control.[51] Likewise, the omission of the 'lessons to be learned' section was intended to leave the Ministry of Aviation to draw its own conclusions. As a result, Granger-Taylor was instructed to prepare a clean copy of the history for despatch to Way and Henderson.[52] Helsby's covering letter, stating that the history was being sent 'on a very personal basis' to them and must not be shown to the minister, stressed that it was 'essentially a Treasury history' indicating what had happened *'as seen from here'* [author's emphasis], thereby pre-empting any controversy based upon rival departmental perspectives.[53] Significantly, Way's reply refrained from doing more than welcoming a narrative history helping to overcome his lack of detailed background on the topic.[54]

At the same time, this history tested yet again the boundaries between divisional officials and historians, as suggested by the way in which PE inserted a note in the THM welcoming Granger-Taylor's study as a 'very valuable contribution to the understanding of an important and complex question *although not necessarily agreeing with all views*' [author's emphasis].[55] Such qualified praise largely reflected Hunt's questioning of the status of the THM's section on 'lessons' because of his belief that Granger-Taylor's role should be confined to writing the history, not identifying lessons.[56] For Hunt, the history, representing the '*individual work* [author's emphasis] of a Treasury historian', should not be presented as an agreed collective Treasury view. Furthermore, in his opinion, only officials were capable of drawing out the lessons from histories. Subsequently his minutes articulating these views, alongside the THM's inclusion of a disclaimer to this effect, was seen by Granger-Taylor as well as Ogilvy-Webb as undermining the validity of her work. Naturally, Granger-Taylor was far from pleased about such qualifications, especially as Vinter had instructed her to codify the lessons as well as guided her on this section.[57]

In November 1965 Granger-Taylor's 116-page history – in fact, a large part of the history comprised appendices – was printed as THM 9. For Vinter, Granger-Taylor's history, fully warranting the extensive time and effort put into writing it, represented, even in its draft form, a 'very useful' and 'worthwhile' project providing officials with 'a better view in depth' of a difficult and 'very expensive' subject.[58] Reading the 'sorry' story of the government's 'tangled' relations with the aircraft industry had proved 'highly relevant to the formation of current attitudes'. In particular, the history had been of 'considerable value in giving us a view in depth of the efforts over the years to get the airways corporations to use British aircraft... [and] been of real use to us in current consideration of B.O.A.C.'s finances'.[59] If nothing else, the history prompted officials to question the economic realism of the government's 'Fly British' policy.[60] As such, the history was welcomed as helping the Treasury to place future policy towards aircraft purchasing, including its dealings with the Ministry of Aviation and aircraft corporations, upon a more satisfactory footing.

Despite Vinter's recognition of the history's utility, in May 1965 Granger-Taylor complained to Hunt that the joint DEA-Treasury submission to the Plowden Committee on the aircraft industry took no account of her history's conclusions.[61] In particular, there was no mention of the serious lack of communication and coordination between aircraft corporations, aircraft manufacturers and the government: 'unless the lessons of this aspect of past experience can be looked at, it seems to me that mistakes will be bound to be repeated'. In many respects, this episode reflected the recurring problem of using completed histories – it was too easy to file them away in a cupboard to gather dust – although the fact that Granger-Taylor's history was somewhat critical of the Treasury did not help the prospects for circulation of shortcomings outside the department.⁶² Like any other Whitehall department, the Treasury remained reluctant to wash its 'dirty linen in public'.⁶³ Unsurprisingly, in 1967, when press reports about the purchase of new aircraft by BEA and BOAC touched upon the role of the Board of Trade, the DEA and Ministry of Technology, the Treasury rejected any possibility of circulating Granger-Taylor's THM to these departments, even those headed by former Treasury staff. Indeed, Henley and Clarke, the PUSs of the DEA and Ministry of Technology respectively, had actually read and commented upon draft versions of this history before leaving the Treasury!⁶⁴

Granger-Taylor's history of the nationalized industries

In Autumn 1964 Granger-Taylor moved on from the somewhat 'diffuse' project on aircraft purchasing – this history was then in its final stages of checking and redrafting – to 'the second stage' of her work for PE, that is a history of the April 1961 White Paper on the economic and financial obligations of nationalized industries (Cmnd 1337).⁶⁵ For PE, this history promised to be 'of considerable advantage' as a reference point for the government's forthcoming review of the targets and financial objectives of the nationalized industries.⁶⁶ Although files proved the prime source from an early stage, Granger-Taylor consulted former Treasury officials involved in the production of the White Paper, including those, like Stevenson, now working in another department.⁶⁷

Once again, Vinter believed that Granger-Taylor had done 'an admirable job' in producing an 'extremely useful and interesting' history.⁶⁸ Despite being 'pretty detailed', the text remained 'highly readable', while possessing an obvious applied value: 'This will stand us in good stead in the further discussions about the development of White Paper policy upon which we shall probably have to embark before very long.' For this reason, Vinter thought it prudent for the draft to be read by Clarke and Hunt, among other senior Treasury staff, as well as by Sir Thomas Padmore and Stevenson, who had been actively involved in drafting the White Paper but had now moved on to other departments.⁶⁹ Typically, Clarke responded by return.⁷⁰ Seconding Vinter's praise, he believed that the relevance of this 'most useful history' would be enhanced through improved coverage of the broader context, including the 'Treasury set-up' and the Coal Board crisis. Following the precedent of Ogilvy-Webb's THM on planning, Clarke proposed an additional covering note 'bringing out the lessons'. Like Vinter, Clarke complained about the history's excessive length resulting in part from the inclusion of superfluous data, 'dreary procedure' and lengthy quotations. In addition, he issued instructions for both the removal of references to named individuals, especially ministers, and 'care in style' to avoid giving offence to other departments in the event of permission being given for external circulation. At the same time, Clarke reaffirmed that when completed this 'secret' history, stamped 'strictly for official use only', must not be shown to ministers.[71]

Stevenson, currently the PUS at the Ministry of Power, made a fairly positive response to the draft. Acknowledging the prominent role performed by officials in the exercise, he confirmed that Granger-Taylor had set out clearly the principal developments, including 'the twist which officials gave to their original remit':

> My recollection is that Ministers were almost exclusively preoccupied with the idea that changes in structure, and in particular decentralisation (whatever that meant) was the open-sesame to the complex problems then surrounding the nationalised industries. Officials took a different view, and manoeuvred the subject accordingly.[72]

Eschewing the temptation to submit a detailed response, particularly upon being informed that names would be deleted from the final text, Stevenson reflected upon the experience of reading about events in which one had been an active participant. Although 'it would be presumptuous of me to pit my recollection of the past against her careful and authenticated marshalling of the facts', the draft history had jogged his memory and made him aware of gaps in the story, such as regarding recoupment when referring to the nationalized industries' lack of contribution to government revenue.

More revealingly, Stevenson reaffirmed the value of learning from the Whitehall past:

> The history itself is, of course, very important. Even more important, however, are the conclusions which are to be drawn from the approach to this subject and from subsequent action on the carrying out of the policy. It is here that the value of recorded experience is to be found.[73]

In particular, the text illuminated ongoing debates about limiting the financial burden placed upon the Exchequer by nationalized industries: 'This is a subject of continuing interest, and may be increasingly important with further extensions of nationalisation.' Even so, according to Stevenson, the principal lesson, that is the difficulty of reconciling contrasting policy objectives, deserved stronger emphasis:

> It would be a good thing if the history provided material for showing how futile it is to make the nationalised industries the handmaiden of other policies, and how unfair it is to make examples of them by restraint of prices when they are already obliged to work on narrow margins. I fear that unless the lessons of the past can be strongly pressed, we may be in for a dreary repetition of history in this matter.

By contrast, Padmore, who had chaired the committee responsible for producing the White Paper and was now the Permanent Secretary at the Ministry of Transport, offered more restrained praise. Indeed, reservations about the merits of generalizing from specific episodes led him to question whether such histories were either 'all that useful' or likely to make an impact upon policy:

> Jobs such as this have to be done in a manner appropriate to *the particular problem and the particular situation* [author's emphasis]. And whether reading about them in detail will ever help anyone else to do a different job in a different situation I cannot but doubt.[74]

Nor was the history's utility for policymakers helped by its excessive length – Padmore suggested excising about half the words – and the occasional error. Like Stevenson, he pressed for the exclusion of names – in fact, this had been agreed by the time his response reached the Treasury – but it is interesting to note their mutual concern about naming specific individuals in Treasury histories, including the implied assumption equating histories with post-mortems on their personal performances.

Overviewing these responses, Vinter identified the way in which Granger-Taylor's history epitomized the distinctive character of the Treasury's "funding experience" work: 'it is comparatively rare for a historian to be in a position to do a serious bit of research on an important turning point & then to get the views of those most prominently involved!'.[75] Notwithstanding Padmore's reservations about using analogies, the contributions provided by officials involved in the events under discussion offered an extra dimension to Treasury's history, such as by allowing Granger-Taylor to record 'the atmosphere in which the exercise was conducted'.[76] In particular, such feedback, going beyond the usual reliance on documentation, illuminated what James Joll has defined as the 'unspoken assumptions' underpinning the thinking of policymakers, as revealed in the following part of Stevenson's response.[77]

> The reference to taxes... reminds me of *thoughts that were around in those days which were seldom overtly stated* [author's emphasis], but found some reflection in the discussion of the appropriate rate of return. Some of us were a good deal concerned about the fact that nationalised industries, with their large and growing investment, and with their low rate of return, made no contribution by way of taxes to the expenses of central government. Thus, the provision in the Statutes confirming their liability to taxes was almost a dead-letter. In thinking about targets, therefore, the possibility of obtaining recoupment, or some reduction in the burden on the Exchequer was present in the minds of some of us.[78]

During April 1965 Hunt, the head of PE, counselled Granger-Taylor about rewriting her draft in accordance with Clarke's instructions for 'greater tightness' and the exclusion of most names.[79] Demands for the removal of explicit criticism of the Ministry of Power and toning down the claim that officials manoeuvred ministers into taking a course they had been reluctant to adopt, though understandable from the Whitehall perspective, undermined the THM's historical pretensions.[80] In the event, Granger-Taylor's commitments, including ongoing research for her next project, meant that almost one year elapsed before the final manuscript was printed in March 1966.[81] Despite being written more concisely, the THM still amounted to 62 pages! Nevertheless, both Hunt and Vinter welcomed the history as both 'first class' and timely, since 'we are working up to a White Paper to succeed Cmnd 1337'.[82] Hitherto, these discussions had stalled, but it was anticipated that the history would help progress the matter. Like most THMs, the memorandum, labelled secret, was denied to ministers. Nor could it be sent outside the Treasury without the permission of the head of the Public Sector Group. Significantly, Hunt, who had originally favoured distribution to other departments, altered his position upon reading the final text, which risked embarrassing the Treasury by recording, say, the low priority attached to economic and social factors when formulating the 'target' philosophy of the nationalized industries.[83]

Following Clarke's advice, Hunt agreed to write the THM's foreword, albeit in Vinter's name, with a view to highlighting the history's principal lessons for policymakers.[84] Recalling Padmore's caution, Hunt inserted a health warning: 'Since the circumstances of 1960–61 are unlikely to be ever repeated, it would be wrong to try and draw too many "lessons" from this history of the White Paper.'[85] Moving on, he claimed, first, that the 1961 White Paper's emphasis upon stricter standards of financial performance meant that the episode offered a classic example of the Treasury's role in establishing a common set of objectives for nationalized industries in place of the vague guidance provided in their individual statutes. As a result, this example of 'legislation by White Paper' represented 'a milestone' in the development of the government's relations with nationalized industries by limiting the need for ministerial interference, prioritizing an improved economic rate of return, and meeting the Treasury's emphasis upon a larger element of self-financing. Secondly, the White Paper reflected the government's growing appreciation of the fact that Britain's much discussed economic problems proved in part a function of the performance of nationalized industries. Thirdly, despite political pressures, nationalized industries must not be treated as 'the handmaidens' of price restraint or other policies. Finally, the THM was presented as relevant to the ongoing discussions about following up Cmnd.1337 with another White Paper.[86]

Granger-Taylor's abortive project

When THM 11 was printed in May 1966, Granger-Taylor had been working already on her next project, that is a history of atomic energy, for over one year. Reviewing PE's future "funding experience" plans in January 1965, Vinter proposed commissioning historical narratives for each nationalized industry covering the past five years: 'Our official memories are short and, to judge by my own experience, can be remarkably distorted according to the events one took part in and perhaps even (sub-consciously) there is an influence according to the success or otherwise of the efforts made.'[87] As a result, Granger-Taylor would be commissioned to collaborate with divisional staff to write a history *pointed towards current requirements* and complemented by an informed commentary based upon 'our *present* knowledge and experience' monitoring how far developments conformed to the original expectations and intentions of policymakers. Lengthy delays in completing previous THMs led Vinter to press the case for making the results available for use by officials as a reference source far more quickly.

Vinter's proposals provided the basis for a discussion of priorities at a divisional meeting held on 13 January 1965. Guided by Granger-Taylor, the division narrowed down the choice so that in May 1965 atomic energy was selected, with the electricity industry being pencilled in as the next project.[88] Of course, these plans assumed the retention of Granger-Taylor's services. However, one of the initial decisions made in January 1966 by the recently established THC was to switch her to another division in pursuit of the newly adopted policy of distributing the Treasury's limited historical resources more evenly across divisions. Paradoxically, PE, having previously stated in its annual "funding experience" return that no extra staffing was required for such work, now entered a lengthy period during which it lacked the services of a specialist historian.[89] Forced to rely entirely upon its own staff, the most immediate consequence was the suspension of work on the atomic energy history.

The Social Services Division moves to the fast lane

Public Enterprises Division's strong performance in the sphere of historical work during the period 1963–66 was far from typical. Lack of access to a historian severely curtailed the efforts of most divisions, even one, like the Social Services (SS) division, seemingly anxious to fulfil the Treasury's "funding experience" goals. Soon after a divisional heads meeting on "Funding Experience", held in April 1964 under Clarke's chairmanship, Jack Rampton, the head of SS, complained that his division – Chapter 4 outlined its initial lack of activity – continued to lag behind other divisions and needed still to implement 'a more effective programme of effort'.[90] Admittedly, "seeded files" were now available on housing subsidies and new towns, but, as one official minuted a few months later, the 'heavy and steadily mounting pressure of *more important work* [author's emphasis]' ensured that progress on low priority "funding experience" activities was slow.[91]

Divisional staff appreciated that history writing could not be undertaken in unpredictable 'snatches with constant interruptions for day-to-day business'.[92] Rather, it required time and concentrated effort. For SS, the position was transformed in May 1965, when it was allocated a new full-time Treasury recruit, Guy Hartcup, to write histories of two topics figuring in its plans: the rebuilding of 10 Downing Street and the rehousing of the Commonwealth Institute.[93] Hartcup worked quickly, so that by September 1965 both drafts were ready for divisional comment, and he had moved onto the next SS project covering the National Land Fund.[94] Even so, as discussed in Chapter 6, the practical impact of Hartcup's efforts was qualified, even negated, by the extensive delay in securing divisional feedback upon drafts and approval for printing. As a result, the histories were not printed until November 1968.

Britain and Europe

Generally speaking, the Treasury adopted an insular, even possessive, approach to its "funding experience" activities. From this perspective, THM 10 on Britain and Europe between 1961 and 1963 was almost unique among Treasury histories, since it differed in origin, type of authorship, form of linkage with ministers, and circulation from other THMs.

Immediately following the breakdown of the talks for British entry to the Common Market in January 1963, Edward Heath, the Lord Privy Seal (1960–63), commissioned members of the delegation to produce a history and analytical commentary of the Brussels Conference.[95] In addition, he asked the Foreign Office to arrange for the writing of a broader history dating back to the late 1950s:

> The primary object of the whole study would not be to produce a defence of our conduct in the negotiations, but to make a searching review of the whole course of the negotiations in order to see where we had gone wrong and what lessons could be learnt for any future negotiations of the same kind.[96]

The history, written while memories were fresh, would help – to quote Pierson Dixon, the head of the British official delegation – 'to get the record clear', given the mutual recriminations following the breakdown of the talks.[97] In particular, Heath sought to identify the reasons for failure, including the extent to which Britain's policy, approach and methods were responsible, as well as the lessons to be learned when formulating future policy. The history would also provide, it was anticipated, material for any official publication, like a Blue Book, required upon the subject.

Although the Foreign Office set up the proposed study and floated the possibility of involving Rohan Butler, one of its historians, the actual task was assigned to the Treasury as the department responsible for coordinating external economic policy.[98] Having taken on the assignment, the Treasury freed Christopher Lucas, an Assistant Secretary in the Finance-Coordination division (FC2), from day-to-day responsibilities to undertake the project working in collaboration with interested departments: the Board of Trade, Colonial Office, Commonwealth Relations Office, Foreign Office, and the Ministry of Agriculture, Fisheries and Food (MAFF).[99] Following an initial trawl through the files, Lucas saw his 'London history' as telling the story 'as seen from Whitehall'; thus, 'the important task of the history seems to me to sketch the evolution of Government thinking' and to 'show where we obviously went wrong'. Perceived similarities between the free trade negotiations of 1957–58 and the 1963 Brussels Conference led him to recognize the need 'to make some comparison between the two to establish whether the lessons of our former experience were fully learned or not; and if not, the reasons for this failure'.

During the next two months or so, Lucas exchanged views about the format, content and scale of the project as well as about his interim drafts with Treasury colleagues and interested departments. Frequently, other departments contributed illuminating perspectives; for example, the Board of Trade reaffirmed the impact of the Suez Crisis:

> The replacement of Mr. Eden by Mr. Macmillan, Mr. Thorneycroft's translation from the Board of Trade to the Treasury and Sir David Eccles's arrival at the Board of Trade played a quite substantial part in the way things developed in the following two years. Equally, of course, the Suez events of the Autumn of 1956 were a strong factor both in the development of opinion in Britain and as expediting the Rome Treaty negotiations.[100]

Despite the usual delays in departmental feedback due to the heavy pressure of current work, by early April 1963 Lucas was able to circulate a revised 155-page draft history for comment by departments.[101] Pointing to the way in which the text glossed over, say, the American and French dimensions, Pierson Dixon saw it as 'very much a Treasury document', which failed to record either the evolution of de Gaulle's thinking throughout the negotiations or the extent to which 'this hindsight tallies with what we were reporting' at the time.[102] Nor did Lucas's history acknowledge that, in Dixon's view, the attempt to join, albeit proving abortive, was better than doing nothing.

Hitherto, the history had moved ahead at a steady rate. However, in mid-1963 the project suddenly hit the buffers; indeed, Lucas's text was not cleared for printing as a 'Whitehall History' in the THM series until September 1965. In part, the problem arose from serious delays in departmental comments upon the revised draft, with MAFF proving the chief culprit, but the loss of momentum was largely a function of Heath's failure to issue instructions about progressing the history, particularly following his switch to the Board of Trade in October 1963.[103] In the end, THM 10, though subject to the Treasury's usual restrictions about circulation to ministers, had a wider distribution than most others in the series, since copies were sent to each department involved in the project.

Significantly, Lucas's 76-page THM was presented not as a comprehensive history, but rather as complementing the 181-page narrative prepared on behalf of the official delegation at the Brussels Conference.[104] Nevertheless, despite its Treasury bias, the history provided a useful reference source upon the course of Britain's negotiations with continental Europe during the past decade or so, while pointing to a series of shortcomings in policies and methods. These included the initial British misjudgement of the strength of the movement towards European unity; the government's failure to educate British opinion about Europe; the exaggerated British expectations about being welcomed into the Common Market; the miscalculations and misperceptions of the French position in general and of de Gaulle's intentions in particular; and the failure of British policymakers to learn the lessons of the earlier free trade negotiations. Despite reversing policy to accept the case for joining the EEC, 'we had not travelled far enough'.[105] As Ogilvy-Webb commented, this THM highlighted 'one of the most important failures in assessment and prediction' by policymakers, including 'a whole series of disastrous assessments' about the likely attitude of other governments' and the impact of the Treaty of Rome.[106]

Similar delays affected the history and commentary on the Brussels Conference, which were submitted to Heath in Spring 1963. Even so, according to Heath, the history impacted upon future policymakers:

> This document proved very important. It contains a full and completely frank account of the development of our negotiating position and the considerations, whether technical or tactical, or of a personal character, that had influenced the course of events. It kept memories of those concerned in Whitehall fresh and, in 1967 when Harold Wilson launched his abortive preparations for new negotiations, it was taken as the starting point of the entire briefing operation. The outcome of the 1970–1 negotiations was also very heavily based on the position reached eight years earlier in Brussels. An even greater achievement, however, was that the methodology for the enlargement negotiations established in 1961–3 is one that has been followed in every enlargement negotiation since then, and is likely to be followed in future.[107]

In 1972, Sir Con O'Neill's confidential Foreign Office history of the negotiations resulting in British entry into the European Economic

Community (EEC) – this internal history is discussed in Chapter 11 – acknowledged the influence exerted upon policymakers by the 1963 Narrative Report, such as in establishing the need for a more informed knowledge of the EEC or the prudence of avoiding confrontation by seeking tariff quotas rather than nil tariffs.[108] However, as O'Neill recognized, the broader international context during the early 1970s, by which time de Gaulle had left the scene, was very different from that encountered one decade earlier.[109] Likewise, during 1970–72 the British delegation, though emulating the practice of its 1961–63 predecessor by travelling between Brussels and London, avoided following the 1963 Report's advice to anchor itself in one spot.[110]

Conclusion

Looking back in 1968, Ogilvy-Webb presented 1962 as a key date for the Treasury's historical activities. For him, his THM on wages policy was seen as effectively inaugurating a 'new series' of THMs.[111] Admittedly, the basic outlines of its "funding experience" programme had been defined already, but the departmental reorganization, implemented at the close of the year, led senior staff, many of whom were already supportive of such activities, to reaffirm the value of "funding experience" in recording collective departmental and divisional memories in a period of rapid change. Soon afterwards, the introduction of the annual monitoring process signalled the adoption of a more systematic and uniform approach to "funding experience".

Notwithstanding the continued support of senior staff, the steady rate of advance in "funding experience" achieved between 1962 and 1965 by the Public Sector Group, particularly in PE, proved atypical in that such progress proved a function of a set of special circumstances centred upon the strong commitment of Clarke and Vinter. Significantly, in January 1964, when reminding divisional heads that the Joint Permanent Secretaries wanted divisions to take "funding experience" work more seriously, Abbot enclosed extracts from one of Vinter's 1963 minutes by way of acquainting them with the practical benefits of such activities alongside ways of balancing the demands of current and historical work.[112] Even so, substantial problems remained, as recognized by the Heads of Division (Public Sector) Group. When meeting in April 1965 under Clarke's chairmanship, the group acknowledged the perceived burden of historical work for busy staff: 'the main difficulty was to find sufficient time in divisions for the work'.[113] Certainly, annual monitoring returns established repeatedly the crucial role played by staffing in influencing the overall level and continuity of historical work. There was – to quote Collier – 'from time to time, a lot of steam behind this exercise', at least in certain divisions, but the way in which delays in making annual returns were often rationalised by limited staffing reflected the relative lack of response by most divisions to pressure for action.[114]

Nor was progress helped by the limited resources available centrally to support such activities. Although the recruitment of Granger-Taylor and then Hartcup brought some improvement, lack of access to a full-time historian severely curtailed the plans of most divisions, since there were strict limits to what could be achieved from their own resources. Also retired staff alleviated the staffing problem, but in practice it was not always easy to persuade such staff to return part-time for such work, as evidenced by the abortive efforts to persuade K. Weston to write a history of debt settlement with the Soviet Union.[115] Occasionally, an outside academic was recruited, as happened with Alan Holmans, an economist from Glasgow University. Working part-time under the supervision of the Economic Adviser, Holmans wrote THM 8 (1965) on the Control of Demand, 1953–58 for the National Economy Group and Economic Section.[116] A longer 159-page version was retained for use within the Economic Section.

At the same time, signs of progress, highlighted by the example of PE, should not obscure the problems, most notably those arising from the 'under-current of resistance' throughout the department to using history. Divisional staff did not always see the Treasury's historical activities as either readily accessible or relevant to his/her everyday work. Far from viewing THMs, divisional notes and "seeded files" as potentially useful working tools for handling current or future problems, most officials treated them as tedious and time-consuming tasks interfering with their everyday responsibilities. Unsurprisingly, it proves difficult to find supportive sentiments expressed about "funding experience" activities by less senior officials, some of whom, like Leo Pliatzky or Douglas Wass, were soon to become senior staff.[117] Admitting that "seeded files" proved 'of some, but limited, value', in 1965 Pliatzky, an Assistant Secretary, raised serious doubts about the practical application of the Treasury's historical activities.[118] In part, this was a question of attitude, but things were not helped by divisional unawareness of their existence due to the restricted circulation list and the lack of a central index. As Pliatzky complained, 'it is of no use funding experience if the fund is not readily available to be drawn on'.

Naturally, Ogilvy-Webb, who was beginning also to see himself as possessing a wider role representing the interests of Treasury historians, retained his belief in the potential utility of "funding experience", but in 1965 his confident espousal of the merits of the Treasury's activities was qualified by the surprising admission that 'the extent to which the information in these works has *in fact* been exploited is unknown to me'.[119] In fact, his relative lack of knowledge about what happened to THMs after they were completed and printed might be taken to reaffirm the Treasury's continuing failure to integrate historians effectively into the work of the whole department. Frequently, Ogilvy-Webb's commentaries proved somewhat downbeat. Despite occasional feedback about specific THMs and regular praise from Clarke, Ogilvy-Webb acknowledged the difficulty of feeding histories easily into the policy-making process: 'I cannot help suspecting that so far there has not been much direct and identifiable use of them.'

6
The 'New Stage' in the Treasury's Historical Work, 1965–68

During 1965 senior officials, led by Vinter, the head of PE, undertook the most searching review to date of departmental mechanisms for managing "funding experience" in general and the Treasury's historians in particular. As Collier, the Deputy Establishment Officer, pointed out, the existing *ad hoc* arrangements were 'unacceptable'.[1] Furthermore, the fact that most staff viewed "funding experience" as a somewhat irrelevant, even disconnected, activity made a strong case for adopting an alternative organizational framework. The resulting changes, centred upon the establishment of a Treasury Historical Committee (THC) and a Treasury Historical Section (THS) located within the Establishment Officer's Branch, sought to integrate such activities more effectively into the department's everyday work by improving the link between divisions and historians. Furthermore, the THC was given the mission 'to spread the gospel more widely' throughout the Treasury, and particularly to encourage divisions to appreciate the value of histories in supporting 'the man at the desk' as well as the case for undertaking more such work through their own resources.[2]

Welcomed by Armstrong and Helsby, the Joint Permanent Secretaries, as 'sensible', even 'forward looking', measures, these changes were presented as marking a 'new stage' in the Treasury's "funding experience" activities.[3] In reality, they represented merely yet another attempt made by the Treasury to translate the theoretical benefits of "funding experience" into practice, and hence to get Brook's 1957 policy initiative back on track. From this perspective, the new THC-based management structure was viewed as allowing the Treasury to perform a macro-role focussed upon 'the total picture'.[4] A stronger central steer, it was anticipated, would enable greater control over the whole process, with specific reference to harmonizing historical work with the current administrative concerns of divisions. As ever, the fundamental objective was to encourage the resulting histories to be treated as a routine part of the Treasury's work. For Collier, hitherto too many THMs had been shelved unread: 'histories should be slotted effectively into the administrative machine. For an historian to write a history, for it then to be circulated (sometimes read, sometimes put in a cupboard) is clearly not enough.'[5]

Bridging the gulf between historians and divisions

Unsurprisingly, Clarke made a substantial input to the discussions leading up to the revised structure, most notably through a minute headed 'Learning from History', in a manner reflecting his longstanding personal enthusiasm for encouraging, protecting and developing such activities.[6] In retrospect, his advocacy of a more realistic future strategy, especially concerning THM-type histories, gained added significance, given his imminent departure in March 1966 to become PUS at the Ministry of Aviation. In part, Clarke's fears that historical work was 'running into a dead end' were prompted by recent conversations with Ogilvy-Webb centred upon the 'very difficult problem' of persuading divisions to find both the time and the inclination to read, let alone use, existing histories. Like Collier, Clarke believed that 'it is obviously nonsense to spend a lot of resources in producing histories and then not to have the histories used'. At the same time, he conceded that it was not easy to force divisions 'to do something which they do not want to do': 'Divisions are so hard pressed anyway that they can't spare the time to think of the past and draw conclusions from it.'

As ever, it was easier to articulate the problem than to find the solution – Clarke advised that the issue should be a priority agenda item for the THC's initial meeting – but for him there was only 'one answer'. And that was *not* to stop "funding experience". Proposing that Vinter should assume a watching brief over this whole sphere of activity, he argued that the historians, who still seemed too often to be doing their own thing, should be placed more tightly in the divisional framework in order to ensure that their work satisfied the needs of current administration and, more importantly, was 'assimilated into our system' effectively and promptly. In part, the problem derived from the nature of the histories: 'They are often rather forbidding in size: they are often SECRET and cannot be taken home.' Some retuning seemed essential: 'The proper use of the histories can therefore be found only if we can relate them to practical problems and to specific proposals for incorporating lessons from the past in our own methods of work.' In this vein, the 'real' Treasury interest in, say, Hartcup's history on 10 Downing Street – Clarke had recently read the draft version being circulated for comment – was in 'the generalisation of the lessons to be learned in order to cover a much wider area of activity' rather than in the specific details about the actual rebuilding project. Henceforth, senior officials, not historians, should be asked to draw out from completed histories the principal conclusions from the point of view of the Treasury *as a whole*, possibly even calling a meeting to examine 'the particular problem of organisation which had been thrown up in these conclusions' to ensure that any lessons were 'discussed and absorbed into our thinking'.

During these exchanges Ogilvy-Webb came to see himself as responsible for presenting both the historians's case for continuing "funding experience" work and the way forward in the light of what had been achieved to date. Revealingly, and notwithstanding his strong belief in the practical administrative value of "funding experience", Ogilvy-Webb was not overly optimistic about bridging the gap with divisions. Thus, his review of progress to date contained a somewhat mixed message:

> Clearly a demand exists for the kind of history which analyses and brings out essential points for future use although there are some who think that history narratives can never be useful because events never repeat themselves exactly. There is, nevertheless, a body of opinion which has stressed the importance of this kind of history in a number of current contexts.[7]

For Ogilvy-Webb, the priority was to encourage officials, especially those responsible for commissioning projects, to read the resulting histories and, more importantly, treat them as a useful policy resource. Searching for an answer, he speculated why officials were deterred from reading, let alone applying, THMs. Was it because long works presented too much of a burden for busy administrators? Alternatively, should Treasury histories be made to appear more accessible and user-friendly through the provision of an index and more informative titles? Ten years on, as recorded in Chapter 8, Ogilvy-Webb was still posing the same questions.

The creation of the Treasury Historical Committee

Following Helsby's formal approval, the revised arrangements emerging from these preliminary exchanges were announced in a divisional heads notice distributed on 3 December 1965.[8] Unsurprisingly, the THC's creation prompted a restatement of the basic principles and priorities of "funding experience", that is 'to produce results which would directly assist current administration' and future work.[9]

Henceforth, the tasks, workload and priorities of the Treasury's small but growing number of historians would be managed by a new committee, the THC, reporting to Helsby and chaired by Peter Vinter, the Third Secretary in charge of Public Sector A. The committee's six members – F.J. Atkinson, F.R. Baldwin, F. Russell Barratt, H.A. Copeman, K.E. Couzens and J.J.B. Hunt – were not seen as representing individual divisions. Rather they were selected for their knowledge and expertise. Likewise, the THC's projected schedule, based upon three to four meetings per year, was designed to allow flexibility when initiating, monitoring and assessing projects. For administrative purposes, the historians would be grouped in a separate THS located within the Establishment Officer's Branch, whose deputy head (Collier) was deputed to liaise with the THC by way of enhancing links between divisions and historians. Collier, the THC's Secretary, was responsible also for liaising with both divisions and historians when following up the committee's decisions. The subordinate role of historians in the revised structure was emphasized by the fact that none of them, not even Ogilvy-Webb, was given membership of the THC. Instead, historians had their own subcommittee, with Vinter acting as both the chairman and the key link with the THC.

Following its initial meetings, as detailed below, Vinter apprised Helsby about the committee's principal guidelines for action:

Looking to the next stage, there seem to us to be several lessons to be drawn from past experience:-

(a) The work needs to be guided and developed rather more purposively;
(b) The balance between major works which lock up our slender resources for long periods, and lesser jobs which spread the results of funding much more widely, has to be watched carefully; the more limited work may in fact be as valuable in teaching a lesson to the present desk-officer as the more ambitious memorandum;
(c) We shall never have many historians...so that a lot of the funding of the experience must be done in Divisions. One of our jobs therefore is to use the historians in such a way as to spread the gospel more widely. Hitherto the balance of funding work between Divisions has been rather marked;

(d) At this stage we all emphatically believe that it is essential to concentrate the funding work on backing up 'the man at the desk'... we are sure that at this juncture we ought to concentrate ouf [sic] slender historical resources on backing up day-to-day work.[10]

The Treasury Historical Section

One of the THC's key roles was to make the best use of the limited resources available for "funding experience" work by directing the work of the historians, advising upon priorities in the light of divisional needs, monitoring progress and appraising outcomes. Henceforth, the Treasury's historians, though undertaking a range of other tasks, were expected to concentrate upon major projects, which divisions valued as *potentially useful to their current and forthcoming work* but lacked the time to do themselves. As Collier reminded Ogilvy-Webb, their role would be 'limited to the funding of experience which is of value to current generations of administrators'.[11] This Treasury-centred approach was reinforced by repeated reaffirmations that research must be confined to departmental papers only.

Of course, within the Treasury as a whole, very few staff were engaged in such work, and hence, as mentioned above, restructuring was intended in part to maximize the use of a scarce resource. Despite Collier's claim that numbers, boosted by recent appointments, had reached 'respectable proportions', in 1965 the Treasury's 'force of historians', or 'funders' as they were often described, totalled only four (Table 6.1).[12] In January 1965 Mrs Terri Banks, a former Principal, joined Ogilvy-Webb and Granger-Taylor. Although she was employed on a part-time basis, it was anticipated that she would return to full-time work when her children were older. Seeking to familiarize her with the technique of "funding experience", Collier commissioned her to produce a history of aid to India and Pakistan in 1956 before moving on to more demanding projects.[13] Later in the year Guy Hartcup, whose previous postings included the Air Ministry Historical Branch and the Cabinet Office, joined the Treasury as a full-time historian.[14] Rated by Collier as a 'considerable addition', he was attached initially to SS to progress its planned projects. In September 1966 Catherine Dennis, another former Principal, began working two to three days per week excluding school holidays.[15] In certain instances, during the late 1960s, specific projects for which the existing historians lacked specialist expertise were undertaken by retired staff, like Russell Bretherton, Colonel Russell-Edmunds

Table 6.1 The Treasury's historians in the mid-1960s

A.K. Ogilvy-Webb	FT	Jul. 1960–76
Barbara Granger-Taylor	PT	Jan. 1963–70
Guy Hartcup	FT	Jun. 1965–Apr. 1976
Terri Banks	PT	Jan. 1965–Sept. 1966
Susan Franks	FT	Sept. 1965–Jul. 1966
Catherine Dennis	PT	Oct. 1966–May 1977
Colonel W. Russell-Edmunds	PT	Jan. 1966–74

Note: FT – Full-time, PT – Part-time.

or R. Symons, who were given room space and paid a proportional fee based upon their former post.

As mentioned above, Ogilvy-Webb had begun to see himself as something more than just a historian undertaking specific projects.[16] Reportedly, he was suspected of hoping that the new THC-centred regime would lead to his promotion to the rank of assistant secretary in charge of the THS.[17] Certainly, during the exchanges conducted about "funding experience" in 1965 with Clarke, Collier and Vinter, among others, Ogilvy-Webb saw himself as responsible for presenting the historians's case, frequently through lengthy memoranda outlining past achievements and future possibilities.[18] However, Collier and Vinter, though generally impressed with the quality, if not the pace, of his historical work, followed Clarke in expressing reservations about Ogilvy-Webb's managerial potential.[19] In the event, the THC, not Ogilvy-Webb, was given the job of managing the Treasury's historians and their work programmes. Nor was Ogilvy-Webb given membership of the THC.

For senior staff, Ogilvy-Webb was viewed as a serial offender ploughing ahead on large multi-volume projects and glossing over projected deadlines. Vinter often worried about Ogilvy-Webb's place in the larger Treasury project: 'Is this becoming a private empire, or even "a world of his own" over which we have lost control?'.[20] At one stage in Spring 1967, when there was talk about Ogilvy-Webb moving temporarily to the DEA to continue his work on planning, prices and wages, Vinter recommended that a senior official therein be deputed to oversee his work: 'unless the general pattern and direction are controlled, he is a little apt to follow up interesting cul-de-sacs too readily'.[21] In brief, the THC sought to contain Ogilvy-Webb's penchant for large projects while simultaneously – to quote Collier – 'riding him on a fairly loose rein' to harness his 'very real talents'.[22]

The THC begins work

When the THC first met on 19 November 1965 (Table 6.2), members began by reaffirming the functional nature of the Treasury's "funding experience" activities: 'the main aim of history writing in the Treasury should be to secure results of practical value to "the man at the desk" '.[23] Looking ahead, members decided that histories should concentrate upon subjects of genuine interest 'from which valuable lessons could be drawn both for the Division concerned, and (where appropriate) more widely', with priority given to shorter self-contained projects. Generally speaking, Treasury historians were seen as undertaking tasks for which divisions lacked the time and resources, even if their small number led the THC to trust that divisions would not be discouraged from conducting their own historical work, at least in the form of divisional notes and "seeded files".

Taking its cue from points raised in the recent intra-departmental exchanges, the THC spent time discussing what had emerged as the fundamental problem: 'Preparation of histories is pointless unless Divisions can be persuaded to make regular use of them. It was therefore agreed that usage was a matter of great concern to the Committee and should be kept under continuous review.' Past experience led the committee to stress the enhanced role expected of divisions in, say, providing clear guidance about the intended use of any history, drawing conclusions from completed projects, and updating histories in the light of their value to current work. Of importance here was the THC's ruling that it was primarily the responsibility of divisions, not historians, to draw conclusions from historical

Table 6.2 Managing history in the Treasury, 1965–70

Treasury Historical Committee	Historians's Sub-Committee
Chair	*Chair*
F.P. Vinter (1965–69); D. Henley (1969–)	F.P. Vinter (1965–69)
Secretary	*Secretary*
A.J. Collier *ex officio* (1965–69); K.T. King (1965–69); E. Yeo (1969–)	K.T. King (1965–69)
Meetings	*Meetings*
1. 19 November 1965	1. 10 December 1965
2. 7 January 1966	2. 23 November 1966
3. 25 October 1966	3. 1 May 1969
4. 14 February 1968	4. 3 June 1969

works, even if historians would be encouraged to prompt divisional thinking through the identification of 'provisional conclusions'. The THC stipulated that future projects, involving 'more limited' tasks and taking no more than two or three months to complete, must promise 'to provide the greatest immediate benefit to Divisional officers'.[24] Concerns about the way in which past projects had often locked up scarce resources for two or more years explained the preference for 'greater flexibility of selection, quicker turnover, and more opportunity for work evaluation'.[25] Even so, more substantial projects, as favoured by Clarke, were not ruled out completely. Looking ahead to the next round of bids for the services of a historian, members agreed on the prudence of a 'severely' selective approach. Rather than conducting another department-wide competition, the plan was to target six divisions – Finance Home; Finance Exports/Imports; Defence Policy and Materiel (DM); Social Services (SS); Agriculture, Towns and Transport (AT); and Management Services – hitherto lacking the services of a historian.

For the THC, use was seen in part as a function of greater accessibility and improved publicity regarding their content. Thus, a central subject index was deemed 'essential' for referencing, planning and monitoring purposes. Acknowledging the seemingly narrow focus of many THMs, members pointed to the careful choice of index headers in order to reference and publicize *all relevant policy possibilities*. For example, a history of British railways, albeit indexed under both 'British railways' and 'history', might well cover issues of broader interest, like writing-off exchequer loans or the appointment of board members to nationalized industries, meriting an index entry.

Historians's Sub-Committee

Three weeks later, that is on 10 December 1965, the Historians's Sub-Committee (HSC), established to act as 'a linking device' between the THC and the historians, assembled for its inaugural meeting.[26] Vinter's chairmanship, alongside the absence of any historian on the THC itself, emphasized the servicing role of Treasury historians, including the fact that henceforth they were expected to work within a tightly circumscribed departmental framework.

Vinter welcomed the historians – Franks, Granger-Taylor, Hartcup and Ogilvy-Webb were in attendance – to what he hoped would be the first of a series of regular meetings forging 'a close relationship' between the THC and the historians, charting the future course of history writing, monitoring the improved dissemination and use of outputs throughout the Treasury, and pooling experience on issues and practical problems.[27] Acknowledging the 'great deal of extremely valuable historical work' already undertaken by the historians of 'direct and immediate benefit to Divisional Officers in dealing with current problems', Vinter communicated the THC's decisions and proposed future strategy. Urging close liaison between divisions and historians at all stages, Vinter expressed the hope that over time the experience of working together would make busy divisions currently 'unsympathetic to historical work' more appreciative of Treasury histories. Reporting the THC's objective to allow a larger number of divisions to benefit from the services of a historian, Vinter stated that Granger-Taylor would be removed from her lengthy placement in PE. Generally speaking, the meeting took the form of a statement by Vinter relaying the views and decisions of the THC. Only when the HSC reached the index as an agenda item did discussion open up. Even so, all present agreed upon the strong case for an index to be prepared by the historians in consultation with divisions and commercial indexers.

Second THC meeting

When meeting again on 7 January 1966, the THC began by briefly reviewing general issues, including the role of divisions, but focused principally upon drafting the department's future historical programme, with an initial preference for short tasks 'while the new system gets into its stride'.[28] Most of the 25 bids submitted by the six nominated divisions were adjudged 'quite good', even 'very good', by reference to an assessment of their 'usefulness'.[29] Seven bids, described variously as either 'topical' or 'offering a number of valuable points of guidance', even of 'considerable importance and urgency', were selected for immediate support. Two proposals, covering the Mantaro and National Research and Development Corporation (NRDC) financing projects, were favoured as limited tasks providing points of entry into more substantial topics pencilled in for a subsequent phase of the programme. The choice of a history of prescription charges reflected Vinter's wish to back one of SS's bids by way of not only building upon Hartcup's previous work but also preparing for the possibility that a future Conservative government might reintroduce the charges abolished recently (1965) by Wilson's Labour Government.[30] Apart from the NRDC project, the AT won support for its bid for a history of government intervention in Fairfields shipyard, a rare success story.

Ogilvy-Webb's 1966 lecture

On 20 October 1966 Ogilvy-Webb delivered a lecture on "funding experience" to some 40 Treasury staff.[31] However, his use of the opportunity to air longstanding grievances regarding, say, the hostility of divisions to historical work or restrictions placed upon both the use of other department's records and the circulation of THMs outside the Treasury caused waves in the higher reaches of the Treasury. For Collier and Vinter, this 'irritating' lecture typified the apparent reluctance of Treasury historians fully to appreciate the actual nature of "funding experience" work or the 'desperate difficulty' experienced by a busy 'front line deskman' in reading and using THMs.[32] Ogilvy-Webb's perceived assumption of a '"High Priest" line', combined with his 'rather foolish remarks', was seen as doing little to bridge the gulf between the historians and the divisions. Certainly, his lecture was interpreted as hindering efforts to 'spread the gospel more widely' in the way favoured by the THC. Despite his claims to represent the views of all Treasury historians, senior staff saw Ogilvy-Webb as pursuing his own personal and intellectual agenda.

Although Vinter opted out of any philosophical discussion with Ogilvy-Webb about the issues raised by the lecture, Collier attempted some 'softening up' of individual historians, like Russell-Edmunds, before calling an informal meeting with all the historians.[33] Dennis, Hartcup and Russell-Edmunds, he reported, seemed reassured, and led Collier to believe that he had succeeded in 'putting a stopper' upon Ogilvy-Webb: 'one can never be sure that he won't come back to it; but as of now he has accepted that it would do great harm to the progress of history writing within the Treasury if he were to talk with people on the lines of his lecture'. Even so, he worried still about Ogilvy-Webb as well as Granger-Taylor, given their apparent penchant to move on from writing history and cross what was seen as the demarcation line between historians and officials by telling Treasury officials what to do in specific circumstances: 'This frightens me; even if our historians were competent to do it, I don't believe it is their function. *I thought I had steered them off this* [author's emphasis] (and indeed I think I have done so successfully with Hartcup, Russell-Edmunds and Mrs. Dennis) but they may come back to it.' Significantly, when reading these sentences, Vinter used marginal notes to second Collier's comment.

The next THC meeting, scheduled for June 1966, slipped until October, when the allocation of new tasks proved the main business. Once again, perceived utility was to the fore when assessing priorities among the proposed topics, which were evaluated as covering problems either 'needed urgently' (provincial differentiation and London weighting), 'always likely to face the Treasury' (debt due to national default) or 'of value in future thinking' (promotion sharing and career management).[34] Conversely, certain topics were ruled out on the grounds of size (government and wages), their ongoing nature (sanctions and Rhodesia), or the need to give other divisions experience of a historian's services (rejection of SS's bid). The refusal to support a proposed history of the TSR2 aircraft project – this was cancelled in April 1965 – reflected the perceived problem of "funding experience" in cases where political considerations were predominant: thus, the THC doubted whether the history 'was likely to produce lessons which could be applied in the future; the reasons for continuing with TSR.2 were so political that the situation could not be said to have been under any administrative control'.

One month later the HSC met.[35] Significantly, prior to the meeting, Collier and Vinter reaffirmed their view that the sub-committee was designed merely to rubberstamp the THC's decisions: 'this mustn't slip into a situation in which they [the historians] go on deciding what they want to do'.[36] Even so, this did not stop the historians – Granger-Taylor's absence on sick leave meant that Dennis, Hartcup and Ogilvy-Webb were the only ones present – using the session to reiterate their usual concerns about working with divisions, delays in progressing histories, and restrictions upon research sources. Vinter listened, but gave little or no ground. For example, responding to Hartcup's observation that access to the DEA's papers would have given greater balance and comprehensiveness to his history about the government's rescue of the Fairfields shipyard (1965–66), Vinter merely reiterated the limited *Treasury* focus of projects. In any case, broadening the 'horizons of history writing' was adjudged likely to cause delays and risk 'destructive publicity'.[37]

Barratt's attendance reflected the new policy of inducing divisions to assume a more proactive role by pointing historians in the right direction when starting a project.[38] Thus, Barratt agreed to brief Ogilvy-Webb about the purpose and deadline date of Civil Pay 2 division's project on provincial differentiation and London weighting:

The aim would be to draw conclusions about the effect of changes in rates upon recruitment and upon the corresponding rates paid by other large employers of staff working in the London area... as a basis for consideration by the Division of the recommendations which should be made about the future form of the allowance when the matter goes before the National Incomes Commission in March 1967.[39]

The HSC was informed also that Bretherton, the head of AT, would be asked to do the same for Granger-Taylor's history of investment grants and Plan E.

Treasury drift

During 1967 the Treasury's historians remained busy on existing projects, including the index. But there were worrying signs of drift. Already, the THC-centred framework was not operating in the manner anticipated. Just as the date of the THC's second meeting had slipped by several months so its next session suffered an even longer slippage, that is until February 1968.[40] As a result, the THC did not meet at all in 1967! So much for the initial plan for three to four sessions per year. Nor was any real effort made to monitor progress of either individual histories or the index. The clearance of draft histories by divisions became an increasingly 'lengthy business'. Too many projects – these included histories of Downing Street, the Commonwealth Institute and Fairfields – got bogged down in divisions for months, even years (Table 6.3).[41] In February 1968, when the THC next met, nine histories still awaited divisional feedback and clearance.

Table 6.3 Treasury histories awaiting divisional clearance, February 1968

Title	Division	Date completed
Downing Street	Social Services	Jul. 1965
Commonwealth Institute	Social Services	Sept. 1965
National Land Fund	Social Services	Feb. 1966
Fairfields shipyard	Agriculture, Towns & Transport	May 1966
NRDC financing	Agriculture, Towns & Transport	Sept. 1966
Aid to India and Pakistan	Finance Overseas Development	Sept. 1966
National Health Stamp	Social Services	Jul. 1967
London weighting	Civil Pay 2	Sept. 1967
Mantaro hydroelectric	Finance Exports/Imports	Sept. 1967

The THC meets again at last

Informed about the forthcoming THC meeting, scheduled for February 1968, the historians prepared a six-page memorandum supporting their claim that "funding experience" work was in a state of crisis.[42] The lengthening list of histories awaiting divisional clearance and approval was presented as symptomatic of their increasingly problematic relationship with divisions at each stage of any project – planning, commencement, production and completion – quite apart from the lack of use of the finished product. As 'producers' of the histories, they advocated a review investigating the actual utility of Treasury histories, with particular reference to the views of the divisions as 'consumers', possibly conducted through a department-wide questionnaire or a survey based on one specific history. The THM on prescription charges was mentioned as a possible case study.

King, the THC's Secretary, conducted a preliminary appraisal of the historians's commentary by way of providing Collier and Vinter with background for the forthcoming THC meeting as well as avoiding the need to submit the actual memorandum to members.[43] To some extent, King sympathized with the historians's complaints: 'If we regard the work of the historians as important, it is equally important to ensure that it is brought as quickly as possible to fruition, and I would favour bringing pressure to bear on divisions who put this aspect of their work to one side for too long.' Nevertheless, for King, the memorandum confirmed that the fundamental problem, the apparent mismatch between what the historians were producing and what hard-pressed divisions viewed as possessing 'immediate practical value', had yet to be resolved. Nor had things been helped by the continued absence of an index; indeed, King proposed delaying any review until divisions had experience of working with an index. Unsurprisingly, the historians's offer to conduct any review themselves evoked a strong riposte: 'Their job is surely to write the histories as best they can, and leave the rest to us and to the divisions.'

The THC met on 14 February 1968. As mentioned above, the historians's memorandum was not circulated to members. Instead, Vinter outlined the key points as a basis for discussion and action. Resolving that prolonged delays – these were attributed to the fact that 'other Divisional work was apparently always being given precedence' – were 'not acceptable', the THC deputed Vinter to take up the matter with AT and SS, the worst offenders.[44] At the same time, the committee pressed for the speedy completion of the index and 'closer oversight' of the work of historians, possibly placing them under the direct control of divisions for the duration of specific projects, in order to 'tailor their approach to the time available' and avoid 'too deep an involvement in a subject'. Most historians, members were informed, were fully occupied with projects, but the premature termination of Dennis' study of promotion policies in the civil service – the Establishments Management division decided that the study was no longer required – led her to be re-allocated to write a history of the Treasury's sanctions against Rhodesia for F(EC), the Finance Exchange Control division.[45] Despite acknowledging the merit of a review, the THC dismissed the attempt made by the historians to concern themselves with the use made of their work: 'this was a matter for the Committee and for the division concerned'. Deciding that a detailed review was inappropriate, pending the lack of an index, the THC concluded that a more modest review, conducted through a case study, might prove useful.

The slow decline, even paralysis, in the THC-based organizational framework was indicated also by the failure to convene the usual follow-up session of the HSC. Instead, Collier merely met Ogilvy-Webb to report upon the decisions, with particular reference to the THC's response to points raised by the historians.[46] At the same time, Collier employed the opportunity to discuss the THC's support for a case study testing the utility of a specific THM. The recent reintroduction of prescription charges made the THM on this topic an ideal choice.

Rebuilding Downing Street and the Commonwealth Institute

As the THC recognized, during the late 1960s, delays to the timely completion of projects emerged as a serious problem, with four histories written for SS experiencing delays lasting years, not months.[47] As a result, in February 1968, the THC delegated Vinter to exert pressure upon the division to expedite clearance. In 1965 Hartcup, a newly recruited Treasury historian, had been allocated to projects proposed by SS with a view to kick-starting its "funding experience" programme. Hartcup worked quickly, and by September 1965 had sent two histories for divisional comment and approval. Divisional delays in giving approval meant that these histories were not printed until November 1968! A third history, submitted in February 1966, was never cleared by officials. For Treasury historians, these delays, epitomizing their difficult relationship with divisions, proved a constant preoccupation and source of irritation.

The SS's bid for a history of the reconstruction of 10–12 Downing Street and the Old Treasury between 1960 and 1963 reflected concern about the project's delays and costs (£3 million), which were well in excess of the original estimate of £1.25 million. Whereas the costs for a new office block varied between £7 to £10 per square foot, the figures for rebuilding Downing Street and the Old Treasury amounted to £26 5 shillings (£26.25) and £20 12 shillings (£20.60) per square foot respectively. Of course, demolition and building afresh would have been both cheaper and easier, but were ruled out for eighteenth-century buildings possessing a heritage value and requiring high standards of workmanship. Fundamental problems identified by Hartcup's history included the choice of a prime cost construction contract, escalating building costs, additional security measures, frequent labour disputes, 'the licence given' to the architect's 'whims', and the Treasury's failure to exert tight fiscal control of the project.[48] Nor were matters helped by the government's failure to learn from similar exercises in the past. In particular, the costly lesson of rebuilding Dover House, another eighteenth-century building, some five years earlier were ignored: 'The story is almost an exact parallel with Downing Street and the Old Treasury with the exception that there were no labour disputes and the work was completed by the scheduled date. There was the same initial under-estimate of work.'[49] As Hartcup observed, the Treasury's failure to learn from the Dover House project highlighted the financial and other penalties of failing to learn from the past.

For Hartcup, the Downing Street project yielded several general lessons for Treasury policymakers:

> The restoration or reconstruction of Government buildings is bound to recur. A number of useful lessons for the future emerged from the unhappy experience of the Downing Street/Old Treasury project which should provide guidance for future reconstruction schemes. Some of the lessons are indeed applicable to other aspects of Treasury work, e.g. defence projects, new buildings, civil aircraft, etc. First, whenever possible, a prime cost contract should be avoided. Secondly, the importance of conducting an initial survey of the building as extensively as possible must be stressed.... Thirdly, care should be taken over the awarding of bonus incentives in order to prevent anomalies arising which, in this case, caused strikes to occur. Fourthly, the responsibilities of an architect outside the Ministry of Public Building and Works must be carefully defined, not only in relation to his fee but in order to ensure adequate supervision. In this

case an unusual precedent was set by the Prime Minister's personal appointment of an architect with extensive responsibility. Fifthly, and finally, the history draws attention to the danger of making guesses at contract prices on the basis of an inadequate survey.[50]

Hartcup's second history covered another project, which was remembered within the division as something of a horror story.[51] During the early 1950s, the Commonwealth Institute's growing reliance upon government support, alongside the apparent decline of empire, raised serious questions about its role, if any, in the contemporary world. Treasury doubts, compounded by an anxiety to check a growing financial burden, led to pressure for the building's closure and demolition.

> These decisions engendered strong vested interests not merely in the preservation but in the expansion of the Institute; and the Treasury's main role thereafter was to try to contain the pressure in favour of expansion. Basically, the Treasury was reacting to events, rather than following a coherent policy of its own. As there was never any real hope of abolishing the Institute, this was perhaps as much as the Treasury could expect to do; but it might have been more effective, even in this limited task, if it had defined more clearly its objectives, and the practical limitations to what it was likely to be able to achieve.[52]

Nor were these 'protracted discussions' helped by the 'unfortunate' intervention of the Royal Fine Art Commission:

> It had not been foreseen that demolition of the Institute would be condemned as vandalism. The lesson to be learned here would seem to be that inadequate attention in the early stages of consultation was given to aesthetic considerations. In the present case the outcry was for preservation of a building on grounds of architectural value, but, equally, there is the possibility of an outcry on another occasion against the design of a new building. The Treasury should therefore be wary on this account.[53]

Quiet apart from drawing attention to the changing character and usefulness of public institutions over time, the THM pointed to the manner in which unforeseen problems, like heritage considerations, complicated negotiations.[54] Like the Downing Street history, this THM reminded Treasury staff about the fiscal consequences of the unexpected, even if the force of this lesson was qualified by the difficulty of knowing precisely what might go wrong.

To a large extent, the division's tardiness in dealing with Hartcup's drafts resulted from the usual everyday pressures. Even so, despite recognizing that the history was written 'most lucidly', divisional staff possessed serious reservations about the content, most notably 'the lessons of the exercise' drawn out of the narrative. Indeed, the difficulty in arriving at agreed conclusions prompted delay as well as serious consideration within the division of proceeding by recording its alternative conclusions.[55] In turn, reservations about Hartcup's conclusions, including his alleged reliance upon 'a good deal of hindsight', led A.J. Phelps, an Assistant Secretary, to articulate doubts whether such histories actually offered useful analogies for policymakers:

> It may be argued that we ought to be more purposive in emphasising the lessons of these historical memoranda. I would accept the argument as a general principle, but I doubt if it applies generally... I think, however, it [the THM] reveals that for the most part this was a case all on its own, and that it really offers little by way of lessons for the future.[56]

Clearly, Phelps was unimpressed by both Hartcup's focus upon learning from recurring general issues, like contractual arrangements and heritage considerations, and emphasis upon the costs of ignoring the lessons of the past.

Hartcup's Downing Street and Commonwealth Institute histories were eventually approved for printing in November 1968 as THMs 13 and 14, but, like their predecessors, remained inaccessible to ministers. Nor could they be shown outside the Treasury without the permission of the divisional head. By contrast, Hartcup's third SS history – this covered the National Land Fund, a project designed to save works of art and great country houses for the nation – raised more substantial concerns within the division, and was never cleared for printing as a THM.[57]

The Treasury's operations against Rhodesia

Soon after the THC's selection in February 1968 of 'The Treasury's operations against Rhodesia' as her next topic, Dennis met Anthony Rawlinson, the divisional head, and A. Glover to be instructed about the history's purpose and scope, possible approaches, and the location of key papers.[58] Faced by the demand for a first draft within three months, Dennis worried about the size of the project and mastering 'voluminous files', even if the preparedness of Glover and Rawlinson to offer support and advice, such as about 'short cuts' through the documentation and prompts about lessons, alleviated her anxieties. As a Treasury history, the files of other interested departments, like the DEA, the FCO and the Ministry of Overseas Development, were excluded from her remit.

For the Finance (Exchange Control) division, the prime requirement was a history of the Treasury's operations against Rhodesia arising out of the illegal declaration of independence (1965), with particular reference to the financial sanctions centred upon exchange control operations, the Reserve Bank of Rhodesia and defaulted Rhodesian Stock. Trade sanctions, which were the responsibility of the Board of Trade, were specifically excluded from the study. Rawlinson and Glover suggested prefacing the narrative with a brief historical overview of financial sanctions imposed to exert political pressure upon another country, such as Egypt in 1956, alongside cases, like Berlin and Gibraltar, where measures were proposed but not implemented. As such, the early stages of this assignment offered a good example of the THC's new approach requiring divisions to play a more proactive role in history writing. However, having started well with the enthusiastic support of divisional officials, the project soon encountered serious problems and delays. In the end, the history remained incomplete, while prompting repeated expressions of concern by Rawlinson and J.G. Littler, his successor, about the way in which the project dragged on.[59] As a result, the whole episode, far from providing in a timely fashion a history supporting the future work of policymakers and demonstrating the value of collaboration between divisions and historians, merely reinforced negative official perceptions about Treasury histories.

Although the topic was described as worth recording for its 'historical interest', the division wanted the history 'just in case' financial sanctions were required for political reasons in the near future: 'there is experience here which may be relevant and useful on a future occasion':

> On such a future occasion, it will be valuable for those then concerned with these matters to have available a summary of what was done, and why, in respect of Rhodesia, how it worked out in practice, and such observations about the matter as now may be offered by those who were concerned with it, while memory is still fresh but it is possible to look back on some of the operations in a more objective way than at the moment when they were happening. It will be especially useful

to have some of this experience put into a single document, not too long, because on a future occasion it is extremely likely that, as in respect of Rhodesia, crucial decisions may have to be taken quickly, and there will be no time to look up, or understand, the experience recorded in the voluminous Treasury files.[60]

What administrators wanted in time of crisis, Dennis was told, was a relatively concise history outlining the lessons to be learned from the Rhodesian case study, with particular reference to the practical effectiveness of alternative types of financial sanctions: 'we want to concentrate on the highlights of the narrative, and the lessons to be drawn'. In brief, the division wanted 'a case study of what can and cannot be done in this way' and what 'could be apposite on a future occasion'.[61] Excessive factual detail must not obscure the key messages.

In the event, a range of personal and other problems, including Dennis' part-time status and repeated allocation to more urgent projects, such as histories of incomes policy (1970) and the import deposit scheme (1970), delayed the conduct of research and the completion of the history.[62] Indeed, it was not even finished within three years in spite of expectations of an initial draft within three months of commencement. By October 1968, when the division demanded the return of the files for contingency planning purposes linked to the forthcoming *Fearless* negotiations, Dennis had made only modest progress.[63] Even worse, during the next year or so, the rapid pace of events – these included the failure of the *Fearless* talks, the imposition of mandatory UN sanctions, the publication of the 1968 Rhodesian trade figures, and the 1969 referendum – not only outdated existing research but also extended the area of study.[64] As a result, in July 1969, the division seriously considered abandoning the project, before deciding to continue work because of the topic's perceived value.[65]

But progress remained slow.[66] In November 1971, Rawlinson was still expressing impatience with the continued unavailability of a history commissioned over three years earlier.[67] In fact, so much time had passed that he confessed to having forgotten the name of the responsible historian.[68] Unsurprisingly, the episode fuelled his growing scepticism about Treasury histories: 'I must confess that I have become rather sceptical about Treasury historical memoranda.'[69] In part, this was a consequence of the delays, but it resulted also from the fact that hitherto 'I have never had any occasion to make use of one.' Following exchanges between divisional staff, including Rawlinson, the project was terminated in March 1972, when sections of the projected history were still either missing (chapter 6 on exchange control, 1966–72) or incomplete (chapter 7 on lessons).[70] As it stood, the history totalled 69 pages plus appendices. For the division, the key section on lessons was merely a slightly modified version of a four-page draft produced by Rawlinson to guide Dennis about the key conclusions. These included insufficient prior discussion about the likely political and economic effects of financial sanctions; the way in which the lack of a coherent set of initial objectives left aims to emerge over time; the failure of financial sanctions to exert significant political or economic impacts between 1965 and 1972; and the fact that the Rhodesian episode did not augur well for future proposals to employ financial sanctions for political reasons.[71] As Day argued in a study published in the same year, the whole problem, though stemming partly from constraints on policy, was in part caused by the government's misunderstanding of the situation due to 'ill-informed' and 'second-class advice'.[72]

Public records, official histories and the Treasury

As outlined in Chapter 2, during the mid- to late-1960s the proposed introduction of the 30-Year Rule and the peacetime official histories series prompted an urgent re-think of the existing lines of Treasury policy in the light of both past experience and the restructuring of "funding experience" work in 1965. The principal areas for debate centred upon the ongoing use of history to fund experience for confidential departmental use; access to Treasury records under the new 30-Year Rule; and the presentation of the Treasury's past to an outside audience through participation in the new peacetime official histories series and/or the publication of edited documents on the *DBFP* model.[73] Once again, these issues required action at the highest official level, as evidenced by the way in which intra-departmental discussions, guided by the Treasury's historians, fed upwards for decision by Armstrong and Helsby, the Joint Permanent Secretaries. Meeting with Abbot on 10 May 1967, they approved the Treasury's submission to the Cabinet Office for discussion at the next session of the interdepartmental Committee on Official Histories of Peacetime Events.[74] As stated in Chapter 3, the Treasury indicated its preparedness to participate in the new peacetime series subject to exerting no detrimental impacts upon existing historical work; thus, its limited historical resources would continue to be targeted principally towards "funding experience" activities conducted for internal use only. In this vein, the THC's meetings, ignoring developments relating to the new official histories series, concentrated upon matters arising from "funding experience" for internal use.

The Treasury, though involved in Keith Hancock's wartime civil series, had commissioned no official histories during the past decade or so. Nor were any projected, even if the idea had been discussed from time to time. As outlined in Chapter 4, Clarke had raised the subject on more than one occasion with regard to both interwar and post-1945 topics. Against this background, Collier recommended that the Treasury should welcome the proposed peacetime official histories 'because historic truth is good in itself'.[75] More specifically, the series was adjudged worthy of support in terms of providing a 'useful' reference source for Treasury staff; improving public understanding and knowledge of government policy through the presentation of an informed and authoritative British version of topics of 'direct Treasury interest'; countering, or at least containing, the impact of official histories published by other governments; and acting as a corrective to 'irresponsible' journalistic and other accounts of the Treasury's past.[76]

Despite the political nature of many topics – for instance, this was seen as ruling out a history of incomes policy – the Treasury had no problem with the fact of publication as such, even within the 30-Year closed period. Indeed, publication was seen as essential in order to meet the above-mentioned objectives as well as to secure the services of good historians.[77] Although it was anticipated that the bulk of any historian's work would remain 'untouched', there were of course limits to what could be cleared for publication; for instance, 'minor deletions' would be required 'to protect current policy-making and negotiations'.[78] Sir Alec Cairncross, the Economic Adviser, indicated a reluctance to allow 'rude things said of Americans to appear in print'.[79] Following a wide-ranging review of potential topics and authors, the Treasury submitted three proposals to the Cabinet Office for possible inclusion in the peacetime series – external economic policy since the war; exchange control; and monetary policy since the war – while indicating support for topics, that is nationalization and town and country planning, already under consideration by the interdepartmental official committee.[80]

The idea of a Treasury variant of the *DBFP*, possibly edited by Richard Sayers, the LSE-based author of the Second World War official history on financial policy, had been floated in 1965, but rejected, partly because of the Treasury's perceived lack of the type of documentation, that is telegrams, published in the *DBFP*.[81] Two years later, Cairncross, Philip Allen and Sayers revisited the issue but saw no reason to reverse the previous decision.[82] In this connection, it is worth noting a minute written in May 1966 by Rohan Butler, the Foreign Office's historical adviser, about a recent conversation with the Treasury's Ian Bancroft recognizing that, whereas documentary collections seemed the most appropriate publishing format for external affairs, narrative histories were best suited for the Treasury and other departments preoccupied with domestic affairs.[83]

Conclusion

When justifying the revised "funding experience" arrangements to the Treasury's General Purposes Committee in December 1965, Collier claimed that, though experience had indicated the case for improved 'central supervision' through the THC, 'the value of a balanced record and analysis of complex and important events was now recognised' in the department.[84] One month later, when reporting the THC's initial sessions to Helsby, Vinter pointed to what had been achieved already as well as to the manner in which the Treasury's historical activities were moving ahead in a way providing a sound foundation for future developments:

> It is impressive in scope, ranging from major studies like those on incomes policy, planning and monetary management, through lesser historical studies, down to Divisional notes and 'seeded files' on numerous topics. There is no doubt at all that a very good start has been made in the past few years on this work.[85]

Even so, these positive assessments, echoed by Armstrong, Clarke and Helsby and repeated by Abbot in 1967, must be interpreted as somewhat optimistic, given the way in which the mere fact of the THC's creation indicated the existence of a perceived problem regarding Treasury histories.[86] In essence, the resulting formalization of the existing somewhat *ad hoc* arrangements acknowledged the urgent need for a stronger central steer. Revealingly, senior officials referred to the HSC in terms implying the use of meetings to control, rather than to empower, the Treasury's historians, whose activities were conducted within a tight framework determined by the perceived needs of divisional heads. Thus, referring to one session, Collier described the 'sub-committee' in top–down terms as 'an interesting talk with Vinter'.[87]

Basically, the changes introduced in 1965 acknowledged the need for retuning the process in order to place a greater emphasis upon the functional role of Treasury histories, user-friendliness, speed of completion and accessibility. Of course, in many respects, these changes were designed to address the fundamental problem articulated in intra-departmental exchanges during 1965, that is the gulf existing between the historians, the 'producers' of Treasury histories, and the 'men at the desk', their 'consumers'. At the same time, the THC was given the mission of spreading the word throughout the Treasury in terms of encouraging divisions to appreciate not only the value of "funding experience" in supporting 'the man at the desk' but also the merits of undertaking more such work through their own resources. From this perspective, the committee's chief task was to build bridges between the Treasury's historians and divisions by ensuring that historical work was directed 'more purposively' towards the needs of present-day policymakers, familiarizing divisions with the nature and utility of "funding experience", and enhancing the level of cooperation between historians and officials in both writing the history and articulating the lessons. An emerging area of debate, as indicated when Hunt queried the status of Granger-Taylor's aircraft purchasing history, concerned the strict demarcation of responsibilities between historians and officials for drawing out the 'lessons to be learned' from any history.

The actual impact of these changes was soon revealed. When informing Jack Rampton, the head of SS, that the THC had agreed to support his division's bid for a history of prescription charges, Collier employed the opportunity to stress that such histories were intended 'to provide lessons for present and future administrators; and this activity is justified, and *only* justified if it can achieve the latter'.[88] Hopefully, the conclusions would possess also a general relevance to the rest of the Treasury, especially as an index was planned to facilitate access by a wider audience. Warning that Ogilvy-Webb and Franks would call upon him in the near future to discuss the project, Collier informed Rampton of the responsibilities and additional work falling upon divisions as well as the THC's guidelines concerning timing, scope and working methods.

In hindsight, the sparring taking place during 1965 between Clarke, Collier, Vinter and Ogilvy-Webb, among others, was historically significant in highlighting the tensions existing about "funding experience" work between historians and officials, even those strongly sympathetic to the concept. Despite agreeing that 'we need to get Divisions taking a greater interest in major bits of historical writing', they disagreed about the fundamentals, as demonstrated by the way in which Collier and Vinter pointed to 'the divergence between history for a purpose and history for its own sake': 'Mr Ogilvy-Webb's views diverge from ours, in that we are necessarily concerned with history writing for a specific administrative purpose, and he tends to think of it as worthwhile in itself.'[89] For Collier and Vinter, the prime focus was placed upon fitness for purpose. Thus, the new THC framework was intended to reaffirm the subordinate servicing role of historians. By contrast, Ogilvy-Webb, though torn repeatedly between the conflicting demands made upon him by functional and academic considerations, viewed things in a less black and white manner. Thus, he presented himself as using good historical methodology to fund past experience, not to write academic history: 'there was no question of attempting an independent and "academic" approach'.[90]

Inevitably, Ogilvy-Webb resented the strict instructions, reaffirmed by the Treasury notice in December 1965, to confine research to 'departmental papers only'. Unsurprisingly, his repeated requests to consult other departments' files were seen by Treasury officials as a function of his desire as a historian to gain a full picture from all perspectives going well beyond the Treasury's more functional requirements. Likewise, interdepartmental links, whether in terms of research, writing or circulation, proved the exception, not the rule. Nor, despite Ogilvy-Webb's lobbying, did senior Treasury officials see this as a serious problem. Indeed, Collier claimed that a one-dimensional picture based only upon departmental sources was what the Treasury wanted, since this enabled past developments to be studied as viewed from its vantage point at the time.

> Since the purpose of funding experience is not to write something which will stand up as an objective and complete picture of an administrative situation but to guide current generations of Treasury administrators in how to carry out Treasury policy, it isn't *necessarily* the case that collaboration with another department is required.[91]

For officials, one-sided was not taken to mean biased, merely realistic. Ogilvy-Webb's enthusiasm to circulate completed THMs to a wide audience within and outside the department by way of fostering an informed knowledge and understanding about the past as a basis for present-day administrative action was not shared by his superiors. Indeed, their reluctance to involve other departments in the research process was paralleled by their relatively illiberal attitude concerning external circulation of the final product.

Notwithstanding the genuine attempt made in 1965 to set Treasury history writing on what was seen as the most appropriate track to meet everyday administrative needs, things soon began to slip. Despite being scheduled originally to meet three or four times a year, the THC only met four times in all between 1965 and 1968 (Table 6.2); indeed, the meeting held in February 1968 proved its last ever. In part, this reflected the emergence of alternative approaches for dealing with the historians, most notably the growing emphasis upon Collier's role in managing individual historians informally, as much as the genuine difficulty of arranging a suitable date for meetings – to quote Collier – 'due to the overwhelming pressure of day-to-day work on the individual membership'.[92] Even so, this feature was yet another symptom of the relatively low priority attached by the Treasury to "funding experience" as compared to the concentration of both senior staff and divisional officials upon present-day business.

7
Retuning the Treasury's Historical Activities after Fulton, 1968–70

During the late 1950s and the 1960s Britain is often characterized as beset by a period of self-examination prompted by a growing sense of decline and a perceived need for radical action in a modernizing direction. Nor was the machinery of government excluded from these debates, as highlighted by Thomas Balogh's 'The apotheosis of the dilettante' (1959). Significantly, the Fabian Society's contribution, 'The Administrators' (June 1964), was produced by a group including both Henderson and Ogilvy-Webb.[1] In many respects, this phase of the debate culminated in the Fulton committee's report on the Home Civil Service. Published in June 1968, this five-volume report possessed the most dramatic implications for the Treasury, whose longstanding control over expenditure had become intertwined over time with managerial responsibilities for the civil service.

Reviewing the civil service's shortcomings – these included amateurism, rigidity, inefficiency and unimaginativeness – the Fulton Report concluded that 'For these and other defects the central management of the Service, the Treasury, must accept its share of responsibility.'[2] In brief, the Treasury was accused of having 'failed to keep the Service up to date'. Most recommendations go beyond the scope of this study, but the report was instrumental in focusing attention upon the generalist/specialist issue as well prompting the hiving off of part of the Treasury's functions to the newly established Civil Service Department (CSD). Sir William Armstrong, replacing Helsby as Head of the Home Civil Service, moved across from the Treasury to become the CSD's Permanent Secretary.

Naturally, such departmental restructuring impacted upon the Treasury's historians. For the time being, they served both departments, even if Armstrong anticipated that the nature of the CSD's work would result in few calls upon their services. Indeed, in time their CSD role was deemed likely to disappear. However, Ogilvy-Webb was not discouraged. On the contrary, as outlined below, he saw the 'completely new general climate of opinion' ushered in by Fulton as an opportunity to develop the historians's contribution to the effective working of government, even to the extent of harbouring unrealistic hopes that Armstrong might exploit the 'moment' to relaunch Brook's 1957 "funding experience" initiative throughout Whitehall.[3]

Reviewing the actual utility of historical work

In fact, 1968 had witnessed already an in-depth review testing the actual utility of the Treasury's internal histories.[4] Despite being conducted in the knowledge of the forthcoming Fulton Report, the exercise was motivated largely by the THC's concern that the Treasury's "funding experience" activities were still failing to impact upon the policy process, thereby indicating the failure of the revised organizational framework to bridge the gulf between historians and divisions.

Rejecting the historians's proposal for a full-scale critical review, in February 1968, the THC decided to conduct a more limited exercise inspired by Ogilvy-Webb's suggestion about using a specific THM as a case study.[5] Following the THC meeting, Collier, who had replaced Abbot as Establishment Officer, contacted Nicholas Jordan-Moss, the head of SS, for comment about the utility of the THM commissioned by his division on prescription charges. This history, one of the initial bids approved for support by the THC in 1966, was produced according to the revised 1965–66 guidelines placing greater demands upon divisions at all stages of the project. Henceforth, as Collier informed Jack Rampton, who was then the SS's head, such histories could *only* be justified in terms of their perceived usefulness for present and future administrators:

> The value to be got from these Historical Memoranda lies in part in their presentation of a series of historical events; but it is doubtful whether this alone would justify the effort put into them, and the major value to be got will be from the conclusions which will be drawn from them, conclusions as to present and future administration. And while these conclusions will help the Division itself, the greatest value will be obtained if it is possible to draw from the Memorandum conclusions which are of wider application in the Treasury. (It will then be for us to ensure, by suitable indexing, that conclusions of wider interest succeed in attracting the wider audience which they deserve.)[6]

Most of the history was written by Susan Franks, a research assistant working with divisional staff under the overall supervision of Ogilvy-Webb.[7] By September 1966 the text, which was finalized by Ogilvy-Webb following Franks' departure from the Treasury, was ready to be circulated for comment by Vinter and Collier as well as members of SS. Pointing to the THC's utilitarian mission, Ogilvy-Webb indicated their attempt to do more than provide a mere narrative outlining the history of prescription charges from their introduction (1952) to abolition (1965). Thus, the analysis, attempting to make '*sense* of the course of events', sought to identify 'lessons to be learned' enabling divisional staff to 'look forwards and not backwards'.[8] Policies towards charges, Franks and Ogilvy-Webb concluded, were decided upon the basis of unsatisfactory hypotheses, incomplete information and unclear objectives.[9] Nor were consequences – these included impacts upon prescribing practice and the drugs bill – adequately considered. Finally, a belief that such lessons were not unique to this topic led Ogilvy-Webb to point also to the THM's broader relevance to other divisions.[10]

Impressed by what he regarded as 'a thorough and competent work', Vinter reminded Rampton about the division's responsibilities, most notably in drawing lessons from such histories.[11] Within SS, officials welcomed the 'first class narrative' as 'a very valuable document', but inevitably concentrated upon its coverage of perceived inadequacies in the policy process. Despite disputing allegations about the lack of clearly defined objectives – they pointed to the Treasury's objective to view prescription charges as part of the policy to contain, if possible reduce, public expenditure – divisional staff conceded that there was some substance in certain conclusions.[12] Indeed, recognition of statistical inadequacies prompted the division to bring in both Alan Holmans, a member of the Economic Section responsible for THM 8, and the Central Statistical Office to discuss remedial measures.[13] For Collier, the resulting discussions, though making slow progress, offered 'a very good example of an historical memorandum leading directly and immediately to further administrative action'.[14]

Notwithstanding the Treasury's ingrained hostility to the external circulation of its histories, SS suggested the prudence of showing the draft history to the Ministry of Health because of the way in which Treasury documents offered inadequate coverage of the differentiation between financial policy – the Treasury's domain – and health policy, which was the concern of another department.[15] As a result, Ogilvy-Webb was instructed to prepare an expurgated version – the Treasury's disinclination to expose its shortcomings to another department meant that the section on lessons was the main omission – for despatch to Arnold France, the PUS at the Ministry of Health (1964–68).[16] Significantly, when sending the history to France, the Treasury followed the precedent of the aircraft purchasing THM by stressing that the draft was for *his personal use only*: 'we would not want anyone in the Ministry apart from yourself to know that this Treasury history exists'.[17] In the event, France refrained from detailed comment about this 'very interesting work', but observed that his department's side of the story would prove rather different.[18] Even so, his reply irritated the Treasury because of a proclaimed reluctance to allocate scarce manpower to improve statistical studies deemed to exert little impact upon Treasury policy.[19] Nevertheless, France's 'frosty' reply cleared the way for Ogilvy-Webb to secure approval from Vinter for printing the history, including the four-page coverage of the 'lessons to be learned'.[20] The resulting history, printed as THM 12 in September 1967 and circulated one month later, was subject to the usual restrictions regarding ministers and other departments.[21] Nor was the Ministry of Health on the circulation list.

Some three months later, that is on 16 January 1968, Wilson, the prime minister, announced a series of austerity measures consequent upon the devaluation crisis of November 1967. Prescription charges were re-introduced as part of a package including the historic decision to withdraw from East of Suez. As a result, when meeting a few weeks later, the THC saw the THM on prescription charges, rated by Collier as 'a good piece of work' throwing up 'a number of useful lessons', as an obvious choice for a 'test case' warranting further investigation about history's impact upon a subsequent major shift in policy.[22] Soon afterwards, in March, Collier asked SS for feedback about the THM's impact upon divisional thinking and actions in the light of the fact that the history was available in both draft and printed form during the period immediately preceding the government's decision to restore prescription charges (Table 7.1). At the same time, he reminded Jordan-Moss, the current divisional head, about the broader context for "funding experience" activities:

> These histories are only worth writing if they are of value to the divisional officers concerned. They may have some marginal historical value (though the fact that they are written on the basis of Treasury papers only must reduce their intrinsic value in this sense), but we wouldn't put staff and money into the operation if it were not for the hope that divisional officers would find it useful.[23]

Table 7.1 History, policy and prescription charges

Date	Policy on prescription charges	Treasury historical activities
1952 June	Charges (1/- per prescription) introduced by 1951–55 Conservative Government	
1956 Dec.	Charges applied to each item (1/- per item) by 1955–59 Conservative Government	
1961 Feb.	Charges doubled (2/- per item) by 1959–64 Conservative Government	
1965 Feb.	Charges abolished by 1964–66 Labour Government	
Dec.		Social Services (SS) Division submits "funding experience" bids to the THC.
1966 Jan.		THC commissioned a history of prescription charges.
Feb.–Mar.		Franks, supervised by Ogilvy-Webb and supported by SS Division, began work on the history of charges.
Oct.		Draft history circulated for comment by SS Division.
1967 Apr.		Expurgated version of history sent on personal basis to PUS of the Ministry of Health.
Sept.		History approved and printed as THM 12.
Oct.		THM on prescription charges circulated.
1968 Jan.	Serious economic crisis led to devaluation (Nov. 1967), major cuts in public expenditure and re-introduction of charges (2/6d per item) by 1966–70 Labour Government	

Table 7.1 (Continued)

Date	Policy on prescription charges	Treasury historical activities
Feb.–June		Treasury review of utility of THM on prescription charges revealed its lack of impact upon the policy discussions resulting in the re-introduction of charges.

Note: 1/-, 2/- and 2/6d were equivalent to 5, 10 and 12½ new pence respectively.

Despite his personal belief in the merits of "funding experience" in general and the THM on prescription charges in particular, Collier's awareness of both the everyday pressures of urgent business and the impact of politico-economic considerations led him to anticipate that 'the answer will be that the history was not of much value in practice'.

The divisional view

Unsurprisingly, Jordan-Moss' reply was delayed, even if this was excused as much on the grounds of having to look back into the files and to consult divisional staff as of the usual everyday pressures.[24] The reply was far-ranging, but the key point emerging from Jordan-Moss' review was that – to quote Malcolm Widdup – 'nobody turned to the history during the months November/February; the decisions then taken rested almost entirely on political judgment'.[25] Despite recording the division's appreciation of the THM as 'a remarkably well-composed piece of historical research', Jordan-Moss' practical administrative experience led him to question the THM's precise purpose and utility, and hence to couch any praise in cautious terms:

> As far as the use of this particular report is concerned – it has been useful as a summary background, though a shorter account would have been more so. And the 'general considerations' section was in fact used in preparing the Civil Expenditure Review of 1967. With Mr. Holmans, the Division did take up the question of the need for further information of various kinds, but there has been no time to pursue this very far: nevertheless it has led to Treasury pressure for better use of *existing* statistics.[26]

For Collier, the outcome, though not unexpected, was still depressing, since it merely reaffirmed the consistent failure of Treasury histories to impact upon policymakers.[27]

The division's reservations about the utility of historical analogies reflected in part a recognition of the discontinuities between past and present: 'In some general sense past experience is always applied to the formation of new policy; and to some extent past experience will always tend to be a shaky guide, because political, social and economic considerations are always changing.'[28] As Jordan-Moss observed, this was especially true of politically sensitive topics, like prescription charges, during a period of economic difficulty: 'the political and economic background has changed so much that the Memorandum in general has been of little use in the immediate situation since January'.[29] In any case, it was always difficult for such histories to strike the appropriate balance:

> As now conceived, they [Treasury histories] seem to be somewhat too perfectionist and consequently too far behind the rapid flow of events by the time they appear – and yet too close to enable all who read them to judge their criticisms with the impartial eye of a later generation.

Addressing Collier's central question of whether divisional staff should make more systematic use of historical memoranda in their everyday work, Jordan-Moss admitted that they helped staff, like him, switched regularly from one part of the Treasury to another to gain a clearer picture of the new division's activities and procedures. Even so, he conceded that 'the case is not good enough, at least until there has been further thought about the precise purposes, the scope and the structure of the Memoranda, and how they are to be handled'. In particular, histories should be 'short enough to be read quickly by busy administrators' or to source a background brief for 'busy ministers'. Divisional staff favoured the inclusion of an 'element of self-criticism and lesson-drawing', but claimed that this was their preserve:

> The historians will tend to mar their work if they themselves draft the critical analysis. In my view they should stop short at presenting the critical questions which their analysis reveals. At that point the Division itself... should set itself to answer the critical questions and do its own heart-searching, either drafting the critical commentary or being responsible for its final form.

No doubt Jordan-Moss' awareness of the ongoing difficulties experienced in agreeing conclusions with the historians on Hartcup's THMs, as mentioned in Chapter 6, coloured this assessment. For instance, it was clear that divisions would question any lessons identified by historians in draft texts if only by way of a defensive reaction and the belief that this task went beyond the historians's role. Even so, Jordan-Moss failed to indicate how his staff would actually find time to write the conclusions required to complete any project. However, on another issue SS, reflecting its close working relationship with the Ministry of Health, sided with the line taken by Treasury historians, that is the value of involving other departments more fully in the whole process. By way of moderating the largely negative tone of his reply, Jordan-Moss informed Collier that the THM would be fed in, whatever that might mean, to future policy discussions about funding the health service.[30]

Generally speaking, the division's response posed more questions than answers, particularly given Jordan-Moss's opinion that Treasury divisions were insufficiently staffed to fund experience systematically. Officials, he argued, lacked the time to read, absorb and use completed THMs, let alone to comment upon and draw lessons from draft histories written by the Treasury historians. By implication, the ability of staff to produce either divisional notes or "seeded files" was even more circumscribed, as spelt out more fully by Jordan-Moss two years later.[31] Finally, recent developments suggested that Treasury histories were 'likely to have a diminishing role in a system where policy is systematically and increasingly subjected to broader critical analysis in the context of P.E.S.C., the work of the Economic Advisers, the Social Services Review, etc., etc.'[32]

What disappointed Vinter and Collier was not so much this history's failure to impact upon divisional thinking about prescription charges between November 1967 and January 1968 but rather during the period beforehand: 'one could not expect them to use a memorandum like this in the midst of their battles, but it might have helped them by suggesting new approaches during the slightly quieter months beforehand'.[33] In May 1968, Collier and Ogilvy-Webb met to conduct a kind of post-mortem on the 'after-history' of the THM on prescription charges. Why had a 'very good' 'forward looking' memorandum 'failed' – they agreed that 'it didn't have the impact it should have done' – despite becoming available at the crucial time when it should have been most useful?[34] Why did the lessons raised by the history remain on the margins of divisional thinking throughout 1968?

Concluding that 'there was something wrong with our system', Collier focused upon the mode of approach, most notably the lengthy narrative, even one prefaced by a three-and-a-half page summary. Glossing over the longstanding failure of Treasury staff to find time to review strategy as opposed to clearing their in-trays – within weeks, this very point was to be pressed by the Fulton Report – he speculated also about the merits of introducing a more open regime drawing in other departments in place of the existing 'under the counter' Treasury-centred system. In the event, little changed. During November 1968 the Treasury refused the request for a copy of the prescription charges THM made by a statistician at the Ministry of Health; indeed, there was considerable concern that the requester even knew that the history existed![35]

Yet another relaunch of Treasury history

In November 1968, Vinter drew together the results of recent exchanges. Richard Sharp, who was taking over as Establishment Officer following Collier's forthcoming move to the CSD, was also involved.[36] The relatively negative outcome of the recent review failed to diminish their confidence that "funding experience" work was 'proceeding on the right lines', as evidenced by the positive spin imparted upon somewhat worrying feedback: 'Our general feeling was that the work was certainly of practical use and should continue.'[37] Even so, they sought a better way of doing things:

> There is a wide potential range of work over which the historians might usefully be employed and we still have much to learn about how to get the best possible value from them. The modified approach we are now proposing should go a long way towards applying these limited resources so as to produce the maximum benefit to current administration.[38]

Yet another sharpening up of procedures followed, centred upon the more precise specification of assignments and methods, greater attention to a project's 'practical current value to the "man at the desk"', and improved publicity of the available histories.[39] Following approval by members of the THC – significantly this was achieved through circulation, not a meeting – the proposed changes, accompanied by a report of the historians's work over the past three years, were submitted to Sir Douglas Allen and Armstrong, the Permanent Secretaries in charge of the Treasury and CSD respectively.[40] The former's approval came quickly, but Armstrong's reply was delayed due to his preoccupation with setting up the new department.[41] Furthermore, his response proved somewhat ambivalent. Despite hoping that the CSD would remain entitled to benefit from Treasury histories, Armstrong did 'not think we shall make great demands on Treasury historians'.[42] In April, N. Forward, a member of the CSD's Machinery of Government division, echoed Armstrong's cautious line during the course of two meetings held with Ogilvy-Webb, but conceded the possible interest of the new training college in selected histories covering the ways in which the Treasury had tackled past administrative problems.[43]

Before formally announcing the proposed 'slight shift of approach' Vinter and Collier agreed also upon the prudence of calling together the historians.[44] The resulting HSC meeting, held on 1 May 1969, enabled another exchange of views about forging 'a stronger and more continuous relationship' between historians and divisions, but largely demonstrated that it was easier to discuss the problem than to find a solution.[45] Nevertheless, the meeting – the first held since November 1966 – cleared the way for Sharp to inform divisions about the revised arrangements. The resulting Treasury notice, dated 2 July 1969, stated that both the Treasury and the CSD would continue to fund past experience under the overall direction of the THC, chaired by the Treasury's Third Secretary.[46] Following the recent departmental reorganization, the committee would be renamed as the Treasury and Civil Service Department Historical Committee (hereafter TCSDHC), and include the establishment officers of both departments. For management purposes, the Treasury's 'small team' of historians would remain a separate section within the Establishment Branch directed by the TCSDHC. In the short term, the THS would continue to service the CSD, but eventually the two departments were adjudged likely to go their separate ways on historical work.

According to the Treasury's notice, experience gained over the past three years suggested the need for 'some modifications' in approach involving, say, greater emphasis upon tasks adjudged 'more immediately relevant to the work of Divisions' and a closer working relationship between historians and divisional staff, possibly even attaching historians to divisions for a temporary period: 'Without close and continuing contact with, and guidance from, the administrator, the work of the historian, and its usefulness, are bound to be impaired.' Henceforth, divisions would be required to provide a clearer specification of both the task and methods undertaken by the historians. Priority would be attached to short-term histories to avoid locking up limited resources on any one project.[47] Nor would there be any shift away from the existing approach confining research to the files of the Treasury and CSD. Proposals to show histories to other interested departments would be treated in an equally restrictive manner.

Using the Fulton Report

Clarke, who was then PUS at the Ministry of Technology (1966–70), saw the Fulton Report as raising the whole question of expertise in government, including the contribution of economists, among others, in helping 'to unlock the door to wise decision-making'.[48] In this vein, Ogilvy-Webb welcomed the report as possessing significant implications for the use of historical expertise in government, thereby offering a window of opportunity for reaffirming the case for "funding experience". As a Treasury historian, Ogilvy-Webb had an understandable desire to feel wanted at a time when the position and role of Treasury historians was under serious debate, even attracting negative divisional feedback.[49] Revealingly, when reporting their recent conversations to Collier, Forward opined that Ogilvy-Webb's 'rather violent views' about post-Fulton Whitehall betrayed a somewhat confrontational personality reflecting his resolve to 'keep up the battle' with Treasury officials on the subject.

Guided by discussions with his fellow historians, Ogilvy-Webb had already presented Collier and Sharp with a 14-page memorandum, entitled 'Fulton and the Histories', arguing that the Treasury's historians occupied an integral place in any future framework: 'Our contention is that histories could be of substantial assistance as an integral part of the "Planning Units" and of the research side of the [Civil Service Training] College.'[50] The issues raised by this memorandum were left for the HSC's meeting scheduled for 22 May 1969. In the event, this session was cancelled and rearranged for 3 June. Postponement, alongside the depressing outcome of the recent review, led Russell Bretherton to write privately to Vinter complaining about the department's 'pretty discouraging treatment' of the historians.[51] As a former divisional head now writing Treasury histories in retirement, his views were not uninfluential:

> They [the historians] have great difficulty in getting reasonably quick comments on their work from most Treasury divisions; their general minutes, asking for guidance and so on, are seldom answered; meetings necessary to discuss their affairs are long delayed and

then cancelled or postponed; and the physical conditions under which they work in 53 Parliament Buildings are a disgrace to any Department, besides underlining their isolation from the rest of the Treasury. Yet much of what they write is very good indeed.

For Bretherton, 'the Treasury really ought to make up its mind – again, reasonably quickly – whether it wants their work or not'. Should the THS be treated as a valued part of the department's work, absorbed in the CSD, or disbanded? Writing as a former divisional head, Bretherton knew 'from bitter experience' that few people in the Treasury from Third Secretary downwards 'have time or energy to deal with anything that is not immediately operational, whatever might be its long-term value. But that, when it goes on year after year, is a pretty damming indictment of the way the Treasury organises its business.' Nor were attempts made to let the historians know 'how current policy is shaping for the fields in which they happen to be working' by way of ensuring relevance. When feeding Bretherton's critique into ongoing exchanges, Vinter could not resist observing that it seemed more a case of the pot calling the kettle black: 'Mr Bretherton was himself one of the worst sinners on consultation on historical projects when he was Head of A.T. – I joined issue with him on this on two or three occasions, without much success.'[52]

Despite accepting the 'inescapable' pressures upon staff, Vinter admitted the case for action: 'It follows from this that if we are to take the historians more seriously – and I think we should – then we have somehow got to *make* time for this purpose.' In the meantime, he recommended that 'the looseness of the connection between the historians and Treasury divisions' could be remedied by attaching a historian – Hartcup's name was mentioned – to a division for a lengthy period:

> He would quite quickly become more an accepted part of the whole scene and I suspect that he would get drawn in more readily and quickly at the working level instead of being propelled into particular jobs, as it were, by you [i.e. Sharp] or me. It would also help to establish Mr Hartcup's ability to press Principals and Assistant Secretaries more readily for comments on his work.

Betraying his irritation with the repeated complaints of Ogilvy-Webb and company, Vinter saw another benefit: 'The more the historians were drawn into the work of particular Divisions, the less time they would have to natter about general topics and, incidentally, their discontents.'

Unsurprisingly, Vinter was far from pleased to receive another note, dated 30 May, in which the historians identified action points for the next HSC meeting.[53]

On 3 June the HSC discussed the revised organizational arrangements, including the proposed temporary attachment of historians to divisions and the CSD's future requirements. Regarding general issues, Vinter reminded the historians that the THC framework had been introduced to contain their apparent preference for writing history. Rather the prime objective was to use the 'special expertise of the historians in the most productive way', that is to fund experience on topics of immediate and continuing practical value to divisions: 'the main purpose of departmental historical work was to produce something to meet the needs of Treasury staff, rather than something for general consumption'.[54]

The historians's frustrations

Clearly, the views of the historians continued to exert minimal impact upon the thinking of senior staff. Unsurprisingly, when meeting Dennis, Granger-Taylor and Ogilvy-Webb in November 1969, E.W. Maude, who was advising the Permanent Secretary on Treasury reorganization in the wake of Fulton, found the historians 'somewhat frustrated in their activities and unhappy about the present role of their section'.[55] Reporting back to Henley, who had taken charge of the Treasury historians following Vinter's move to the Ministry of Technology in 1969, Maude urged giving some thought to the matter, if only on the grounds of staff morale. At the same time, he drew attention to what he saw as the 'basic flaw' inherent in the present system, that is the fact that other Whitehall departments, though often intimately involved in the events, were neither consulted nor shown the finished histories.[56] If they were to be written on an interdepartmental basis, the Cabinet Office's Historical Section or the CSD, not the Treasury, might prove the best base. Henley shared Maude's concerns, but pointed out that such questions had been under active discussion within the Treasury for some time, frequently prompting 'fairly strong policy views'.[57] Nor, in his view, did the reported lack of "funding experience" activities in other Whitehall departments enhance the prospects for interdepartmental collaboration.

In the meantime, Henley called together the historians in January 1970 for an informal discussion designed partly to make direct contact with the historians as a group – there were no plans to call a formal meeting of the HSC – and partly to contain their growing sense of frustration.[58] Although the session did little more than go over the usual ground, Henley left sympathizing with their complaints and the consequent need to do more to encourage divisional interest in their work.

History and the PE Division

Some three years had elapsed since the THC's last trawl for proposals, and hence the Treasury notice, distributed in July 1969, was employed also to invite divisions to bid for future projects.[59] At the same time, Sharp warned that the department's 'very limited history-writing resources' necessitated a highly selective approach prioritizing bids adjudged of 'real current interest and value to the sponsoring Divisions'.[60] Significantly, interdepartmental topics were rated a low priority. In the event, the resulting bids were mislaid – this seemed to typify the growing drift of "funding experience" work – thereby resulting in the issue of a revised invitation in February 1970![61]

Although nil returns proved relatively common, one division responding positively to the renewed invitation to bid was PE, which had led the way in "funding experience" during the early to mid-1960s. Following extensive discussions, PE submitted three topics capable of completion within two to four weeks.[62] Forced to rely upon its own resources following the loss of Granger-Taylor's services in 1966, the pace of progress slowed. No more THMs had been completed. Granger-Taylor's history of atomic energy remained unfinished. Ogilvy-Webb's paper on 'The criteria of efficiency in the nationalised industries', written some years earlier, still awaited updating.[63] The only real advance came in the sphere of divisional notes, which increased in number from 28 in 1966 to 33 in 1969.

One divisional note, Lawrence Airey's nine-page history of 'The Aluminium Smelter Negotiations' between June 1966 and August 1968, written in 1969 and drawing upon some 20-plus PE files, demonstrated what divisions could achieve with their own resources *if* they valued the historical dimension. Basically, Airey's history outlined the way in which initial plans for a single 60,000-ton smelter expanded some two years later into a scheme for three separate smelters with a total capacity of 260,000 tons funded through £33m in investment grants and £63m in loans. For PE, the history's prime aim was to identify 'the lessons which may be learned from the handling of this subject in Whitehall', even if Airey recognized that the immediacy of his history – certain events covered therein had occurred within the past year – qualified the sense of historical perspective: 'we cannot at this stage know what will and what will not turn out, in the long run, to have been a mistake'.[64] According to Airey, the historical narrative suggested that the principal policy shortcomings included informational inadequacies, most notably the absence of an economic reference point for measuring the costs of the various schemes; the fact that political pressures were allowed to override economic considerations; and the failure of Whitehall departments to formulate a coherent agreed negotiating strategy.

Re-reading Airey's history in September 1969 by way of preparing the PE bid, Miss J. Kelley reaffirmed its utility in not only drawing out 'lessons of the future' but also highlighting the problematic nature of learning from the past.[65] Over time, changing economic circumstances, including variations in world prices, might establish the misconceived nature of any scheme to promote a British aluminium smelting industry or cast doubt upon the prudence of the methods – these included a reliance upon three smallish projects and special electricity tariffs – employed to implement the plans.

> None of them can yet be evaluated. All we can learn at the moment is lessons relating to the handling of the issues: could we have set up more effective inter-Departmental machinery? Could we have preserved a better negotiating position with the companies? Was internal Treasury consultation effective? and so on.[66]

Furthermore, the history offered only a partial view based upon research 'as recorded on Treasury papers'. As such, it failed to take account of either the records of other government departments or discussions, such as those held during 1966 between the UKAEA, Rio Tinto Zinc and the Central Electricity Generating Board, 'which the Treasury did not know of at the time'.

In September 1969, the Treasury's adoption of yet another 'new course' for its historical work led to Hartcup's temporary attachment to the General Expenditure division (GE) – he remained still a member of the THS – to analyse and record annual public expenditure reviews. According to Vinter, 'a proper record' of these complex exercises, involving seven divisions, was required in order to ensure that the history of individual items was not lost in the general mass of documentation.[67] Three studies resulted, with the third study, entitled *Decisions on Public Expenditure for 1971–72 and 1974–75*, being printed as THM 17 in November 1971. Reportedly, 'the memoranda were much used in GE with whom the conclusions (1 page) were discussed and agreed for each study'.[68] Meanwhile, Hartcup remained available to undertake occasional short-term projects, such as the topics shortlisted by PE as relevant to its work.[69] Hartcup completed a divisional note, entitled 'Public dividend capital' in July 1970, and this was soon followed by a history of 'Specific subsidies'.

The abortive index project

In many respects, the demise of the THC's plans for an index epitomized the increasingly uncertain place of "funding experience" work in the Treasury. When this project was first taken up in December 1965, Vinter indicated that a central subject index was a priority task to be completed within months in order to improve accessibility, usage and the flow of historical information across the department.[70] An index would also, the THC anticipated, inform future plans and priorities. From the start, the prime focus was placed upon the index's utility and user friendliness, such as in ensuring that the choice of headers pointed staff to histories whose relevance might not be immediately obvious from their titles. As Collier noted, both the THM on 10 Downing Street and a divisional note on the Chieftain tank, albeit on very different topics, covered estimating costs and forecasting policy and procedures.[71]

In the event, the exercise, advised by J.L. Jolley, a firm of Information Handlers, proved, or rather became, more complex than anticipated. Notwithstanding the project's priority, the completion date increasingly slipped, since occasional bursts of activity by Ogilvy-Webb and Granger-Taylor had to be coordinated with their other commitments. Nor did the THC in general and the Establishment Officer's Branch in particular maintain a close watch over the progress. Almost three years passed before an experimental version of the index was ready for testing by 14 divisional 'guinea-pigs' in Summer 1968 with a view to making the index operational in the near future.[72] Six months later, Ogilvy-Webb complained that only two triallists had 'uttered a squeak', thereby forcing him to conduct several interviews in order to secure meaningful feedback from divisional staff.[73] But comment was discouraging; indeed, the underwhelming response from divisions raised serious questions about whether or not to continue work. Following his meeting with the historians in November 1969, Maude confessed that he was not convinced by the case for an index and advised its abandonment.[74] Nor did Henley see any reason to differ.[75] Soon afterwards, the index project was shelved, as recorded by Dennis: 'at the very last fence, the decision was taken not to proceed'.[76]

Conclusion

Generally speaking, in 1970, the overall state of "funding experience" activities in the Treasury remained as patchy as ever.[77] During 1968–69 the conduct of yet another review of the Treasury's historical work, following those undertaken in 1962–63 and 1965, reaffirmed the fundamental problem of translating theory into practice as well as of overcoming the barrier dividing historians from divisions. Despite frequent assertions of its theoretical benefits and the repeated retuning of procedures, things continued to turn out differently in practice.[78]

Within this context, perhaps the most revealing response to the July 1969 notice – among other things, this had invited divisions to comment upon what had been achieved to date – emanated from Jordan-Moss, the head of SS, a division which had not only received an above average level of support from Treasury historians but also been the subject of the 1968 review on the utility of THMs. Reportedly, his hard-pressed staff had made minimal progress seeding files and writing divisional notes: 'the procedure of seeding files and compiling divisional notes does not justify the time and effort spent on it'.[79] Jordan-Moss reaffirmed the potential theoretical value of "funding experience", but admitted his reluctance to burden staff with work 'which is of insufficient practical use to justify the time spent on it' and could only be justified if 'sufficient actual use is made of the results'.[80] For Jordan-Moss, 'this adds up to a strong prima facie case for discontinuing the exercise'.[81]

The preceding discussions within the division feeding into Jordan-Moss's response were useful in revealing the way in which divisional officials continued to see things differently from senior staff. In many respects, M. Stuart, an Assistant Secretary in charge of one of the SS's branches, expressed what might be interpreted as a typical view: 'Judged by the opportunity cost criteria these ways of funding experience are not worthwhile.'[82] Moreover, as W. Smith observed, such activities required 'relatively prolonged and uninterrupted periods' and 'sections have not yet been able to devote sufficient time for completion of the task'.[83] Generally speaking, individual branches regarded "seeded files" and divisional notes as having 'little practical use' for either present-day guidance or induction purposes.[84] Reportedly, newcomers found a period of overlap with their predecessors of greater value in terms of introducing them to the work and location of relevant documents: 'they have found little help from such "seeded files" as already exist (and indeed did not know that some of them existed until the present review)'! In any case, events moved on, thereby making any history, except those covering complex procedural matters, like the control system for starts in hospital building programmes, somewhat 'academic' and irrelevant to current policy requirements and legislation: 'the issues which are currently important subjects are seldom identical with what has been important in the past'. Thus, any list of topics adjudged worthy of coverage at the present moment was bound to be very different from a selection made in a few years' time.[85]

During the late 1960s the THC-based framework never really operated in the way intended. Preoccupied with higher priority everyday concerns, Vinter and Collier experienced difficulty in finding time to call THC and HSC meetings, monitor progress of individual historical projects, and enforce relevance and target dates. The abortive index project was paralleled by the repeated slippage in the completion of Treasury histories, like Russell Edmunds' history of debt situations. In October 1967, when still awaiting divisional comments on his Mantaro history, Russell-Edmunds began working part-time on debt situations for the Overseas Finance division. The first instalment on Argentina, based upon 72 files, was not ready until May 1969.[86] Although the next section on Colombia soon followed, the projected coverage of Brazil, Ghana, Indonesia and Turkey ensured that the project extended into the early 1970s; in fact, the 738-page history was not completed until 1973.[87]

Looking back, problems arose also from the gradual loss of high level support as senior officials supportive of "funding experience" either retired or, like Clarke, Collier and Vinter, moved to another part of Whitehall. Generally speaking, their replacements, like those who remained, were less committed, if not hostile, to "funding experience" work. Another constraint derived from the THS's diminishing size in the light of Granger-Taylor's departure at the close of 1970.[88]

8
Moving Towards the Closure of the Treasury Historical Section, 1971–76

On 30 September 1976, the Treasury formally closed the THS and called a halt to writing Treasury histories. Looking back at the THS's history, it is easy to view closure as almost inevitable, given the problematic course of the Treasury's "funding experience" activities, their continued inability to impact significantly upon the everyday work of policymakers, and the repeated failure of remedial measures to retrieve the situation.

Nevertheless, during the early 1970s the Treasury continued to support the THS's work. Moreover, paradoxically, the THS's final years proved its most productive when measured by the number of histories completed during this period. The list of THMs expanded at its fastest ever rate, with 14 of the Treasury's 30 THMs being printed between 1971 and 1976.[1] Four topics predominated: sterling and exchange control (Symons); the control of demand (Bretherton); external financial relations (Owen); and incomes policy (Ogilvy-Webb). As mentioned in the previous chapter, Hartcup was given a kind of roving commission resulting in the production of THMs and unprinted histories for six different divisions. Even so, an enhanced historical output produced in a more expeditious fashion than hitherto failed to prevent the THS becoming perceived increasingly as a serious problem, even an insoluble problem. As a result, its position within the Treasury, which had always proved somewhat tenuous and marginal in both the policymaking and geographical senses, became even more insecure.

The effective demise of the Treasury Historical Committee

During the early 1970s, the THS's position within the Treasury was undermined further by recognition of the *de facto* demise of both the THC (TCSDHC) and the HSC. Neither had met for some time. Nor was either committee convened ever again. In fact, the resulting vacuum had been filled already during the late 1960s by an *ad hoc* informal group, which assumed responsibility for supervising the choice of the THS's new projects as well as for liaising with Ogilvy-Webb about the allocation of historians to individual tasks.[2] Chaired by Douglas Henley, who had succeeded Vinter as chair of the THC in 1969, this group decided to target the Treasury's limited historical resources towards projects adjudged as meeting genuine divisional requirements and promised support from relevant officials: 'properly written histories (drawing the right conclusions etc.) are possible only through a close and continuing relationship between the historian and the division'.[3] By implication, the previous policy of generating demand by inviting bids for the services of historians, as happened in 1969–70, was dropped.

For staffing purposes, the THS remained part of the Establishment Officer's Branch. Inevitably, the total number of Treasury historians, which had never been large anyway, followed the THS's overall declinist trend. Typically, Granger-Taylor, who left in 1970, was not replaced. Even worse, in 1972 Sharp, the Establishment Officer, was giving serious consideration to signing off Russell-Edmunds on completion of his current assignment. Staffing calculations were of course complicated by the usual mix of full- and part-time appointments as well as by the *ad hoc* use of retired officials, like Ronald Symons, whose links with the THS proved – to quote Sharp – 'a bit fuzzy'.[4] As happened in the mid-1960s, when Alan Holmans was instructed to write THM 8 on the Control of Demand, 1953–58 (1965), occasional commissions were given to outsiders, with Professor Fred Hirsch of the University of Warwick being contracted in 1975 to write a history of the 1969 wages explosion.

Although the post-1965 THC-based framework never functioned well and soon fell into disuse, these arrangements had at least linked the THS formally into the work of the department. However, during 1971–72 discussions, centred upon the Establishment Officer's Branch, gave serious thought to further organizational changes, even including the THS's closure, in the wake of the perceived need to update the THC's membership following the departure from the Treasury of both its chairman (Vinter) and secretary (Collier) to the Ministry of Technology and CSD respectively.[5] From the Treasury's viewpoint, the existing informal arrangements seemed to be working so well that the THC might be scrapped, given the infrequency of its meetings and the lengthy gap since it last met in 1968. At the same time, D. Truman urged caution, since the Treasury's historians were adjudged liable to interpret such moves as a retrograde step leaving them 'in limbo'.

Doubting the prudence of formally reconstituting the THC, Henley agreed to retain overall responsibility for the informal group supervising the work of the THS, while keeping the situation under review in the light of current realities and 'new ideas'.[6] Truman's review of the THS's current projects caused Henley to worry that some ongoing projects fell into the category of 'substantial' histories, possibly more akin to 'fundamental research', failing to conform to the functional guidelines laid down in the Treasury notice issued in July 1969. Thus, he reaffirmed the priority attached to utility, even floating the idea of conducting a systematic review of the actual usefulness of Treasury histories:

> The emphasis should continue to be for the most part on studies which promise to be of practical and immediate relevance to the work of divisions. This need not exclude the preparation from time to time of a more substantial 'history', rather on the lines that some fundamental research is justified even though one cannot see specific practical applications.

Revisiting the question of 'the way in which a memorandum is written' to fund experience, Henley asserted that historians should do far more than produce a mere historical narrative:

> Divisions presumably do not want so much a detailed and accurate chronicle of events, but a study which while narrating the main developments also draws out 'the lessons'. I accept that some recent experience has illustrated certain snags about the historians drawing lessons; but unless they do so, or the narrative provides its own lessons, I cannot believe that the study would be of much practical value.

For Henley, utility was in part also a function of accessibility. As a result, he pointed to the case for ensuring that divisions were better informed about the THS's work through the regular circulation of lists of Treasury histories. In January 1972 the debate was joined by Hunt, a Deputy Secretary, whose intervention in support of the continuation of the existing informal arrangements acquired significance from his subsequent promotion to succeed Trend as Cabinet Secretary (1973). Despite doing little to hide either his fundamental lack of enthusiasm for "funding experience" activities or limited view of the historians's sphere of responsibility, that is to write the history but not to identify the lessons, Hunt focused upon the 'perennial problem' of building 'some sort of bridge' between divisions and the historians: 'otherwise the historians will only tend to drift on to work which is fascinating to them but of no great relevance to the rest of us'.[7]

Seeking to draw these exchanges to a close, at least for the time being, Sharp accepted both the THC's *eventual* formal demise and the continued functioning of the informal group. Following Henley's recommendation, in March 1972, he circulated a notice updating the list of Treasury histories, while reminding divisional heads that 'the histories assembled in a coherent form a large quantity of information not otherwise quickly obtainable, and they therefore constituted useful works of reference'.[8] However, on two questions, he took issue with Henley.[9] The historians were *not*, Sharp asserted, doing their own thing. On the contrary, as evidenced by Barratt's enthusiasm for Hartcup's work on Treasury control of defence expenditure between 1946 and 1971, existing historical projects were fulfilling specific divisional requirements.[10] Perhaps, he conceded, Russell-Edmunds' history of debt situations was somewhat esoteric, but was 'in principle desirable because of the increasing variety of them'.[11] Nor did Sharp deem it prudent to conduct an in-depth review of the utility of Treasury histories, given the predictability of the outcome.

> The responses we have had in the past have been very dispiriting, and could easily lead to the conclusion (which we have rejected) to give up writing histories. We now hope that the histories will be more relevant, through greater contact with the divisions concerned, and therefore more read.

Preparing for the Treasury Historical Section's closure

In fact, in 1975 the long-running debate about the actual utility of Treasury histories resumed in earnest. For once, this chapter in the story had a decisive outcome, albeit with consequences unwelcome to the Treasury's historians in general and Ogilvy-Webb in particular.

Despite the expanding list of histories covering a wide range of topics, as circulated with synopses in January 1975, Ogilvy-Webb continued to worry that Brook's aspirations about the applied value of "funding experience", as expounded in December 1957, remained a chimera.[12] THMs were still not treated as a routine element within the Treasury's administrative processes. At the same time, the generally negative attitude assumed by divisions towards the THS's work failed to dent Ogilvy-Webb's belief in the fundamental value of funding past experience to support the work of the Treasury. Taking advantage of their personal friendship, in October 1975, Ogilvy-Webb made a direct approach to Douglas Wass, the Permanent Secretary. Responding to the departmental reorganization introduced on 20 October 1975 following the 1974–75 Management Review, he pressed the case for renewed action intended to reaffirm the usefulness of Treasury histories, and especially to urge divisions to make greater use of them in their everyday work. As ever, Ogilvy-Webb's vision of "funding experience" work extended beyond the Treasury to Whitehall in general: 'Might it not be a good thing if a letter were sent to Departments reviving ideas of Sir Norman Brook's letter of 1958 [sic] to Permanent Secretaries?'.[13] Citing contemporary Treasury realities and the heavy everyday pressures placed upon staff, Wass switched their conversation to an alternative focus, that is the THS's 'low cost effectiveness': 'It was an undeniable fact that the histories were not in fact being read by the operational divisions.'[14] Far from taking up Ogilvy-Webb's proposals, Wass rationalized his refusal to take action in terms of worsening staff workloads and the limited utility of THMs. In reality, what largely explained his negative response was knowledge that action was already underway to close the THS with effect from the end of September 1976. From this perspective, Ogilvy-Webb was swimming against a fast-running tide.[15]

When planning staffing levels for 1976–77 the Treasury's Management Group was under strong pressure to reduce civil service staffing as part of public expenditure cuts. As far as the THS was concerned, the Management Group's discussions about staff economies were framed by evaluations of the costs and benefits of historical work conducted in the light of the broader departmental context and the Treasury's recent Management Review. As Wass subsequently reminded Ogilvy-Webb, he was 'obliged to make savings in any area where they can be made *without detriment to the current business of the Treasury*' [author's emphasis].[16] From this perspective, the THS, though cheap to run, was an easy target when trying to remove costs on the Treasury vote, especially as the Management Review team had raised serious questions about its utility when recommending that 'the role of the section should be reviewed'.[17] Furthermore, as conceded by David Hancock, who succeeded Sharp as Establishment Officer and led the Review team, the THS's abolition secured 'the very important presentational advantage' of showing the rest of the Treasury that the Establishment Officer's Branch was cutting its own staff first.[18] More immediately, Ogilvy-Webb, who had been promoted to Senior Principal as Head Historian in February 1975, would not be replaced upon his retirement in January 1976. Ogilvy-Webb's scheduled retirement, though opportune, represented a secondary consideration.

Thus, when Ogilvy-Webb met Wass in October 1975, David Hancock was already implementing measures for the THS's eventual demise by way of response to the Management Review's recommendation that any action should be pursued by the Establishment Officer's branch through normal departmental procedures rather than through further intervention by the Review team. Even so, he delayed finalizing the draft closure notice pending 'delicate' discussions with individual historians about their current work and future plans.[19] By mid-December 1975, David Hancock had met each historian, noted their current assignments, agreed projected completion dates, and drafted individual action plans, thereby clearing the way for Wass to reply formally to the aide-memoire left by Ogilvy-Webb when they met in October. Reporting the recent decisions taken by the Management Group to close the THS as well as the reasons thereof, Wass indicated that henceforth any historical work would be undertaken on 'a much reduced scale', possibly modelled upon the *ad hoc* contract placed with Hirsch.[20] When preparing in 1974 for the forthcoming Management Review of the Treasury, the Treasury Steering Committee, acting upon the advice of Sir Bryan Hopkin, the Chief Economic Adviser, agreed upon the prudence of conducting a case study to evaluate the Treasury's performance in one self-contained area, that is dealing with the 1969 wages explosion.[21] Significantly, senior staff decided against asking Ogilvy-Webb and the THS to undertake the task.[22] Instead, in February 1975, Hopkin commissioned Professor Fred Hirsch of the University of Warwick to write the history. The resulting study, completed in December 1975 but not printed as a THM, identified the way in which the Treasury focused upon the short-term, at the expense of the medium and long-term, 'pay-off' and lacked any proper framework for conducting a comprehensive policy review.

Fearing the worst, Wass and David Hancock were both surprised and relieved by the fact that Ogilvy-Webb, though extremely disappointed by news about the THS's forthcoming closure and his non-replacement, reacted in a somewhat philosophical manner.[23] Detecting 'no sign of resentment', David Hancock believed that Ogilvy-Webb 'showed complete understanding of reasons leading us to wind down the Treasury Historical Section'. Indeed, the aide-memoire left with Wass in October 1975 established that Ogilvy-Webb's strong sense of commitment for "funding experience" failed to prevent him possessing an informed appreciation of departmental realities, thereby making it difficult for him to deny claims about the marginal impact of the THS's output upon the policymaking process. Undoubtedly, his demeanour was helped also by the fact that senior staff went out of their way to consult him as well as to prove responsive to his requests for ensuring the THS's orderly closure: the careful treatment of individual historians; the completion of ongoing historical projects, especially the Industry and Agriculture division's 'Financial Rescue Operations by Government' and the Overseas Finance division's 'Collapse of the Gold Exchange Standard, 1968–73'; improved publicity about the availability of Treasury histories; the commissioning of an internal history of the THS; the reconsideration of the proposal for using THMs at the Civil Service Training College; and the archiving of the THS's records.

Closing down the Treasury Historical Section

The early months of 1976 saw the progressive dismantling of the Treasury's "funding experience" work. Bretherton and Symons had already completed their final tasks. Ogilvy-Webb's final project, a collaborative history written with Dennis and Watts on the control of public expenditure, was completed in January. Ogilvy-Webb himself retired at the end of the month. In June Owen, a former divisional head, completed his history of the collapse of the gold exchange standard, with a copy being sent to the Cabinet Office to support Pressnell's work on the peacetime official history on external economic policy.[24] Watts was offered the choice of switching to either an administrative role as a higher executive officer or to another department as Research Officer. The principal uncertainty concerned Hartcup, who was adjudged likely to be 'extremely distressed' if made redundant before the age of 60.[25] Neither David Hancock nor Wass wanted a permanent historian on the department's complement, but were prepared, if necessary, to retain Hartcup as the sole Treasury historian undertaking short histories on demand for senior officials. In the event, the problem was resolved on 14 June when he obtained a post in another Whitehall department.

Although the completion of the history of the control of public expenditure brought her allocated tasks to an end, Dennis's employment was extended until the end of September 1976 in order to clear up any loose ends, but was then prolonged into 1977.[26] Initial plans for her to assist research for the history of the Treasury's financial rescue operations – this was often described as the 'lame ducks history' – were foiled by Hartcup's sudden departure. Subsequently, Dennis finalized Hartcup's history, such as by adding an introduction and a conclusion, but undertook no further research in spite of the fact that only three of ten projected case studies from different industries (e.g. British Leyland, Ferranti) had been conducted. Completed in October 1976, the 45-page history, entitled 'Some Financial Rescue Operations 1963–1971', used three case studies based upon Beagle Aircraft, Handley Page and Rolls Royce to identify lessons arising from the Treasury's rescue of companies in imminent danger of insolvency. Problem areas foregrounded by the history included the way in which the companies concerned had underestimated the costs of projects and failed to monitor budgets; the strong pressure exerted upon governments to rescue firms previously given financial assistance; and the need for governments to conduct a more thorough investigation of the financial soundness of companies applying for rescue. Forwarding the history to David Hancock, Dennis conceded its limitations consequent upon the scaling down of Hartcup's initial plans: 'I am conscious of the limited validity of the tentative conclusions drawn from only three cases all in one sector of industry.'[27] Nevertheless, David Hancock believed that the history represented a self-contained document identifying lessons likely to prove of 'very real help' as 'a training document for those coming new to industrial support work'.[28] In November 1976 copies were sent to selected divisional heads to support their future work as well as to provide a 'useful addition' to 'newcomers' kits'.[29]

Meanwhile, Dennis undertook editorial work on outstanding histories, drafted a lengthy narrative history of the Treasury's historical activities between 1957 and 1976, and assisted work preparing the THS's documentation for archiving.[30] Finally, in June 1977, David Hancock circulated a departmental notice pointing to the THS's closure 'as a contribution to the Civil Service cuts exercise', listing available THMs, urging their use, and pointing out that a copy of Dennis' internal history of the THS was available upon request from the Establishment Office.[31] Encouraged by news that there was 'quite a demand' to read her history of the THS, Dennis apprised Hartcup of the fact that 'we all have posthumous fame if we were not appreciated when we were here!'.[32]

Conclusion

During the late 1960s, the THS's position had become even more problematic. Nor did things improve during the early 1970s, when the Treasury's historical activities, though still presented in some quarters as having potential utility, were viewed increasingly by senior Treasury officials as a problem. Repeated talk about bridging the divide between historians and divisions established the fundamental difficulties arising from the reluctance of divisional officials to read and use THMs. Naturally, the morale of the Treasury's historians was not helped by speculation about Henley's relinquishment of the THC's chairmanship, the proposed scrapping of the THC and their increasingly informal position within the Treasury. Even worse, senior staff lacked the commitment to "funding experience" exhibited by Brook, Clarke and Vinter.

Writing in 1978, Peter Hennessy observed that 'The Treasury ... had an excellent historical section until the retirement of Mr. James Ogilvy-Webb in 1976 was used as a pretext for closing it down as part of a general economy drive'.[33] Admittedly pressures for economies and staffing reductions, like Ogilvy-Webb's retirement, were relevant factors, but the THS's termination resulted primarily from the failure of senior staff to accept that "funding experience" was making a useful contribution to the work of the Treasury. Indeed, as Wass implied, there seemed little risk of the section's closure exerting a detrimental impact upon current business.[34] Nor was this the first time that senior staff had admitted the point, as evidenced by Jordan-Moss' confirmation that the THM on prescription charges failed to impact upon the policymaking process in 1967–68. Equally revealing were Sharp's negative observations, as quoted earlier in this chapter, when opposing Henley's proposal for a review investigating the utility of Treasury histories.[35] Sharp's pessimism was justified. Indeed, some three years later, even Ogilvy-Webb was forced to reaffirm that THMs remained still largely unread and unused as far as the department's policymaking processes were concerned. Faced by demands for staffing reductions, the THS, and hence the Treasury's "funding experience" work, was a natural focus for downsizing, even termination. Among the Treasury's senior staff, Hopkin represented almost a lone voice arguing to save the THS.[36]

9
Using History in the Treasury

In June 1963, Peter Vinter, the head of the Public Enterprises division (PE) but soon to take effective charge of the newly created THS (1965–69) through chairmanship of the THC, circulated a memorandum to divisional staff: 'Much attention has been given in the Treasury in recent years to means of "funding experience".... The general aim is to ensure that past experience is more readily available in future to both us and to our successors than it sometimes has been in the past.'[1] This typified the manner in which the Treasury rationalized historical activities in overtly functional terms, that is to support the work of 'the man at the desk in current and future operations'.[2] Placing the Treasury's version of the past on record for the sake of posterity was a secondary consideration. From long experience, Vinter appreciated the interdependence of past, present and future, most notably the manner in which revisiting the recent past provided background and perspective for current issues as well as guidance about future possibilities.[3] In particular, looking again at past successes and failures, especially at what one official described as 'gigantic errors', promised to be a useful learning exercise.[4] Nor could Treasury forecasting be divorced from studying either past or current trends.[5] Unfortunately for the Treasury's historians, Vinter's vision was shared over time by a declining number of Treasury staff at all levels.

Types of historical outputs

During the period between 1950 and the late 1970s the Treasury's "funding experience" work resulted in a wide range of historical outputs (Box 9.1): official histories; large scale historical studies, normally printed in the THM series; divisional notes; and "seeded files". Proposals for a Treasury variant of the *DBFP* proved abortive. Official histories were intended for publication as part of the wartime series managed by the Cabinet Office's Historical Section. During the 1950s the Treasury was still processing the remaining volumes in the Second World War Civil Series – for instance, Sayers' history of *Financial Policy* was published in 1956 – but remained relatively unenthusiastic about proposals for a new peacetime series pending the government's adoption of a central framework for such studies. Subsequently, as discussed in Chapters 2–3, during the mid-1960s the government's introduction of the peacetime official histories under the auspices of the Cabinet Office's Historical Section led the Treasury to give support to the project in principle, subject to exerting no detrimental impacts upon resourcing the work of the THS.

Box 9.1 The Treasury's "funding experience" outputs

> (i) large scale histories, written by the Treasury's historians and often printed as THMs;
> (ii) divisional notes – shorter histories produced within divisions;
> (iii) "seeded files" – selected key documents prepared by senior divisional staff;
> (iv) official wartime and peacetime histories – written by outside historians;
> (v) published collections of documents – considered but rejected.

Building upon Gowing's legacy, Treasury historians worked principally upon THMs, which covered both general (for example, economic planning, wages policy) and specialist (for instance, Acts of God, Civil Service Superannuation) topics.[6] Despite their diverse range, most histories shared, Ogilvy-Webb claimed, common features: 'each constitutes an analysis as well as a description of events, and from this conclusions are, or can be, drawn'.[7] Exceptions included THM 3, a mere chronological listing of relevant legislation covering civil service superannuation, and THM 6 specifying the form of estimates. The fact that most divisions had to rely largely upon their own resources led them to adopt a 'less ambitious' course concentrating upon divisional notes and "seeded files", even if Organisation and Methods, among other specialized divisions, sought exemption from the whole exercise on the grounds that the nature of its work rendered it difficult to find suitable historical subjects.[8]

Normally, histories written as divisional notes were prepared by divisional staff, not Treasury historians. Like THMs, such histories attempted to 'bring together in a useful way the work which has been done on a particular subject, for use either when it comes up again or for its intrinsic importance... or as examples of an incident and handling which may be valuable in other connections'.[9] Even seemingly narrow topics covering, say, the aluminium smelter project or the proposed Highland air subsidy possessed a broader relevance. By contrast, "seeded files" represented only an edited selection of the principal papers on specific topics or episodes. Offering timesaving shortcuts to the leading documentation on a past question, "seeded files" were described by Vinter as 'very useful, particularly where subjects have gone on for a long time and much ephemeral paper has accumulated'. A brief historical covering note accompanied some files.

"Funding experience" more systematically

Traditionally, Treasury evaluations of the performance of past policies and administrative procedures were 'based on general impressions or individual instances known to the person giving views' rather than upon 'solid information about what actually happens'.[10] In part, this reflected the department's relatively unsystematic approach to staff induction, training and development, at least during the pre-Fulton period. Nor did the frequent mobility of staff across divisions – writing in the mid-1960s as head of the Public Sector Group, Clarke described rapid staff turnover as a major problem – help the formation of a collective departmental memory.[11] During the early 1970s, Sharp, the Establishment Officer, was still complaining that 'inherited divisional memories are short'.[12] Over time, the work of the THS began to fill this lacuna in a more formal and systematic manner, or at least this was the theory, as claimed by Ogilvy-Webb:

> Instead of sticking to generalisations about official attitudes to public business, we [Treasury historians] have asked ourselves the crude question: 'Does the system work?' We have decided that it is fair, to a very great extent, to impute to officials the outcome of events, for good or ill... we think that there is enough solid material in our histories to justify some prima facie conclusions.[13]

Like official histories, Treasury histories had a functional purpose, that is to fund past experience with the benefit of privileged access to departmental files and oral testimony taken from those involved at a time when the decisions taken were not yet forgotten. But there was a significant difference. Whereas official histories were produced for publication – they relied also upon a more extensive research base – the Treasury's historical outputs were strictly reserved for confidential departmental use:

> We in the Treasury are doing something quite new. We are trying to relate the internal administrative process to the policy problems of Government in a much more intimate way than has previously been attempted and indeed in a way designed to help to solve problems. The histories do not consist therefore of an analysis of the subject itself, as, for example, an economist might write, nor a general account of Government policy and public reactions to it as an outside historian would write. It is an analysis of how policy evolved from what administrators believed or knew and from the institutional pressures to which they were subjected.[14]

As a result, the work made slightly different demands upon staff as compared to official histories:

> Because publication of the results was precluded (completed studies are circulated strictly within the confines of Whitehall and given a stringent security classification), academics on the whole were unlikely to find it appealing. Despite this major disadvantage by comparison with the Cabinet Office scheme, however, the Treasury one has the compensation that it permits of a considerably more penetrating approach. By virtue of being known to be non-disclosable outside Government circles, the Treasury studies are able to be more rounded and a good deal more forthright in their conclusions. To this extent they are likely to serve as a much better training-ground for academic researchers than the Cabinet Office scheme (bearing in mind as well the limitations of Cabinet papers themselves).[15]

Or at least this represented Ogilvy-Webb's view on the matter.

Successive THMs highlighted the way in which hitherto – to quote Ogilvy-Webb – 'the absence of feedback masks the failure of policies and methods'.[16] From this perspective, THMs provided 'useful feedback' capable of closing the Treasury loop by providing informed guidance about how departmental procedures and policies left room for improvement, thereby providing the basis for the more effective formulation and execution of future policies and methods. As Peter Middleton acknowledged, the Treasury's historians had a 'special contribution' to make to the work of the Treasury, especially post-Fulton: 'they were one of the few groups who had evidence to support what they said, and much of this evidence was based on fairly up-to-date studies'.[17]

What did Treasury histories offer policymakers?

When seeking to consolidate the place of "funding experience" work in the Treasury as well as to press its broader relevance to Whitehall as a whole, Ogilvy-Webb articulated what the Treasury historians saw as the specific utility of their work.[18] In brief, they claimed Treasury histories provided:

- insights into *how* things really happened, and particularly the process of administration *at work* in the Treasury, including the complex interplay of ideas, events and people within the institutional framework;
- working tools for evolving criteria by which the Treasury's performance in formulating and executing policy over time could be critically assessed at a time when the civil service was being placed increasingly under the spotlight. The historical narrative established what happened, when and why things worked or went wrong. Thus, they allowed users to investigate, say, the extent to which short-termism characterized administrative actions or short-term successes obscured long-term failures;
- an invaluable resource for staff training and development in the civil service, meeting calls, such as advanced by the 1968 Fulton Report, for improved professionalism and the greater use of specialist expertise;
- an improved sense of historical perspective by way of highlighting the 'real issues' underlying past topics/problems as well as the unspoken assumptions of administrators;
- practical lessons to be drawn from the historical narrative in order to provide a clear framework for action by indicating how problems could be tackled more effectively in the light of past experience.

Within this context, Ogilvy-Webb saw Treasury historians as using departmental files to investigate in depth 'the process of policy formation and execution *from the inside*'.[19] THMs and, albeit to a lesser extent, divisional notes offered an informed critical commentary upon the policy process as a whole and individual stages in particular

(Box 9.2): 'whatever faults the histories may have they give more insight into real administrative issues than practically any other material available'.[20] More specifically, THMs possessed several purposes. First, by recording the departmental memory, they represented an authoritative source of reference for policymakers when undertaking their current responsibilities. Based upon extensive research using departmental files, these historical narratives promised to save 'the man at the desk' time and effort, most notably avoiding the need to consult large numbers of files when drafting an urgent background briefing or seeking a sense of perspective on present-day matters. Secondly, their frequent ability to draw upon the oral testimony of participants in the events under discussion meant that THMs provided an additional dimension to departmental files, and hence to the Treasury's collective memory. Thirdly, they offered an effective method for recording Treasury precedent, with specific reference to indicating and contextualizing changing practice over time, as evidenced by the way in which Gowing's *Acts of God* THM recognized that the doctrine of governmental non-interference in the consequences of natural disasters was dead. Fourthly, the problem-centred agenda of THMs made them an invaluable resource for staff development and induction purposes.[21] Finally, and most importantly as regards "funding experience", THMs were seen as yielding lessons 'of direct use as working tools' for divisions when handling analogous current or future problems.[22]

Box 9.2 Policymaking stages studied by Treasury histories

---

1. *Assessing the nature of the question requiring attention*
   Officials often failed to undertake this assessment in an appropriate or timely fashion and/or relied upon faulty and outdated reasoning (THM 5; THM 13).
2. *Formulating a hypothesis to guide official thinking about appropriate ways forward*
   The frequent reliance upon common sense meant that clear sets of objectives were rarely articulated or seriously tested (THM 7; THM 9).
3. *Obtaining and assembling relevant facts to establish the basis for the proposed policy*
   There was a relative lack of interest in collecting empirical material to assess alternative possibilities, partly due to the failure to take initial stages seriously (THM 7; THM 12).

Box 9.2 (Continued)

> 4. *Feeding official thinking upwards to senior staff and ministers*
>   Despite the primacy of ministers in making policy and the consequent impact of political factors, officials often exerted a significant, even decisive, influence (THM 11).
> 5. *Selecting methods for putting policy into practice*
>   Frequently decisions were made hurriedly, with inadequate consideration of alternative policies and methods, thereby resulting in unforeseen, often intractable, problems (THM 12).
> 6. *Checking the results and amending policy/methods in the light of experience*
>   Little or no effort was made to learn from the past by securing feedback about the impact of relevant past policy decisions and methods (THM 12; THM 15).
>
> *Note*: Only a sample of findings is summarized above. Their critical tone reflected the fact that most THMs were commissioned for perceived failures in policies and/or methods. The appendix, p. 252, lists THMs.

For the Treasury, the principal value of THMs lay in their conclusions, frequently headed as the 'lessons to be learned', which were seen as providing policymakers with a practical framework guiding their day-to-day work at each stage of the policymaking process (Box 9.2). According to Ogilvy-Webb, any lessons should emerge naturally from the final historical narrative through exchanges conducted between the historians and divisional staff, even if the latter's commitment to the process proved somewhat variable and served to undermine as well as to delay the THS's work.[23] "Funding experience" would not work, Ogilvy-Webb argued, if the history was written to justify what had been decided in advance: 'this would be inconsistent with the urge to get the lesson of our histories learned'.[24]

The THM's limitations

At the same time, Ogilvy-Webb conceded the limitations of THMs, given the fact that by their very nature they were commissioned normally to investigate something which had gone wrong. From this perspective, THMs gave a rather one-sided negative impression of the Treasury's past. Hartcup's history (1966) of the Fairfields Shipyard rescue focused upon a rare success story. Moreover, the interdepartmental nature of modern government, alongside the Plowdenite emphasis upon government as a cooperative enterprise, raised questions about the somewhat blinkered approach of THMs.[25] Based narrowly upon Treasury documentary sources, THMs made little or no effort to take account of either the files or the standpoint of other departments actively involved in the developments under discussion in spite of indications that they often saw things somewhat differently from the Treasury. Despite being heavily dependent upon Treasury sources, THM 10 on *Negotiations with the European Economic Community* drew also upon contributions from several departments, and was the exception proving the rule. Otherwise, the attitudes and roles of other departments were viewed only through the Treasury's eyes and documentation.

The Treasury's responsibilities for the management and overall efficiency of the civil service prior to the creation of the CSD might be interpreted as requiring the Treasury to share the fruits of its "funding experience" programme with Whitehall departments, especially as most THMs were seen as possessing a broader relevance. As Clarke argued in his 1964 Stamp Memorial Lecture, the Treasury needed to be far more proactive in introducing improved administrative and management techniques: 'Instead of being a back-seat driver, the Treasury's job is to ensure that every Department has the best possible cars and drivers and is properly equipped with maps.'[26] In the event, as reaffirmed by repeated departmental notices, the Treasury maintained its restrictive attitude towards proposals for the circulation of THMs to other departments because of an ingrained, albeit understandable, reluctance to expose either its past mistakes or its methods when doing battle with other departments over budgets.

Significantly, the Treasury was unwilling to let other departments know about the existence of THMs, let alone to read them! Even the rare exceptions, occurring only after high-level exchanges drawing in the Joint Permanent Secretaries, resulted in histories being sent to the relevant PUSs on a personal basis, *not* to the departments. Unsurprisingly, Keeling's frequent requests to use bowdlerized versions of THMs for training purposes attracted the backing of Ogilvy-Webb, but not that of senior staff.[27] In any case, generally speaking the Treasury was disinclined to amend, even dilute, the content of any history to avoid infringing the sensitivities of another department. Indeed, their actual value to the Treasury in terms of identifying lessons for the future was viewed as a function of the openness, ruthlessness and comprehensiveness with which topics were discussed.

Any toning down of the content was deemed liable to undermine their rationale and utility.

Despite being specifically produced to improve the machinery of government in general and Treasury procedures in particular, THMs were invariably stamped to the effect that they could *not* be shown to ministers. Although this was, of course, a matter of constitutional propriety arising from the fact that most histories covered previous governments and topics of domestic political controversy, Ogilvy-Webb saw this restriction as yet another 'impediment to their usefulness'.[28] Obviously, the principal responsibility of ministers for providing political leadership should not be under-estimated, but there was no bar on the content, including the lessons to be learned, being filtered to ministers through official advice about the pros and cons of specific policies and methods. In any case, many issues never reached ministers, being processed by officials within the overall policy framework laid down by the government. Indeed, as Ogilvy-Webb recorded, THMs established that officials frequently performed a far from insubstantial role in the machinery of government:

> Our researches tend to show however the very great influence of officials and their ability, when they are so minded, to persist with proposals, in spite of the reluctance of Ministers, until official views come to be more or less accepted.... Within the general framework of Ministers, officials, we think, produce triumph or disaster.[29]

"Seeded files" as a policy resource

"Seeded files", albeit a relatively modest historical strategy, helped to streamline the reference process within several divisions, most notably those within the sphere of responsibility of Clarke and Vinter. For example, in 1962 Derek Mitchell, when advising Rickett about history-related matters, pointed to the way in which Vinter had personally "seeded" 15 files on German support costs into one file and then added a narrative: 'he tells me that it has since proved invaluable to a number of people from Ministers down'.[30] Mitchell reported also the way in which HOPS had incorporated into one "seeded file" the key documentation on reflation plans previously contained in 10 files:

> This strikes me as a file which would be invaluable to anyone faced with the same kind of problem on some future occasion. It is not that the circumstances would be exactly the same but that the file would

illustrate the procedures that would have to be gone through and enable the organiser of a new exercise to produce a work programme quickly with much less risk of overlooking some essential stage, for example, of consultation with other Departments or outside bodies.[31]

HOPS's growing collection of "seeded files" owed much to Clarke, who expounded their merits in finding the needles in the haystacks. For example, in February 1964, when supplying Armstrong, the Joint Permanent Secretary, with specific papers requested on the control of investment in 1956–57, Clarke presented it as a vivid example of the utility of "seeded files": 'Never say that the system of having selected files [i.e. "seeded files"] does not yield very large returns when you want to go back into history!.'[32]

Divisions and historians

For any historian, whether working in government or academia, communication with the intended audience is important.[33] Treasury histories had a clear target, that is 'the man at the desk', but generally evoked a less than enthusiastic reaction from that audience, which proved reluctant to read THMs, let alone to incorporate their findings into the administrative process.

> For Ogilvy-Webb:
>
> The important thing in the case of the Historical Memoranda is to consider whether they have been acted upon. We cannot always be certain.... It would be interesting to know what use Divisions have made so far from the kind of feedback represented by the histories.[34]

In this sense, 'acted upon' was not necessarily taken to mean followed and implemented to the letter, but rather consulted and read by officials to provide information, guidance, lessons and perspective in appropriate cases. In reality, as demonstrated by Chapters 3–8, the Treasury encountered problems in translating the concept of "funding experience", as articulated by Brook in 1957, into practice. Despite being presented as a useful working tool yielding accessible assessments of the performance of the Treasury's past policies and methods, the concept of "funding experience" always looked better in theory than practice.

Notwithstanding his vested interest in believing and proclaiming that the Treasury had built up an impressive and useful collection of histories, even Ogilvy-Webb remained uncertain about their real utility. During 1969–70 he conceded that 'only in a few cases is advantage being taken of them for practical purposes', thereby prompting him to express the Treasury historians's continuing concern 'at what seems to us to be a poor return on investment, secured from our work and partly (and of course related to this) because reactions to and discussion of one's work is an important stimulus which we still lack, in spite of efforts to get over this'.[35] As late as 1975, that is when the Treasury had been "funding experience" for almost two decades, he admitted that 'it is difficult for the Historians to know how successful this venture has been': 'There is little feedback. But as so few officers seem to be aware of the histories or to use them we feel that they have not made much impact.'[36]

Previous chapters establish that most divisional staff in the Treasury held a rather different view of the nature and utility of departmental histories from that espoused by Ogilvy-Webb and his fellow historians. As Sharp recognized during the THS's final years, 'Divisions, and people, have very mixed attitudes – some think histories are valuable, and take an interest in them; others do not.'[37] Unfortunately for the THS, the 'others' referred to by Sharp represented the large majority. In fact, the enduring gap existing between historians and divisions, a kind of "us" and "them" divide, reflected the fact that most officials never saw "funding experience" outputs as providing useful support for their day-to-day work. On the contrary, whenever they gave some thought to the matter, THMs were seldom viewed in positive terms as 'working tools' worthy of divisional support and collaboration.

Yet "funding experience" could only work in the way envisaged by Brook through continuing dialogue between the historians and divisional staff. Thus, divisions were expected to set out a history's purpose in meeting an actual divisional need, and then to collaborate with the historians to ensure that the resulting history fulfilled its original objective. As Ogilvy-Webb asserted when the THC was created, 'the historians must not get shut up in an ivory tower'.[38] In practice, the Treasury's historians frequently came up against a virtual dead end through the lack of timely responses to their requests for, say, divisional feedback on interim drafts or help in drawing out the lessons from completed histories. Throughout the period of study the Treasury's historians suffered constantly from their peripheral involvement in the department's everyday work. Gowing's early sense of isolation and feeling unwanted was replicated by Ogilvy-Webb and company, whose marginal role and status were accentuated by their continued geographical detachment from the main Treasury building.

When looking back at the THC's first year of work, Collier pointed out that 'in the Historical Committee we have always recognised the need for close cooperation between Historian and Division.... In time, it [this doctrine] will take root; but it is bound to be a slow process.'[39] Repeated calls for building a bridge between divisions and historians – in 1972, Hunt, who was soon to leave the Treasury to become Cabinet Secretary, acknowledged yet again this omnipresent gulf – recognized the failure of this collaborative doctrine to take root.[40] Despite repeated efforts upon the part of senior staff to resolve the problem, the establishment of an effective dialogue between divisions and historians constantly proved an elusive aspiration, never a reality. Four years later, when announcing the THS's abolition, the Treasury was in effect conceding that the problem was probably insoluble.

What was the problem?

Despite rationalizing its nature and timing in terms of the urgent 'need for economy' and Ogilvy-Webb's retirement, in reality the decision to abolish the THS reflected longstanding doubts about the actual utility of "funding experience" work.[41] After all, the small number of staff involved meant that any financial savings were minimal. By 1976 the THS's position, as viewed from the perspective of the perceived costs and benefits of its activities, had become increasingly problematic and insecure. Successive attempts to harness the administrative potential of "funding experience" had proved abortive. In particular, the new THC-centred regime, introduced in 1965, never worked well, soon lost momentum, and failed to put the Treasury's "funding experience" work back on what was viewed as the right track. Responding in December 1975 to Ogilvy-Webb's aide-memoire pointing to the failure of Treasury's histories to make a significant impact upon policymakers, Wass agreed: 'you are right to say that we have not made full use of them'.[42] Or rather, to quote David Hancock – as the Establishment Officer he proved a prime mover in the THS's closure – the histories 'were, on the whole, not what the Department needed'.[43]

Why did Treasury histories fail to make an impact?

The THC's 1968 review investigating the utility of the prescription charges history vividly highlighted the failure of THMs to feed into divisional discussions resulting in a major shift in policy, even one occurring soon after the history's completion. To some extent, the problem was part of the wider question of using expertise in British government. Despite its growing reliance upon professional economic expertise as a 'new source of advice', the Treasury encountered difficulties in integrating professional economists into an administrative machine dominated still by Bridges' vision stressing the virtues of the generalist exercising commonsense administrative standards.[44] Even during the late 1960s Alec Cairncross, the Director of the Treasury's Economic Section (1961–68), was complaining that administrators and economists represented 'two groups without effective contact between them'.[45] Was it realistic to expect historians in the Treasury to fare any better when dealing with divisions?

In the meantime, Ogilvy-Webb made repeated attempts, frequently through lengthy memoranda, to identify the causes of the problem. Indeed, during 1975–76, when searching for a way to safeguard the THS following his forthcoming retirement, he was still searching for answers. Was the problem, he speculated, because lengthy histories presented too much of a challenge to 'the digestion of administrators'?[46] For Treasury historians, a lengthy history was seen as essential to provide comprehensive coverage of a topic, while saving busy officials considerable time and effort: 'a history is, in effect, a quick and easy way of absorbing the results of, say, 18 months of someone else's work on the files'.[47] But, for officials seeking urgent guidance, 'voluminous' Treasury histories proved a challenging read and an unwelcome distraction from more pressing business.[48] To some extent, this difficulty was mitigated by the THM's inclusion of executive summaries as well as by the production of shorter versions of Treasury histories for printing as THMs, although even these histories risked being too long from the point of view of officials. THM 5 on wages policy, an abbreviated version of the original three-volume 120,000 word plus history, still totalled 34 pages!

Use was in part also a function of perceived contemporary relevance. Acknowledging the lengthy period taken to complete many histories, Ogilvy-Webb accepted the need to produce results more quickly, even prioritizing short-term projects. From this perspective, histories had to become available in a timely manner in order to play a meaningful role in the policymaking process. Things moved on while any project was in progress. There was always the risk that any history, when completed, might have been overtaken by events, and hence too late to feed into the work of officials. In a fast-moving world, as Miss J. Forsyth, the head of a branch in the Social Services division, remarked, 'the issues which are important today are seldom those which were important yesterday'.[49]

Furthermore, staff mobility, though frequently cited as a good reason for "funding experience", meant that a history commissioned by one divisional head was often received upon completion by his/her successor, who would not necessarily treat the final history as useful to, let alone as still wanted by, the division. Nor was their utility helped by the limited involvement and cooperation from relevant divisional officials at each stage of the production process, particularly in drawing out the lessons to be learned from the history. Even worse, divisions, though treating the identification of lessons as their specific sphere of responsibility, rarely went out of their way to find time and space to undertake this stage of the project.

As noted by the 1968 Fulton Report, the civil service culture of concentrating upon the in-tray often overrode the adoption of a more measured and strategic approach to policy analysis and research involving the in-depth reading of papers unconnected with immediate events.[50] According to Ogilvy-Webb, there lingered 'in official minds the feeling that an account of what has happened in the past is not relevant to the present or the future'.[51] For instance, when commenting in 1971 upon a history of exchange control going back to the late 1950s, Rawlinson opined that 'the world of the fifties is too remote and too different to be relevant to future policy-making'.[52] Of course, most THMs had a more limited time span, even if the historians argued that a long-term view provided a more balanced and comprehensive picture for those dealing with contemporary issues. Nor were civil service recruitment and training procedures irrelevant. As the 1968 Fulton report noted, the civil service's 'generalist' approach encouraged recruits, including history graduates, to view their university studies as merely a test of ability for recruitment purposes, not a useful framework for their work.[53] Nor was history's image helped by the way in which procedures, as noted by the Fulton report, had moved on from old style learning 'on the job' strategies to an enhanced focus in training courses upon vocational relevance.

In part, Brook saw "funding experience" as one way of offering postmortems critically assessing past performance by reference to what Ogilvy-Webb came to describe as 'the empirical tests of history'.[54] However, as implied by the strong reservations expressed about naming individual officials in THMs, Treasury staff exhibited – to quote Collier – 'mixed feelings' about exposing what had happened in the past: 'there are many activities of T.I. [Trade and Industry division] in the early fifties which I personally would prefer to see hidden under a shroud of historical mystery!'.[55] Even worse, the fact that THMs focused chiefly upon past failures meant that the histories often reflected unfavourably upon officials, as noted by Forward in 1969:

> According to some of the histories [civil servants] seem constitutionally incapable of doing anything right – perhaps because there was a bias against problem-solvers at the selection stage or because success in one's career depended on emptying one's in-tray and getting into 'good habits' instead of tackling the fundamental questions.[56]

For example, the history of aircraft purchasing policy disclosed – to quote Vinter – 'a not particularly happy or creditable account of the Government's relations with the Aircraft corporations or of their own activities on the purchase of civil aircraft. Circumstances, occasions and performance have varied but I doubt whether anyone could say that the average score has been satisfactory.'[57]

To some extent, the above-mentioned problems resulted from the failure of divisional staff to understand the nature of the historical process. Overlooking the fact that the standards of research required for writing a sound Treasury history were – to quote Ogilvy-Webb – 'more exacting than those required for producing an ordinary administrative memorandum', officials were inclined to view history writing as 'too slow a business'.[58] Busy officials, seeking to clear their in-trays, regarded THMs as synonymous with academic histories rather than as useful contributions to long-term policy analysis:

> The pressure to concentrate on immediate matters of procedure and mechanics (which the historians document) may discourage administrative officials from addressing themselves to the policy implications of the histories, even when these implications are vigorously spelt out by the historians.[59]

A matter of presentation

For Ogilvy-Webb, there was also an urgent need to 'do something about selling our stuff' more effectively to 'consumers', that is the divisions.[60] Treasury histories had to be *presented* as not only potentially useful but also available in order to overcome the perceived 'impediments' preventing officials reading the histories by way of absorbing, thinking about, and drawing out any lessons adjudged relevant to their current and future work.

Generally speaking, Treasury histories were viewed as not very user-friendly. Apart from what was regarded as their excessive length, titles often obscured the broader relevance of specialist histories. Nor was the utility of THMs enhanced by divisional 'unawareness of their existence' consequent largely upon the lack of a detailed index. As Pliatzky, an Assistant Secretary in AT, complained, 'it is of no use funding experience if the fund is not readily available to be drawn on'.[61] Typically, the index project, albeit taken up as a priority by the THC during 1965–66, never reached fruition. Successive Treasury notices listed titles and urged divisions to use THMs, but did little to break down the indifference, even negative mindsets, characteristic of most divisional staff.

In January 1975 Sharp circulated another Treasury notice rationalizing and publicizing the case for the Treasury's historical activities:

> Because of staff changes in divisions it has often been found that people do not know about historical work affecting their own divisions. Yet the object of preparing these histories is to save people a lot of time on background reading when they are trying to familiarise themselves with a new subject, as well as to provide on occasion a useful survey of some of the wider problems with which the Treasury has to deal.[62]

Revealingly, in October 1975 Ogilvy-Webb continued to debate causes and solutions with senior staff.[63] Wass, who was, of course, preparing for the THS's closure, did little more than to acknowledge the problem. For Wass, 'chronically overworked' officials conducting 'severely stressed jobs' had neither the time nor the inclination to use THMs in support of their everyday administrative work.[64] Nor had it proved possible for Wass to meet Ogilvy-Webb's proposal for a handover period allowing staff moving divisions the opportunity to read up material, including THMs and "seeded files", relevant to his/her new duties: 'It is often impossible to allow time to enable people to read even the most recent files before they are totally immersed in the despatch of current business.'

For Collier, blame for the failure of "funding experience" work to establish itself within the Treasury was difficult to apportion: 'The fault is partly theirs [the historians]; they expect their work to be accepted as something much more important and helpful than it could ever be – but equally Divisions have not yet got used to the idea of getting the fullest value from these reports.'[65] Writing as a divisional head, Jordan-Moss believed that the historians failed either to pitch their histories at the right level or to keep up with fast-moving events.[66] At the same time, divisions, like that headed by Jordan-Moss, were often uncertain about what they wanted, made little effort to explain their requirements clearly, and failed to allocate time for either commenting upon drafts in progress or reading and acting upon completed histories. Nor should the Treasury itself be excluded from blame, given the extent to which "funding experience" work came to depend upon the support of senior staff. Even Brook's words of support were rarely translated into resources. Despite limited additions in the mid-1960s, the small number of historians ensured that their impact was always bound to be both limited and fragmentary across the department as a whole.

The Ogilvy-Webb factor

As indicated above, Ogilvy-Webb came to see himself as performing a representational role acting on behalf of the Treasury's historians, most notably in presenting the case for "funding experience" and taking on the doubters. Certainly, Ogilvy-Webb gave considerable thought to what the historians were doing and what went wrong, as evidenced by his frequent lengthy memoranda covering all aspects of the topic.[67]

However, for senior staff, Ogilvy-Webb, the administrator turned historian, was part of the problem. Notwithstanding polite remarks made during 1975–76 about his long and successful career as a Treasury historian as well as reassurances that the THS's abolition should not be interpreted as reflecting adversely upon him, Ogilvy-Webb was often criticized for pursuing his own personal agenda through missing tight deadlines, writing overlong histories, and requiring close supervision to avoid the production of academic-type histories.[68] Reportedly, his confrontational style when pressing the interests of Treasury history or exposing the Treasury's shortcomings did the historians's cause more harm than good, as indicated by the irritation displayed by Vinter and Collier about his 1966 lecture. Likewise, Sharp's marginal comment on one of his memoranda – he minuted 'Oh dear' – typified the exasperation of senior staff with Ogilvy-Webb's pontificating at length and assumption of what Vinter called a 'Superior Confessor role'.[69]

Conclusion

Lecturing to Treasury staff in October 1966, Ogilvy-Webb quoted one senior official as having said recently 'that, in effect, history is bunk.

Lessons cannot be learnt because nothing is ever the same as before'.[70] No indication was given of the speaker's identity, but such sentiments proved far from uncommon. For instance, despite, or perhaps because, of his membership of the THC, Kenneth Couzens, the head of AT, had minuted a few weeks earlier that he had 'never been vastly impressed with the usefulness of all this': 'all the experience of the last 2 years casts doubt in my mind on whether "funded experience" is of more than historical interest. Even when a situation recurs to some extent, the differences are such as to invalidate much of the old material'.[71] Unsurprisingly, Ogilvy-Webb went out of his way to use his lecture to confront such negative thinking:

> Of course it is true that history never repeats itself, (though the historian of Wages Policy may sometimes be tempted to think otherwise). But officials remain the *same*, and the attitudes and procedures which cause one mishap have an extraordinary aptitude for creating another.[72]

However, this divide, representing a continuing undercurrent throughout the text in Chapters 3–8, meant that the Treasury's historians faced a constant uphill struggle to make a meaningful impact upon the everyday work of divisions. Certainly, Vinter, albeit better disposed as a divisional head to the concept than most of his counterparts, was not alone in acknowledging the conundrum for a busy division:

> It is no simple matter to give general guidance on how this 'funding experience' should best be pursued. On the one hand its use is undoubted and must not be overlaid by the pressure of current business – indeed as more experience is funded, some current pressures will be eased: on the other hand, current business has got to be despatched and we are a hard-pressed Division.[73]

Against this background, perhaps the key question for the historian to answer is not so much what was achieved by the Treasury's "funding experience" activities, why did they fail to impact upon policymakers, or why the THS was abolished after a relatively short life, but rather why did the THS survive as long as it did. Regular recitals of the same problems, alongside abortive efforts to relaunch "funding experience" work, raise serious questions about why this historical experiment was not terminated much earlier. In particular, why was there a constant search for a better way of doing things in order to make "funding experience" work in the way envisaged by Brook?

Possibly one of the principal reasons centred upon the high-level Treasury support enjoyed by "funding experience" during the late 1950s and 1960s, when Brook, Clarke and Vinter, among others, saw such activities as capable of contributing to the more effective formulation and conduct of public policy. Undeterred by repeated setbacks, in 1969, Vinter was still trying to get "funding experience" to work better:

> There is a wide potential range of work over which the historians might usefully be employed and we still have much to learn about how to get the best possible value from them. The modified approach we are now proposing should go a long way towards applying these limited resources so as to produce the maximum benefit to current administration.[74]

What changed over time was the decline, or rather the virtual disappearance, of such backing, as influential supporters either retired, like Brook (1962), or moved to another department, like Clarke (1966) and Vinter (1969).[75] By the mid-1970s senior staff, like Wass and David Hancock, viewed the THS's role far less positively. Neither had been impressed with the applied value of "funding experience" outputs when moving up through the Treasury, and saw little reason to change tack when assuming senior managerial roles during the 1970s.[76] Looking back, Sir David Hancock confirmed that "funding experience" represented 'a secondary or even tertiary responsibility – priority was given to getting on with the business'.[77] Although much time was spent writing notes for the departmental record, this was of course 'not the same as funding experience which was a separate exercise'. Significantly, during 1974–75 David Hancock led the Treasury Management Review team which called 'into question whether the efforts of the Historical Section are properly directed': 'The general view seems to be that they take too long in writing over elaborate histories of little immediate interest and that they are not able to produce quick reports for which a real need is expressed by operational staff'.[78] In many respects, the resulting call for a critical review of the THS's utility provided a key prompt for decisive action.

Changes at the Cabinet Office merely accentuated this process. In 1973 Trend was replaced as Cabinet Secretary by Sir John Hunt, whose service in the Treasury had familiarized him with THMs but failed to provide convincing evidence about their applied value. Commiserating with Hartcup in 1976 about the THS's demise, Gowing reflected upon

Trend's retirement: 'Hunt seems very poor exchange for Trend who, like Norman Brook, really believed in history as something worthwhile.'[79] Of course, throughout the period 1957–76, "funding experience" work had never really attracted much support from less senior officials. The reservations articulated during the late 1950s by Shirley Littler and Peck about Gowing's history of colonial aid typified the contrasting perspectives adopted from an early stage by senior and other staff towards such activities.

Inevitably, the THS's closure in 1976, alongside the problematic course of the relationship between historians and divisions, encourages somewhat negative appraisals of the Treasury's "funding experience" programme. Generally speaking, THMs, like other historical outputs, exerted no more than a spasmodic and marginal impact upon the formulation and execution of Treasury policy, even if Chapters 3–8 quote several senior officials, like Vinter, espousing both the theoretical case for such work and the actual utility of specific Treasury histories, even in draft form. Such support was based largely upon an informed appreciation of the practical utility of "funding experience" to the 'man at the desk' in providing historical knowledge, guidance and perspective because of the frequent feeling of 'having been there before' (Clarke) and the consequent value of learning from the past.[80] Even so, there remained the need to make allowances for changing circumstances, as evidenced by Clarke's qualified praise for the utility of Ogilvy-Webb's THM on wages policy:

> As regards the use of the document, we have certainly ourselves found it very useful during the last year, but... the circumstances have changed a great deal as a result of the events of the last twelve months, and there is clearly an interruption in the continuity at this stage. But I think there is some value, nevertheless, in the experience of the past, although it may not bite very sharply upon our preoccupations at the moment.[81]

There was also, as the THC recorded in 1966, the problem of "funding experience" in cases, like the TSR2 project, where political pressures overrode official advice.[82]

Nevertheless, any evaluation should not lose sight of the positives. For almost two decades the Treasury, doing far more than other Whitehall departments to implement Brook's 1957 policy initiative, offered an excellent case study in the use, and non-use, of history in a public policy context. Indeed, in 1967 Abbot even informed the

Cabinet Office that 'we do however go in for "funding experience" in a pretty big way'.[83] Perhaps, this was an exaggeration, at least in-so-far as "funding experience" failed to become a routine formal input to the Treasury's policy process. However, reading the histories allowed at least some officials to remember the past more accurately, and possibly improve the quality of their work. Significantly, even David Hancock, who played a key role in the THS's closure, admitted that he had 'derived great profit from reading Mr Owen's history about the collapse of the Bretton Woods system' (THM 30).[84] Nor should it be forgotten that the claims made for "funding experience" by Brook were relatively modest in the sense that history was never intended to be more than one part of a package of resources feeding into the policy process. In many respects, this book complements Hugh Pemberton's *Policy Learning and British Governance in the 1960s*, whose theoretical approach demonstrated the way in which policy networks based upon pressure groups and think tanks drew in external economic expertise and reinforced official concerns to remedy past policy failures.

Between 1957 and 1976, the historians built up a substantial Treasury resource – already in 1968 Ogilvy-Webb was praising the THS's 'pretty rich tapestry' recording the history of a wide range of the department's activities – comprising 30 printed THMs, some 22 unprinted histories, and a substantial number of divisional notes and "seeded files".[85] There was also an internal history of the THS written by Dennis to provide both a reference source and a guidance note in the event of any future decision to revive such work![86]

Notwithstanding their variable use by divisional officials, the Treasury's historical outputs offer an invaluable yet hitherto under-used primary source for historians. The work of Treasury historians, though produced in a different manner to academic history, represents a useful research resource recording the department's activities, most notably supplementing the documentary evidence with unique oral testimony revealing the unspoken assumptions of officials involved in those events. Furthermore, the fact that the historians were asked to mark for preservation any files used enhanced the prospects of key documents surviving the weeding process for use at Kew. Finally, Treasury histories, like official histories, offer illuminating insights for studies about the nature and use of history, most notably the art of writing for a target audience, while yielding illuminating examples of the way in which historians working in government were faced with repeated conflicts between professional historical standards and public policy practice.

Part III
Using History in the Foreign Office

Part III
Using History in the Foreign Office

10
The Foreign Office's 1962 Abadan History

Faced by the breakdown of his dictatorial authority, in January 1979, Mohammad Reza Shah Pahlavi, the Shah of Iran (1941–79), abandoned his throne and fled into exile.[1] Returning to London a few days later from a five-year posting as British ambassador in Teheran, Sir Anthony Parsons articulated his anxieties about the experience of living through events prompting comparisons with France in 1789.[2] For Parsons, recent developments raised serious questions for British policymakers: 'Where did we go wrong?'; 'How did we fail to read the signs in time?'.[3] Why had his embassy failed to warn London about the imminence of revolution? If he had read the situation better, 'would I have advised my government to adopt different policies? . . . . And again, if we had adopted different policies across the broad spectrum of our dealings with Iran, would this have lessened the damage to British interests when the collapse came?'.[4]

The perceived significance of these developments for British foreign policy led Sir Michael Palliser, the PUS at the Foreign and Commonwealth Office, to arrange a series of lunchtime meetings enabling Parsons to think aloud about learning from the Anglo-Iranian past. For John Dickie, an experienced diplomatic correspondent, these sessions provided an invaluable input into the foreign policymaking process.

> To have a senior ambassador stand up in front of everyone . . . and admit he made a big mistake required a large measure of courage. For many in his audience the meetings were a textbook example of how it can be worthwhile to learn the lessons of diplomacy by hindsight.[5]

However, as Dickie acknowledged, Parsons's master class in diplomacy proved a rare 'exception to the normal ostrich posture in the Foreign

Office over learning lessons from mistakes': 'Diplomatic post-mortem examinations of policy are rare inside the Foreign Office.... It is unusual for the policy-making process to be reviewed after a major event.'[6] Dickie's conclusion was confirmed in a more recent study by Zara Steiner. Preoccupied with today's world and the immediate future, busy ministers and officials, though prepared to use history for rhetorical effect and occasional background information, made – to quote Steiner – 'only limited use' of history in actually making foreign policy.[7]

The importance of the Abadan crisis

When reviewing the events bringing Ayatollah Khomeini to power at the head of an Islamic Republic, Parsons soon became aware of the way in which rightly or wrongly many Iranians saw the 1979 revolution as reversing events in the early 1950s, when the 1951 Abadan crisis resulted in an Anglo-American coup returning the Shah to power as 'the creature of the United States'.[8] Memories of this earlier dispute, sparked off by the Iranian nationalization of British oil interests and resulting in Britain's evacuation of Abadan, remained influential in 1979, at least in Iran, where 'Oil Nationalization Day' is still celebrated today. By contrast, in Britain, this earlier dispute has been pushed to the margins of people's memories, if not completely obscured, by the 1956 Suez Affair. Then, the British resort to force, resulting in part from the portrayal of President Nasser by Anthony Eden (prime minister, 1955–57) as another dangerous and unappeasable dictator in the Hitler mould, failed to reverse Egypt's nationalization of the Suez Canal Company, let alone achieve the projected regime change.

As outlined in Chapter 1, the Suez Crisis has been presented frequently as a formative moment in Britain's post-1945 history and figured prominently in declinist historiography. In this vein, David Goldsworthy observed that, though lack of economic strength, nationalist pressures within the empire, and growing reliance upon the USA were already apparent as forces driving British policy, 'at no stage up to the time of Suez did *all* these relevant factors come together in a way that might cause Britain serious difficulty in its imperial role'.[9] "Suez" became also an enduring element in British political vocabulary employed repeatedly, even today, to frame contemporary political controversies. By contrast, "Abadan" strikes no real political chord today. Even worse, the 1951 Abadan crisis, like the history of Britain's troubled relationship with Iran, is normally glossed over in histories and international relations texts, excepting several publications by William Roger Louis and a spate of recent studies prompted in part by the release of files previously subject to extended closure.[10]

What was the Abadan crisis? Why does it rate a stop *en route* from Munich to Suez? Following Goldsworthy, did the Abadan crisis pre-empt the Suez dispute in highlighting the mounting pressures upon British power, even serving as a kind of dress rehearsal for 1956? In brief, the Abadan dispute came to a head in May 1951, when Mohammad Mossadegh's government nationalized the Iranian oil industry and took over the assets of the Anglo-Iranian Oil Company (AIOC), including the British government's majority shareholding therein. Escalating tension, punctuated by abortive diplomatic initiatives, culminated in the refinery's closure (31 July) and eventual British evacuation of the Abadan refinery (3 October).[11] Anglo-Iranian diplomatic relations were ruptured in October 1952. In August 1953 Mossadegh's fall from power, arising from a covert Central Intelligence Agency (CIA) and British Military Intelligence Section 6 (MI6) operation ushering in the dictatorship of Mohammad Reza Shah, prepared the way for the resumption of diplomatic relations (December 1953) and the Anglo-Iranian settlement secured in August 1954. Iran's oil industry remained nationalized, but henceforth effective control was exercised by an international consortium, including five American oil companies, but leaving the AIOC (renamed British Petroleum, 1954) as the largest single stakeholder with a 40 per cent holding.

Anthony Eden, who took over as Foreign Secretary in the new Churchill Government (1951–55) soon after the evacuation of Abadan, admitted that the resulting settlement was far from perfect, but marked nevertheless 'a remarkable improvement on what might have been expected three years before'.[12] Profits were shared 50/50 between the Iranian government and the consortium, so that the AIOC (BP) continued to benefit financially from Iranian oil, while receiving compensation for 'surrendering' most of its holding. Nevertheless, the new consortium arrangements, alongside its influence over the Shah, marked a substantial advance in America's position in the Middle East in general and in Iran in particular, and led many to see the USA as the real winner of the Anglo-Iranian dispute, at least in the short term.

For Sir Roger Stevens, who went to Teheran as British ambassador in 1954, the Abadan dispute was one of the more serious of the kaleidoscopic problems facing the British government during the decade or so following the end of the Second World War: 'the Persian Oil question became, during those years, the dominant international question after the cold war itself'.[13] Historians might interpret things more circumspectly, but there is no denying the fact that the resulting crisis proved a major test of post-1945 British power and influence. For *The Times*, the evacuation of Abadan proved 'a humiliating defeat'. *The Daily Telegraph* agreed: 'From today, the word Abadan passes as a common noun into the vocabulary of national humiliation.'[14] According to Rohan Butler, the Foreign Office historian, withdrawal resulted from 'one of the heaviest decisions taken by any British Government since the close of the Second World War'.[15] Apart from the fact that the AIOC's Abadan refinery represented – to quote Butler – 'the greatest single British investment overseas', Iranian oil exerted substantial impacts upon the British economy, the balance of payments, gold and dollar reserves, and government revenue through taxation and AIOC dividends. For the Treasury, the vital importance of Iranian oil precluded any break point in negotiations with Iran.[16]

According to William Roger Louis, 'there was much to be learned from the Persian oil crisis'.[17] Indeed, on 5 October 1951, *The Times* used Britain's withdrawal from Abadan to draw attention to serious 'Faults in diplomacy':

> An opportunity of learning from mistakes rarely presents itself on this scale.... It is not a failure that Britain can afford to repeat.... The cumulative evidence of failure is so great that an urgent case clearly arises for the relevant documents on the dispute to be given to the country in the fullest possible form.... It is not for the sake of finding scapegoats that these matters need to be made clear; the lessons of a muddle have to be learned so what happened in Persia will not be allowed to happen – as it could easily happen – elsewhere.[18]

For historians, the resulting crisis yields revealing insights into a wide range of issues: post-1945 British policy, power and global role, including the constraints imposed upon policymakers by such factors as Britain's declining military capabilities and the United Nations; the longstanding controversy about appeasement, Munich and warmongering; the problematic Anglo-Iranian relationship; the evolving Anglo-American relationship; the clandestine activities of the CIA and MI6; the emerging challenge of nationalism; the strategic role of oil diplomacy; the growing frailties of the British economy; the interface between big business and government; the World Bank's attempt to act as 'a global corporatist manager of international economic relations' offering an alternative approach to international diplomacy; the contrasting foreign policy priorities of British political parties and government departments;

the BBC's role in British government propaganda; and the outcome of the October 1951 General Election, as Clement Attlee's Labour administration gave way in the midst of the Abadan crisis to Winston Churchill's Conservative government.[19]

Butler's history

Following Wm. Roger Louis, there was much to be learned by British policymakers, as demonstrated in 1959 when the Abadan dispute was selected by the Foreign Office as the subject of an experimental internal history designed less to record what happened but rather to test the value of history as a formal input to the policymaking process. As such, the resulting study, pre-dating Parsons's 1979 exercise in learning from the Anglo-Iranian past, offers useful insights informing any appraisal of the case for and against the systematic use of history in the everyday work of government.

The history was the work of Rohan Butler, who had been working part-time for the Foreign Office since 1944 and was currently the senior editor (1955–65) of the *DBFP* series. Butler's part-time status – he was a Fellow of All Souls, Oxford (1938–84) – gave him a foothold in both academia and government.[20] His history was far from being a Foreign Office initiative. Rather it represented a departmental response to Brook's 1957 "funding experience" proposal.[21] In fact, one of the few positive departmental reactions emanated from the Foreign Office, where the question was taken up in April 1958 by the Steering Committee.[22]

The Foreign Office's historical activities

Chaired by Sir Frederick Hoyer Millar, the PUS (1957–62), the Foreign Office's Steering Committee evaluated Brook's proposal in the light of the historical work already undertaken within the department. Like other Whitehall departments, the Foreign Office codified precedents concerning standard administrative procedures appertaining to, say, the presentation of an ambassador's letters of credence, the rupture of diplomatic relations, or the evacuation of British nationals. In addition, the Research department, managed by the Director of Research and Librarian, met requests for information, including historical background, on current and future work.[23] Its utility was aptly summarized in evidence submitted to the Plowden Committee in 1963 by the Foreign Office branch of the Institution of Professional Civil

Servants (IPCS): 'The rapid turnover of officers in the political and functional Departments is such that only rarely is an officer in these Departments in charge of the same duties for more than a couple of years. Departments in consequence lack what may be called medium-term memory.'[24] However, as the IPCS reported, much of its historical work was concerned with furnishing *ad hoc* background for ongoing problems – the Guatemala/British Honduras dispute was cited as one example – rather than the routine funding of past experience in the way advocated by Brook in 1957. As William Wallace noted, 'The Foreign Office Research department has not been able to re-examine assumptions about international developments, because its status has been too low and its main function has been to provide background material for policy departments.'[25] Even worse, during the late 1950s, 'it remained physically separated from the policy departments, its different sections scattered on either side of the Thames'.

By contrast, publication figured prominently in the Foreign Office's historical activities. Pointing to the nineteenth-century *Blue Books* and the *British and Foreign State Papers* dating back to the mid-1820s, the Foreign Office claimed to have a longer tradition of historical publication than most other Whitehall departments.[26] Following the Second World War, its publications policy, though intended in part to provide a historical record and to meet the professional needs of historians, among others, was designed principally to give a wide audience at home and abroad an informed, hopefully sympathetic, understanding of British foreign policy: 'The aim of the Foreign Office in the field of historical publication must be to secure a truthful presentation of British foreign policy which will carry the greatest possible weight and conviction with the public at home and abroad.'[27]

Building upon the *Documents on the Origins of the War, 1898–1914* (1926–38), during the post-1945 period the Foreign Office prioritized edited collections of archival documents published in the *DBFP* series. As Cecil Parrott, the Director of Research and Librarian, noted in 1960, 'It has been official policy to disclose the course of British foreign policy in time of peace, not by a series of narrative histories, but by means of a published series of documents from our archives.'[28] Rohan Butler, who succeeded Llewellyn Woodward as senior editor in 1955, presented the *DBFP* as offering readers 'a balanced view of British foreign policy'.[29] As an Oxford-based academic, Butler felt justified in claiming that the series, edited by university-based 'independent historians' working part-time for the Foreign Office, was accepted within academia for its reliability and accuracy as a historical record, even representing the 'objective basis of historical truth'. Furthermore, he saw the *DBFP* series as meeting the preference of historians for the actual documents as opposed to 'an official write-up' thereupon.

Of course, Butler's claims glossed over the fact that the *DBFP* represented an *edited selection* of documents. In fact, the deliberate exclusion of Foreign Office minutes and memoranda meant that the series merely recorded the nature and conduct of British diplomacy. As Woodward admitted, there was *no intention* of publishing a documentary account of the process of British foreign policy in the making.[30] Moreover, the series presented the British side of the story, thereby proving – to quote Woodward – 'a good corrective' to existing histories.[31] Indeed, for some commentators, the series was more concerned with propagating a propagandist message. Typically A.J.P. Taylor, who saw the *DBFP* as having 'the deliberate purpose of vindicating the British foreign service', emerged as one of the sharpest critics.[32]

The Foreign Office's preference for the *DBFP*-type format was reinforced by concern about the perceived ability of official histories to harm British foreign policy interests. The long-running saga centred upon Woodward's history of British foreign policy during the Second World War merely reaffirmed this belief. During the late 1950s, Woodward's five-volume official history, commissioned during the early 1940s and completed in the mid-1950s, was still awaiting the removal of the ruling against publication made in December 1950 by Attlee, the prime minister (1945–51).[33] When starting work upon the project, Woodward recognized that the history was unlikely to be cleared for publication 'for a very long time to come' because of the predictable, yet understandable, anxieties of policymakers about its potential for exerting adverse impacts upon *present-day British relations* with France, the Soviet Union and the USA, among other countries.[34] Even so, this did not prevent Woodward venting his frustrations about the ruling's impact:

> This policy of carefully locking our own stable door while all the American and French horses are gaily let out to do their circus tricks is a great mistake... we lose politically not a little by leaving students, journalists and everyone else to get their detailed accounts of our wartime diplomacy mainly from American writers.[35]

By this time, that is 1956, Woodward had moved from Oxford to Princeton in the USA, where he complained about being exposed to 'so much nonsense about British policy'.

Nor did the passage of time enhance the prospects for early publication. In 1958 de Gaulle's return to power in France accentuated concerns arising from the history's 'exceedingly critical' coverage of his wartime role.[36] Indeed, Gladwyn Jebb, the British ambassador in Paris, feared that the publication of such 'explosive material' would prompt an anti-British campaign in France.[37] Parrott agreed that it 'might cause damage to Anglo-French relations if an official history of British Foreign Policy were published which exposed the French president and national figurehead to considerable criticism, if not sometimes ridicule'.[38] Wartime references to the abdication of Reza Shah of Iran and the accession of the current Shah offered further cause for anxiety.

Despite Woodward's hopes that his study would be published within a decade of its completion in 1956, or at least within his lifetime, the book was not cleared for publication until 1970–72 in the wake of the accelerated release of Second World War files.[39] Even then, approval for publication was sought first from Attlee and Eden, now Lord Avon, as former ministers actively involved in the wartime period. In the event, Woodward, who died in March 1971, lived only long enough to see the first volume in print, even if he was still revising the text for publication during the weeks immediately preceding his death.[40]

Progressing Butler's history

When taking up Brook's "funding experience" proposal in April 1958, the Steering Committee acknowledged the relatively limited amount of historical work already undertaken within the Foreign Office, particularly for internal use as opposed to publication. A background paper, prepared by Robin Hooper, guided members about the value of doing more, and particularly to contemplate moving on to fund experience for use within the Foreign Office in a more systematic manner:

> Looking back can be a salutary exercise. If we could spare the time or the staff we should probably derive great benefit from examining in retrospect the accuracy of the information on which policy was based and the correctness of the conclusions drawn from it.[41]

As Hooper pointed out, 'there may be issues... when past experience can be a useful guide to recurrent problems. For example, the Persian oil crisis was a major trouble which may one day be followed by others sufficiently similar to make its history relevant to their handling.' Acknowledging the proposal's merits, alongside the problems consequent upon staff mobility and short official memories, the committee accepted the case for action on a historical topic yet to be agreed.

Subsequently Hoyer Millar commissioned Rohan Butler to undertake a 'pilot project', with particular reference to assessing the extent to which the Foreign Office's original forecasts and judgements stood the test of time. The resulting request for suggestions from departmental heads for recent cases of which 'historical accounts might be useful in the future' prompted a 'voluminous list of subjects', many of which were dismissed as 'not practicable'.[42] Following a review led by Parrott, a seven-topic shortlist – subjects included the 1950–53 Korean War, the 1951 Abadan crisis and the 1954 Geneva conference on Indochina – was placed before the Steering Committee in February 1959. Looking back, the 1956 Suez Affair seems a notable omission, but, as Butler himself noted subsequently, the time was not yet right for even a confidential internal history of this event because of its continued high sensitivity in both political and official circles.[43]

In the event, the Steering Committee selected Abadan. Described as involving 'a complex concentration and critical balance of factors, political, economic, juridical and military', the topic promised to yield 'a particularly instructive case history'.[44] The fact that the committee had devoted a large proportion of its time during the previous year to redefining British policy towards the Middle East reinforced the case for the choice of Abadan, especially as Selwyn Lloyd, the Foreign Secretary (1955–60), devoted close attention to the policy draft's coverage of Iran.[45] Significantly, this topic, quite apart from its mention in Hooper's background paper, was favoured also by Butler; thus, his covering note attached to the shortlist to guide the Steering Committee's selection process stated that this project promised to be 'important, revealing and not too dispersed from point of view of treatment'.[46]

The Abadan history

In March 1962 Butler completed what had proved a challenging, often difficult, research study entitled 'British Policy in the Relinquishment of Abadan in 1951'.[47] The time taken to complete the project, though partly explained by its size, reflected also the fact that Butler, a fellow of All Souls and Sub-Warden (1961–63), worked only part-time for the Foreign Office, principally on the *DBFP* series.

Despite claiming to approach the topic like any other academic historian, Butler acknowledged his functional role in giving practical effect to both the 'expressed intentions' of Brook's "funding experience" initiative and the brief set by the Steering Committee.[48] From this perspective, the concluding section covering the lessons to be learned from the historical narrative was of central importance. Recalling Woodward's assertion that 'while history does not repeat itself, historical situations do recur', Butler urged caution when using the history, especially as hindsight rendered it easy to appear wise after the event. Account had to be taken also of an ever-changing international context.

> To attempt to reduce this to too rigid an exercise would, I fear, be unduly mechanistic and unrealistic in view of the complexity of ever-shifting diplomatic problems, of their particularly high political content by comparison with the work of most other Government departments, and of the tiresome fact that diplomacy deals with foreigners not subject to the authority of the Secretary of State.[49]

The history, totalling 324 pages, was rather long, but according to Butler, a more concise approach would have reduced its utility by oversimplifying and distorting complex issues relating to, say, the evaluation of alternative policy options, the decision-making process and the lessons to be learned. Nevertheless, an awareness of the pressures upon busy policymakers led Butler to signpost key points for readers through headers as well as to codify the lessons in a 16-page concluding section cross-referenced to the text. Rejecting the use of oral testimony because of time pressures, Butler's research was based largely upon Foreign Office records supplemented by limited use of Cabinet Office files, *Hansard* and press sources.[50] Even so, and contrary to his initial expectations, relevant departmental documentation was withheld, thereby prompting Butler 'as a matter of historical principle, to disclaim in advance all responsibility for all errors or omissions of fact or inference due to this cause'.[51] The fact that his history glossed over the 1953 coup suggests that intelligence files came into this 'top secret' category.[52] Nor was he allowed access to the records of the Ministry of Fuel and Power and the Treasury, other departments prominent in the Abadan crisis. Inevitably, the archives of the AIOC, like the American, Iranian and other governments, were closed to him.[53]

The lessons to be learned

Butler's conclusions prioritized 'political' and 'administrative' lessons. Glossing over 'personal' issues, he left readers to draw their own conclusions about the performance of individual ministers and officials.

Nevertheless, Butler took the opportunity to identify the apparent correlation between bureaucratic shortcomings and staff inexperience as well as to stress the need for high quality recruits to the Foreign Service. His conclusions were numerous and often overlapped, but for the sake of study the principal lessons can be categorized under six headers (Box 10.1).

Box 10.1 The lessons of Butler's history

> (i) the revelation of Britain's declining power and capacity for independent action, including a growing dependence upon the USA;
> (ii) the decision not to use force undermined images of British power and prestige;
> (iii) policymakers failed to respond to Britain's 'changed circumstances';
> (iv) the failure to adopt a proactive strategy allowed the Iranian government to set the agenda;
> (v) the need for a range of methodological improvements;
> (vi) administrative reforms were required to deal with a crisis situation.

First, the Abadan crisis, ranking alongside the 1956 Suez Crisis as a major British foreign policy reverse, revealed Britain's relative weakness in power, as evidenced by its declining capacity for independent action and growing dependence upon the USA. The American government proved a 'heavy power-factor' impacting upon British policy:

> One is left with the impression that if a mark of the greatest among great Powers be the capacity to influence the government of smaller Powers by its extreme displeasure then, in relation to Persia, that greatest Power, over against Russia, was now the United States and no longer Great Britain as in the days of her recently relinquished Indian Empire.[54]

Iranian intransigence meant that 'probably, as came to be recognised in the Foreign Office, only British military force could at the last, have prevented the abandonment of Abadan'.[55] But the military option, whether in the form of large ('Operation Buccaneer') or small-scale (movement of warships) operations, was repeatedly rejected. Nevertheless, in public, the Labour government assumed a strong, even 'rigid', stance towards Abadan. Responding to Harold Macmillan's challenge, on 30 July 1951, Attlee reassured Parliament that 'our intention is not to evacuate entirely'.[56] One day later, Lord Jowitt, the Lord Chancellor, reaffirmed that 'we accept *all the implications* that follow from this decision'.[57] In reality, the Attlee government had no intention of standing by its words. For example, on 7 September the prime minister undermined the force of parliamentary reassurances when writing that 'we should not threaten to use force unless we mean to do so and *we do not* [author's emphasis]'.[58] A few weeks later, on 27 September, Attlee told the Cabinet that 'he did not think it would be expedient to use force to maintain the British staff in Abadan'.[59] By contrast, the hawkish stance assumed by Herbert Morrison, the Foreign Secretary (1951), elicited minimal support within the Cabinet, as evidenced by the way in which Hugh Dalton, the Minister of Local Government and Planning, dismissed Morrison as a 'bloody little fool' handicapped by a 'political blind spot on this'.[60]

Throughout a fundamental lack of power in the region, and especially the dearth of adequate forces readily available for action, was paramount in government thinking: 'British economic and political weakness after the Second World War spelt British weakening in the Middle East.'[61] Pointing to the dispatch of troops based in India to protect British interests in Iran in July 1946, Butler claimed that Indian independence (1947) was also relevant: 'the decline of the British Empire, notably in India, lay behind the Abadan Crisis'.[62] For Attlee, strong American opposition to the use of force strengthened the case for restraint. In the Cabinet, Hugh Gaitskell, the Chancellor of the Exchequer, pointed to 'how much we needed them [i.e. USA] on Defence, Dollar, etc' by way of support for Attlee's caution: 'we couldn't afford to go agst. U.S. on this'.[63] For Butler, the 'effective lack of American support for British policy... underlay the whole development of the crisis in 1951' in terms of inclining the British government to reject the military option.[64]

Even worse, the US government's attitude facilitated 'the Persian game of playing Great Britain off against the United States'. Whereas British policymakers prioritized the maintenance of control over Iranian oil, their American counterparts, though not unaffected by either US oil interests or Iran's anti-imperial rhetoric, adopted a Cold War paradigm towards the issue. The Korean War, reinforcing Washington's tendency to view Iran primarily as a potential ally, ensured that the British government was 'more immediately influenced by pressure from the American government' to appease, not oppose, Iran.[65] The last thing that the American government wanted in 1951 was British military action launched against a potential ally.

In time, the resolution of the Abadan crisis, including the 1953 CIA/MI6 coup overthrowing Mossadegh in 1953, was facilitated by closer Anglo-American cooperation – for Eden, it resulted also from curing the Americans of their 'Mussadeq mania' – but this failed to disguise the way in which events revealed serious tensions in the "special relationship" arising in part from a growing divergence of interest in the Middle East.[66] Contrasting, frequently conflicting, approaches assumed towards events in Iran meant that the Abadan crisis illuminated the limits of the "special relationship" being forged between Britain and the USA. From this perspective, the crisis has often been interpreted as a dress rehearsal for the rift occasioned by the 1956 Suez Affair in terms of indicating the possibility of not only Anglo-American disagreement over the Middle East but also American opposition to unilateral British action therein.[67] In this manner, the Abadan dispute revealed the ongoing transformation in the post-1945 balance of power, including the growing dependence of Britain upon the USA, even in traditional spheres of interest, like the Middle East. As such, this episode marked a further stage in Britain's declining capacity for independent action, following on from, say, the way in which the USA, acting through the Truman Doctrine (March 1947), filled the gap left by Britain's retreat from its commitments in Greece and Turkey.

Secondly, the failure to use force, compounded by media coverage of the evacuation of Abadan, undermined images of British power and prestige in the world as a whole and in the Middle East in particular: 'The relative British decline and American ascendancy in the Middle East generally (e.g. Saudi Arabia, Palestine, Greece, Turkey) extended to Persia and underlay the Abadan Crisis.'[68] Quoting from Eden's recently published memoirs to the effect that 'the troubles fomented on the Shatt al Arab, festered on the Nile', Butler saw events in Iran as stimulating 'strong political currents' working against British interests throughout the region, but beginning in Egypt: 'The gravest and most prompt repercussion of the British eviction from Abadan occurred in Egypt with special significance for the British position on the Suez Canal.'[69] Within days of leaving Abadan, the British government was confronted by Egypt's denunciation of the 1936 Anglo-Egyptian Treaty as well as serious unrest in the Suez Canal zone.[70] Reporting from Baghdad, Sir John Troutbeck remarked that images of the British allowing themselves to be pushed around by Iran did little for Britain's standing in Iraq.[71] Unsurprisingly, during 1950–51, the Conservative party, when in opposition, found it easy to criticize the consequences of the Attlee government's policy of drift in a manner implying that it would have done better if in power throughout the period. Thus, speaking at an Empire Day rally in May 1951, Eden attacked the government's shortcomings in Egypt, Korea and Iran in emotive terms: 'That was appeasement at its worst. We had been pushed around a little too much of late.... We should call a halt to that process.'[72]

Thirdly, despite rejecting force, policymakers were adjudged guilty of failing to adjust to the 'changed circumstances' of the post-1945 world, while doing little to exploit Britain's vital role in the Cold War:

> It may be that in 1950–51 the background of British power and prestige (e.g. Second World War, Indian Empire) was too close to permit a full adjustment to changed circumstances wherein Great Britain might need to reinforce her position of strength in relation to lesser Powers such as Persia by exploiting the techniques of bargaining from weakness with greater Powers such as the United States. Hence, perhaps, the impression sometimes that British policy regarding Persia was at once too rigid and too weak.[73]

According to Butler, Washington's Cold War preoccupations should have been used as leverage to ensure that American pressure was exerted upon Iran, not Britain, to do the appeasing. Of course, it is always easier to identify trends and lessons after the event, particularly as compared to politicians and officials confronted by present-day pressures and weighed down by inertia, but, as happened with the Suez Crisis, the Abadan dispute raised serious questions about how far British policymakers understood and were keeping pace with what was happening in a fast-moving world.

Fourthly, the crisis revealed the failure of British policymakers to adopt a proactive strategy. Notwithstanding the occasional use of robust language by ministers, the impression of drift and indecision allowed the Iranian government to set the agenda: 'British policy often seemed to be waiting upon, or catching up with, Persian propulsion of events.'[74] Despite accepting Strang's maxim that normally it was preferable to make no agreement than to make a bad one, Butler concluded that the 'precarious' situation confronting the Attlee government in September 1951, when only the 'extreme alternatives' of withdrawal from Abadan or the eviction of Mossadegh remained, exposed the 'bankruptcy' of British policy.[75] For Butler, drift, compounded by inertia, proved a function of the Labour government's small parliamentary majority; the lengthy illness of Ernest Bevin, the Foreign Secretary (1945–51), including the 'especially heavy burden placed upon [Sir William] Strang', the PUS at the Foreign Office; the inadequacies of Herbert Morrison, Bevin's successor; the contrasting perspectives adopted by the Treasury, the Ministry of Fuel and Power, and the Foreign Office; and the lack of support from Washington.[76] Nor during the formative stages of the crisis was the British government helped by its uneasy relationship with the AIOC, which was viewed and presented by Iranians increasingly as a reactionary instrument of British imperialism. Within this context, Butler lamented the relative lack of political control exercised over what he described as an 'independently minded' company engaged in activities which were not only capable of exerting substantial impacts upon British power and prestige but also adjudged of vital importance to British economic performance.[77] In particular, the company failed to acknowledge the need to adopt an alternative strategy allowing Iran a more equitable share of profits along the lines of Aramco's 50–50 deal with Saudi Arabia (December 1950).

Equally worrying was the Foreign Office's relative lack of influence within Whitehall, so that the international dimension was rarely treated seriously enough during the crucial early phase of the dispute. The varying agendas, contrasting perspectives and rivalries of the Treasury, Ministry of Fuel and Power, and the Foreign Office meant that no consensus existed within Whitehall about either the nature of the problem or the most appropriate way forward. Was Iranian nationalization an economic, financial and technical issue, as argued by the Treasury and Ministry of Fuel and Power, or an international political question, as claimed by the Foreign Office? Initially, Whitehall treated Abadan more as a technical and economic issue rather than as a matter of diplomacy and high policy, as evidenced by the lead role assumed initially by the Working Party on Persian Oil, chaired by the Treasury.[78] This problem was not remedied until the change of government brought in Eden as Foreign Secretary in late October 1951, that is after the relinquishment of Abadan. Even worse, the British government showed itself incapable of responding effectively to the nationalist movement emerging in Iran, let alone dealing with political leaders like Mossadegh, 'a demagogic xenophobe and fanatical eccentric' skilled at mobilizing popular support, using the UN as a global platform, and playing upon the USA's Cold War angst.[79] Whatever the reason, British governments failed to develop policies adjudged capable of managing change in a world where the growing challenge from lesser powers was compounded, as in the case of Iran, by aggressive anti-British nationalism.

Fifthly, the British failure to consider *in advance* a range of alternative strategies in the event of the AIOC's nationalization revealed a range of methodological shortcomings, most notably a fundamental lack of intelligence, research, forward thinking and contingency planning. For Butler, the Teheran embassy's lack of reliable local contacts, fragmentary grasp of the Iranian nationalist movement, and difficult relationship with its American counterpart meant that policymakers were handicapped by an inadequate information base upon which to make decisions. This failing was compounded during the actual crisis when 'action under pressure' and 'the endless rustle of the in-tray' allowed officials 'little or no time for philosophic brooding upon the heavy issues' or looking 'back to historical precedents and warnings or forward to the remoter but in the long run possibly more important implications and consequences of immediate action'.[80] Hence, the micawberite tendency to muddle through, not control, the crisis.

Finally, the fast-moving nature of events tested the performance of the administrative 'machine' in time of crisis, when ideally both the government as a whole and individual departments should prove – to quote Morrison – 'as efficient as a military operation in war'.[81] Bureaucratic shortcomings revealed in his Abadan history included the Foreign Office's failure to prepare adequate briefing historical memoranda providing background on, say, the constitutional relationship between the government and the AIOC or the growing pressure building up in Iran for the nationalization of oil. Seeking to overcome this problem, Butler advocated the appointment of 'continuity men', combining the tasks of historians with those of planners, with time and space to 'look around, back to historical precedents and warnings' as well as to engage more effectively in forward and contingency planning.[82] In particular, they would assume responsibility for reviewing the department's handling of any recently concluded crisis in order to judge performance and to fund experience for future use. More seriously, Butler highlighted surprising delays in dealing with urgent dispatches. Reportedly, one dispatch, sent by the British ambassador in Teheran on 31 December 1950 and received in the Foreign Office on 4 January 1951, was not seen by the head of the Eastern department until 24 January! Such examples led Butler to recommend procedural improvements, like placing the Foreign Office on "Crisis Alert" in order to prioritize important and urgent communications through the addition of more streamlined procedures.

Conclusion

When Butler completed his history during the early 1960s, Robert McNamara was the US Secretary of Defense (1961–68). Looking back in 2003 to a period when he performed an influential role in international affairs serving both Presidents Kennedy and Johnston, McNamara opined that 'My rule has been to try to learn. Try to understand what happened. Develop the lessons and pass them on.'[83] Of course, as McNamara's detractors have claimed, it is easy to present oneself as a 'Mr I-have-all-the-answers', and hence to overlook both the challenge of making sense of past experience and the risks of identifying the wrong lessons. Much depends also upon the next stage, that is incorporating the lessons into the policy process as the basis for discussion, perhaps even for action and implementation. In practice, this process proved far from straightforward, most notably because of the ever-changing domestic and international context. As Herbert Morrison discovered when Foreign Secretary in 1951, 'one never knows what will turn up at the Foreign Office. Other countries often shape the agenda.'[84] More seriously, there remained the fundamental practical difficulty of introducing historical inputs formally and systematically into the policymaking process.

As a result, when Rohan Butler handed over his history to the Foreign Office in March 1962, several question marks remained about its use. After all, when commissioned, the history was not intended to be treated primarily as an account of what happened, when and why, with a view to being filed away in the archives as a possible reference resource at some future date. Rather it was intended as a pilot case study investigating the value of using history to fund experience as a working tool in the foreign policy process. The nature of the readership was equally significant. Would Butler's history, particularly its conclusions, reach only a few medium-ranking officials or would it impact upon the thinking of senior officials, including the PUS, perhaps even making waves extending at least as far as the Foreign Secretary?

In many respects, past experience was not encouraging. Although 1962 saw the publication of an abridged and heavily sanitized version of Woodward's official diplomatic history of the Second World War, the five-volume version was still awaiting clearance. As Woodward had already complained, his vast history, including its lessons, was destined to 'be locked in the archives for goodness knows how long'.[85] In theory, copies were available for confidential use by policymakers, but from experience of working for the Foreign Office, 'I very much doubt whether any of the senior members of the Department who might have access to a copy will ever read it – I expect the copies will go into the same dusty cupboard as my history of the origins of the war.'[86] Would Butler's history suffer the same fate?

11
Using Butler's Abadan History to Reappraise British Foreign Policy

In Autumn 1962, Lord Home's advocacy of the case for adopting a 'modern edition of British foreign policy' reflected the ongoing questioning of British policies and methods in the wake of the Suez debacle, the retreat from empire, the debate about British entry to the Common Market, economic setbacks, and the growing gap between power and commitments.[1] For Rohan Butler, Home's period as Foreign Secretary (1960–63) brought a new sense of mission to British foreign policy, most notably as articulated in a speech he delivered in Autumn 1962:

> I believe that we hide our head in the sand if we do not recognise that when we deliberately shed an empire we shed with it a lot of wealth, influence and power. I believe that the knowledge of this, which has been felt throughout the nation, has accounted very largely for the unsureness of the nation and the discontent which I have observed in recent years, because although people recognised the facts, they did not see how to redress the balance.[2]

Inevitably, during 1963–64 this broader debate about Britain's changing role in the world framed the Foreign Office's response to Butler's Abadan history, while helping to explain why exchanges thereupon were overtaken increasingly by a broader reappraisal of British foreign policies and methods rather than an in-depth concentration on the Anglo-Iranian dimension.

Initial responses to Butler's history

Despite gaining strong praise from officials allowed an early read in 1962, there was no intention of giving Butler's history a wide circulation in the Foreign Office, let alone Whitehall. Only 100 copies were printed in September 1962 for 'confidential official use' within the Foreign Office as well as for circulation to selected embassies (e.g. Washington, Paris, Teheran, Kuwait, Cairo, Baghdad) and missions (UN, NATO), as well as a few Whitehall departments.[3]

Notwithstanding its limited distribution, Butler's history exerted a far from insubstantial impact upon policymakers. Generally speaking, most readers acknowledged its utility, most notably in stimulating rethinking about past events and looking forward with the benefit of past experience. Revisiting the 1950s prompted several readers to go beyond the Anglo-Iranian past to reappraise Britain's current international position alongside future courses of action adjudged capable of enabling Britain – to quote Butler's history – 'to regain a larger measure of initiative in her foreign policy'.[4] Commentaries, drawing frequently upon personal memories of the actual crisis or a recent posting in Teheran, reflected also a growing appreciation of the shifting balance of power in the Middle East during the past decade. Moreover, Butler's grasp of the Iranian scene and personalities won praise from officials who had returned recently from Teheran.[5]

In many respects, the tone of departmental responses was set by Roger Stevens, a deputy PUS, who welcomed Butler's 'extremely interesting' paper as offering 'valuable lessons for Whitehall and for the administration of this office'.[6] The fact that Stevens had been chosen as ambassador following the resumption of diplomatic relations with Iran in December 1953 imparted an extra significance to his comment. Likewise, a lengthy minute, written by Frederick Mason, the head of the Foreign Office's Economic Relations department, praised Butler's history as 'a most valuable document, not only for its substance but for the lessons it draws'.[7] For Mason, three key points emerged from Butler's story. First, the Attlee government's narrow parliamentary majority and ailing Foreign Secretary impacted adversely upon 'the vigour of our approach'. Secondly, the AIOC did 'not come well out of this account'. Finally, 'the whole story is full of *the lesson that Her Majesty's Government can no longer act on their own in major matters* [author's emphasis] of this kind', particularly given the constraints imposed by the USA upon British policy:

> If anyone ever doubted the paralysing effect which United States actions had on the negotiations, this history is there to dispel such doubts. Again and again our actions were frustrated by American warnings, threats and above all by their day to day interference

and attempts to mediate or influence one side or the other.... Our Ministers and negotiators are constantly complaining that if only the Americans would do nothing at all for a while, we might be able to get on with the negotiating job.... The Americans, by their interferences, and the Russians, by doing nothing at all, gave the Iranians their opportunity to play us off against each other.

Mason moved on to highlight the time taken by the American government to realize the futility of supporting Mossadegh, the impact of the 'disastrous Mr. Grady', the US ambassador in Teheran, and the readiness of American oil companies to profit from Britain's misfortune. Indeed, he feared that, if published, Butler's history would revive strong anti-American feelings in Britain, possibly reversing the post-Suez improvement in the relationship. At the same time, Mason pressed the case for a sense of perspective when discussing the 'great shift of power' in the Middle East after 1945, since experience of living in post-Abadan Iran – he had returned recently from a four-year posting therein – revealed evidence of growing anti-American hostility.[8] Paradoxically, the 1956 Suez debacle might be interpreted as helping Britain's position therein: 'Suez emphasised that our teeth had now been drawn and that the Iranians had nothing more to fear from us.' Nor was Mason disinterested in the organizational aspects covered by Butler's study concerning, say, the need in any fast-moving international political crisis for the Foreign Office to assume the lead role in any interdepartmental machinery or the case for moving onto a 'war footing' capable of dealing with developments in an efficient and expeditious manner.

Impressed by the memorandum's value in illuminating contemporary realities and offering meaningful discussion points for policymakers, Harold Caccia, Hoyer Millar's successor as PUS (1962–65), asked Lord Strang, who had served as PUS (1949–53) during the Abadan dispute, to review Butler's history in order to 'draw what lessons he can both as to the conduct of affairs in the circumstances of the time, and as to the possible bearing of these lessons upon the conduct of affairs in the circumstances of today'.[9] In addition, Caccia forwarded Butler's concluding section to Lord Home, who found the lessons a 'very interesting' read. Undoubtedly, his attentiveness – Home, trusting that 'we are better geared to an emergency now', indicated his willingness to discuss any issues raised therein – reflected also his recent involvement in the Cuban missiles crisis (October 1962) and active role in publicly articulating the lessons thereof.[10] Following receipt of the Foreign

Secretary's comments, Caccia asked Strang to investigate also the case for any special administrative preparations.[11]

Meanwhile, Caccia used the Christmas holiday break to look again at Butler's study, and particularly to re-read the illuminating, often 'cogent', conclusions.[12] In his view, the outcome fully justified the time and effort required to produce the memorandum, even if recent events reaffirmed his reservations about the problematic nature of any attempt, no matter how well intentioned, to draw lessons from past events. For example, Caccia noted that the recent nationalization of the Burmah Oil Company's assets in Burma (now Myanmar) undermined the force of Butler's praise for this company's more enlightened approach as compared to that of the AIOC in Iran.[13] Notwithstanding such reservations, Caccia believed that Butler's 'Abadan history lends practical point' to ongoing discussions about the future course and methods of British foreign policy, such as those conducted by the Cabinet Future Planning Working Group (1962–64) or the Plowden Committee on representative services overseas.[14] Suspecting correctly that the Plowden report would recommend that the Foreign Office should adopt a stronger economic focus in future, Caccia deemed it prudent to reaffirm his department's pivotal role in speaking with authority on 'the political effects abroad of British activities'. As a result, he sent Lord Plowden a copy of the Butler's memorandum alongside a covering letter drawing attention to such issues.

Strang's commentary

Meanwhile in February 1963, that is soon after giving evidence to the Plowden Committee reflecting upon future developments in British diplomacy, Strang submitted an informed and thoughtful commentary on what he described as Butler's 'instructive case history'.[15] Indeed, his handwritten commentary amounted to 64 pages, or 44 pages when typed up![16] Furthermore, marginal and other notes written when reading the history – these comments did not always find their way into his final report – offer additional insights about his attitude.

Strang began by praising an extensive case study written by a historian whose 'profound understanding' and 'almost unrivalled acquaintance' with Foreign Office papers of the interwar years enhanced his 'study of a post-war episode of *lasting significance* [author's emphasis] in British foreign policy'.[17] Nor did Strang attempt to evaluate the pros and cons of British policy towards the Abadan issue, particularly as something was saved for Britain in the end through the consortium scheme. Despite his preparedness to identify lessons viewed 'in the circumstances of the time', Strang confessed diffidence about articulating their present-day relevance because of changes in both international affairs and departmental practice since his retirement. Strang admitted also that he had a personal case to answer in the sense that the Abadan crisis was only one of a number of questions requiring his attention as PUS; indeed, from May 1951 he conceded that, apart from the ongoing Korean War, his prime focus was the defection of Burgess and Maclean to the Soviet Union, not the Abadan crisis.[18] At the same time, Strang used recent events in Cuba to offer a sense of perspective about power in the modern world, when asking how much more successful the United States had been in preventing and securing redress for the confiscation of American property in Cuba: 'The Americans, so far at any rate, have in fact been less successful. Castro has not yet suffered the fate of Musaddiq.'[19]

On the whole, Strang found Butler's conclusions somewhat lengthy and written a 'shade pedantically', but basically sound, excepting an occasional problem of interpretation: 'Butler is hard to satisfy. If Persian proposals are accepted, this is a retreat. If they are rejected, this is a failure to negotiate. If we consult the Americans, we are waffling; if we do not, we are reckless.'[20] Responding to recent events, including the Cuban missiles crisis, Strang asserted that the key lesson centred upon the fact that 'US not UK the Great Power', so that 'The whole Abadan crisis bedevilled by US theory about Russia.'[21] Like Butler, he complained that in 1951 the British government failed to 'face America with grave consequences of breach between us' because of Washington's cultivation of Iran as a potential Cold War ally.[22]

Looking back, Strang recalled that Britain's failure to pursue 'an adroit and purposeful diplomacy' towards Iran largely reflected 'the lack of strong ministerial direction at the highest level', since the problems consequent upon Bevin's ill health were compounded by Morrison's inexperience of foreign affairs, ignorance of the historical dimension, and relative lack of ministerial authority.[23] As a result, as Strang recorded, the prime minister settled policy: 'In Mr. Attlee's mind, that course meant retreat rather than resort to force.'[24] For Strang, who believed at the time that only military force could have prevented British withdrawal, these policy weaknesses were remedied only after the General Election in October 1951, when Eden's assumption of the Foreign Secretaryship restored the Foreign Office's primacy over international issues.[25] Henceforth, a streamlined Ministerial Committee worked alongside a new interdepartmental Persian (Official) Committee, chaired by the Foreign Office, in place of the Working Party on Persian

Oil operating under the Treasury's chairmanship. Of course, Britain had already withdrawn from Abadan by this stage, but Eden's 'strong hand' and 'clear mind' helped secure what Strang saw as 'not a bad result' in the 1954 settlement.[26]

Churchill opened his party's 1951 General Election campaign at Liverpool with a speech blaming the Labour Government for the loss of Abadan, while implying that things would have developed differently if the Conservative Party had been in power since 1945.[27] Subsequently, Churchill complained that the British government 'had scuttled and run from Abadan when a splutter of musketry would have settled the matter'.[28] Whether or not a Churchill-led government would have made any difference remains debatable, but Strang opined that *stronger political direction* by the Foreign Office when dealing with other departments, the AIOC and foreign governments might 'have avoided some of the grosser humiliations which we had to suffer': 'When ministers know their own minds and can convey their policies to their officials, the advice tendered by the latter can be more securely based and more clearly expressed than where officials have to try to make up their Ministers' minds for them.'[29] Such quotes reflect the way in which Strang drew upon his experience as PUS to provide the 'personal conclusions' – he saw them as 'an essential element of any post mortem' – omitted by Butler.[30] For Strang, Butler's history established that 'the calibre of the Foreign Secretary himself does matter tremendously, and his relationship with the Prime Minister perhaps no less. He cannot get the best out of his officials, unless he can inspire, stimulate and control them'. Morrison, Strang believed, failed on all counts. Strang's praise for Eden, alongside implicit condemnation of his Labour predecessors, needs to be qualified however by Strang's strong admiration for Bevin *'in his prime'*.[31]

Looking ahead with history

Reviewing the past encouraged Strang also to look forward by way of advocating the serious re-think of both policies and methods adjudged necessary to enable Britain to play 'the active game of diplomacy' more effectively.[32] Building upon Butler's critique of the 'temper' in which British diplomacy had been conducted in 1951, Strang developed arguments outlined already in both his recent book entitled *Britain in World Affairs* (1961) – here, he compared the 'quiet tradition' of Castlereagh, Salisbury and Grey with the 'rumbustious tradition' associated with Canning and Palmerston – and oral evidence given to the Plowden Committee.[33] The perceived failure of a 'quiet' strategy in the Abadan crisis, viewed alongside indicators of declining power, imperial retreat and the fact that 'you can never be sure of complete US support', led Strang to use his closing paragraphs to speculate whether, 'in our present international situation', Britain could afford any longer to maintain existing foreign policies and methods. Was there a case, he asked, to give British diplomacy 'a new look', even bringing about 'a revolution' in policies and methods?[34] Pointing to de Gaulle's selfish independent course, he presented France as a possible role model. The alternative – Strang raised the spectre of 'international impotence' – was unwelcome, even unacceptable.

Strang's comments about Butler's 'administrative' conclusions were framed in part by his belief that the fundamental problem was more the lack of political leadership and will than departmental shortcomings.[35] Despite occasional failings, he believed that the Foreign Office had adapted well to the rapidly changing demands of the Abadan crisis, but would have done much better if allowed more influence in directing policy, particularly *vis à vis* the Treasury. Otherwise, Strang displayed a distinct lack of enthusiasm for Butler's proposed organizational reforms. Despite looking good on paper, they posed practical difficulties. For example, he feared that any 'continuity-men' would be drawn inevitably into day-to-day work, thereby qualifying their ability to undertake the dual role envisaged by Butler.[36] Likewise, long experience led Strang to observe that it would not be easy to decide when to give the department a 'war-look' by declaring a 'political alert'. Crises varied markedly in character. Some erupted suddenly, whereas others – Strang cited the case of the Abadan dispute stretching between 1947 and 1954 – developed gradually over a lengthy period of time, and rendered it difficult to decide when to call an alert. For Strang, Butler's proposed historical studies would 'supply a historian with evidence upon which to come to a judgment upon the formulation and conduct of our foreign policy. . . . The definition and analysis of a problem in its widest implications can be enlightening both for the writer and the reader.'[37] But he questioned whether such histories would possess real practical utility for policymakers.

Looking forward with history

Having already commented upon Butler's conclusions, Lord Home found Strang's commentary a stimulating and thought-provoking read:

> I am particularly interested in paragraph 73 to the end. Are we a bit too altruistic in our foreign policy? We could reach a point when

we are so careful to appease this or that interest that we have no recognisable line of our own and have no identity. That would mean that we would lose influence and authority and command no function in our own right. I would like you to give some thought to this danger of 'international impotence', paragraph 75.[38]

The Foreign Secretary's positive response and request for further 'thought', alongside the government's perceived need to consider alternative policy options in the wake of Britain's recent failure to join the Common Market (January 1963), led Caccia to reproduce the paragraph attracting Home's attention in the recently introduced monthly letter to heads of mission: 'While we are re-considering our methods rather than our long-term objectives, I would ask you to consider a thought which has been recently put to me by Lord Strang.'[39] Most of paragraph 75 followed:

Would it be possible to give our diplomacy a new look? The example is here before our eyes. The French have traditionally employed a highly efficient diplomacy for self-regarding national ends. Unlike ourselves, they have not as a rule thought it to their long-term advantage to cast their bread upon the waters by taking account of the general interest side by side with the national interest. Can we any longer afford, indeed do we now need, to be to this extent altruistic? President de Gaulle has shown how a European Power, alliance or no alliance, can follow an independent, nationally-based policy, paying scant regard to the interests of others. France has shown how to exploit the advantages of the weaker party. As M. Massigli is reliably reported once to have said: 'France, though no longer so powerful as of old, has always a stopping card to play in the game of diplomacy'. She can, and does, make the most of her nuisance value. Having no effective parliamentary check, and little public sentiment in favour of the United Nations, and a deep scepticism about the reliability of the United States and the effectiveness of NATO, she can follow courses on a number of international issues which one would say are not open to any British Government in the face of prevailing Parliamentary and public opinion. And yet, unless we break free from these shackles, may we not be condemned to relative international impotence? Is it not time, as Sir Ivone Kirkpatrick once asked, for us to force someone to appease *us* for a change? If we cannot bring about a revolution in our international outlook and procedures, can we not at least make a modest start? We have a Foreign Secretary today who, more than any of his recent predecessors, has the necessary qualities. And might we not, in our training, try to instil into our new recruits some insight into the active game of diplomacy, as the French have shown that it can still be played?

No indication was given in the letter of what actually prompted Strang's speculations. Reportedly, most readers thought mistakenly that he was reacting to the abortive Common Market talks. As a result, Caccia used his next monthly letter to disclose the actual source in a manner merely acknowledging the existence, not the contents, of Butler's Abadan history. More importantly, Caccia took the opportunity to place on record what he saw as the contemporary relevance of the lessons of the Abadan dispute.

> Then [i.e. 1951], in the main, we employed an accommodating diplomacy in an ugly and most difficult situation, with results that were far from wholly satisfactory, even though we ultimately salvaged a large amount economically by the consortium agreement of 1954. The defence of our stake in Persian oil in 1951 was severely handicapped by the fact, among others, that for the Americans it was rather too readily subordinated to their fear of provoking Russian intervention and to their calculation that in order to obviate that danger it was desirable to appease, not us, but the weaker Persians. The latter surpassed themselves in techniques of bargaining from relative weakness, techniques which only the very strong can afford to neglect all the time. Such instances are worth recalling, even while they clearly need to be balanced against those more familiar ones e.g. from the Suez Crisis the dangers inherent in any attempt to go it nearly alone: a situation, indeed, which all diplomacy so far as possible must surely try to prevent.[40]

Prompted by Strang's praise for Gaullist vigour in promoting French interests as well as Butler's critique of British policy towards Iran in 1951, Caccia speculated whether Britain was 'too apt... to do the giving and leave the taking to others'.

Caccia's monthly letter to overseas embassies and missions, like the ensuing exchanges with individual diplomats, indicated the emergence within the Foreign Office of a slightly more open approach. In particular, the procedure was welcomed by many diplomats as allowing the expert meeting of minds required to encourage fresh thinking about the future course of British diplomacy in a rapidly changing world.

For example, Sir Paul Gore-Booth (New Delhi), who was soon to succeed Caccia as PUS, welcomed a discussion which 'has obviously been most valuable and could go on – and indeed profitably go on – forever'.[41] Likewise, Butler welcomed improved transparency and dialogue within the Foreign Service, but believed that much more was needed, most notably in terms of targeting a broad audience ranging beyond both the diplomatic service and what Lord Home called the 'intellectual fringe'.[42]

Thinking about a new perspective for British diplomacy

Caccia's receipt of some 30-plus responses from overseas missions showed that Strang's thoughts struck a chord within the British diplomatic community. Naturally, his views did not always win support, but, like Butler, most respondents exploited the opportunity to comment, frequently by way of expressing disquiet, about current policies and methods.

Revealingly, many experienced difficulty in finding an appropriate agreed descriptor for Britain's current status. Was Britain, though no longer a major power 'in the sense that we once were and the Americans and Russians now are' (Patrick Dean, UN), still 'a world-wide power' (Dean), a 'leading European nation' (Lord Robert Hankey, OECD, Paris) or merely 'a declining power' of 'one and a halfth rate importance' (Gore-Booth, New Delhi)?[43] Within this context, Sir Geoffrey Wallinger (Rio de Janeiro) offered perhaps the most vivid description of Britain's fundamental dilemma: 'Our difficulties seem to have turned us into the rather muscle-bound policeman of the Western world... primarily engaged in the somewhat negative task of trying to stop the fast-moving traffic all about us from getting out of hand.'[44] Prompted by Caccia's reference to the Abadan crisis, Gore-Booth offered a 'footnote' for Butler's history. For Gore-Booth, who was responsible in 1951 for explaining British policy to the American public through the British Information Service, the Abadan crisis established that Britain was 'a declining power' preoccupied with packing up an empire: 'our problem is to learn how to behave like a smaller power than we were, while retaining those of the qualities of an ex-great power which are relevant and discarding those which are not'.[45] Nor had much thought been given to broader issues:

> I suppose the real difficulty was, – and this is why I have taken up a pen again, – that we had at the time no policy about what... we... should do in mid-twentieth century when a major economic

interest abroad is threatened e.g. by nationalisation without consent. It was indeed difficult to have such a policy in the abstract. I think we have in fact arrived, as a country, at the conclusion (China, Iran and Suez) that there is really not very much we can do about it, except negotiate as best we may and hope that our interests will have made sufficient profit in the past to have made the original venture worth while. Our nineteenth century forefathers would find this pretty pusillanimous. The question no doubt is can we or ought we to try to do anything else?

Several respondents advocated updating British diplomacy through sharper thinking, plainer speaking and the adoption of a 'greater ruthlessness in discarding inherited axioms and sentiments' (John Maud, Cape Town) by way of moving on from the usual nostalgia about 'the old spacious days' (Sir Roderick Parkes, Amman).[46] Although Strang had never proposed slavish adherence to the French model, but rather a more selfish assertive form of diplomacy, this failed to prevent respondents expressing reservations about emulating the French example because of marked differences between the two countries arising from France's greater economic self-sufficiency and continental location. In any case, as Dean observed, de Gaulle, who was subject to 'no effective parliamentary check', had 'no conscience about the United Nations'.[47] Moreover, the French model, perceived to depend heavily upon one person, might easily, some suggested, end in failure; thus, both Hankey (OECD) and Maud (Cape Town) believed that de Gaulle was repeating the mistakes of Emperor Napoleon III (1851–70) by pursuing his grandiose imperial ambitions in Europe upon inadequate geopolitical and strategic foundations.[48] Even so, as Butler noted, he was 'pursuing them with impressive clarity of purpose and strength of will'.[49]

Generally speaking, respondents displayed a keen, indeed revealing, appreciation of perceived constraints hindering the future conduct of British diplomacy in a more positive, dexterous and flexible manner than had happened during and since the Abadan crisis. Britain's straitened economic circumstances, including its poor performance relative to other countries, proved a perennial theme. None felt able to minimize the economic drags on policy; indeed, as Wallinger observed, 'diplomacy by itself... cannot make a great power out of an economic question mark'.[50] Failure at Suez was often cited as casting a long shadow over policymakers, most notably by discouraging strong independent action. For Hankey, the Suez precedent undermined Strang's case for 'going it alone': 'we saw in 1956 that we could not do this effectively even in association with France, and even against the Egyptians'.[51] At the same time, Suez led countervailing evidence to be ignored, as indicated by the fact that only one respondent mentioned Britain's armed intervention at Kuwait in 1961.[52] Revealingly, several responses betrayed continuing official sensitivities about Suez; in fact, Maud questioned whether this episode, when 'diplomacy was short circuited' by Eden, warranted description as a diplomatic failure.[53]

In this manner, the informed reflections of senior diplomats prompted by Butler's Abadan history and Strang's commentary thereupon – appropriately, these exchanges occurred soon after Dean Acheson's infamous remark in December 1962 about Britain's loss of empire and failure to find a new role – fed into and complemented ongoing policy reviews conducted by ministers and officials about the future course and methods of British foreign policy.[54] In particular, Butler's history encouraged a greater official preparedness to recognize contemporary realities and consider new directions based upon a more realistic assessment of recent trends.

The Steering Committee moves on from Abadan

Encouraged by the 'stimulating, if critical', range of views submitted by fellow diplomats, Caccia instructed Butler to summarize responses by way of guiding the Steering Committee's future discussions about giving British diplomacy a 'new and more enterprising look'.[55] The resulting memorandum, entitled 'A new perspective for British diplomacy', codified the key themes articulated by respondents. Despite downplaying organizational issues because of the ongoing work of the Plowden Committee, Butler took the opportunity to reinforce recommendations advanced in his Abadan history. In particular, he presented a Planning Committee as one way of imparting 'extra thrust' to British diplomacy and harmonizing policy with current economic realities.[56] Chance and accident could not be ruled out, but the use of planning to identify priorities, contingency options, bargaining and fall-back-positions, break points, worst-case scenarios and so on promised to avoid the existing tendency to muddle through, particularly given the fact that the small policy planning department established during the late 1950s tended to prioritize current work.[57]

Once again, a substantial part of the resulting memorandum, presenting Britain as 'a somewhat impotent middleweight' power, was circulated both within the department and to overseas missions as the next stage in the ongoing exchanges about alternative ways forward enabling the Foreign Secretary to lead 'a modern Britain in a modern world'.[58] The text was sent also to Edward Heath, the Lord Privy Seal, given his recent discussions with the historian, David Thomson, about a projected history of Gaullism.[59] More importantly, Butler's memorandum provided the basis for discussion at two meetings of the Steering Committee, held on 30 July and 23 August 1963, with Butler attending upon the second occasion to guide members.[60] In the event, the committee, eschewing a point-by-point focus upon Butler's themes, gravitated towards more practical issues, like planning, being discussed already by the Plowden Committee (1962–64) and the Foreign Office's existing planning staff.[61] In fact, the latter had already sent the Steering Committee comments about the 'new perspective' memorandum.[62]

In the event, as recorded by Sir John Nicholls, a deputy undersecretary, most policy and methodological issues raised by Butler's history and subsequent commentaries were not acted upon straightaway. Rather they would be taken into account, but not necessarily followed, by the Foreign Office over time in the future work of the Steering Committee and planning staff.[63] Significantly, within weeks of taking over as head of the restructured planning staff in January 1964, Michael Palliser – as mentioned in Chapter 10, some 15 years later he arranged Parsons's sessions looking back upon recent events in Iran – acknowledged that Butler's Abadan history and subsequent memoranda, alongside 'the ideas generated as a result of the numerous letters sent last year by Heads of Mission have been to some extent responsible for the "new look" that we are now trying to give to our planning arrangements': 'I think it is fair to say that the present experiment is designed to give Planning greater punch and precision and I hope we shall therefore meet many of the criticisms made in Butler's paper.'[64]

In any case, radically shifting direction, as opposed to gradually readjusting course, was a complex and time-consuming business requiring a fundamental transformation in the mindsets of both ministers and officials. After all, the latter were just beginning to address seriously the case for a major reappraisal of both foreign policy and methods. What these exchanges had done was to carry forward, at least at the official level, the process of diagnosis and prognosis about Britain's role in a rapidly changing world, particularly regarding Europe, the Middle East, the empire, the USA and the Soviet Union. As such, they were part of what Saki Dockrill described as the 'incremental' series of twists and turns culminating during the late 1960s in the landmark decision to withdraw from east of Suez.[65] The genuine interest shown by Home and Heath in Butler's lessons indicated that the Abadan history exerted significant impacts also at the political level; indeed, in October 1963, Heath specifically asked to be kept apprised of any follow-up to Butler's 'new perspective' paper, but within days moved out of reach to the Board of Trade in Douglas-Home's new government.[66]

From Abadan to Suez again

Butler's history also reached the desk of Michael Stewart, when Foreign Secretary (1965–66) in the 1964–70 Wilson governments. Impressed by this 'interesting' study, Stewart suggested that Butler should undertake a confidential history of the 1956 Suez Crisis for which 'The Abadan report would be the pattern and precedent': 'I think that just as we have learned some useful lessons from Abadan, so something worthwhile could emerge from a study of Suez.'[67] Quite apart from recognizing the value of learning from the past, Stewart saw himself as giving effect also to the perennial demands of Labour MPs for an official history of what was seen as the Conservative party's Achilles heel.

Inevitably, Stewart's proposal alarmed officials, who feared that any Suez history would open up a veritable Pandora's Box highlighting, say, the failure of politicians to consider, let alone follow, official advice.[68] For Gore-Booth, Caccia's successor as PUS (1965–69), the proposal raised unwelcome memories of 1956 when he had been a deputy under-secretary of state:

> The lesson to be learned from Suez was a simple one. It was this: if Ministers consulted their officials and then rejected their advice this was perfectly proper and might on many occasions give the right answer. If, however, a government undertook operations by a process of deliberately refraining from taking official advice, or keeping officials informed, then the result would in due course be disastrous.[69]

Stressing the topic's enduring domestic and political sensitivity, Gore-Booth sought to dissuade Stewart from pressing the matter.[70] As a result, he placed great emphasis upon the fact that a departmental review indicated that the records 'thin out' after the nationalization of the Suez Canal Company. Reportedly, there existed 'no confidential evidence in the Foreign Office official archives at all' documenting the crucial events leading up to hostilities. In this instance, official advice prevailed. Stewart backed down, at least 'for the present'.

In fact, unknown to Stewart, there existed already a 1957 Foreign Office study of the lessons of Suez prepared at Eden's request by his private secretary, Guy Millard. Significantly, when commissioning the project, Eden acknowledged the need to strengthen Britain's economic base and scale down existing military commitments, but still opined that Britain was capable of playing 'an independent part in the world'.[71] Unsurprisingly, Millard's account, albeit focused principally upon Britain's relations with France, the USA and the United Nations and deliberately omitting planning and operational aspects, identified many of the themes developed a few years later by Butler's history, including the limitations upon British power. Of particular interest were the links drawn by Millard between the Abadan and the Suez disputes, including the way in which 'strong memories of Abadan' appeared to influence both British and Egyptian policymakers in 1956. Thus, he saw Iran's example as reinforcing Egypt's 'intense nationalism' by demonstrating that 'the "imperialist" Powers could successfully be defied'. Conversely, concern about the resulting damage to British interests and prestige in the Middle East was presented as a 'strong' influence determining the nature of the British response in 1956:

> The abdication by Britain since the war of her overseas responsibilities is one of the greatest of revolutions.... Successive retreats in Asia and the Middle East had made further retreats increasingly repugnant.... An earlier crisis had left strong memories of Abadan. Their lesson seemed to be that in the defence of important British interests it is sometimes necessary to take risks.[72]

For Millard, the Eden government's big mistake arose from the attempt to resolve at the same time two different problems, that is those posed by nationalization and the Nasser regime. As happened during the Abadan crisis, London and Washington entered the crisis with conflicting interests and contrasting policies; thus, unlike Britain, the US government viewed Egyptian nationalism 'less as a hostile force than as something with which an accommodation must be sought and reached'.[73] Even worse, the divide widened as the crisis developed, and helped explain why for Britain the Suez Crisis represented a 'political defeat of the first magnitude':

> For Britain, Suez was a climacteric. It had severely shaken the basis of Anglo-American relations and exposed the limitations of our strength. This fact defined the conditions within which British

foreign policy must henceforth operate. . . . But we could never again resort to military action, outside British territories, without at least American acquiescence. Our capacity to act independently had been seen to be closely circumscribed by economic weakness. The experience of Suez may have led to a re-assessment of British interests and of our relative position in the world.[74]

Internal histories

Despite attracting widespread praise and exerting significant impacts upon departmental thinking about policies and methods, Butler's history failed to persuade the Foreign Office to make "funding experience" a routine part of its activities. Nevertheless, as outlined in Chapter 2, soon afterwards the introduction of the 30-Year Rule and the peacetime official histories series led the Foreign Office to review existing strategies towards historical activities. The resulting reaffirmation of the longstanding policy of prioritizing the *DBFP* was accompanied by a somewhat negative response to the Foreign Office's inclusion in the peacetime histories project partly because of the desire to target its limited historical resources to the *DBFP* and related projects and partly because of the perceived adverse impacts of *published* official histories upon British foreign policy interests.[75] Even so, as Gore-Booth told the interdepartmental Committee on Official Histories of Peacetime Events in October 1966, his department did not rule out commissioning histories funding peacetime experience upon an *ad hoc* basis for *internal use*: 'The Foreign Office does not set its face against narrative histories for its own confidential purposes (e.g. Mr Butler's confidential history of the Abadan crisis), and it must reserve the freedom which it has always exercised to commission such histories for its own use,' as opposed to publication.[76] Reporting back afterwards, Gore-Booth informed Rohan Butler that by way of example 'I mentioned your very valuable work on "What went wrong at Abadan" and how useful we had found it.'[77]

In 1979 the FCO's submission to the Wilson Committee on Public Records – Gowing was one of its members – indicated that little changed during the next decade or so: 'A very few narrative accounts of particular episodes have been written but in the Foreign and Commonwealth Office *funding of experience* [author's emphasis] is (in continuation of Foreign Office tradition) carried out by published collections of documents.'[78] In fact, the 'narrative accounts' referred to included occasional internal histories written by Butler, most notably upon the Katyn Massacre. Prepared in the wake of an upsurge in public and parliamentary interest in the Katyn question during 1971–72, Butler's history documented what British governments knew about the Katyn Massacre as well as why throughout the Cold War they failed publicly to accuse the Soviet authorities of responsibility for the crime. Apart from drawing together material from the archives, the 68-page history was intended largely to forewarn the government in case further revelations caused unwelcome embarrassment.[79] Recognized as timely, given its completion days prior to the 30th anniversary of the discovery of the massacre in April 1943, Butler's history was praised by both Julian Amery, the Minister of State at the FCO, and senior officials as 'very useful' in terms of both providing a reference source possessing 'lasting value' and reaffirming the prudence of existing lines of British policy.[80] The resulting historical memorandum, based upon confidential government records, was printed in April 1973 for internal circulation as part of the Eastern European and Soviet Department's departmental series.[81]

As mentioned in Chapter 5, in 1972 Sir Con O'Neill, the head of the British official delegation, produced a confidential internal history of the multilateral negotiations providing for British entry to the European Community in 1973. Reading the history soon after it was written, David Hannay, a First Secretary attached to the British negotiating team, praised the manner in which O'Neill illuminated a complex series of multilateral mechanisms and processes, provided in-depth insights into the British negotiating position, and critically evaluated the outcome.[82] Likewise, Douglas-Home, the Foreign Secretary (1970–74), welcomed a history of events providing the vital framework for Britain's future: 'a full report of those negotiations was essential both for present and future consideration of British policy'.[83] Like such histories drawing primarily upon closed public records, it was written 'for official purposes', that is for only a small official audience of policymakers, with copies being sent only to named and numbered recipients. However, as O'Neill conceded, the history, drawing only upon FCO files occupying some 150 foot of shelving, was very long – comprising *circa* 200,000 words, it totalled 394 pages – perhaps even 'too long for its purpose' in the sense 'that the only people able to read it will lack the time to do so'.[84] The perceived sensitivity of the European issue meant that the circulation list was tightly restricted, especially as the government had no desire to provide anti-marketeers with ammunition to use against the government.[85] Unsurprisingly, as stated in parliamentary answers, the government had no intention of commissioning an official history on the subject.[86]

Conclusion

Following the arrest of several British servicemen on the Shatt al Arab waterway in June 2004 for allegedly entering Iran's territorial waters, Jack Straw, the British Foreign Secretary, drew upon history to explain to BBC radio listeners the problematic course of Anglo-Iranian relations.[87]

> Part of the problem that we have in terms of our relations with Iran go back to our domination of that region. We had been instrumental in putting the Shah's father on the throne and many aspects of the Shah's regime were brutal, repressive, sought to strike out Iran's past and also its Islamic heritage and its Islamic beliefs. So those things are associated in many Iranians' minds with the United Kingdom.

Straw's exploitation of history's present-day rhetorical value in presenting and explaining present-day policy and relationships possessed added contemporary meaning given Britain's recent role in the overthrow of Saddam Hussein in Iraq (2003).

Within this context, Butler's Abadan history, covering a controversial episode in Anglo-Iranian relations, offered an illuminating case study trialling Brook's 1957 "funding experience" initiative. Despite failing to make "funding experience" a routine part of its everyday activities, the Foreign Office continued to commission the occasional internal history, such as Butler's study of the Katyn question, by way of codifying past experience to support current and future work. In turn, the Foreign Office's concentration upon the *DBFP*-type publications reflected in part a fundamental lack of enthusiasm about participation in the peacetime official histories series, given the perceived potential of such volumes to damage present-day international relationships.[88] Dismissing the new series as a further stage towards 'instant history', the Foreign Office warned that in any case the inevitable need to dilute the historical content to enable publication risked making the end product 'completely anodyne and uninformative and acceptable to none'.[89] Finally, the Abadan history, reaffirming Butler's reputation in the Foreign Office as 'a historian of distinction', reinforced the case for his appointment in May 1963 as the Foreign Secretary's historical adviser (1963–82).[90] Significantly, this part-time post specified responsibility for providing historical background on policy as well as drafting historical memoranda for internal use. In addition, Butler continued to act as senior editor of the *DBFP*, but with a brief to expedite production and extend coverage to the post-1939 period.

12
Using History in the Foreign Office

Lecturing to new Foreign Office recruits in 1958, Strang drew attention to the disjunction between academia and Whitehall:

> Those of you who have read history or politics at the University will probably know a great deal about the matters dealt with by diplomatists, as seen from the outside. You are now about to see them from the inside, and I am pretty sure that they will wear a rather different aspect for you. It is one thing to pass Olympian judgments upon the past acts of one Foreign Secretary or another: it is quite another to have to advise him, in precise terms, with adequate reasons given, what exactly he ought to do next in a developing crisis.[1]

A few years later, when commenting upon Butler's Abadan history dealing with events taking place during his period as PUS, Strang confessed that he was 'keenly interested in seeing himself through the candid eyes of the historian': 'Like others, indeed perhaps more than others, I should have a case to answer – without being obsessed by it.'[2] As such, Strang gave substance to the observation made in his lecture in a manner raising important questions about history's role in the foreign policymaking process.

Historians, officials and Britain's past

Within this context, one interesting aspect revealed by the Abadan history episode was the contrasting perspectives adopted by the historian and the official, even when the former was acting in effect as an official historian and the retired diplomat concerned possessed a strong sense of history.

Naturally, Butler welcomed the fact that Strang, though questioning certain interpretations, largely accepted the validity of both his historical narrative and principal conclusions. Responding to Strang's critique of his excessively detailed and long history, Butler observed that this was an inevitable consequence of their different priorities and agendas: 'It is perhaps only too understandable that a subsequent historian, who laboriously and conscientiously tries, as I did try, to strike the fine balance of the truth in complicated issues, should sometimes appear a little pedantic to one who has first-hand knowledge of them and who had the far harder task of grappling with the contemporary swirl of events.'[3] Despite acknowledging the force of Strang's criticism, Butler argued his case, at least in part, in terms of the specific circumstances characteristic of the Abadan crisis:

> A historian can comparatively easily compress his story when it is of a strong government pursuing a clear and consistent policy, so that only variations and deviations from it need be recorded... quite disproportionably long, on the other hand, are the annals, if conscientiously presented, of weak governments with confused and vacillating policies – no two shifts in them are ever quite the same so that generalising compression in their narration is only too liable to be dangerously inaccurate.

Butler quoted his research on eighteenth-century French history to make the point that undue compression tended to oversimplify and distort the story, thereby making it more difficult to record properly what happened, how and why. Even so, in 1980 the publication of the first volume of his academic monograph on Choiseul suggested that Strang had a point in complaining about Butler's overly detailed approach to the past.[4] Thus, this 1000-page plus volume, in which Butler even named the pear trees in an orchard at Stainville in 1720, concluded by asserting that 'The diplomatic and political career of the Duke of Choiseul had begun'!

Responding to Butler's complaints about occasional gaps in the documentary record, including the apparent lack of substantial minutes written by him, Strang observed that 'the historian can note only what is written: not what is spoken', particularly if, as in this case, no attempt was made to solicit oral testimony from those involved in events.[5] Strang conceded that 'for the sake of the historian, the record should carry as clear an explanation as possible of why things happened as they did, and a fair representation of the part which he himself played'.[6]

In particular, he acknowledged that 'if public servants wish to stand up to the scrutiny of historians their first recourse is to put everything down on paper. Try as they will to qualify the thought, historians tend to assume that if something is not set down in writing in the archives it was not said or not done.'[7] For Strang, Butler overlooked everyday departmental realities in a crisis: 'Absence of record does not necessarily mean absence of action. Much that is done informally by word of mouth passes unrecorded. Without the telephone and the informal talk, the machine would break down.'[8] By implication, the better the documentary record of a crisis, the worst the government's performance because too much time was spent recording developments, not taking action. For Strang, the successful conduct of policy in a crisis was a function of dealing with matters quickly and efficiently, frequently through ways inadequately recorded in writing at the time. This point acquired added impact from Strang's reminder that at the time his sphere of responsibility – this contrasted with Butler's narrow focus upon the Anglo-Iranian crisis – extended far beyond the Abadan question; indeed, other issues, like the Korean War and the Burgess–Maclean affair, often acquired priority to the exclusion of almost everything else.

In any case, as Strang emphasized, British diplomacy was neither conducted nor recorded for the benefit of historians: 'Archives are not written for the sole delectation of historians', but rather for departmental use and reference. Butler agreed; indeed, archives so written would possess only a limited historical value.[9] Even so, there remained, Butler indicated, a dilemma. As a historian, he wanted 'the important issues to be well documented. . . . But the remorseless accumulation of enormous masses of paper is in fact apt to fill the modern historian – certainly this one – with a gloom second only to that of the administrator himself.'[10] Inspired by Strang's contribution to this exercise, Butler identified the merits of introducing the practice by which, upon retirement, PUSs should provide a 'high level record', a kind of 'inner history' documenting past experience for future use by officials and historians. Even so, he possessed reservations still about the value of oral testimony as historical evidence.[11]

Using Butler's history

Notwithstanding its impact upon ministerial and official thinking, as outlined in the previous chapter, Butler's Abadan history was commissioned principally as a pilot study testing the case for implementing Brook's 1957 "funding experience" initiative in the Foreign Office.

Writing from Prague, Parrott, who had helped Butler set up the project, urged the institutionalization of what he saw as a 'fascinating' and worthwhile activity.[12] Likewise, George Vaughan (Panama) welcomed Butler's history as emphasizing the 'lessons for us, as diplomats, in what has happened.... First, which ought not to need repeating, is how important is a knowledge of history, if blunders and pitfalls are to be avoided.'[13] In turn, the Abadan history – a copy was sent to Lord Plowden a few weeks before his committee heard evidence from Strang – encouraged the 1964 Plowden Report to identify the utility of historians's expertise in departmental activities, most notably planning: 'Full use should be made of their services by executive departments so as to ensure that action on current problems is not taken in ignorance of the lessons of the past.'[14]

Despite presenting himself as an academic 'outsider looking inwards at the problems confronting British diplomacy today', Butler found it difficult to avoid acknowledging that in reality he was acting as an official historian enjoying privileged access to departmental records.[15] Conceding the functional nature of his brief – he saw his principal task as being less to record what happened, when, how and why, but rather to draw out lessons about policies and methods for policymakers – Butler hoped that his history would make 'a small but constructive contribution towards strengthening British foreign policy for the great tasks and great opportunities which now lie ahead'.[16] From this viewpoint, the priority was to discover 'the basis for a more compact and positive policy' more appropriate for Britain's status in the contemporary world, but preventing any further serious loss of power and prestige.[17]

In 1996, Butler's obituary in *The Times* claimed that 'Among the special studies that he made, his analysis of the lessons to be learnt from the Abadan crisis of 1951 permanently influenced Foreign Office thinking.'[18] Perhaps, this view, albeit influenced by Butler's post as special historical adviser to the foreign secretary (1963–82), rather overstated the long-term impact of his Abadan history, but what had been supported by the Foreign Office as an experimental project seemed worthy of emulation, even if such histories would not always prove either as timely or possess a similar wide-ranging utility.[19] Inevitably, the principal influence was exerted upon officials, but the interest shown by Home, Heath and Stewart established that the history impacted directly upon ministerial thinking across parties without having to be filtered upwards through officials. Despite regretting that his history was reserved for confidential departmental use only, Butler appreciated that, if published, the Abadan study would have exerted unwelcome impacts upon both domestic and international affairs. For example, the Labour government's role was compared unfavourably to that of its Conservative successor, with strong praise for Eden contrasting with critiques of both Attlee and Morrison. Nor, as Frederick Mason minuted, would publication help the cause of Anglo-American relations.[20]

Policymakers and analogies

Looking back from 1962, it seemed natural for Butler to view the Abadan and Suez crises as 'contrasting yet largely complementary' elements in Britain's 'scuttle' from the Middle East.[21] Withdrawal gathered pace in 1956, when Nasser's action led parallels to be drawn with not only Hitler and Mussolini but also Mossadegh. At the time, Abadan was easily viewed as both a cause and a dress rehearsal for 1956, as suggested by the way in which the opening lines of Keith Kyle's history of the Suez Affair focus upon the 1951 Abadan crisis.[22] Pointing to the lack of coincidence in American and British interests, Verbeek argued that 'the events in Iran between 1951 and 1954 could have taught Great Britain some important lessons'.[23] For Wm. Roger Louis, Britain's failure to intervene militarily over Abadan 'became one of the root causes of the Suez crisis five years later'.[24] Even so, the Suez Crisis's cataclysmic and divisive nature soon rendered it easy for politicians, among others, to gloss over, even forget, what had happened at Abadan a few years earlier. In reality, as Speller argued, 'the non-use of military force during the Abadan crisis in 1951 is as interesting and instructive as its use five years later against Egypt'.[25]

As Mossadegh ratcheted up the pressure on British interests in Iran, Emanuel Shinwell, the Minister of Defence (1950–51), articulated the need 'to show that our tail could not be twisted interminably'; thus, in May 1951, he told the chiefs of staff that 'if Persia was allowed to get away with it, Egypt and other Middle East countries would be encouraged to think that they could try things on: the next thing might be an attempt to nationalise the Suez Canal'.[26] In this vein, the Suez debacle, in which Nasser not only posed a more demanding challenge than Mossadegh but also sought to avoid the latter's mistakes, demonstrated vividly that Eden – in 1956 he looked back to the 1930s rather than 1951 – had learned little from Abadan.[27] Of course, in 1956 the lessons of the Abadan dispute had yet to be codified formally in the way undertaken by Butler, but in August 1951, that is at the height of the crisis and a few months before Eden returned to the Foreign Office in Churchill's government, Sir Roger Makins, a deputy under-secretary, drafted what Strang, then the PUS, described as a 'brilliant and sound' appraisal of the fundamental principles underpinning British foreign policy.[28] In particular, Makins recognized the growing pressures upon British power consequent upon economic underperformance, the emerging nationalist challenge, and the USA's character as 'an awkward ally'. Nor was the ongoing Abadan dispute helping Britain's standing in the Middle East: 'The dispute with Persia has dealt a heavy blow to our prestige. . . . We cannot afford another mistake of this magnitude.' From this perspective, the key lesson of the Abadan question was clear, that is 'we now need American support to keep our end up in this area', and particularly 'to maintain our position as a great Power'.

Despite Donald Cameron Watt's assertion that the chief lesson of Suez 'was largely to discredit the conduct of foreign policy by the light of historical analogy in Britain', politicians, officials and journalists have continued to use analogues, frequently centred upon Suez, to frame present-day debates about methods and policies.[29] Nor did Suez deter either Brook from launching his "funding experience" initiative one year later or the Foreign Office from commissioning the Abadan history in 1959 to investigate history's policy potential. As discussed in the previous chapter, it proves difficult to evaluate Butler's pilot study in terms of having a clear-cut outcome; indeed, neither Steiner nor Neustadt and May anticipated more than marginal improvements in policymakers's behaviour to result from incorporating history more formally into the policy process.[30] Rather the Abadan history, including related commentaries, fed into, guided and influenced ongoing discussions and reviews within Whitehall by juxtaposing the lessons of history with both contemporary realities and speculation about new directions in foreign policies and methods.

However, this episode, albeit casting light upon history's utility as a policy input, demonstrated also the need for caution. Admittedly, the lessons resulted from in-depth research referenced back to the actual events, but they were – to quote Butler – 'historical conclusions' applicable to the political, economic, military and administrative context of the early 1950s.[31] As Strang noted, the domestic and international context changed, was even transformed, during the next decade, and hence the contemporary relevance and application of Butler's lessons was rarely obvious and largely a matter for conjecture upon the part of policymakers. Reviewing Eden's Suez memoirs a few years earlier, Strang articulated his strong belief that every diplomatic event was *sui generis* when pointing to the central issue underpinning attempts to learn from history: 'The question that will be long debated is whether the analogy with the 1930s was a true one, and how far it is wise in any event to shape a course of action upon an analogy from history.'[32]

In this vein, the Abadan history raised several questions, but without necessarily providing the answers, about history's utility as a policy resource *within the Foreign Office*. How far could specific diplomatic problems be managed, even resolved, through the application of general rules derived from past experience? How useful for policy purposes is a 324-page history which takes years, not days, to complete? Is even a 16-page summary of key lessons too lengthy for policymakers to use easily during a fast-moving crisis? To what extent is the utility of lessons a function of the quality of a history's research base? Was a history of a topic, involving several other Whitehall departments and governments but based principally upon Foreign Office documentation, a useful policy resource? Or did this give a more realistic indication of the situation actually facing Foreign Office policymakers, who unlike historians were unable at the time to consult the files of other departments and governments?[33] How far should such internal histories make use of oral testimony? Should the identification of the lessons be undertaken by the historians responsible for writing the history or the diplomats involved in the events covered therein? Was there a serious problem in writing a history, as in this case, a decade or so after the event, when the improved sense of historical perspective was qualified by the risks of hindsight as well as of filtering lessons through subsequent events?

In addition, the Abadan episode raised interesting questions about the ability of history to challenge, even to transform over time, the traditional worldview of a foreign policymaking elite imprisoned by structural, ideological and other factors.[34] As Strang pointed out in his commentary, contemporary events repeatedly challenged conventional ways of thinking about Britain's role in the world, particularly regarding continental Europe, the USA and smaller powers, like Egypt and Iran. From this perspective, Abadan-type histories, using the historical narrative to yield lessons based upon past experience, appeared potentially capable of reinforcing the impact of events, *but only* if read, digested and fed into the policymaking process.

Despite frequent praise for their content and perceived relevance, in practice it proved difficult for internal histories to make a decisive impact upon the policymaking process. Butler's Abadan history exerted a stimulating impact upon the thinking of both ministers and officials, but proved influential only on the margins. Within this context, it is worth noting the fate suffered by another confidential internal history, albeit one produced across the Atlantic, on the Abadan crisis.

Donald N. Wilber, the author of the CIA's secret history of the 1953 Iranian coup, believed that covert operatives, like diplomats, had much to learn from history, even if in practice he found that few either read about or took much notice of past experience. Viewing the coup as a long-running irritant in Teheran–Washington relations culminating in the anti-Americanism displayed in the 1979 Iranian Revolution and the subsequent American hostages crisis (1979–81), Wilber used his memoirs – reportedly, prior to publication these were heavily 'sanitized' by the CIA – to regret the failure of American policymakers to learn from history.[35] For Wilber, the success of the 1953 coup derived from giving the people of Iran a choice between established institutions, represented by the monarchy, and the uncertain future offered by Mossadegh:

> If this history and this conclusion had been read by the planners of the Bay of Pigs, there would have been no such operation. The Cubans were *not forced* by circumstances to make a choice between two possibilities. From time to time, I gave talks on the operation to various groups within the Agency, and, in hindsight, one might wonder why no one from the Cuban desk ever came or read the history.[36]

Of course, Wilber's assertions, though furnishing opportunities for counterfactual histories, cannot be proved, but such examples highlight the fundamental problem of convincing policymakers to read internal histories, let alone to make use of their lessons in the policymaking process.

Looking at Whitehall in general and the Foreign Office in particular, Butler opined that 'ministers and officials are in constant danger of being swamped by remorselessly multiplying papers and committees'.[37] If nothing else, Butler's history, and particularly the exchanges conducted thereupon, encouraged busy ministers and diplomats snowed under with urgent paperwork to find time to review the basic principles of British foreign policy and hence to comprehend better present-day issues and future scenarios. As Sir Andrew Noble (The Hague) complained to Butler, 'We are writing too much and thinking rather too little.'[38] Nor did things improve, as evidenced by Sir David Hannay's comments about O'Neill's confidential internal history of Britain's 1970–72 EC negotiations:

> When I first read this report, shortly after it was written in 1972, I can recall feeling regret that, for some thirty years or so, it was fated to

be read by relatively few people and that, as Sir Con O'Neill himself observed, 'the only people able to read it will lack the time to do so'.[39]

At the time Douglas-Home, the Foreign Secretary, had dismissed such fears on the grounds that 'time is short but not so short as that', whereas of course departmental realities worked against the use of 394-page histories.[40]

Internal histories were viewed also as a potential historical resource recording events for posterity, as claimed by Lord Greenhill, a former PUS at the FCO (1969–73), when contributing in 1977 to ongoing debates about history and public records.

> The sheer volume of documents, the inevitable decline in the standards of filing, the mass of unrecorded telephone conversations, all contribute to the fact that the course of events can no longer be followed from the original documents, and individual documents of special interest may well be over-looked. Why and when decisions were taken will be hard to divine.... The answer, which could apply to other departments of state equally, may be to record factually selected episodes of history currently. As is known this has been done in the case of the entry into Europe by Sir Con O'Neill who has written a confidential history of the negotiations. There is also in the Foreign and Commonwealth Office a consolidated account of the Musaddeq affair. Other episodes should be recorded by the employment of historians who could consult the living participants and be guided to the documents whilst memories are fresh. When such histories should be released to the public is another question. But they would do much to maintain the truth for future generations.[41]

Conclusion

Perhaps Guy Millard, currently a departmental head in the Foreign Office, identified the central dilemma for British foreign policymakers during the early 1960s. Responding to Butler's 'new perspective' memorandum, he pointed to the failure of successive governments to accommodate foreign policy to post-1945 realities, and particularly to recognize that 'our reduced circumstances' meant that Britain could influence events but no longer command them, Millard opined that 'There is a lot of truth in the suggestion, made by Mr. Acheson in his celebrated speech, that we have failed to find our true role in the world.'[42]

The creation of new pieces of machinery is not a substitute for policy. If there is a lesson to be learned from General de Gaulle's methods it is... that the influence which any state can exert is vastly increased if it has clearly defined national objectives. One of our troubles is that we lack what one might call a philosophy of foreign policy. To a large extent we go on answering telegrams without having any very clear idea of where exactly we want to get to... we do not know what our national ends are supposed to be. This lack of philosophy is more marked now than before in contrast with the Russians, the French.

As happened in the Abadan crisis, policy proved increasingly a function of 'what was negotiable within Whitehall... the highest common factor of agreement between entrenched bureaucrats' rather than a function of an informed evaluation of Britain's current and future interests and power.

Part IV
Conclusion

13
Making British Policy, Using and Ignoring History

In theory, the use of past experience recorded through history should enable ministers and officials to improve both policies and methods. For Peter Nailor, a historian with a background of working in government, history offered British policymakers the ability 'to devise something better than a one-dimensional response' to complex multi-dimensional problems:

> More often than not, the problem that faces government today has its roots in the past; it has grown out of circumstances that will have created problems for governments before. And insofar as there will have been some discussion in the past about which of several optional policies to follow, it will be sensible to find out what the options were, and why one rather than another was chosen. When you have done that – which comes close to what social scientists call 'policy analysis' – it does not mean that you have either discovered, or eschewed, a novel solution. All it means is, to use a rather old-fashioned term – that you 'have done your homework'.[1]

In practice, during the period between the late 1950s and the mid-1970s the historical dimension was more frequently ignored than used by policymakers. Although this might not seem a very startling conclusion, it proved a disappointing outcome for supporters of the Whitehall "funding experience" initiative launched by Norman Brook in 1957. As a result, as outlined in this book's opening lines, Margaret Gowing used her 1978 Rede lecture both to criticize this state of affairs and to argue that public policy in Britain, and by implication the state of the country, was all the poorer for the continued neglect of history by ministers and officials.

Admittedly, government departments still undertook historical work, such as to provide background for current events, search for precedents, or write in-house histories of particular crises 'both to make sure that details are not lost and that lessons are learned'.[2] However, such activities proved largely reactive and *ad hoc*, rather than proactive, integral and routine in the way envisaged by Brook. In addition, British governments continued to support the peacetime official histories series – indeed, Gowing herself was the UKAEA's official historian – but such histories were targeted at an external audience outside of Whitehall and not at the ministers and officials involved in the policy process.

Unsurprisingly, Gowing's private papers include numerous items touching upon history and public policy, including the transcript of lectures delivered at Aspen by Alan Bullock, an Oxford colleague and the biographer of Ernest Bevin, prior to her Rede lecture. In many respects, Bullock's message, though framed in more academic terms, reinforced Gowing's thinking when preparing this lecture, especially as many points echoed those made by Keith Hancock when working together in the 1950s:

> The good historian knows too much about past events to expect that they will ever repeat themselves mechanically. It is his constant endeavour to discover both the continuing and contingent elements in human experience. He does not regard recorded history as a lesson book that contains all the answers. He does expect to find in it questions that are likely to be worth asking both now and in the future.[3]

Sharing Keith Hancock's scepticism about "the lessons of history" – this phrase gave 'too mechanical description of a rather subtle relationship' – Bullock presented history as a potentially useful resource for policymakers dealing with today's world:

> I would hardly suggest that there were *lessons* one could automatically extract from the past and directly apply to the present. Rather than teaching lessons, the study of history, and familiarity with it, provides useful insights which give public policymakers a perspective on almost all of our problems, an understanding of the tendency of peoples to resist innovation, and an avoidance of absolutisms in predicting human behavior and affairs.[4]

Using history, he argued, would warn policymakers about the dangers of presentism and their consequent need to accommodate an unpredictable future: 'If we realize how different both the past and the present are from what men expected or foresaw, we will find it easier to conceive of a future that may be as different from the present as the present is from the past.'[5] Acknowledging that historical knowledge and understanding would not necessarily provide policymakers with *the answer*, Bullock argued that history was capable of being used to reveal possible solutions, most notably recording what had been tried in the past, whether or not the policies and/or methods had worked, and the reasons explaining success or failure in each case. In particular, looking back through history might suggest also what was *new*, perhaps even insoluble, about a current problem.

From this perspective, historians working in government, though easily depicted as performing a marginal ivory tower type role, were presented as maintaining, in operational terms, the institutional memory for the benefit of ministers and officials, whose mobility within and between Whitehall departments meant that their mindsets tended to be both short term and partial. As Richard Clarke, a senior civil servant, observed, without histories, 'the "accumulated experience" of the Department is almost literally reduced to what is in the memories of people on the jobs'.[6] At times, this meant that on many issues – to quote Rawlinson, a Treasury colleague – 'our ignorance is surprisingly comprehensive!'.[7] Providing permanently available historical expertise and knowledge, historians helped to ensure that present-day pressures were not allowed to obscure relevant insights drawn from past experience.

> It is not simply a question of a safety net to prevent errors which can arise through ignorance of essential facts. Rather it concerns the vital nuance, the shaded judgement. In a more general sense this depth and the longer view should also act as a buttress against short-termism.[8]

Internal histories, like "seeded files", provided working tools expediting access for busy officials to relevant past experience through voluminous files, unhelpful filing systems and the lack of efficient finding aids.[9] Moreover, as Brook argued in 1957, "funding experience" through history helped fill a gap in the existing machinery of government by furnishing useful informed feedback on the performance of past policies and methods.[10] Hopefully, this would prevent Whitehall constantly re-inventing the wheel, or, to use the Admiralty variant cited in Chapter 5, going around the same buoy again and again. Despite his irritation with Ogilvy-Webb's tendency to bombard him with lengthy memoranda extolling the merits of Treasury histories, Vinter conceded that he made 'one good point, namely his repeated insistence on the need for a closer look at the hypotheses upon which current work, and indeed public policy generally, are based. This is a good point and one of which we need to be reminded from time to time.'[11]

Of course, this was the theory. In practice, it proved difficult to integrate historical outputs, or rather the historical knowledge, perspectives and lessons contained therein, into the actual policymaking process. Generally speaking, during the period between 1957 and 1976 British policy, though often presented within and outside Whitehall in a manner making rhetorical use of history, displayed little or no evidence of any genuine historical input. This book's case studies covered the two departments responding most positively to Brook's proposal, but neither offers much encouragement to those seeking evidence about the way in which "funding experience" actually made a difference. Even Butler's much praised Abadan history exerted only limited impacts. Admittedly, the study prompted busy diplomats and ministers to think seriously both inside and outside the box – for many, even this was deemed a major achievement – but in the event his history exerted few measurable consequences, except perhaps in terms of reinforcing ongoing developments concerning the restructuring of planning or the discussion of new policy directions. Although this conclusion might be deemed disappointing, Neustadt and May, like Steiner, warned against exaggerating the consequences of incorporating history more formally into a policy process influenced by a wide range of political and other considerations.[12]

In any case, the utility of internal histories depended upon a number of factors including their perceived relevance and usefulness to the busy desk officer's current tasks as well as their user-friendliness, as regards indexing and accessibility. Naturally, ministers and officials possessed a very different agenda to historians; indeed, for policymakers, preoccupied with present-day and future concerns, history's backward-looking character meant that its relevance was seldom immediately apparent. As one Treasury official admitted, 'It would seem that what is historical (or potentially so) to A is useless clutter to B', especially given the 'pretty elastic' nature of the phrase 'background of a policy'.[13] Whereas Clarke extolled the 'considerable topical interest' of most THMs – when reading Treasury histories, he often encountered 'a strong smell of *déjà vu*' – most Treasury staff proved far more circumspect.[14] Reviewing his past experience of historical work in both the Air Ministry and the

Treasury, M. Stuart, who currently headed a branch of the SS division, offered a typically negative response when concluding that 'the game isn't worth the candle': 'History is (for me, at least) a fascinating subject, but seldom of direct practical significance for current administration.'[15] As Leo Pliatzky observed, their prime focus was making history, not writing or using it: 'I should record that, while we are so stretched trying to cope with the history that is now being made, I personally can hardly apply myself to the problem of writing up past history, nor is the Division in general in a position to do so.'[16]

Moreover, as Henderson complained, civil servants proved extremely sensitive about the conduct of post-mortems upon past performance.[17] The fact that most histories were commissioned to examine past failures – as Malcolm Widdup noted, this meant that they were 'very largely directed to the shortcomings on our own part' – proved a further constraint upon utility.[18] Nor was the impact of Treasury histories helped by their restricted circulation within and outside the department. Unsurprisingly, the Treasury, where Abbot and Vinter feared drifting into a more liberal circulation policy by accident, proved reluctant to let other departments know about the existence of THMs, let alone to expose its past policy failures to a wider Whitehall audience.[19] Furthermore, Treasury ministers were specifically forbidden on constitutional grounds from reading THMs, even if this would not prevent either the content or any lessons reaching them as part of official advice. By contrast, the Foreign Office took a different view, as indicated by the way in which ministers were routinely allowed access to internal histories.[20]

At the same time, "funding experience", albeit presented by Brook as one way of improving the efficiency of government by saving time and money, had a cost in terms of staff, money and space. Lacking the status of a front-line task and frequently located separately from the policy sections, historical work found it difficult to attract resources for either start-up or continued support, let alone expansion. More seriously, during periods of pressure upon public expenditure it proved vulnerable to cutbacks, as evidenced by the way in which the THS was targeted for closure in 1976.

Historical activities in other government departments

Obviously, limited historical work for internal use and/or publication through edited documents and official histories continued to be undertaken by government departments, but the THS's closure in 1976 effectively concluded Whitehall's attempt to enhance history's contribution to the policymaking process in the formal proactive way advocated by Brook's 1957 initiative.[21] Despite its problematic course, "funding experience" had fared much better in the Treasury than in the rest of Whitehall. Butler's Abadan history was used to good effect, but failed to prevent the Foreign Office deciding to concentrate its limited resources primarily upon historical publications. Henceforth, internal histories, like those written on the Katyn massacre or the EEC negotiations, were produced on only an occasional *ad hoc* basis upon such topics as the Icelandic cod wars, developments in Iran [presumably centred upon 1979], and negotiations concerning the sovereignty of Gibraltar and Hong Kong.[22]

Generally speaking, Whitehall's overall response to Brook's proposal proved extremely disappointing. Previous chapters have outlined examples of historical work conducted by other departments, including the Board of Trade and the Ministry of Transport, but such histories were produced only spasmodically, not as part of a formal "funding experience" programme. In 1962, when Butler completed his Abadan history, A. Woods, the head of the Cabinet Office's Historical Section, informed the Foreign Office that, excepting the Treasury, hitherto no other Whitehall department had done very much.[23] Nor did the position change substantially during the next decade or so, as indicated when the post-Fulton Management Review of the Treasury's historical activities raised questions about how far other departments were "funding experience". Revealingly, given its pre-1968 responsibilities for the civil service, the Treasury lacked detailed knowledge on the point.

Ruling out the circulation of a questionnaire throughout Whitehall, the Establishment Officer's Branch decided to collect relevant information during the course of the scheduled visits of Treasury staff to other departments on the basis that history writing might be defined as part of their 'planning' activities.[24] An early progress report, based upon visits to Customs, Revenue, and the Departments of Education and Science, Housing and Local Government, and Overseas Development, was submitted by G. Crane in August: 'In all five cases the answer has been a straightforward "No" and the question is now becoming somewhat of an embarrassment.'[25] Despite drawing 'a complete blank', Crane agreed to continue his enquiries, even if he opined that 'we can fairly safely take it that our Historians are unique'. Recalling mention of the Ministry of Transport's 'very informative' history about the Joint Steering Group responsible for supervising the reorganization of British railways, Ogilvy-Webb suggested that Crane might use his forthcoming visit there to solicit further information about the history and its impact.[26] In the event, Henley, a former member of the Joint Steering Group now working at the Treasury in charge of the Treasury's historians, provided the answer when reporting that it was a one-off history receiving a very restricted circulation, and not part of a regular "funding experience" programme.[27]

Academic and administrative history

Within the Treasury, one enduring issue concerned the perceived conflict between what was described as "academic history" and "practical history", that is the tension between on the one hand history understood as a process of in-depth critical analysis and on the other hand history viewed as a set of clear lessons. For Collier, 'history qua history and history qua funding are two quite separate things':

> The purpose of funding experience is not to write something which will stand up as an objective and complete picture of an administrative situation, but to guide current generations of *Treasury* administrators in how to carry out Treasury policy.[28]

As a result, Treasury histories were viewed and presented differently from academic histories. Thus, when writing the history of sterling balances commissioned to contextualize the recently concluded Sterling Agreements (September 1968), Ronald Symons, a retired Treasury administrator, specifically stated his intention to avoid either making the study too academic or duplicating work done in academia.[29] By implication, an ivory tower approach ranging widely to draw upon documentation from other departments and governments would produce accounts which would be seen by administrators as both irrelevant to their current work and a waste of scarce Treasury resources. In this vein, senior Treasury officials often adjudged Ogilvy-Webb, among others, guilty of deviating from the departmental script: 'we are necessarily concerned with history writing for a specific administrative purpose, and he (Ogilvy-Webb) tends to thinks of it as worth while in itself'.[30] Naturally, Ogilvy-Webb saw things rather differently.

Therefore, the Treasury's view of "history" was both relatively limited and contemporary, given the inevitable concentration upon the very recent past, frequently defined as covering merely the past few years or so, but occasionally going back to 1945. Moreover, Treasury histories were specifically required to be produced and written in what professional historians would regard as an unhistorical manner, that is by setting out deliberately to offer a blinkered one-sided view of the department's past through almost total reliance upon Treasury papers. Treasury historians were strictly instructed *not* to consult the files of other departments, even when working upon inter-departmental topics. However, they did benefit from an ability to interview and to solicit feedback from participants in past events; thus, as one Treasury official observed, 'The difference between any old commentary and our Treasury histories is that the latter are naturally more authoritative, and may contain comment and observations not readily obvious in the record. This is more likely to be because the writer had inside knowledge.'[31] Also THMs, like Butler's Foreign Office histories, were produced primarily for overt practical present-day purposes. As one Treasury divisional head admitted, they were intended to do far more than place on record an accessible historical narrative:

> A history of this kind is obviously a valuable work of reference. But its main usefulness is not so much to provide a record of the past as to enable us to learn for the future – especially from the way in which policy issues were handled and the extent to which officials were able to make a proper analysis of the facts and arguments on which decisions were based.[32]

Differing from academic histories in nature, purpose, methodology and audience, did these "funding experience" outputs merit the descriptor "history"? Or was "history" merely 'a convenient term for the recording and analysis of recent policy over a wide field'.[33] Certainly, Maude believed that 'the Historical Memoranda can hardly claim to be "histories" in any proper sense of that term. They merely record actions taken and trains of thought pursued within the Treasury on questions where Treasury thinking was only one part of the total.'[34] Although this narrow departmental perspective might be dismissed as unhistorical, such one-sided histories provided what both the Treasury and the target readership required, that is 'an analysis of how policy evolved from what administrators believed or knew and from the institutional pressures to which they were subjected'.[35] For these reasons, Gowing preferred to present her Treasury histories as ' "policy evaluation" rather than straight history'.[36] Against this background, in July 1974 Sharp, the Establishment Officer, provided an apt summary clearly differentiating THMs from both academic and official histories:

> These Treasury 'histories' are purely departmental and can be based only on Treasury files. It becomes a different, and much larger exercise

to try to write a complete history of some aspect of Government; and in general we do not attempt it. All we try to do is to cull from the files and sum up the essence of a subject, as seen through Treasury eyes, in the hope that Treasury administrators who have to continue to deal with it may have a ready guide to the past and the lessons of previous experience. The nearer it gets to a complete history, of course, the better; but it cannot avoid being partial.[37]

Thus, it proves difficult, even unfair, to attempt any evaluation of the quality of Treasury histories as "history", since they never claimed this status in the first place. Rather they should be treated very much as products of their time, handicapped by both a limited research base and a lack of historical perspective, and hence as merely interim partial assessments of the Treasury's past experience. Even so, for present-day historians, they supplement working files in terms of offering informed insights on a wide range of topics, most notably illuminating the unspoken assumptions of policymakers. Hitherto THMs have been under-used as a historical source, although Alan Booth has made effective use of selected studies in his publications on the political economy of post-1945 Britain, even describing Ogilvy-Webb's 1962 history of wages policy as providing 'an excellent summary' of Treasury policy.[38] When writing his peacetime official history of *External Economic Policy since the War*, Leslie Pressnell relied primarily upon the Treasury's 'day to day working files', but part of his closing chapter drew upon two THMs but 'not upon their author's views, which are not necessarily acceptable'.[39]

Of course, the functional character of the Treasury historians's work does not necessarily impugn its historical integrity, even if its quality naturally varied. Frequent praise for Hartcup and Ogilvy-Webb's contributions contrasted with more measured comments for other historians. Moreover, the fact that they were required to satisfy a strict task specification, restrict their research base, adhere to official rules and regulations, and prompt divisional staff to identify lessons did not prevent them acting like any other historian. As Ogilvy-Webb stressed 'we have always tried to be impartial and to take account of all the facts available to us', even if readers of his histories might conclude that he adopted a rather subjective definition of 'impartial'.[40] Nor were things helped perhaps by the way in which most Treasury historians were recruited from the ranks of former administrators, who converted to historical work for a range of personal and other reasons. Admittedly, some, like Gowing and Hartcup, studied history at university, but others, like Ogilvy-Webb – he had a languages degree – had not.

In many respects, Con O'Neill echoed the Treasury line when sending Douglas-Home, the Foreign Secretary (1970–74), his lengthy account of the 1972 EEC negotiations. Presenting his study as 'a Report, not a History', O'Neill saw himself as 'too close' both in time – in fact, he began writing the history within days of the signature of the accession treaty – and position, that is as a diplomat heading the official negotiating team, to claim otherwise.[41] By contrast, Rohan Butler presented his internal histories very much as products of his historical training and ongoing academic role, even if he felt compelled to deliver health warnings arising from the enforced narrowness of his research base.

Conclusion

Within the Treasury, occasional demarcation disputes highlighted the disputed boundary between policymakers and historians as well as the subordinate and marginal roles assigned to the historical dimension in the policy process. Historical outputs, it was stipulated, must be focused, policy relevant and potentially useful, but policy neutral in the sense of allowing policymakers to decide whether or not to act upon the information provided therein. As John Hunt stressed when working at the Treasury prior to becoming Cabinet Secretary, the historian was 'essentially working as an historian and not to advise on future policy'; thus, the historians's contribution should be confined to writing the history with a policy objective in mind, leaving officials to draw out the lessons.[42] Providing working tools for policymakers, their role fell well short of being allowed to act as a policy department.

More seriously, throughout the period of study there remained the fundamental problem of actually slotting histories into the government machine, particularly in terms of ensuring that they were consulted whenever relevant. In reality, the histories were left largely unread, let alone used to inform and improve policies and methods. Even after the Treasury had been actively "funding experience" for over a decade, senior Treasury officials were expressing concern still about the department's failure to use the work of its historians. For example, in 1972 Sharp pointed to the latter when urging Henley to 'Remember Belloc? When I am gone, I hope it may be said "his sins were scarlet, but his books were read". But it may still be a hope only partially realised.'[43] In the event, these hopes were foiled in 1976, when the perceived lack of utility of Treasury histories merely reinforced the case to close the THS.

Writing in 1976, Michael Lee expressed concern about the way in which recent developments appeared to mark a retreat in Brook's attempt to build a historical dimension into the everyday practice of British administration, even threatening the future of the peacetime official histories:

> The demise of the Treasury Historical Section is not a good augury.... The pace of administrative work in the higher echelons of the civil service militates against an historical understanding. 'Water under the bridge' is a phrase used all too often. The Treasury and the CSD have lost the Whiggish *hauteur* of Norman Brook's day.[44]

Whether or not public policy in Britain during the period between the late 1950s and the mid-1970s was all the poorer for the neglect of history by ministers and officials, as claimed by Gowing and Lee, remains an open question, but what this study has established is the difficulty of providing a meaningful common meeting ground between public policy and history in Britain.

Appendix: Treasury Historical Memoranda

1.	Treasury and Acts of God	1957
2.	Festival Pleasure Gardens	1957
3.	Civil Service Superannuation	1960
4.	The Convertibility Crisis of 1947	1962
5.	The Government and Wages 1945–60	1962
6.	Form of Estimates	1963
7.	Long Term Economic Planning, 1945–51	1964
8.	Policy to Control the Level of Demand 1953–58	1965
9.	History of Aircraft Purchasing for the Air Corporations	1965
10.	Negotiations with the European Economic Community 1961–63	1966
11.	Economic and Financial Obligations of the Nationalised Industries	1966
12.	History of Prescription Charges	1967
13.	Rebuilding of Downing Street and the Old Treasury 1960–63	1968
14.	Rehousing of the Commonwealth Institute	1968
15.	Provincial Differentiation and London Weighting	1969
16.	Sterling Balances since the War	1972
17.	Decisions on Public Expenditure for 1971–72 and 1974–75	1971
18.	Control of Demand 1958–64	1972
19.	The Sterling Agreements, 1968	1972
20.	The Gold Crisis, March 1968	1975
21.	The Control of Credit in the Private Sector, 1965–71	1975
22.	The Control of Demand 1964–70	1975
23.	Exchange Control, 1959–72: UK attitudes and reactions	1975
24.	Incomes Policy 1961–64	1975
25.	International Liquidity, 1962–68	1975
26.	The Defence Budget 1946–71	1976
27.	Prices and Incomes Policy 1968–70	1976
28.	Incomes Policy 1964–68	1976
29.	Special Study of Incomes Policy	1976
30.	The Collapse of the Bretton Woods System, 1968–73	1976

Note: THMs are in T267/1–36, TNA. THM 2 is available on-line at http://archive.treasury.gov.uk/pub/html/thm/thmlist1.html.

Notes

1 British policymakers and history

1. Peter Hennessy, 'Civil Service accused of neglecting history', *The Times*, 28 Apr. 1978.
2. Margaret Gowing, *Reflections on Atomic Energy History: The Rede Lecture 1978* (Cambridge: Cambridge University Press, 1978), p. 4.
3. Gowing to Guy Hartcup, 17 Dec. 1976, Private papers of Guy Hartcup (GH).
4. Jeremy Black, *Using History* (London: Hodder Arnold, 2005), pp. ix, 1–11; Christopher Hill, 'Academic international relations: the siren song of policy relevance', in C.R. Hill and P. Beshoff (eds), *Two Worlds of International Relations: Academics, Practitioners and the Trade in Ideas* (London: Routledge/LSE, 1994), pp. 1–21.
5. W. Palmer, *Engagement with the Past: The Lives and Works of the World War II Generation of Historians* (Lexington, Ky.: The University Press of Kentucky, 2001), pp. 297, 303.
6. See http://www.historyandpolicy.org/.
7. Peter Mandler, *History and National Life* (London: Profile Books, 2002), pp. 141–2, 163.
8. G.R. Elton, 'Second thoughts on history at the universities', *History*, 54 (1969), 66.
9. John Tosh, *The Pursuit of History: Aims, Methods and New Directions in the Study of Modern History*, 3rd edn (Harlow: Longman, 1999), p. 4.
10. John Tosh (ed.), *Historians on History* (Harlow: Longman, 2000), pp. 2–8.
11. See Peter J. Beck, 'History and policy-makers in Argentina and Britain', in Hill and Beshoff (eds), *Two Worlds*, pp. 164–87; Black, *Using history*, pp. 72–84.
12. Donald Cameron Watt, 'The political misuse of history', in *Trends in Historical Revisionism: History as a Political Device* (London: Centre for Contemporary Studies, 1985), p. 11.
13. Quentin Skinner and Russell Price (eds), *Machiavelli, The Prince* (Cambridge: Cambridge University Press, 1988), p. 53.
14. William Lamont, 'Introduction', in W. Lamont (ed.), *Historical Controversies and Historians* (London: Routledge, 1998), p. xv; Arthur Marwick, *The New Nature of History: Knowledge, Evidence, Language* (Basingstoke: Palgrave Macmillan, 2001), p. 42.
15. Michael Howard, *The Lessons of History* (Oxford: Clarendon Press, 1991), pp. 9–11; Tosh, *Pursuit of History*, pp. 213–14.
16. There is not space to develop this point here, but even A.J.P. Taylor, whose advocacy of the role of accident and contingency underpinned his critique of learning from history because it merely taught policymakers how to make new mistakes in the present, was not immune from this approach: A.J.P. Taylor, 'Men of 1862: Napoleon III' in Chris Wrigley (ed.), *A.J.P. Taylor, From Napoleon to the Second International: Essays on Nineteenth-Century Europe*

(London: Hamish Hamilton, 1993), p. 279. For example, Taylor's 1977 television lecture on the causes of war in 1914 concluded with an attack on the concept of deterrence by way of reinforcing the case for nuclear disarmament: Chris Wrigley (ed.), *A.J.P. Taylor: British Prime Ministers and Other Essays* (London: Penguin, 1999), p. 204.
17. Eric Hobsbawm, *On History* (London: Abacus, 1998), pp. 32–3.
18. Eric Hobsbawm, 'Introduction: Inventing traditions', in Eric Hobsbawm and Terence Ranger (eds), *The Invention of Tradition* (Cambridge: Cambridge University Press, 1983), pp. 1–14.
19. Palmer, *Engagement with the Past*, pp. 292–7; Tosh, *Pursuit of History*, p. 214.
20. Andrew Roberts, 'An inadvertent history lesson', *Evening Standard*, 29 Oct. 1994.
21. Eric J. Hobsbawm, 'Spreading democracy', *Foreign Policy*, Sept./Oct. 2004, http://www.foreignpolicy.com/story/files/story2666.php, accessed 14 Dec. 2004.
22. Hobsbawm, *On History*, p. 33.
23. Ibid., pp. 46–7.
24. Yuen Foong Khong, *Analogies at War: Korea, Munich, Dien Bien Phu, and the Vietnam Decisions of 1965* (Princeton, NJ.: Princeton University Press, 1992), pp. 3–18, 174–205; Jeffrey Record, *Making War, Thinking History: Munich, Vietnam and Presidential Uses of Force from Korea to Kosovo* (Annapolis: Naval Institute Press, 2002), pp. 11–18, 146–55.
25. David Dutton, *Anthony Eden: A Life and Reputation* (London: Arnold, 1997), pp. 1–19; Peter J. Beck, 'Politicians versus historians: Lord Avon's "appeasement battle" against "lamentably, appeasement-minded" historians', *Twentieth Century British History*, 9 (1998), 396–419.
26. Eden to Sir Toby Low, 21 Apr. 1961, AP23/4/44A. The Lord Avon papers (AP) are located at the Library, University of Birmingham.
27. Encl. Lord Avon to Spanel, 4 June 1965, AP24/64/28A.
28. Anthony Eden, 'Foreword', *The Memoirs of Sir Anthony Eden: Full Circle* (London: Cassell, 1960). See Eden to Viscount Chandos, 29 Sept. 1959, AP23/17/36B.
29. Eden, *Full Circle*, p. 431.
30. Ibid., p. 518.
31. Anthony Gorst and Lewis Johnman (eds), *The Suez Crisis* (London: Routledge, 1997), pp. 32–3; Dutton, *Anthony Eden*, pp. 356–63; Sue Onslow, ' "Battlelines for Suez": the Abadan Crisis of 1951 and the formation of the Suez Group', *Contemporary British History*, 17 (2003), 21–2.
32. Evelyn Shuckburgh, *Descent to Suez: Diaries, 1951–56* (London: Weidenfeld & Nicolson, 1986), p. 75.
33. Anthony Nutting, *No End of A Lesson: The Story of Suez* (London: Constable, 1967), pp. 7, 12–16.
34. John W. Young, *Britain and the World in the Twentieth Century* (London: Arnold, 1997), pp. 166–7; W. Scott Lucas, *Divided We Stand: Britain, the US and the Suez Crisis* (London: Sceptre, 1996), pp. 324–30.
35. David Carlton, *Anthony Eden: A Biography* (London: Allen Lane, 1981), p. 478; Richard English and Michael Kenny, 'Conclusion: decline or declinism?', in R. English and M. Kenny (eds), *Rethinking Decline* (Basingstoke: Macmillan, 2000), pp. 279–96. For an alternative revisionist view arguing that Eden was

right to stand up to Nasser's 'piratical confiscation', see Andrew Roberts, 'Betrayal of the brave at Suez', *Sunday Times*, 20 Oct. 1996.
36. Peter Hennessy, 'The pleasures and pains of contemporary history', *History Today*, 44 (Mar. 1994), 17.
37. Margaret Thatcher, *The Downing Street Years* (London: HarperCollins, 1993), p. 186.
38. *The Falkland Islands. The Facts* (London: HMSO, 1982), p. 10; Peter Beck, *The Falklands Islands as an International Problem* (London: Routledge, 1988), pp. 29–56.
39. Tony Blair, 'Doctrine of the international community', Chicago Economic Club, Online NewsHour Select, 22 Apr. 1999: http://www.pbs.org/news hour/bb/international/jan-june99/blair_doctrine4-23.html accessed 25 June 2004. Seldon sees Roy Jenkins' influence in encouraging Blair's adoption of a historical perspective drawing upon the Munich analogy: Anthony Seldon, *Blair* (London: Free Press, 2004), p. 519.
40. *Hansard Parliamentary Debates, House of Commons* (hereafter *Hansard Commons*), 14 Sept. 2001, vol. 372, col. 618: http://www.parliament.thestationery-office.co.uk/pa/cm200102/cmhansrd/vo010914/debindx/10914-x.htm, accessed 20 June 2004.
41. Straw, 2 Oct. 2001: http://politics.guardian.co.uk/labour2001/story/0,1414, 561867,00.html, accessed 20 June 2004.
42. Robin Cook, *The Point of Departure* (London: Simon & Schuster, 2003), p. 121.
43. Cook, *Point of Departure*, pp. 203, 224; Robert Fisk, 'New crisis, old lessons', *The Independent*, 15 Jan. 2003; Robin Cook, 'The invasion of Iraq was Britain's worst foreign policy blunder since Suez', *The Independent*, 19 Mar. 2004.
44. *Interviews with Historians: Margaret Gowing with Charles Webster* (London: Institute of Historical Research, 1988). The rare distinction of election as a fellow of the Royal Historical Society (1970), the British Academy (1975) and the Royal Society (1988) recognized her authority on both history and science.
45. Gowing to Sir Douglas Wass, 31 Oct. 1978, MG Corresp. Wass. The Margaret Gowing Papers (MG) are located at the Library, Museum of the History of Science, Oxford.
46. Hennessy, 'Civil service accused of neglecting history'; J. Ford to Miss Court, 5 July 1978, EO22/85/01. EO (Establishment Officer's branch) files were read at the Treasury.
47. See Denys Hay, 'British historians and the beginnings of the civil history of the Second World War', in M.R.D. Foot (ed.), *War and Society: Historical Essays in Honour and Memory of J.R. Western, 1928–1971* (London: Paul Elek, 1973), p. 54.
48. Lorna Arnold, 'A letter from Oxford: the history of nuclear history in Britain', *Minerva*, 38 (2000), 202–10; Sarah White, 'Nuclear historian', *New Scientist*, 28 Nov. 1974, 656–9.
49. Margaret Gowing, *Britain and Atomic Energy, 1939–1945* (London: Macmillan, 1964); Margaret Gowing with Lorna Arnold, *Independence and Deterrence, Britain and Atomic Energy, 1945–1952*, vols 1–2 (London: Macmillan/UKAEA, 1974). Frequently, academic reviewers, like F.S. Northedge, praised Gowing for her 'detached' approach: *History*, 61 (1976), 476–7. Likewise, Roger Carey recorded her sympathy with the project, but acknowledged that 'no punches

are pulled, and the book is far from sycophantic': *International Affairs*, 51 (1975), 397-9.
50. Gowing to Sir Robert Armstrong, 19 July 1983, MG Misc. Corresp. 1983-86.
51. Gowing, *Reflections*, p. 5.
52. Ibid. p. 6. On Anglo-American comparisons, see Gowing to Armstrong, 19 July 1983, MG Misc. Corresp. 1983-86.
53. Gowing to Trevor-Roper, 8 Dec. 1977, MG Rede Corresp.
54. Bancroft to Gowing, 31 May 1978, MG Corresp. Bancroft.
55. Gowing to Bancroft, 7 June 1978, MG Corresp. Bancroft.
56. *House of Commons, Education, Science and Arts Committee, Public Records, Minutes of Evidence, 4 May 1983*, Gowing, n.d. p. 83; Margaret Gowing, 'Modern public records: selection and access. The report of the "Wilson Committee" ', *Social History*, 6 (1981), 351-7.
57. *House of Commons, Education, Science and Arts Committee, Public Records, Minutes of Evidence, 4 May 1983*, p. 86. Gowing reported that only 6 per cent of records requisitioned from the Public Record Office (now called The National Archives) were for current use by government departments.
58. Gowing to C.W. France, 31 Jan. 1978, MG Corresp. Wass.
59. Richard E. Neustadt and Ernest R. May, *Thinking in Time: The Uses of History for Decision Makers* (New York: The Free Press, 1986), pp. xxii, 1-4.
60. Lord Strang, *The Diplomatic Career* (London: Andre Deutsch, 1962), p. 119.
61. Zara Steiner, 'The historian and the Foreign Office', in Hill and Beshoff (eds), *Two Worlds*, p. 46; P.K. Kemp, 'War studies in the Royal Navy', *RUSI Journal*, 111 (1966), 155.
62. Neustadt and May, *Thinking in Time*, p. 79.
63. Charles Kurzman, *The Unthinkable Revolution in Iran* (Cambridge, Mass.: Harvard University Press, 2004), pp. 1-9.
64. Steiner, 'The historian', p. 45; Zara Steiner, 'On writing international history: chaps, maps and much more', *International Affairs*, 73 (1997), 538; Hill, 'Academic international relations', pp. 3-21.
65. J.L. Gaddis, 'New conceptual approaches to the study of American foreign relations: interdisciplinary perspectives', *Diplomatic History*, 14 (1990), 423; John Tusa, 'A deep and continuing use of history', in David Cannadine (ed.), *History and the Media* (Basingstoke: Palgrave Macmillan, 2004), p. 131.
66. Jose Harris, 'Economic knowledge and British social policy', in Mary O. Furner and Barry Supple (eds), *The State and Economic Knowledge: The American and British Experiences* (Cambridge: Cambridge University Press/Woodrow Wilson International Center for Scholars, 1990), p. 383.
67. Peter Hennessy, *Whitehall* (London: Pimlico, 2001), p. 133; George C. Peden, 'Old dogs and new tricks: the British Treasury and Keynesian economics in the 1940s and 1950s', in Furner and Supple (eds), *The State and Economic Knowledge*, pp. 210-11, 236-7; Peter Clarke, 'The Treasury's analytical model of the British economy between the wars', in Furner and Supple (eds), *The State and Economic Knowledge*, pp. 206-7; George C. Peden, *The Treasury and British Public Policy, 1906-1959* (Oxford: Oxford University Press, 2000), pp. 425, 521-2.
68. Jean Nunn to P. Rogers, 18 Sept. 1964, CAB21/5230. Cabinet (CAB) records are located at The National Archives (TNA), Kew.

69. G.K. Fry, *The Administrative Revolution in Whitehall: A Study of the Politics of Administrative Change in British Central Government Since the 1950s* (London: Croom Helm, 1981), pp. 3, 44; Mary O. Furner and Barry Supple, 'Ideas, institutions, and state in the United States and Britain: an introduction', in Furner and Supple (eds), *The State and Economic Knowledge*, pp. 4–5; Roy Macleod, 'Introduction', in Roy Macleod (ed.), *Government and Expertise: Specialists, Administrators and Professionals, 1860–1919* (Cambridge: Cambridge University Press, 1988), pp. 1–24.
70. Howard, *Lessons of History*, pp. 10, 97–112.
71. Kemp, 'War studies', 153. There are exceptions: see AIR20/9306, AIR20/10843. Air Ministry files (AIR) are located at TNA.
72. *The Times*, 29 Aug. 1978.
73. A. Collier to L. Petch, 24 Oct. 1966, T199/1025. Treasury (T) records are located at TNA.
74. Sir Alec Cairncross (ed.), *Sir Richard Clarke, Public Expenditure, Management and Control* (London: Macmillan, 1978), pp. vii–6.
75. Relevant texts include Michael Fry (ed.), *History, the White House and the Kremlin: Statesmen as Historians* (London: Pinter, 1991); Alexander L. George, *Bridging the Gap: Theory and Practice in Foreign Policy* (Washington DC.: United States Institute of Peace, 1993); Hill and Beshoff, *Two Worlds*; Robert Jervis, *Perception and Misperception in International Politics* (Princeton, N.J.: Princeton University Press, 1976); Scot Macdonald, *Rolling the Iron Dice: Historical Analogies and Decisions to use Military Force in Regional Contingencies* (Westport, CT.: Greenwood, 2000); Khong, *Analogies at War*; Ernest R. May, *'Lessons' of the Past: The Use and Misuse of History in American Foreign Policy* (New York: Oxford University Press, 1973); Neustadt and May, *Thinking in Time*; Stephen R. Rock, *Appeasement in International Politics* (Lexington, Ky.: The University Press of Kentucky, 2000); and Record, *Making War*. For an economic dimension, see Paul A. David and Mark Thomas, 'Introduction: Thinking historically about challenging economic issues', in Paul A. David and Mark Thomas (eds), *The Economic Future in Historical Perspective* (Oxford: British Academy/OUP, 2003), pp. 6–26.
76. Peter Nailor, *Learning from Precedent in Whitehall* (London: ICBH/RIPA, 1991), pp. 25–9, 47.
77. George Peden to the author, 4 Feb. 2004; Leslie Hannah, 'Economic ideas and government policy on industrial organization in Britain since 1945', in Furner and Supple, *The State and Economic Knowledge*, p. 365, note 25.
78. Hugh Pemberton, *Policy Learning and British Governance in the 1960s* (Basingstoke: Palgrave Macmillan, 2004), pp. 16–24, 172–5, 180–2.
79. Peter Hennessy, 'A crack appears in the door to Treasury documents', *The Times*, 18 July 1978; Hennessy, *Whitehall*, pp. xiii–xix.
80. Hennessy, 'A crack appears'; Wass to Hennessy, 10 July 1978, EO22/85/01. In the event, two THMs were soon released, but they were atypical and 'incredibly boring': Court to France, 30 Aug. 1978, Ford to P. McCaffrey, 23 Oct. 1978, EO22/85/01; Peter Hennessy, 'Studies requested by The Times released', *The Times*, 6 Nov. 1978.
81. Black, *Using History*, p. 7; Adrian Smith, 'Tony Blair, the Iraq War and a sense of history', *The Historian*, 79 (2003), 6–8.
82. Tusa, 'Deep and continuing use of history', pp. 131–2.

2 Using official histories and public records to present Britain's past to a global audience

1. Burke Trend to Brook, 4 Oct. 1957, Trend to Brook, 21 Oct. 1957, CAB103/562; Richard Aldrich, 'Policing the past: official history, secrecy and British intelligence since 1945', *English Historical Review*, CXIX (2004), 935–9, 951.
2. For example, see *The Times*, 27 Jan. 1960, 7 Oct. 1961, 10 Oct. 1961.
3. S. Wilson to J. Nunn, 31 Jan. 1967, CAB103/621; Donald C. Watt, 'Contemporary history: problems and perspectives', *Journal of the Society of Archivists*, III (1965–69), 512; Hay, 'British historians', p. 39.
4. Jeffrey Grey, 'Introduction', in J. Grey (ed.), *The Last Word?: Essays on Official History in the United States and British Commonwealth* (Westport, CT: Praeger, 2003), p. ix.
5. D.J. Mitchell to Sir D. Rickett, 20 Feb. 1962, T199/921.
6. Brook to Heads of Departments, 5 Dec. 1957, CAB103/562. On Brook, see Kevin Theakston, *Leadership in Whitehall* (Basingstoke: Macmillan, 1999), pp. 95–126.
7. R. Symons to Rickett, 30 Sept. 1959, T236/5982.
8. Brook to Heads of Departments, 5 Dec. 1957, CAB103/562.
9. Hancock to Gowing, 14 Nov. 1986, Hancock to Richard A. Chapman, 29 May 1985, MG Corresp. Hancock; W.K. Hancock, *Country and Calling* (London: Faber and Faber, 1954), pp. 196–7. Henceforth Professor Sir Keith Hancock will be referred to as 'Keith Hancock' to avoid confusion with 'David Hancock'.
10. Edward Bridges to Winnifrith, 4 Apr. 1955, CAB103/596; Hay, 'British historians', pp. 41–52.
11. Trend to Brook, 4 Oct. 1957, CAB103/562.
12. Robin Higham, 'Introduction', in R. Higham (ed.), *Official Histories: Essays and Bibliographies from around the World* (Manhattan, Kansas: Kansas State University Library, 1970), pp. 1–4; Sir Keith Hancock, 'British civil histories of the Second World War', in Higham (ed.), *Official Histories*, pp. 518–25; Hay, 'British historians', pp. 39–55; Sir J.R.M. Butler, 'The British military histories of the war of 1939–45', in Higham (ed.), *Official Histories*, pp. 511–14. On the First World War, see Andrew Green, *Writing the Great War: Sir James Edmonds and the Official Histories, 1915–1948* (London: Frank Cass, 2003), pp. 5–20, 195–208.
13. For example, on Medlicott's first volume of *The Economic Blockade* (1952), see Hancock to W.N. Medlicott, 1 Nov. 1950, Medlicott to E. Playfair, 4 Nov. 1950, T199/662.
14. *Interviews with Historians, Gowing*.
15. W.K. Hancock and M.M. Gowing, *British War Economy* (London: HMSO, 1949), p. ix.
16. C.I. Savage, *Inland Transport* (London: HMSO, 1957), pp. xv–xvi.
17. Professor Sir W. Keith Hancock, 'Official history of the war civil series. Report', Jan. 1957, CAB103/562.
18. Hancock to Gowing, 27 Oct. 1967, MG Corresp. Hancock; Hancock, Foreword to Reprint of Civil Histories, n.d. (1972–73), MG Cabinet Office War Histories.

19. Gowing, 'Keith Hancock and official history', p. 21, n.d., MG Official History.
20. Hancock, *Country and Calling*, p. 203.
21. Hancock, Report, Jan. 1957, p. 9, CAB103/562.
22. Ibid., pp. 9–10, CAB103/562; Margaret Gowing, 'Peacetime Official History', *SSRC Newsletter*, 21 Jan. 1974, 2. According to Gowing, some 226 unpublished narratives on individual topics were written by historians working on the civil histories: Note, p. 17, n.d., MG Official History.
23. Hancock, 31 July 1946, Titmuss 7/44/1, Richard Titmuss papers. The Titmuss papers are located at the British Library of Political and Economic Science Archives, London School of Economics (hereafter LSE).
24. Higham, 'Introduction', p. 3; Grey, 'Introduction', p. xi. Note the claim, attributed to Philip L. Graham, that the press provides the 'the first rough draft of history'.
25. Hancock, 'British civil histories', p. 521. Note also the example during the late 1960s when F. Hinsley's history of intelligence was commissioned to help restore the 'battered' image of British intelligence: Aldrich, 'Policing the past', 923–4.
26. Hancock and Gowing, *British War Economy*, p. ix.
27. Print and stock quantities are given in B. Waye to Miss Merrifield, Apr. 1972, 10 May 1972, MG Cabinet Office War Histories. Titmuss' volume was out of print and out of stock despite being reprinted for a total print of 5000 copies. See also 'History "en masse"', *The Times*, 3 Mar. 1955.
28. Trend to Brook, 4 Oct. 1957, CAB103/562.
29. Higham, 'Introduction', pp. 1–2; Stephen W. Roskill, 'Some reasons for official history', in Higham (ed.), *Official Histories*, pp. 10–18.
30. Aldrich, 'Policing the past', 923.
31. Herbert Butterfield, *History and Human Relations* (London: Collins, 1951), p. 186.
32. W. McIndoe to Trend, 14 Jan. 1966, CAB103/598; J.R.M. Butler, 'Letter: official war histories', *The Times*, 10 Oct. 1961.
33. Brook, n.d., encl. Brook to Bridges, 7 May 1953, T273/72.
34. Hancock to Chapman, 29 May 1985, MG Corresp. Hancock. On changes affecting Medlicott's second volume on the economic blockade: Hancock to Parrott, 10 Mar. 1958, FO370/2551/LS6.
35. Titmuss to Hancock, 21 July 1949, Titmuss ADD1/33.
36. Hancock to Gowing, 27 Oct. 1967, Hancock to Chapman, 29 May 1985, MG Corresp. Hancock; Hancock, *Country and Calling*, pp. 203–5.
37. Hancock, 'British civil histories', p. 521; Hancock to Gowing, 27 Oct. 1967, MG Corresp. Hancock.
38. Hancock, *Country and Calling*, p. 204.
39. Hancock to Titmuss, 23 Mar. 1949, Titmuss 7/44/4.
40. Bridges, quoted, Hancock to Chapman, 29 May 1985, MG Corresp. Hancock.
41. Brook to Churchill, 19 Nov. 1951, Churchill, 26 Nov. 1951, CAB103/368.
42. Hancock and Gowing, *British War Economy*, p. xii.
43. In fact, such documents were not always preserved: Christina J.M. Goulter, 'British official histories of the Air War', in Grey (ed.), *The Last Word?*, p. 143.
44. Hancock to C.B. Behrens, 6 Aug. 1947, BEHR Add 17. The Behrens Papers (BEHR) are located at the Churchill Archives Centre, Cambridge University.
45. Hancock to Behrens, 6 Aug. 1947, BEHR Add 17.

46. Hancock, Report, Jan. 1957, p. 8, CAB103/562.
47. Hancock, *Country and Calling*, pp. 197, p. 203.
48. Hancock, Report, Jan. 1957, p. 9, CAB103/562.
49. Gowing, 'Peacetime official history', 2. Gowing pointed also to the fact that Michael Howard's volume (1970) in the Grand Strategy series won the 1972 Wolfson Prize.
50. Margaret Gowing, 'Hancock: some reminiscences', *Historical Studies*, 13 (1968), 303.
51. Hancock to R. Makins, 10 Mar. 1958, T199/662.
52. Brook to Hancock, 19 Feb. 1958, CAB103/562; Hancock to Makins, 10 Mar. 1958, T199/662. Only a few titles remained in press/preparation, like Medlicott's second volume on *The Economic Blockade* (1959) and R.J. Hammond's *Food*, Vol. 3 (1962), but D.J. Payton-Smith's *Oil* was delayed until 1971.
53. Brook to departments, 31 July 1957, CAB103/562.
54. Trend to Brook, 4 Oct. 1957, CAB103/562.
55. Ibid. Trend read a draft version of Gowing's history prior to printing in November 1957.
56. Brook to Hancock, 13 Feb. 1958, CAB103/562; *The Times* 23 Nov. 1957.
57. *Eighth Report from the Select Committee on Estimates*, *The Times* 23 Nov. 1957; *The Glasgow Herald*, 25 Nov. 1957. As mentioned above, only the unpublished versions retained within departments were fully referenced.
58. 'War histories and historians: the dead-hand of secrecy', *The Glasgow Herald*, 25 Nov. 1957; Cassandra, 'Words and wars', *Daily Mirror*, 25 Nov. 1957. The figures covered all Second World War series, including the more substantial military histories.
59. In the event, *Victory at Sea* (1958), contracted originally to Sir Arthur Bryant in 1946, was completed by Lt Cdr P.K. Kemp, head of the Admiralty's Historical Section: letter, J.C. Reynolds, *The Bookseller*, 7 Dec. 1957; letter, Sir Arthur Bryant on 'Official war histories', *The Bookseller*, 14 Dec. 1957.
60. Robert Oppenheimer made a similar point: quoted, Hancock, *Country and Calling*, p. 205.
61. Presumably the references are to R.C. Sherriff's *Journey's End* (1929) and Erich Remarque's *All Quiet on the Western Front* (1929).
62. Brook to Heads of Departments, 5 Dec. 1957, CAB103/562.
63. A.K. Ogilvy-Webb to R. Clarke, 18 Apr. 1962, T230/1048. Despite extensive searches, assisted by the Cabinet Office's Historical Section, the actual responses have not been found.
64. For examples of 'The Novel' during the late 1950s, see WO350/9-11. War Office files (WO) are located at TNA.
65. Sir John Maud to Brook, 24 Sept. 1958, quoted Ogilvy-Webb to Clarke, 18 Apr. 1962, T230/1048.
66. Ogilvy-Webb to Clarke, 18 Apr. 1962, T230/1048.
67. Sir E. Playfair to Brook, 18 Feb. 1958, quoted Ogilvy-Webb to Clarke, 18 Apr. 1962, T230/1048.
68. Michael Cary to Trend, 11 Dec. 1962, CAB103/598.
69. Trend to Douglas-Home, 22 Nov. 1963, CAB21/5230.
70. Cary to Trend, 11 Dec. 1962, CAB103/598; *The Times*, 27, 29 Jan. 1960; Brook to Eden, 7 Mar. 1960, AP23/56/72.

Notes   261

71. C(65) 114, 27 July 1965, CAB129/122, Pt. 1, fol. 195; Minute 7, ACPR Meeting, 13 July 1964, CAB21/5230; Watt, 'Contemporary history', 512; Llewellyn Woodward, 'The study of contemporary history', *Journal of Contemporary History*, 1 (1966), 3–5.
72. Cary to Trend, 11 Dec. 1962, CAB103/598.
73. Aldrich, 'Policing the past', 953.
74. Minutes of Meeting, 14 Jan. 1964, CAB21/5230; W. McIndoe, 11 Jan. 1966, CAB103/598; Rohan Butler, 3 Feb. 1964, FO370/2771/LS17. Foreign Office (FO) records are located at TNA. On the historians's campaign, see H.G. Nicholas to Cary, 12 Nov. 1963, CAB21/5230; Butler, 21 Nov. 1963, FO370/2725/LS17; Colin Holmes, 'Government files and privileged access', *Social History*, 6 (1981), 335; Watt, 'Contemporary History', 515–18.
75. Charles Webster and Noble Frankland, *The Strategic Air Offensive Against Germany, 1939–1945*, vols 1–4 (London: HMSO, 1961).
76. H.G. Nicholas, 'Foreign historians get first say', *The Times*, 19 June 1962; Trend to Douglas-Home, 22 Nov. 1963, CAB21/5230.
77. Bligh to Trend, 24 Nov. 1963, I. Bancroft to Abbot and Cairncross, 10 Dec. 1963, CAB21/5230; *Hansard (Commons)*, 20 Feb. 1964, vol. 689, col. 1393; *Hansard (Commons)*, 9 June 1964, vol. 696, col. 234.
78. Trend to Douglas-Home, 22 Nov. 1963, CAB21/5230.
79. *Hansard (Commons)*, 6 Dec. 1962, vol. 668, cols 1496–7; 11 Dec. 1962, vol. 669, cols 207–209; Douglas-Home to P. Noel Baker, 26 Mar. 1964, PREM11/4660. Prime Minister's Office (PREM) records are located at TNA.
80. *Hansard (Commons)*, 9 June 1964, vol. 696, cols 233–4.
81. Trend to Douglas-Home, 22 Nov. 1963, Trend to H. Caccia, 19 Mar. 1964, Trend to Sir G. Coldstream, 8 June 1964, CAB21/5230.
82. Trend to Douglas-Home, 22 Nov. 1963, CAB21/5230. The presentation of colonial history was a prime concern: Garner to Trend, 5 Aug. 1964, CAB21/5230.
83. Trend to Douglas-Home, 22 Nov. 1963, CAB21/5230.
84. P. Allen to Trend, 17 Jan. 1964, encl. McIndoe, 11 Jan. 1966, CAB103/598.
85. *The Times*, 11 July 1964; ACPR Minutes, 13 July 1964, encl. Gowing to Woods, 12 Aug. 1964, CAB21/5230.
86. Clifton Child, 5 Jan. 1965, FO370/2811/LS23; D.C. Watt, 'Restrictions on research: the Fifty-Year Rule and British foreign policy', *International Affairs*, 41 (1965), 89–95.
87. Lord Denning, ACPR chairman, to Lord Gardiner, Lord Chancellor, 26 Oct. 1964, CAB21/5231.
88. Trend to Wilson, 29 Jan. 1965, CAB21/5230; Trend to Wilson, 9 Apr. 1965, CAB21/5231.
89. Trend to Nunn and Woods, 11 Feb. 1965, CAB21/5230; Harold Wilson, *The Labour Government, 1964–1970: A Personal Record* (London: Weidenfeld and Nicolson & Michael Joseph, 1971), pp. 203–4.
90. Trend to Wilson, 29 Jan. 1965, CAB21/5230; Trend to Wilson, 9 Apr. 1965, CAB21/5231.
91. Trend, 30 Apr. 1965, CAB21/5231.
92. Ibid.
93. Trend to Coldstream, 27 July 1965, CAB21/5231. At one stage, Wilson proposed a 25-Year Rule.

94. Quoted, Butler, 26 May 1966, FO370/2906/LS13.
95. Cabinet 5 Aug. 1965, meeting 45, CAB128/39 Pt 3, fols 343–4; C(65) 114, 27 July 1965, CAB129/122 Pt 1, fols 194–7.
96. Grimond gave his support relatively quickly, but the Conservative Party's preference for a 40-year period meant that Heath's approval for the 30-Year Rule was not received until June 1966: Child, 18 Jan. 1971, CAB164/887; Wilson, *Labour Government*, p. 204.
97. Wilson, *Hansard (Commons)*, 9 Mar. 1966, vol. 725, cols 561–3.
98. W. Reid to Trend, 9 May 1966, CAB103/598.
99. Wilson, *Hansard (Commons)*, 10 Aug. 1966, vol. 733, cols 1706–8; Wilson, *Hansard (Commons)*, 8 June 1967, vol. 747, cols 1291; Child to P. White, 21 Feb. 1974, MG Cabinet Office War Histories.
100. R. Butler to Nicholls, 8 Sept. 1966, FO370/2906/LS13.
101. *Hansard (Commons)*, 10 Aug. 1966, vol. 733, cols 1706–8; Butler, 8 Sept. 1966, FO370/2906/LS13.
102. Butler, 26 May 1966, FO370/2906/LS13; 'Talking points', n.d. (Oct. 1966), FO370/2906/LS13.
103. F. Ashton Gwatkin to C. Syers, Treasury, 31 July 1941, FO366/1221/X6167.
104. L. Woodward to William Strang and Bridges, 13 Oct. 1944, FO370/1082/L4925.
105. Butler, 1 July 1964, FO370/2771/LS17; FCO Questionnaire for Public Records Committee, p. 4, encl. M. Palliser to Aylett, 7 Mar. 1979, LCO27/21. The Lord Chancellor's Office (LCO) records are located at TNA.
106. Child, 12 Sept. 1966, FO370/2906/LS13; Gore-Booth to George Brown, 3 Oct. 1966, FO800/983.
107. Aldrich, 'Policing the past', 935–41, 944.
108. *Hansard (Commons)*, 10 Aug. 1966, vol. 733, cols 1706–8; Butler, 8 Sept. 1966, FO370/2906/LS13.
109. Butler, 3 Feb. 1964, FO370/2771/LS17; Butler, 18 Oct. 1966, FO370/2906/LS13.
110. Gore-Booth, 31 Oct. 1966, FO370/2906/LS13.
111. Gore-Booth to Sir John Nicholls, 19 Sept. 1966, 'Talking points', n.d. (Oct. 1966), FO370/2906/LS13.
112. Wilson, n.d. (Apr. 1968), PREM13/2144.
113. Trend to Wilson, 11 Apr. 1968, PREM13/2144. Douglas-Home's membership is interesting given his limited vision of official histories: 'I do not quite see the point of the 30 years rule if Official Historians have access to all the material long before it is up': quoted, D.R. Thorpe, *Alec Douglas-Home* (London: Sinclair-Stevenson, 1996), p. 395.
114. Wilson, *Hansard (Commons)*, 18 Dec. 1969, vol. 793, cols 411–13.
115. Wilson, n.d. (Apr. 1968), PREM13/2144. Wilson specifically mentioned this topic in his memoirs: Wilson, *The Labour Government*, p. 204; Alec Cairncross (ed.), *The Wilson Years: A Treasury Diary, 1964–1969* (London: The Historians' Press, 1997), p. 316.
116. *The Times*, 1 July 1967.
117. Wilson, *Hansard (Commons)*, 22 Mar. 1960, vol. 620, col. 231; *Hansard (Commons)*, 14 May 1964, vol. 695, col. 602; *Hansard (Commons)*, 11 June 1964, vol. 696, col. 629.

118. *Hansard (Commons)*, 26 Nov. 1964, vol. 702, col. 1468.
119. Wilson, *Hansard (Commons)*, 24 May 1966, vol. 729, col. 279; 8 June 1967, vol. 747, cols 1290–91.
120. Trend to Douglas-Home, 22 Nov. 1963, CAB21/5230.
121. Reid, 4 Oct. 1966, T199/1025; Gowing, 'Peacetime official history', 2.
122. Trend to Wilson, 11 Apr. 1968, PREM13/2144; Child to P. White, 21 Feb. 1974, MG Cabinet Office War Histories.
123. Hay, 'British historians', p. 53.
124. Nailor, *Learning from Precedent*, p. 30.
125. Woodward to Cadogan, 26 May 1956, 13 June 1956, ACAD 4/6. The Alexander Cadogan Papers (ACAD) are located at the Churchill Archives Centre, Cambridge University. Brook approved Eden's request to consult Woodward's text when writing his memoirs: Brook to Eden, 30 May 1962, AP23/56/95A.
126. Aldrich, 'Policing the past', 941–50.
127. Gowing, *House of Commons, Education, Science and Arts Committee, Public Records, Minutes of Evidence*, 4 May 1983, p. 95.
128. Gowing, 'Peacetime official history', 3; C. Child to A. Allen, UKAEA, 19 July 1972, T319/2709.
129. Cabinet Office Historical Section, 6 June 1972, MG Cabinet Office War Histories.
130. Aldrich, 'Policing the past', 924.
131. Trend to Wilson, 29 Jan. 1965, CAB21/5230; Sir John Hunt to Sir A. Part, 31 Dec. 1973, T319/2706.
132. Quoted, Butler, 18 Oct. 1966, FO370/2906/LS13. See Peter J. Beck, 'The conflict potential of the "dots on the map" ', *The International History Review*, 13 (1991), 124–33.
133. Sir John Hoskyns, 'Conservatism is not enough', *Political Quarterly*, 55 (1984), 12.
134. David Henderson, 'Two costly British errors', *The Listener*, 27 Oct. 1977, 530. As indicated in Chapter 6, Henderson, who was Professor of Political Economy at University College, London, in 1977, had acted previously as an economic adviser at both the Treasury and the Ministry of Aviation before moving to the World Bank. Subsequently, he gave the 1985 Reith lectures and worked for the OECD.
135. David Henderson, 'Under the Whitehall blanket', *The Listener*, 17 Nov. 1977, 635.
136. Gowing to SSRC, 'Official histories', Mar. 1972, MG Cabinet Office War Histories; Hoskyns, 'Conservatism is not enough', 9.
137. Abbot to W. Armstrong, 4 Dec. 1962, T199/921.
138. The impact of the FOI provisions, introduced in 2005, warrants further study as yet another step-change in the management of official secrecy.
139. Gowing to Child, 23 Jan. 1974, MG Cabinet Office War Histories; Coll. Misc.0817, files 1–4, Treasury 1967–69, Papers of Michael Lee. Lee's papers are located at LSE.
140. Hancock to Chapman, 29 May 1985, MG Corresp. Hancock.
141. Hancock, *Country and Calling*, p. 197.

3 The Treasury becomes 'very historically minded', 1957–60

1. A.K. Ogilvy-Webb to P. Vinter, 14 Oct. 1966, T199/1025.
2. I. Bancroft to K. Weston, 11 Mar. 1963, T199/921.
3. Abbot to W. Armstrong and Helsby, 5 May 1967, T199/1025.
4. Collier to Petch, 24 Oct. 1966, T199/1025.
5. Collier to Lee, Hartcup, 7 Apr. 1967, Abbot to D. Heaton, Cabinet Office, 12 May 1967, T199/1025.
6. Collier to J.D. Rae, 22 Apr. 1964, T199/921.
7. Sir Alexander Johnston to Brook, 28 Jan. 1957, T199/664.
8. Johnston, 19 Mar. 1957, T199/664.
9. Brook, 29 Jan. 1957, T199/664; Brook to Johnston, 4 Feb. 1957, MG War Economy.
10. Johnston, 19 Mar. 1957, T199/664. Gowing's 'Monetary policy and the control of economic conditions: a note on recent experience' paralleled the Bank of England's 'Some features of monetary history in the last five years'. The Radcliffe Committee's report on the British monetary system was published in 1959.
11. Sir Edmund Compton, 19 June 1957, T233/1692; Gowing, 3 July 1957, MG War Economy.
12. Compton to Gowing, 16 Sept. 1957, T233/2129.
13. Johnston, 12 Nov. 1957, 15 Nov. 1957, 17 Jan. 1958, Brook, 27 Dec. 1957, T199/664.
14. Treasury Historical Memorandum (THM) 1: *The Treasury and Acts of God*, Nov. 1957, T236/5982.
15. *Acts of God*, p. 4, T236/5982. See Hilda Grieve, *The Great Tide: The Story of the 1953 Flood Disaster in Essex* (Chelmsford: Essex County Council, 1959).
16. *Acts of God*, p. 2, T236/5982.
17. Ibid., p. 6, T236/5982.
18. Although the government's pound-for-pound promise in 1953 resulted in a potential liability of £4.5m, the Treasury had to pay out only *circa* £2m, thereby resulting in suggestions that the difference should be used to improve coastal defences. Speaking in July 1956, Harold Macmillan, the Chancellor of the Exchequer, informed Parliament that the resulting surplus would make the government more ready to help in the case of future disasters. Significantly, Gowing noted that hitherto the Treasury had made no effort to examine the implications of this pledge: *Acts of God*, pp. 9, 11, T236/5982.
19. *Acts of God*, p. 7, T236/5982.
20. THM 2: *Festival Pleasure Gardens*, Nov. 1957, T236/5982; Trend to Brook, 4 Oct. 1957, CAB103/562.
21. Becky E. Conekin, *'The Autobiography of a Nation': The 1951 Festival of Britain* (Manchester: Manchester University Press, 2003), pp. 203–31. Conekin used public records, but *not* Treasury files.
22. *Festival Gardens*, pp. 4, 6, 7, T236/5982.
23. Ibid., p. 8, T236/5982.
24. Ibid., p. 8, T236/5982.
25. Ibid., p. 9, T236/5982.

26. Peter Vinter to Sir Robert Hall, 9 Aug. 1957, T234/716. George Bradshaw's railway timetables, as published between 1839 and 1961, were regarded as a national institution.
27. Vinter, 16 Oct. 1957, T234/716.
28. Sir Robert Hall, 9 Aug. 1957, R. Clarke, 12 Aug. 1957, Vinter, 16 Oct. 1957, T234/716.
29. Vinter to Clarke, 8 May 1958, Clarke, 21 May 1958, T234/716.
30. Abbot, 9 July 1958, T234/716.
31. Johnston, 16 Oct. 1957, T199/664.
32. Johnston, 19 Mar. 1957, 16 Oct. 1957, T199/664.
33. G.R. Bell to divisional heads, 7 May 1958, T199/664.
34. P. Nicholls to Abbot, 9 Oct. 1958, Nicholls, 21 Jan. 1959, T199/664.
35. Abbot, 3 July 1958, T199/664.
36. Bell, 26 June 1958, T199/664.
37. Johnston to Brook, 26 June 1958, T199/664.
38. Brook, 30 June 1958, T199/664.
39. Ibid.
40. Clarke, 21 May 1958, T234/716; Clarke, 30 June 1958, Clarke to Brook, 9 July 1958, T199/664.
41. Cairncross, *Richard Clarke*, p. 139.
42. Clarke to Brook, 9 July 1958, T199/664.
43. Clarke to Brook, 9 July 1958, T199/664.
44. Clarke, 21 May 1958, T234/716.
45. Brook, 11 July 1958, 8 Aug. 1958, T199/664.
46. Lee, 14 Aug. 1958, Bell, 1 Oct. 1958, T199/664.
47. Bell, 1 Oct. 1958, T199/664.
48. Abbot to Clarke, 2 Oct. 1958, T199/664.
49. Clarke, 3 Oct. 1958, T199/664.
50. Abbot, 21 Nov. 1958, T199/664.
51. P. Nicholls, 2 Jan. 1959, T199/664.
52. Gowing to Peirson, 2 May 1962, MG Corresp. UKAEA. Pension arrangements remained a perennial cause of concern: Gowing to John Patten, 4 Feb. 1982, MG Civil Service Pension 1973–86.
53. Brook to Gowing, 22 Nov. 1962, MG Misc. Corresp. Pre-1966.
54. Technically, Gowing was still employed by the Cabinet Office. Soon afterwards, Sir Roger Makins (later Lord Sherfield) followed her from the Treasury to become the UKAEA's chairman.
55. Nicholls, 21 Jan. 1959, 5 June 1959, T199/664.
56. Gowing, Draft Introduction, May 1959, p. 1, T220/1382.
57. W. Russell Edmunds to Gowing, 21 Nov. 1958, T220/1382. Upon retirement, Russell-Edmunds became a part-time Treasury historian!
58. Gowing, May 1959, p. 1, T220/1382.
59. Ibid., pp. 2–3, T220/1382.
60. Nicholls to Littler, 2 June 1959, T199/664.
61. Gowing to A. Peck, 23 July 1958, Littler to Gowing, 4 Nov. 1958, Littler to Peck, 12 June 1959, T220/1382.
62. Littler to Peck, 12 June 1959, T220/1382.
63. Peck to Littler, 9 June 1959, Peck to Nicholls, 5 Aug. 1959, T220/1382. The term 'memoranda' reflects its nature as a series of separate memoranda on individual countries.

64. Littler to Peck, 12 June 1959, T220/1382.
65. Peck to Littler, 9 June 1959, Peck to Nicholls, 5 Aug. 1959, T220/1382.
66. Gowing, May 1959, p. 1, T220/1382.
67. Littler to Peck, 12 June 1959, Peck to Nicholls, 5 Aug. 1959, T220/1382.
68. Nicholls to Abbot 15 Sept. 1959, T199/664. One unresolved matter concerned the extent to which Gowing's permission was required to amend the text, particularly as compared to the view that 'the decision to make amendments rests entirely with the Treasury' as the commissioning authority. In the event, shelving the history avoided the need to press this point to a conclusion: Littler to Peck, 12 June 1959, T220/1382.
69. Douglas Wass, *Government and the Governed: BBC Reith Lectures 1983* (London: Routledge & Kegan Paul, 1983), pp. 88–9; Hennessy, 'A crack appears'.
70. Gowing to Wass, 18 Sept. 1978, 31 Oct. 1978, MG Corresp. Wass.
71. Wass to Gowing, 23 Oct. 1978, MG Corresp. Wass.
72. Gowing to Wass, 31 Oct. 1978, MG Corresp. Wass.
73. Gowing to PRO, July 1969, MG Job Applications.
74. *Festival Gardens*, p. 7, T236/5982.
75. Quoted, Minutes of SSRC Social Science and Government Committee, 20 Oct. 1972, MG Cabinet Office War Histories; Wass to Gowing, 29 Nov. 1978, MG Corresp. Wass.
76. Gowing to Wass, 1 Aug. 1980, MG Corresp. Wass.
77. Littler to Peck, 12 June 1959, T220/1382.
78. Littler to Gowing, 4 Nov. 1958, T220/1382.
79. Clarke to Brook, 25 Apr. 1962, CLRK1/3/2/1. Sir Richard Clarke's papers (CLRK) are located at the Churchill Archives Centre, Cambridge University.
80. Ogilvy-Webb to Vinter, 13 Oct. 1965, T230/1048.
81. Douglas Henley to Sharp, 22 Dec. 1971, T199/1240.
82. Gowing to France, 31 Jan. 1978, MG Corresp. Wass; *The Times*, 13, 20 Jan. 1978.
83. C.W. France to Gowing, 7 Feb. 1978, MG Corresp. Wass.
84. Gowing to Wass, 1 Aug. 1980, MG Corresp. Wass.
85. Gowing to France, 23 Feb. 1978, France to Gowing, 27 Feb. 1978, MG Corresp. Wass.
86. Brook to Gowing, 22 Nov. 1962, MG Misc. Corresp. Pre-1966.
87. Clarke to Brook, 30 July 1959, T199/664.

4 Pushing ahead with "funding experience", 1960–62

1. Clarke to Brook, 30 July 1959, T199/664.
2. Samuel Goldman, 'Clarke, Sir Richard William Barnes (1910–1975)', *Oxford Dictionary of National Biography*, Oxford University Press, 2004 [accessed 26 Oct. 2004: http://www.oxforddnb.com/view/article/30938]; Theakston, *Leadership in Whitehall*, pp. 148–69. One of Clarke's sons, Charles, held ministerial office in the Blair governments, becoming Home Secretary in 2004.
3. Peden, *Treasury and Public Policy*, pp. 493, 523–4; Cairncross, *Richard Clarke*, pp. xxi–ii.
4. Clarke to Brook, 25 Apr. 1962, CLRK1/3/2/1.
5. Clarke to Brook, 30 July 1959, T199/664.

Notes   267

6. Clarke to Brook, 25 Apr. 1962, CLRK1/3/2/1.
7. Clarke to Brook, 30 July 1959, T199/664.
8. Brook to Clarke, 13 Aug. 1959, T199/664.
9. Office Notice, G. Bell, 7 May 1958, T199/664.
10. Nicholls to Abbot, 15 Sept. 1959, T199/664.
11. Ibid.
12. Clarke to Brook, 30 July 1959, T199/664.
13. A. Phelps to Bancroft, 28 Sept. 1962, T320/128.
14. THM 5: *The Government and Wages, 1945–1960*, July 1962, p. 1, T267/7; Peden, *Treasury and Public Policy*, pp. 481–6.
15. Clarke to Ogilvy-Webb, 9 Oct. 1961, T311/21.
16. Ibid., 1 Feb. 1961, 17 Jan. 1962, T311/21.
17. Clarke to Abbot, 1 Feb. 1961, CLRK 1/3/1/3; Clarke, 27 June 1961, T311/21; Clarke to Abbot, 27 Apr. 1962, CLRK 1/3/2/1; Cairncross, *Richard Clarke*, pp. vii–ix.
18. Clarke to Ogilvy-Webb, 1 Feb. 1961, T311/21.
19. Ogilvy-Webb, 15 Nov. 1961, T311/21. The three-volume version included occasional narrator's comments in square brackets. For example, in *The Government and Wages*, vol. 3, p. 5, Ogilvy-Webb commented that a claim made in the *Manchester Guardian*, 26 May 1956, about a government appeal to trade unions was 'perhaps an exaggeration': CLRK 1/1.
20. Clarke to Ogilvy-Webb, 9 Oct. 1961, T311/21; *Government and Wages*, p. 1, T267/7.
21. Clarke to Ogilvy-Webb, 9 Oct. 1961, Clarke to Stevenson, 15 Nov. 1961, T311/21.
22. Clarke to Ogilvy-Webb, 16 Jan. 1962, T311/21.
23. Stevenson, n.d. (Nov. 1961), Stevenson to Clarke, 16 Mar. 1962, Clarke to Sir L. Helsby, 11 Apr. 1962, T311/21.
24. Helsby to Clarke, 5 June 1962, T311/21; Ogilvy-Webb to Sharp, 28 Feb.1969, p. 6, T199/1240.
25. The three volumes were sub-divided as follows: *The Government and Wages 1945–1960*: vol. 1, 1945–51; vol. 2, 1952–56; vol. 3, 1956–60.
26. Ogilvy-Webb to Clarke, 30 Nov. 1961, T230/1048.
27. *Government and Wages*, vol.1, pp. 1–2, CLRK 1/1.
28. Ibid., pp. 4–5, CLRK 1/1.
29. *Government and Wages*, p. 1, T267/7.
30. Ibid., pp. 2–3, T267/7.
31. Ibid., p. 1, T267/7; Clarke to Helsby, 5 June 1962, T311/21.
32. *Government and Wages*, p. 3, T267/7.
33. Clarke, July 1962, CLRK 1/1; Clarke to Lee, 7 Mar. 1962, CLRK 1/3/2/1; Clarke to Brook, 25 Apr. 1962, CLRK1/3/2/1; Clarke to Maude, 9 May 1962, T311/21.
34. Clarke to Lee, 7 Mar. 1962, CLRK 1/3/2/1.
35. Clarke to Ogilvy-Webb, 9 Oct. 1961, T311/21; Clarke to Lee, 7 Mar. 1962, CLRK 1/3/2/1.
36. Clarke to Lee, 7 Mar. 1962, CLRK 1/3/2/1.
37. Clarke to Brook, 25 Apr. 1962, CLRK1/3/2/1; Clarke to Helsby, 5 June 1962, T311/21.
38. Examples of generally positive feedback include E. Maude to Clark, 8 Mar. 1962, Vinter to Clark, 12 Mar. 1962, Stevenson to Clark, T311/21.

268 *Notes*

39. Clarke to Lee and Brook, 1 Dec. 1961, T230/1048.
40. Clarke to Lee, 7 Mar. 1962, Clarke to Helsby, 5 June 1962, T311/21.
41. Maude to Clarke, 8 Mar. 1962, T311/21.
42. Clarke to Trend, 14 June 1962, CLRK 1/3/2/1.
43. Clarke to Abbot, Cairncross, 14 Feb. 1962, T311/21; Clarke to Brook, 25 Apr. 1962, Clarke to Trend, 14 June 1962, CLRK1/3/2/1.
44. Clarke to Trend, 14 June 1962, CLRK 1/3/2/1.
45. Clarke to Brook, 25 Apr. 1962, CLRK1/3/2/1; Clarke to the Warden, Nuffield College, Oxford, 13 Jan. 1964, CLRK 1/3/3/1.
46. Quoted, Bancroft, 1 Feb. 1962, T199/921.
47. Clarke to Brook, 25 Apr. 1962, CLRK1/3/2/1.
48. See Chapter 3 for these exchanges.
49. Clarke to Brook, 25 Apr. 1962, CLRK1/3/2/1.
50. Clarke to Abbot, 27 Apr. 1962, CLRK 1/3/2/1.
51. Symons to Rickett, 30 Sept. 1959, T236/5982.
52. M.E. Johnston to Isaac, 23 June 1958, T236/5982.
53. J.E. Lucas to A.W. Taylor, 31 Aug. 1959, Symons, 30 Sept. 1959, T236/5982.
54. Lucas to Taylor, 31 Aug. 1959, T236/5982. Given the focus of Chapters 10–12 on the 1951 Abadan dispute, it is worth noting that Lucas' history merely glossed over this episode in a few lines.
55. Symons to Rickett, 30 Sept. 1959, T236/5982.
56. Taylor to Rickett, 15 Mar. 1960, T236/5982.
57. HD 63(8), Abbot, 19 Feb. 1963, T319/1158.
58. THM 3: *Civil Service Superannuation – A Chronological Narrative of Legislation*, R.C. Sugars, Jan. 1960, T227/2082. Reportedly, Sugars died before its completion.
59. Gowing to Wass, 31 Oct. 1978, MG Corresp. Wass. For one Treasury official, it was 'incredibly boring': Miss Court to France, 30 Aug. 1978, EO22/85/01.
60. THM 4: *The Convertibility Crisis of 1947*, Dec. 1962, p. 1, T267/4.
61. *Convertibility Crisis*, p. 49, T267/4.
62. Ibid., p. 53, T267/4.
63. Ibid., p. 49, T267/4; Peden, *Treasury and Public Policy*, pp. 386–90.
64. Convertibility Crisis, p. 58, T267/4.
65. Clarke to Brook, 9 July 1958, T199/664; Clarke quoted, Mitchell to D. Allen, 20 Feb. 1962, T199/921. See Chapter 13 for the comments of L.S. Pressnell, the official historian, about this THM.
66. Playfair quoted, Mitchell to Allen, 20 Feb. 1962, T199/921. In 1941 Rickett was involved in the initiation of the wartime official histories.
67. Mitchell to Allen, 20 Feb. 1962, T199/921; Abbot to Collier, 4 May 1964, T311/202.
68. J. Hansford to Douglas, 28 Aug. 1962, T199/798.
69. Clarke to Brook, 25 Apr. 1962, Clarke to Trend, 14 June 1962, CLRK 1/3/2/1.
70. Mitchell, 20 Feb. 1962, Bancroft to Abbot, 13 Dec. 1963, T199/921.
71. W. Webster, 27 May 1959, T222/1029.
72. Clarke to Brook, 30 July 1959, T199/664.
73. Bancroft, 29 Mar. 1962, T199/921.
74. Quoted, Bancroft, 1 Feb. 1962, T199/921.
75. Catherine Dennis, 'A note on funding experience and Treasury histories, 1957–1976', May 1977, p. 7, EO22/85/01.
76. Sir Frank Lee to Clarke, 16 Apr. 1962, T311/21.

77. Nicholls to Abbot, 15 Sept. 1959, T199/664.
78. Clarke, n.d. (July 1962), T311/21.

5 The Public Enterprises Division (PE) as a case study, 1962–65

1. Board of Trade, 'Historical Memoranda', 10 Oct. 1961, BT296/52; 'Historical Memoranda', 31 Oct. 1962, T199/921.
2. Board of Trade, 10 Oct. 1961, BT296/52.
3. P.D. Nairne, Admiralty, 'Digging up the past', n.d. (Oct. 1961), BT296/52.
4. 'Historical Memoranda', 31 Oct. 1962, T199/921.
5. Nairne, 'Digging up the Past', n.d. (Oct. 1961), BT296/52.
6. R. Clarke, 'The reorganisation of the treasury', lecture at LSE, 4 Dec. 1962, CLRK 6/1/3; Richard A. Chapman, *The Treasury in Public Policymaking* (London: Routledge, 1997), pp. 43–5.
7. Abbot to Armstrong, 4 Dec. 1962, T199/921.
8. L.J. Taylor to Henley, 18 Sept. 1962, T199/798.
9. Abbot to Armstrong, 4 Dec. 1962, T199/921.
10. Abbot, H.D.(62)31, 13 Aug. 1962, T319/1158.
11. Abbot to Armstrong, 4 Dec. 1962, T199/921.
12. Bancroft to Abbot, 13 Dec. 1963, T199/921.
13. Abbot, H.D.(63)8, 19 Feb. 1963, T319/1158.
14. Ibid. (62)31, 13 Aug. 1962, T319/1158.
15. Ibid. (63)8, 19 Feb. 1963, T319/1158.
16. Bancroft to Abbot, 13 Dec. 1963, T199/921.
17. R. Lloyd, 27 Sept. 1962, Lloyd to Abbot, 6 May 1963, T276/39.
18. Clarke to Brook, 25 Apr. 1962, CLRK 1/3/2/1.
19. Clarke to Ogilvy-Webb, 19 Feb. 1963, 11, 12 June 1963, T311/202.
20. Ibid., 11 June 1963, 27 Nov. 1963, T311/202.
21. Douglas Allen to Clarke, 31 Dec. 1963, T311/202.
22. Ogilvy-Webb to Clarke, 30 June 1963, T311/202.
23. Clarke to Ogilvy-Webb, 19 Feb. 1963, T311/202.
24. A.K. Rawlinson to Ogilvy-Webb, 1 July 1963, T311/202.
25. Cairncross, *Richard Clarke*, pp. 70–6.
26. THM 7: *Long-Term Economic Planning, 1945–1951*, vol. 1, Apr. 1964, p. 1, T267/11.
27. Helsby to Clarke, 6 May 1964, T230/1048; Collier to Anson, 12 May 1964, T311/202.
28. Collier to Ogilvy-Webb, 27 Oct. 1964, T311/202.
29. Rawlinson to Ogilvy-Webb, 1 July 1963, T311/202.
30. *Economic Planning*, pp. 93–4, T267/11; Peden, *Treasury and Public Policy*, pp. 375–83.
31. *Economic Planning*, pp. 1–3, T267/11.
32. Ibid, p. 2, T267/11.
33. Ibid, p. 3, T267/11.
34. Vinter to Littlewood, 4 June 1963, T319/1158; Vinter to L. Petch, 31 Oct. 1963, T139/141.
35. Vinter, 11 June 1963, T319/1158.

36. Vinter, 9 Oct. 1963, T319/1158.
37. J.J.B. Hunt to Collier, 13 May 1965, R. Middleton, 4 Jan. 1966, K.T. King to Miss Kelley, T319/1158.
38. Hunt to Collier, 13 May 1965, T319/1158.
39. Hunt to Granger-Taylor, 10 Mar. 1965, T319/1158.
40. Granger-Taylor to Vinter, 9 July 1963, Oct. 1963, T319/140.
41. Vinter to Granger-Taylor, 7 Oct. 1963, 31 Oct. 1963, 20 Dec. 1963, T319/141.
42. Granger-Taylor to Barratt, 30 Oct. 1964, T319/142.
43. Granger-Taylor to Vinter, 17 Feb. 1965, T319/142.
44. Vinter to Clarke, 8 Mar. 1965, Vinter to Helsby, Cairncross, Clark, 29 Mar. 1965, T319/142.
45. Helsby to Clarke, 5 Apr. 1965, T319/142.
46. Hunt to Vinter, 12 Mar. 1965, A.K. Cairncross to Vinter, 22 Mar. 1965, T319/142.
47. Clarke, 1 Apr. 1965, T319/142.
48. Cairncross, *Richard Clarke*, p. 174.
49. Cairncross to Clark, 29 Mar. 1965, T319/142.
50. Henderson's interest in monitoring the performance of British governments was outlined in Chapter 2.
51. Helsby to Clarke, 5 Apr. 1965, T319/142.
52. Vinter to Hunt, 20 Apr. 1965, T319/142.
53. Helsby to Way, 30 Apr. 1965, Collier to Abbot, Anson, 15 June 1965, T319/142.
54. Way to Helsby, 3 May 1965, T319/142.
55. THM 9: *A History of Aircraft Purchasing for the Air Corporations*, Nov. 1965, T267/13.
56. Hunt to Vinter, 12 Mar. 1965, Hunt to L. Airey, 13 May 1965, T319/142.
57. Granger-Taylor, 20 May 1965, T319/142.
58. Vinter to Granger-Taylor, 7 Oct. 1963, T319/140; Vinter to Petch, 31 Oct. 1963, L. Petch, 4 Nov. 1963, T319/141.
59. Vinter, 4 Jan. 1965, T319/1158; Vinter to Helsby, Cairncross, Clark, 29 Mar. 1965, T319/142.
60. The resulting balance sheet of pros (for example, saving dollars and enhancing national prestige) and cons (resulting in unsuitable aircraft for export and higher operating costs), though somewhat tentative, suggested that the debits far outweighed the gains: Vinter to Granger-Taylor, 4 Nov. 1963, 7 Jan. 1964, T319/141; Granger-Taylor to Vinter, 29 Jan. 1965, 17 Feb. 1965, T319/142.
61. Granger-Taylor to Hunt, 28 May 1965, Hunt to Granger-Taylor, 3 June 1965, T319/142.
62. Collier to Abbot, 15 June 1963, T319/142.
63. Ogilvy-Webb, 26 Oct. 1965, T199/987.
64. *The Observer*, 19 Mar. 1967, *The Times*, 27 July 1967, Collier to Granger-Taylor, 29 Aug. 1967, Bancroft to Hunt, Lee, 2 Aug. 1967, T319/142.
65. Granger-Taylor to Stevenson, 27 Oct. 1964, T319/52; Vinter to Clarke, 3 Feb. 1965, T319/53.
66. Vinter, 4 Jan. 1965, T319/1158.
67. Granger-Taylor to Stevenson, 27 Oct. 1964, T319/52.
68. Vinter to Clarke, 3 Feb. 1965, Vinter to Stevenson, 16 Feb. 1965, Minute, Vinter to Hunt, 30 Apr. 1965, T319/53.

69. Vinter to Stevenson, 16 Feb. 1965, T319/53.
70. Clarke to Vinter, 4 Feb. 1965, T319/53.
71. Vinter to Stevenson, 16 Feb. 1965, T319/53.
72. Stevenson to Vinter, 22 Feb. 1965, T319/53; Cairncross, *Richard Clarke*, pp. 13–14.
73. Stevenson to Vinter, 22 Feb. 1965, T319/53.
74. Sir Thomas Padmore to Vinter, 12 Apr. 1965, T319/53.
75. Vinter to Hunt, 30 Apr. 1965, T319/53.
76. Vinter to Padmore, 24 Feb. 1965, T319/53.
77. James Joll, *1914: The Unspoken Assumptions. An Inaugural Lecture delivered 25 April 1968* (London: Weidenfeld & Nicolson, 1968), pp. 6–7, 23–4.
78. Stevenson to Vinter, 22 Feb. 1965, T319/53.
79. Hunt to Granger-Taylor, 15 Mar. 1965, Hunt to Vinter, 21 Apr. 1965, T319/53.
80. Hunt, 15 Apr. 1966, T319/53.
81. Granger-Taylor to Hunt, 16 Mar. 1966, T319/53; THM 11: *The Economic and Financial Obligations of the Nationalised Industries: White Paper of 1961*, May 1966, T267/15.
82. Hunt to Vinter, 25 Mar. 1966, Vinter, 29 Mar. 1966, T319/53.
83. Hunt to Collier, 19 July 1966, T319/53.
84. Hunt, 15 Apr. 1966, T319/53.
85. *Economic and Financial Obligations*, p. i, T267/15.
86. Another White Paper was published in 1967, but the results of the new strategy towards the nationalized industries proved disappointing: Hannah, 'Economic ideas', pp. 364–71.
87. Vinter, 'Granger-Taylor's Historical Work', 4 Jan. 1965, T319/1158.
88. Granger-Taylor to Vinter, 17 Feb. 1965, Hunt to Granger-Taylor, 10 Mar. 1965, Hunt to Collier, 13 May 1965, T319/1158.
89. King, 4 July 1969, T319/1158.
90. J. Hansford to J. Douglas, 28 Aug. 1962, T199/798; J. Rampton, 13 Apr. 1964, T224/2235.
91. P.G. Myers, 25 Nov. 1964, T224/2235.
92. Hansford to Douglas, 28 Aug. 1962, T199/798.
93. Miss M. Moody to Phelps, 10 May 1965, Rampton to Collier, 11 May 1965, T227/3221; author's interviews with Guy Hartcup, 20 June, 4 July 2003.
94. A. Phelps, 30 Sept. 1965, Rampton, 14 Oct. 1965, T227/3221.
95. Edward Heath, *The Course of My Life: My Autobiography* (London: Hodder & Stoughton, 1998), p. 238; Narrative Report on the Brussels Negotiations, 9 Sept. 1962, Commentary on the Narrative Report, 8 Mar. 1963, T312/1112.
96. Sir Patrick Reilly, Foreign Office Librarian, 30 Jan. 1963, T312/1111.
97. Pierson Dixon, British ambassador in Paris, to Reilly, 1 Feb. 1963, T312/1111.
98. A. France, 31 Jan. 1963, Sir Eric Roll, MAFF, to Henry Hainworth, Brussels, 25 Feb. 1963, T312/1111.
99. Lucas to Ken Gallagher, 25 Feb. 1963, 27 Feb. 1963, T312/1111.
100. S. Edwards, Board of Trade, to Lucas, 14 Mar. 1963, T312/1111.
101. G.B. Shannon, CRO, to Lucas, 27 Feb. 1963, Edwards to Lucas, 14 Mar. 1963, T312/1111; John Owen to Reilly 9 Apr. 1963, FO371/171441/M1091; Lucas to Owen, 9 Apr. 1963, T312/405.

272 Notes

102. Dixon to Reilly, 7 May 1963, FO371/171441/M1091.
103. Reportedly Heath had some doubts about the commentary but never saw Lucas' text: Reilly to Dixon, 13 May 1963, Owen to A. France, Treasury, 10 Dec. 1963, FO371/171441/M1091; R. Symons to Owen, 17 Dec. 1965, T312/1112.
104. THM 10: *Negotiations with the European Economic Community, 1961–1963*, Apr. 1966, p. 1, T267/14.
105. *Negotiations with EEC*, p. 1, T267/14.
106. Ogilvy-Webb to Vinter, 3 Nov. 1966, p. 7, T199/987.
107. Heath, *Course of My Life*, p. 238.
108. Sir David Hannay (ed.), *Britain's Entry into the European Community: Report on the Negotiations of 1970–1972 by Sir Con O'Neill* (London: Frank Cass, 2000), pp. 49, 192–3. The history is also in FCO75/1.
109. Hannay, *Britain's Entry*, pp. 341–5.
110. Ibid., pp. 32–3.
111. Ogilvy-Webb to Collier, n.d. (Feb. 1968), T199/1241.
112. Abbot to Cairncross, 3 Jan. 1964, T230/1048.
113. HD (P.S.) G (64) 3rd Meeting, 6 Apr. 1964, T224/2235.
114. Collier, 9 April 1965, T319/1158; Collier, 3 May 1965, T224/2235.
115. Bancroft to Weston, 11 Mar. 1963, Collier to J.D. Rae, 22 Apr. 1964, T199/921; THC, 19 Nov. 1965, 1st Meeting, para 15(ii), T199/1148.
116. The history, using confidential Treasury papers, was intended as a supplement to a projected book by J.C.R. Dow, a former Treasury official (1946–54). Based upon published sources, Dow's book, entitled *The Management of the British Economy, 1945–1960*, was published in 1964, and included a foreword written by Sir Robert Hall. Subsequently, Holmans became a full-time member of Treasury staff.
117. Interview with Sir Douglas Wass, 15 July 2005.
118. Pliatzky, 18 Oct. 1965, T224/2235.
119. Ogilvy-Webb to Vinter, 13 Oct. 1965, T230/1048.

6 The 'new stage' in the Treasury's historical work, 1965–68

1. Collier to Abbot, 2 July 1965, Abbot, 9 July 1965, T199/986.
2. Vinter to Helsby, 21 Jan. 1966, T230/1048.
3. Helsby, Armstrong, 25 Jan. 1966, T199/1240.
4. Collier, n.d. (Oct. 1967), T199/1240.
5. Collier to Ogilvy-Webb, 29 Oct. 1965, T199/987.
6. Clarke, 25 Oct. 1965, T199/986.
7. Ogilvy-Webb to Vinter, 13 Oct. 1965, T230/1048.
8. Helsby, 12 July 1965, T199/986; THC 1, Collier, 28 Sept. 1965, T230/1048; HD(65)42, 3 Dec. 1965, in Dennis, 'A Note on funding experience', May 1977, EO22/85/01.
9. THC 1, Collier, 28 Sept. 1965.
10. Vinter to Helsby, 21 Jan. 1966, T230/1048.
11. Collier to Ogilvy-Webb, 29 Oct. 1965, T199/987.
12. Collier to Abbot, 2 July 1965, T199/986.

Notes 273

13. In fact, she soon moved on from historical work, eventually becoming Registrar-General of England and Wales!
14. Collier, 2 July 1965, T199/986; author's interviews with Guy Hartcup, 20 June, 4 July 2003. At the Air Ministry, his work included a history of Operational Research.
15. Collier, 30 Mar. 1966, T199/1240. Reportedly, Dennis, who had left the Treasury upon marriage, had been teaching British Constitution in a further education college.
16. Bancroft, 1 Feb. 1962, T199/921.
17. Abbott, 11 Aug. 1965, Collier, 12 Aug. 1965, T199/986.
18. Ogilvy-Webb to Vinter, 13 Oct. 1965, T230/1048.
19. Vinter, 4 Aug. 1965, Collier, 12 Aug. 1965, T199/986.
20. Vinter to Collier, 26 Sept. 1966, T199/1240.
21. Vinter to Sir Douglas Allen, DEA, 7 Apr. 1967, T199/1240.
22. Collier to Vinter, 21 Nov. 1966, T199/1240.
23. THC, 19 Nov. 1965, 1st Meeting, T199/1148.
24. HD(65)42, 3 Dec. 1965, in Dennis, 'A Note on funding experience', May 1977, EO22/85/01.
25. THC, 19 Nov. 1965, para 4, T199/1148.
26. Ogilvy-Webb to Vinter, 9 Dec. 1965, T199/987; D.A. Truman to Lee and Henley, 11 Nov. 1971, T199/1240.
27. HSC, 10 Dec. 1965, p. 1, T199/987.
28. THC, 7 Jan. 1966, para 10, T199/1148.
29. Vinter to Helsby, 21 Jan. 1966, T230/1048.
30. J. Rampton to Vinter, 15 Dec. 1965, T227/3221. Paradoxically, the 1967 devaluation crisis led the Wilson government to re-introduce prescription charges. The resulting THM is discussed in Chapter 7.
31. Encl. Ogilvy-Webb to Collier, 3 Nov. 1966, T199/987.
32. Vinter to Collier, 7 Nov. 1966, Collier to Vinter, 21 Nov. 1966, T199/1240.
33. Collier to Vinter, 21 Nov. 1966, T199/1240.
34. THC, 25 Oct. 1966, paras 4–5, T199/1148.
35. HSC, 23 Nov. 1966, T199/987; Vinter to Collier, 7 Nov. 1966, T199/1240.
36. Collier to Vinter, 3 Nov. 1966, T199/1240.
37. HSC, 23 Nov. 1966, T199/987.
38. Collier to Vinter, 21 Nov. 1966, T199/1240.
39. HSC, 23 Nov. 1966, para 6(i), T199/987. In the event, the history was not submitted to Barratt for comment until September 1967.
40. King to Collier, 12 Oct. 1967, T199/1240.
41. Ogilvy-Webb for Collier, n.d. (Feb. 1968), T199/1241.
42. Treasury Historians, n.d. (Feb. 1968), T199/1241.
43. King to Collier, 12 Feb. 1968, T199/1241.
44. THC, 14 Feb. 1968, T199/1148.
45. Collier to Pitchforth, 28 June 1967, T199/1241.
46. Collier to Ogilvy-Webb, 21 Feb. 1968, T199/1241.
47. Vinter, 7 Nov. 1966, T199/1240.
48. *THM13: Rebuilding of No.10 Downing Street and Old Treasury*, Nov. 1968, pp. 9, 16, T267/17. Unlike a fixed price contract, a prime cost contract covered the actual costs.
49. *Downing Street*, Nov. 1968, p. 15, T267/17.

50. Ibid., p. 16, T267/17.
51. A.J. Phelps, 26 Apr. 1967, T199/1241.
52. *THM 14: Rehousing of the Commonwealth Institute*, Nov. 1968, p. 16, T267/18.
53. Commonwealth Institute, Nov. 1968, p. 17, T267/18.
54. The institute was moved to a new site and opened in 1962. In 2005 it prompted renewed controversy, given the way in which the building's listed status thwarted demolition plans: *The Times*, 21 July 2005, 23 July 2005.
55. Phelps, 26 Apr. 1967, T199/1241; King to Collier, 12 Oct. 1967, T199/1240.
56. Phelps, 26 Apr. 1967, T199/1241.
57. THC, 19 Nov. 1965, para 5(i), T199/1148; Phelps, 26 Apr. 1967, T199/1241. Archival evidence on this history is sketchy but, reportedly, it was adjudged 'worthless', and hence destroyed: D. Matthew, n.d. (June 1977), EO22/85/01.
58. Collier to Dennis, 20 Feb. 1968, T199/1241; A.K. Rawlinson to Dennis, 26 Feb. 1968, T295/887. See John Day, 'A failure of foreign policy: the case of Rhodesia,' in Michael Leifer (ed.), *Constraints and Adjustments in British Foreign Policy* (London: George Allen & Unwin, 1972), pp. 150–71; John W. Young, *The Labour Governments, 1964–1970: international policy*, vol. 2 (Manchester: Manchester University Press, 2003), pp. 169–88.
59. Rawlinson, 9 June 1969, Littler to Rawlinson, 10 July 1969, T295/887.
60. Collier to Dennis, 20 Feb. 1968, Rawlinson to Collier, 21 Feb. 1968, T199/1241; Rawlinson to Dennis, 26 Feb. 1968, T295/887.
61. Rawlinson to Owen, 22 Nov. 1971, T199/1241.
62. Ogilvy-Webb, 7 Oct. 1968, T199/1240.
63. Dennis to P. Gordon, 29 Oct. 1968, T295/887.
64. Gordon to Littler, 13 June 1969, Dennis to Littler, 1 July 1969, T295/887.
65. Littler to Rawlinson, 10 July 1969, Rawlinson to Littler, 10 July 1969, T295/887.
66. Dennis to Littler, 23 Nov. 1971, T295/887.
67. Rawlinson to Owen, 22 Nov. 1971, T199/1241.
68. Rawlinson to Littler, 22 Nov. 1971, T295/887.
69. Rawlinson to Owen, 22 Nov. 1971, T199/1241.
70. Littler to Rawlinson, 25 Nov. 1971, Dennis to Littler, 16 Mar. 1972, T295/887.
71. Day, 'Failure of foreign policy', p. 151.
72. Rawlinson to Dennis, 26 Feb. 1969, Draft history, pp. 65–9, Mar. 1972, T295/887. See Day, 'Failure of foreign policy', pp. 157–64.
73. Collier to Petch, 4 Oct. 1966, T199/1025.
74. Collier to Abbot, 29 Mar. 1967, Abbot to Armstrong and Helsby, 5 May 1967, A. Bailey, 10 May 1967, T199/1025.
75. Collier to L. Petch, 24 Oct. 1966, T199/1025.
76. When advising Vinter and Collier, Ogilvy-Webb proved critical of the existing coverage of the history of government and administration by the media and academics as well as by the Royal Institute of Public Administration (RIPA): Ogilvy-Webb to Vinter, 14 Oct. 1966, T199/1025.
77. Some questioned publications involving people still alive and active in political life: Samuel Goldman, 3 May 1967, T199/1241.
78. Collier to Abbot, 24 Apr. 1967, T230/984; Abbot to Armstrong and Helsby, 5 May 1967, T199/1025.
79. Cairncross to Petch, 21 Oct. 1966, T199/1025.

Notes 275

80. Abbot to D. Heaton, Cabinet Office, 12 May 1967, Collier to Abbot, 4 July 1967, T199/1025; Roy to Abbot, 20 Apr. 1967, Collier to Abbot, 24 Apr. 1967, T230/984. In 1958 Clarke suggested a history of external economic policy to Brook: Clarke, 9 July 1958, T199/664. In due course, Sayers' commitments to write a history of the Bank of England led Leslie Pressnell to be commissioned for the official history of external economic policy: Cairncross, *The Wilson Years*, p. 363.
81. Cairncross, 11 Oct. 1965, P. Allen, 20 Oct. 1965, T230/984; Cairncross, *The Wilson Years*, p. 85.
82. Cairncross to Abbot, 18 Apr. 1967, T230/984.
83. Quoted, Butler, 26 May 1966, FO370/2906/LS13.
84. General Purposes Committee, item 8, 20 Dec. 1965, T199/987.
85. Vinter to Helsby, 21 Jan. 1966, T230/1048.
86. Clarke to Vinter, 25 Oct. 1965, T199/986; Helsby, Armstrong, 25 Jan. 1966, T199/1240.
87. Collier to Vinter, 21 Nov. 1966, T199/1240; Collier to Granger-Taylor, 24 Nov. 1966, T199/1241.
88. Collier to Rampton, 24 Feb. 1966, T199/987.
89. Collier to King, 19 Oct. 1965, T199/986; Collier to Ogilvy-Webb, 29 Oct. 1965, T199/987.
90. Ogilvy-Webb to Collier, 26 Oct. 1965, T199/987.
91. Collier to Ogilvy-Webb, 29 Oct. 1965, T199/987.
92. James Collier to the author, 9 Nov. 2005.

7 Returning the Treasury's historical activities after Fulton, 1968–70

1. Chapman, *Treasury*, p. 46; Hennessy, *Whitehall*, pp. 170–4; Thomas Balogh, 'The apotheosis of the dilettante: the establishment of mandarins', in H. Thomas (ed.), *The Establishment* (London: Anthony Blond, 1959), pp. 102–12, 119–26; *Fabian Tract 355: The Administrators* (London: The Fabian Society, 1964).
2. *The Civil Service: Report of the Committee 1966–68, Chairman: Lord Fulton, Cmnd 3638: Report*, vol. 1 (London: HMSO, 1968), para 21, p. 13; Henry Roseveare, *The Treasury: The Evolution of a British Institution* (London: Allen Lane, The Penguin Press, 1969), pp. 351–6; Hennessy, *Whitehall*, pp. 203–8.
3. Ogilvy-Webb, 28 Feb. 1969, pp. 6, 7, T199/1240.
4. Vinter to Sharp, 12 Nov. 1968, T199/1240.
5. Ogilvy-Webb to Collier, n.d. (Feb. 1968), T199/1241; THC, 14 Feb. 1968, T199/1148; Collier to Ogilvy-Webb, 21 Feb. 1968, T199/1076.
6. Collier to Rampton, 24 Feb. 1966, T199/1107.
7. J. Anson, 2 June 1966, T227/2522.
8. Ogilvy-Webb to Rampton, 22 Sept. 1966, T199/1107.
9. Anson to O. Williams, 27 Oct. 1966, Rampton to Williams, 26 Jan. 1967, T199/1107.
10. Ogilvy-Webb to Rampton, 22 Sept. 1966, T199/1107.
11. Vinter to Rampton, 12 Oct. 1966, T199/1107.

12. F. Quinlan, 18 Oct. 1966, Anson to O. Williams, 27 Oct. 1966, T199/1107; Rampton to France, 31 Mar. 1967, T227/2522.
13. Holmans, 25 Jan. 1967, T199/1107; Rampton, 24 May 1967, T199/1076.
14. Collier to Vinter, 21 July 1967, T199/1076.
15. Williams to Rampton, 16 Nov. 1966, Rampton to Williams, 26 Jan. 1967, T199/1107.
16. Ogilvy-Webb, 9 Feb. 1967, Anson to Williams, 29 Mar. 1967, T199/1107.
17. Rampton to France, 31 Mar. 1967, T227/2522.
18. Rampton, 24 May 1967, T199/1076.
19. France to Rampton, 27 June 1967, T227/2967.
20. A. Langdon to Williams, 11 July 1967, T227/2967; Collier, 21 July 1967, Vinter, 21 July 1967, T199/1076; John Eversley, 'The history of NHS charges', *Contemporary British History*, 15 (2001), 56–69. See the peacetime official history: Charles Webster, *The Health Services Since the War: Problems of Health Care, The National Health Service before 1957*, vol. 1 (London: HMSO, 1988), pp. 143–8, 188–94, 213–15; Charles Webster, *The Health Services Since the War: Government and Health Care, The National Health Service, 1958–1979*, vol. II (London: HMSO, 1996), pp. 138–9, 190–2, 214, 226.
21. THM 12: *History of Prescription Charges, 1948–1966*, Sept. 1967, T267/16; Circulation List, 25 Oct. 1967, T199/1076.
22. Collier to Vinter, 21 July 1967, Collier to Ogilvy-Webb, 20 May 1968, T199/1076; Collier to N. Jordan-Moss, 1 Mar. 1968, T227/2967.
23. Collier to Jordan-Moss, 1 Mar. 1968, T227/2967.
24. Jordan-Moss to Collier, 22 Apr. 1968, T227/3221.
25. Malcolm Widdup to Anson, Jordan-Moss, 8 Mar. 1968, T227/2967.
26. Jordan-Moss to Collier, 22 Apr. 1968, T227/3221.
27. Collier to Ogilvy-Webb, 20 May 1968, T199/1076.
28. Jordan-Moss to Collier, 22 Apr. 1968, T227/3221.
29. Widdup to Anson, Jordan-Moss, 8 Mar. 1968, T227/2967. On the political dimension, see Janet Morgan (ed.), *Richard Crossman: The Diaries of a Cabinet Minister, 1966–68*, vol. 2 (London: Hamish Hamilton and Jonathan Cape, 1976), pp. 619, 637–8, 643–6, 654; Webster, *Health Services Since the War*, vol. II, pp. 199–203, 764.
30. Collier to Ogilvy-Webb, 20 May 1968, T199/1076.
31. Jordan-Moss's subsequent comment is outlined in this chapter's conclusion.
32. Jordan-Moss to Collier, 22 Apr. 1968, T227/3221.
33. Collier to Vinter, 12 June 1968, T199/1076. Nor does the THM appear to have been used by Webster's official histories cited above.
34. Collier to Ogilvy-Webb, 20 May 1968, Ogilvy-Webb to Collier, 24 May 1968, Collier to Vinter, 12 June 1968, T199/1076; Ogilvy-Webb, 31 Oct. 1975, EO25/85/01.
35. Jordan-Moss to Sharp, 25 Nov. 1968, Sharp, 26 Nov. 1968, T199/1076.
36. Vinter, 7 Nov. 1968, T199/1241.
37. Vinter to Sharp and Collier, 12 Nov. 1968, T199/1240.
38. Vinter to Allen and Armstrong, 4 Feb. 1969, T199/1240.
39. Vinter to Allen and Armstrong, 4 Feb. 1969, T199/1240.
40. K.T. King to Sharp, 3 Dec. 1968, King, 21 Jan. 1969, Vinter to Allen and Armstrong, 4 Feb. 1969, T199/1240.
41. Allen, 7 Feb. 1969, T199/1240.

42. Armstrong to Vinter, 8 Apr. 1969, T199/1240.
43. N.S. Forward, CSD, to Collier, 2 May 1969, T199/1240.
44. King to Sharp, 3 Dec. 1968, T199/1240.
45. HSC, 1 May 1969, T199/1240.
46. Sharp, HD(69)14, 2 July 1969, T199/1241.
47. Vinter to Sharp and Collier, 12 Nov. 1968, T199/1240.
48. Clarke to Professor S. Beer, 17 July 1968, CLRK 4/3/1.
49. Forward to Collier, 2 May 1969, T199/1240.
50. Ogilvy-Webb, 20 Nov. 1968, p. 4, T199/1240; *Fulton Report*, vol. 1, paras 99–103, 172–7.
51. Bretherton to Vinter, 21 May 1969, T199/1240.
52. Vinter to Sharp, 27 May 1969, Sharp, 3 June 1969, T199/1240. On AT's delays, see Chapter 6.
53. Treasury historians to Vinter, 30 May 1969.
54. HSC, 3 June 1969, p. 2, T199/1240.
55. E. Maude to Henley, 9 Jan. 1970, T199/1241.
56. Maude to Henley, 9 Jan. 1970, T199/1241.
57. Henley to Maude, 12 Jan. 1970, T199/1241.
58. Henley to Sharp, 23 Jan. 1970, T199/1240.
59. K.T. King, 24 Oct. 1968, Collier, 25 Oct. 1968, T199/1240; Sharp, HD(69)14, 2 July 1969, T199/1241.
60. Sharp to Figgures, 24 Jan. 1969, T199/1241.
61. E. Yeo to HoDs, 19 Feb. 1970, T227/3221.
62. Kelley to McKean, 4 Sept. 1969, McKean, 5 Sept. 1969, T319/1158.
63. King, 4 July 1969, King to Kelley and McKean, 28 July 1969, App. 1, T319/1158.
64. 'The Aluminium Smelter Negotiations', n.d. (1969), T319/1158. For Cairncross, the episode offered an 'excellent case study' of a project in which the government got into 'deeper and deeper water': Cairncross, *The Wilson Years*, pp. 160–1, 278.
65. J. Kelley to D. McKean, 4 Sept. 1969, T319/1158.
66. 'The Aluminium Smelter Negotiations', n.d. (1969), para 1, T319/1158.
67. Vinter to Sharp, 27 May 1969, T199/1240; Vinter, 10 Sept. 1969, T199/1241; Kelley, 14 May 1970, D. Andren 31 July 1970, T319/1158.
68. Dennis, 'A note on funding experience', May 1977, p. 30, EO22/85/01.
69. Kelley, 14 May 1970, T319/1158.
70. HSC, 10 Dec. 1965, p. 3, T199/987; Ogilvy-Webb to J. Archer, 14 Dec. 1965, T199/1082.
71. Collier, 18 Mar. 1968, T199/1082.
72. Ogilvy-Webb to Collier, 23 Feb. 1968, T199/1241.
73. Ogilvy-Webb to Sharp, 28 Feb. 1969, T199/1240; Ogilvy-Webb, 2 Jan. 1970, T199/1241.
74. P. Middleton, 27 Nov. 1969, Maude to Henley, 9 Jan. 1970, T199/1241.
75. Henley to Sharp, 26 Jan. 1971, T199/1243.
76. Dennis to Hancock, 13 Nov. 1976, EO25/85/01.
77. J. Ford, 6 May 1970, T199/1240.
78. Sharp to Figgures, 24 Jan. 1969, T199/1241.
79. Jordan-Moss to Sharp, 24 Mar. 1970, T227/3221.
80. Jordan-Moss to Widdup, Miss Forsyth, Airey, 6 Nov. 1969, T227/3221.

81. Jordan-Moss to Sharp, 24 Mar. 1970, T227/3221.
82. M.F.H. Stuart, 16 Feb. 1970, T227/3221.
83. W.C. Smith to Jordan-Moss, 16 Oct. 1969, T227/3221.
84. Widdup to Jordan-Moss, 19 Nov. 1969, T227/3221.
85. R. Jones to Forsyth, 25 Nov. 1969, Forsyth to Jordan-Moss, 26 Nov. 1969, T227/3221.
86. Russell-Edmunds to King, 8 Aug. 1969, T199/1241.
87. King, 11 Aug. 1969, T199/1241.
88. King to Collier, 12 Oct. 1967, T199/1240.

8 Moving towards the closure of the Treasury's Historical Section, 1971–76

1. See the appendix, p. 252.
2. James Collier to the author, 9 Nov. 2005.
3. Sharp to Henley, 1 Feb. 1972, T199/1240.
4. Ibid.
5. D.A. Truman to Lee and Henley, 11 Nov. 1971, D.C. Lee, 16 Nov. 1971, T199/1240.
6. Henley to Sharp, 22 Dec. 1971, T199/1240.
7. Hunt to Sharp, 5 Jan. 1972, T199/1240.
8. Sharp, 14 Mar. 1972, HD(72)10, 'A note on funding experience', May 1977, p. 35, EO25/85/01.
9. Sharp to Henley, 1 Feb. 1972, T199/1240.
10. Barratt to Sharp, 16 June 1971, T199/1241.
11. Sharp to Henley, 1 Feb. 1972, Henley, n.d. (Feb. 1972), T199/1240.
12. Sharp, 21 Jan. 1975, HD(75)3, in EO25/85/01.
13. Sharp, HD(75)23, 'Reorganisation', 11 Sept. 1975, T199/1374; Ogilvy-Webb to Wass, 31 Oct. 1975, EO25/85/01; author's interview with Wass, 17 July 2005. Note Wass wrote Ogilvy-Webb's obituary published in *The Guardian*, 15 Dec. 1988.
14. Wass to David Hancock, 5 Nov. 1975, EO25/85/01.
15. Hancock to Wass, 17 Dec. 1975, EO25/85/01.
16. Wass to Ogilvy-Webb, 18 Dec. 1975, EO25/85/01.
17. Supplementary Report on the Preliminary Survey by the Management Review team, n.d., P.R. Gordon to D.C. Lee, 3 Dec. 1974, T199/1361.
18. Hancock to Wass, 28 June 1977, EO25/85/01.
19. Hancock to Gordon/Hawtin, 12 Dec. 1975, EO25/85/01.
20. Wass to Ogilvy-Webb, 18 Dec. 1975, EO25/85/01.
21. Dennis, 'A note on funding experience', May 1977, App. G, pp. 8–9, EO22/85/01.
22. Hopkin to Wass, 3 Oct. 1974, M. Folger to Wass, 17 Oct. 1974, T199/1320.
23. Ogilvy-Webb to Wass, Jan. 1976, Hancock to Wass, 8 Jan. 1976, Hancock to Gordon, 14 Jan. 1976, EO25/85/01.
24. J.G. Littler to Owen, 15 June 1976, EO25/85/01.
25. Hancock to Gordon, 14 Jan. 1976, Hancock, 29 Jan. 1976, EO25/85/01.
26. Hancock to Brazier, 16 Jan. 1976, Hancock to Dennis, 3 Dec. 1976, EO25/85/01.

27. Hancock to Whitaker, 10 May 1976, Dennis to Hancock, 23 June 1976, 20 Oct. 1976, EO25/85/01.
28. Hancock to Dennis, 25 June 1976, 2 Nov. 1976, Hancock to Gordon, 14 July 1976, EO25/85/01.
29. Hancock to J. Beastall, J. Caff, W. Norton, W. St. Clair, J. Whitaker, 18 Nov. 1976, EO25/85/01.
30. Dennis to Hancock, May 1977, EO22/85/01; J. Ford to Miss J. Court, 20 June 1977, Court to Hancock, 24 June 1977, EO25/85/01. Like official historians, Treasury historians were required to stamp any files used in their work for preservation with the instruction 'Do not destroy. Historical value': Y. Woodbridge, 17 Nov. 1976, EO22/85/01.
31. HD(77) 8, 9 June 1977, Hancock, EO22/85/01.
32. Dennis to Hartcup, 13 July 1977, GH.
33. Hennessy, 'A crack appears'.
34. Wass to Ogilvy-Webb, 18 Dec. 1975, EO25/85/01.
35. Sharp to Henley, 1 Feb. 1972, T199/1240.
36. Hancock to Wass, 28 June 1977, EO25/85/01.

9 Using history in the Treasury

1. Vinter, 11 June 1963, T319/1158.
2. Vinter, 7 Nov. 1968, T199/1241.
3. Vinter to Hall, 9 Aug. 1957, T234/716.
4. The 'errors' referred to the CEGB's policy adopted towards the atomic energy industry: C. Fogarty, 13 Oct. 1961, T230/1048.
5. A.D. Roy, 7 Aug. 1968, T230/1048.
6. Vinter, 11 June 1963, T319/1158.
7. Ogilvy-Webb to Vinter, 13 Oct. 1965, T230/1048.
8. Mitchell to D. Allen, 20 Feb. 1962, T199/921; W. Webster, 27 May 1959, T222/1029.
9. Vinter, 11 June 1963, T319/1158.
10. Ogilvy-Webb to Vinter, 3 Nov. 1966, T199/987.
11. Cairncross, *Richard Clarke*, p. 135.
12. Sharp to Henley, 1 Feb. 1972, T199/1240.
13. Ogilvy-Webb to Vinter, 3 Nov. 1966, T199/987.
14. Ibid., 9 Dec. 1965, T199/987.
15. Ogilvy-Webb quoted, Minutes of SSRC Social Science and Government Committee, 20 Oct. 1972, MG Cabinet Office War Histories.
16. Ogilvy-Webb, 2 Jan. 1970, T199/1241.
17. P. Middleton, 27 Nov. 1969, T199/1241.
18. Ogilvy-Webb, 20 Nov. 1968, pp. 2–4, 9, 11, T199/1240.
19. Ogilvy-Webb to Vinter, 3 Nov. 1966, T199/987.
20. Ogilvy-Webb, 3 Nov. 1966, T199/987; Ogilvy-Webb to Sharp (28) Feb. 1969, p. 3, T199/1240; Ogilvy-Webb, 2 Jan. 1970, T199/1241.
21. Ogilvy-Webb to Collier, 3 Nov. 1965, T199/986.
22. Abbot, H.D.(63)8, 19 Feb. 1963, T319/1158.
23. Ogilvy-Webb, 20 Nov. 1968, pp. 3–4, T199/1240.
24. Ogilvy-Webb to Collier, 3 Nov. 1965, T199/986.

25. Ogilvy-Webb to Wass, 31 Oct. 1975, Ogilvy-Webb, 27 Nov. 1975, EO25/85/01.
26. Cairncross, *Richard Clarke*, p. 174.
27. Collier to Keeling, 21 Oct. 1965, T199/987; Ogilvy-Webb, 31 Oct. 1975, EO25/85/01.
28. Ogilvy-Webb, 27 Nov. 1975, EO25/85/01. On the broader issue: Sir Edward Boyle, 'Who are the policy makers? Minister or civil servant. 1. Minister', *Public Administration*, 43 (1964), 251–9; Sir Edward Playfair, 'Who are the policy makers? Minister or civil servant. 2. Civil servant', *Public Administration*, 43 (1964), 260–8.
29. Ogilvy-Webb, 3 Nov. 1966, p. 2, T199/987.
30. Vinter to Clarke, 8 May 1958, T234/716; Mitchell to Allen, 20 Feb. 1962, T199/921.
31. Mitchell to Allen, 20 Feb. 1962, T199/921.
32. Clarke to Armstrong, 25 Feb. 1964, CLRK 1/3/3/1.
33. Marwick, *New Nature of History*, pp. 49, 227.
34. Ogilvy-Webb to Vinter, 3 Nov. 1966, p. 23, T199/987.
35. Ogilvy-Webb to Sharp, (28) Feb. 1969, p. 9, T199/1240; Ogilvy-Webb, 2 Jan. 1970, p. 9, T199/1241.
36. Ogilvy-Webb, 27 Nov. 1975, EO25/85/01.
37. Sharp to Henley, 1 Feb. 1972, T199/1240.
38. Ogilvy-Webb to Vinter, 9 Dec. 1965, T199/987.
39. Collier to Vinter, 3 Nov. 1966, T199/1240.
40. Hunt to Sharp, 5 Jan. 1972, T199/1240.
41. Hancock to Wass, 28 June 1977, EO25/85/01.
42. Wass to Ogilvy-Webb, 18 Dec. 1975, EO25/85/01.
43. Hancock to Wass, 28 June 1977, EO25/85/01.
44. Chapman, *Treasury*, pp. 42–3; Peden, *Treasury and Public Policy*, pp. 437–41, 521–2; Hannah, 'Economic ideas', pp. 360–3.
45. Cairncross, *The Wilson Years*, p. 284; Alan Booth, 'New revisionists and the Keynesian era: an expanding consensus?', *Economic History Review*, 56 (2003), 125–30.
46. Ogilvy-Webb to Vinter, 13 Oct. 1965, T230/1048; Ogilvy-Webb to Hancock, 7 Oct. 1974, T199/1320; Ogilvy-Webb to Wass, 31 Oct. 1975, EO25/85/01.
47. Ogilvy-Webb to Sharp, (28) Feb. 1969, p. 3, T199/1240.
48. Vinter to Allen and Armstrong, 4 Feb. 1969, T199/1240.
49. Forsyth to Jordan-Moss, 26 Nov. 1969, T227/3221.
50. *Fulton Report*, vol. 1, para 172, p. 57; Middleton, 27 Nov. 1969, T199/1241.
51. Ogilvy-Webb, 27 Nov. 1975, EO25/85/01.
52. Rawlinson to Owen, 22 Nov. 1971, T199/1241.
53. *Fulton Report*, vol. 1, paras 59–122, pp. 24–42.
54. Ogilvy-Webb, 27 Nov. 1975, EO25/85/01.
55. Collier to Rae, 22 Apr. 1964, T199/921. Henderson's critique, referred to in Chapter 2, is relevant here.
56. Forward to Collier, 2 May 1969, T199/1240.
57. Vinter to Petch, 31 Oct. 1963, T319/141.
58. Ogilvy-Webb to Vinter, 9 Dec. 1965, T199/987.
59. Ogilvy-Webb, 27 Nov. 1975, EO25/85/01.
60. Ogilvy-Webb to Sharp, (28) Feb. 1969, p. 2, T199/1240.

61. Pliatzky, 18 Oct. 1965, T224/2235.
62. HD(75) 3, 21 Jan. 1975, EO25/85/01.
63. Ogilvy-Webb to Wass, 31 Oct. 1975, EO25/85/01.
64. Wass to Ogilvy-Webb, 18 Dec. 1975, EO25/85/01.
65. Collier to Vinter, 3 Nov. 1966, T199/1240.
66. Jordan-Moss to Collier, 22 Apr. 1968, T227/3221.
67. J.M. Lee, 'Public administration and official history', *Public Administration*, 54 (1976), 128.
68. Wass to Ogilvy-Webb, 18 Dec. 1975, EO25/85/01.
69. Vinter to Collier, 7 Nov. 1966; Sharp, n.d. (Feb.–Mar. 1969), p. 7; Vinter to Sharp, 27 May 1969, T199/1240.
70. Quoted, Ogilvy-Webb, p. 2, 3 Nov. 1966, T199/987.
71. K. Couzens, 1 Sept. 1966, T224/2235.
72. Ogilvy-Webb, 3 Nov. 1966, p. 2, T199/987.
73. Vinter to Littlewood, 11 June 1963, T319/1158.
74. Vinter to Allen and Armstrong, 4 Feb. 1969, T199/1240.
75. On an earlier phase in the generational issue, see Alec Cairncross (ed.), *The Robert Hall Diaries, 1954–61*, vol. 2 (London: Unwin Hyman, 1991), p. 165.
76. Author's interview with Sir Douglas Wass, 17 July 2005; Sir David Hancock to author, 11 Oct. 2005.
77. Sir David Hancock to author, 30 Sept. 2005, 11 Oct. 2005.
78. Supplementary Report on the Preliminary Survey by the Management Review team, n.d., P.R. Gordon to D.C. Lee, 3 Dec. 1974, T199/1361.
79. Gowing to Hartcup, 17 Dec. 1976, GH; Aldrich 'Policing the past', p. 924.
80. *Government and Wages*, p. 1, T267/7; Clarke to Brook, 25 Apr. 1962, CLRK1/3/2/1; Stevenson to Vinter, 22 Feb. 1965, T319/53.
81. Clarke to Helsby, 5 June 1962, T311/21. Recent events included the creation of "Neddy" and government support for a policy of wage restraint.
82. THC Minutes, 25 Oct. 1966, 3rd. Meeting, para 3, T199/1148.
83. Abbott to D. Heaton, 12 May 1967, T199/1025.
84. Hancock to Wass, 28 June 1977 EO25/85/01.
85. Ogilvy-Webb, 20 Nov. 1968, T199/1240; Ogilvy-Webb, 27 Nov. 1975, EO25/85/01. See the appendix. Although 'unprinted' histories were still firmly bound and duplicated, printing was adjudged useful 'because of the much greater seriousness with which printed documents tend to be taken': Ogilvy-Webb to Clarke, 10 Jan. 1964, T311/202.
86. Dennis to Hancock, May 1977, EO22/85/01.

10 The Foreign Office's 1962 Abadan history

1. The text uses 'Iran', as adopted in 1935, but retains 'Persia' when part of quotations.
2. Anthony Parsons, *The Pride and the Fall: Iran, 1974–1979* (London: Jonathan Cape, 1984), p. 131.
3. John Dickie, *Inside the Foreign Office* (London: Chapmans, 1992), pp. 236–7; Parsons, *Pride and the Fall*, pp. ix–x. Nor did the American authorities read events better: Kurzman, *Unthinkable Revolution*, pp. 1–11.
4. Parsons, *Pride and the Fall*, pp. x, 137–40.

5. Dickie, *Inside the Foreign Office*, p. 237.
6. Ibid., p. 236.
7. Steiner, 'The historian and the Foreign Office', p. 50; Neustadt and May, *Thinking in Time*, pp. xxii, 4.
8. Parsons, *Pride and the Fall*, p. xi.
9. D. Goldsworthy, 'Keeping change within bounds: aspects of colonial policy during the Churchill and Eden Governments, 1951–57', *Journal of Imperial and Commonwealth History*, 18 (1990), 103.
10. J.H. Bamberg, *The History of the British Petroleum Company: The Anglo-Iranian Years 1928–1954*, vol. 2 (Cambridge: Cambridge University Press, 1994), pp. 383–511; Mary Ann Heiss, 'The United States, Great Britain, and the creation of the Iranian oil consortium, 1953–1954', *International History Review*, 16 (1994), 511–35; Wm. Roger Louis, 'Mussaddiq and the dilemmas of British imperialism', in J.A. Bill and Wm. R. Louis (eds), *Mussaddiq, Iranian Nationalism, and Oil* (London: I.B. Tauris, 1988), pp. 228–56; Wm. Roger Louis, *The British Empire in the Middle East, 1945–1951: Arab Nationalism, the United States and Postwar Imperialism* (Oxford: Clarendon Press, 1984); Wm. Roger Louis, 'Britain and the overthrow of the Mosaddeq government', in Mark J. Gasiorowski and Malcolm Byrne (eds), *Mohammad Mosaddeq and the 1953 Coup in Iran* (Syracuse: Syracuse University Press, 2004), pp. 126–77; Steve Marsh, 'HMG, AIOC and the Anglo-Iranian oil crisis: in defence of Anglo-Iranian', *Diplomacy and Statecraft*, 12 (2001), 143–74; Steve Marsh, *Anglo-American Relations and Cold War Oil: Crisis in Iran* (Basingstoke: Palgrave Macmillan, 2003), pp. 169–94; Onslow, 'Battlelines for Suez', 1–22; Ian Speller, ' "A splutter of musketry?": the British military response to the Anglo-Iranian oil dispute, 1951', *Contemporary British History*, 17 (2003), 39–66; Amy L.S. Staples, 'Seeing diplomacy through bankers' eyes: The World Bank, the Anglo-Iranian oil crisis, and the Aswan High Dam', *Diplomatic History*, 26 (2002), 397–418; 'Document: a very British coup', *BBC Radio Four*, 22 Aug. 2005; Donald N. Wilber, *Clandestine Service History: Overthrow of Premier Mossadegh of Iran, November 1952–August 1953* (Washington DC.: CIA, Mar. 1954): http://www.nytimes.com/library/world/mideast/041600iran-cia-index.html accessed 24 Apr. 2004.
11. *HMS Mauritius* Log, 3 Oct. 1951, ADM53/130664; *The Times*, 4 Oct. 1951; Norman Kemp, *Abadan: A First-hand Account of the Persian Oil Crisis* (London: Allan Wingate, 1953), pp. 239–50.
12. Anthony Eden, *The Eden Memoirs: The Reckoning* (London: Cassell, 1965), p. 218.
13. Sir Roger Stevens, *Middle East Oil in International Relations* (Leeds: Leeds University Press, 1973), p. 13.
14. *The Times*, 3 Oct. 1951; *Daily Telegraph*, 4 Oct. 1951.
15. Butler, Sept. 1962, p. 308, FO370/2694/LS18/3.
16. Ibid., pp. 15, 310–11, FO370/2694/LS18/3.
17. Louis, *The British Empire*, p. 689. Attlee, the prime minister (1945–51), agreed: C.R. Attlee, *As it Happened* (London: Heinemann, 1954), p. 176.
18. *The Times*, 5 Oct. 1951.
19. Alec Cairncross (ed.), *The Robert Hall Diaries: 1947–53*, vol. 1 (London: Unwin Hyman, 1989), pp. 168, 173; Staples, 'Seeing diplomacy', 397. On appeasement, Munich and warmongering, see: *Times*, 4,9,20 Oct. 1951; *Daily*

Mirror, 9,24,25 Oct. 1951; 'Middle East Munich', *The Economist*, 6 Oct. 1951, 779–80.
20. The publications of Rohan D'Olier Butler (1917–96) included *The Roots of National Socialism, 1783–1933* (London: Faber & Faber, 1941) and *Choiseul, Father and Son, 1719–1754*, vol. 1 (Oxford: Clarendon, 1980).
21. Brook to heads of departments, 5 Dec. 1957, CAB103/562.
22. Minutes, 8th meeting, Steering Committee (hereafter SC), 1 Apr. 1958, FO371/135611/ZP2/12G.
23. Office Notice, G. Hampshire, 21 May 1965, FO366/3457/DSE103; *Report of the Committee on Representational Services Overseas Appointed by the Prime Minister under the Chairmanship of Lord Plowden, 1962–63, Cmnd 2276* (Feb. 1964), p. 79. Confusingly, the Foreign Office equivalent of a Treasury division was a department.
24. IPCS, 12 Feb. 1963, p. 1, FO366/3309/XS243.
25. William Wallace, *The Foreign Policy Process in Britain* (London: Royal Institute of International Affairs, 1975), pp. 66–7, 78.
26. Keith Hamilton, 'Historical diplomacy: Foreign ministries and the management of the past', in J. Kurbalija (ed.), *Knowledge and Diplomacy* (Malta: DiploProjects, 1999), pp. 47–59.
27. Butler, 18 Oct. 1966, FO370/2906/LS13.
28. C. Parrott to A.J. Woods, 13 Apr. 1960, FO370/2597/LS6.
29. Butler, 8 Mar. 1960, FO370/2597/LS6.
30. L. Woodward, 17 Sept. 1941, FO370/643/L2090; Woodward, 18 Mar. 1946, FO370/1195/L3751; Butler, 23 Aug. 1963, FO370/2724/LS17; Rohan Butler, 'Sir Llewellyn Woodward, 1890–1971', *Proceedings of the British Academy*, LVII (1971), 506–11; Aldrich, 'Policing the past', 948.
31. Woodward to Strang, 13 Oct. 1944, FO370/1084/L4925; Woodward to Cadogan, 26 May 1956, ACAD 4/6.
32. Kathleen Burk, *Troublemaker: The Life and History of A.J.P. Taylor* (New Haven: Yale University Press, 2000), pp. 271–4. Woodward responded that such 'unscrupulous' charges were 'entirely untrue': Woodward to Strang, 12 May 1956, STRN3/3. The Lord Strang Papers (STRN) are at Churchill Archives Centre, Cambridge.
33. Strang, 11 Dec. 1950, Attlee to Brook, 24 Dec. 1950, PREM 8/1211; Hoyer Millar to Brook, 18 Feb. 1959, 26 Aug. 1959, FO370/2571/LS6.
34. Woodward to Strang and Bridges, 13 Oct. 1944, FO370/1082/L4925.
35. Woodward to Cadogan, 27 Apr. 1956, 26 May 1956, ACAD 4/6.
36. Parrott to Hoyer Millar, 10 Feb. 1959, FO370/2571/LS6.
37. Gladwyn Jebb, Paris, to Hoyer Millar, 30 Dec. 1958, FO370/2571/LS6.
38. Parrott to Hoyer Millar, 10 Feb. 1959; Parrott to Trend, 24 Feb. 1959, FO370/2571/LS6.
39. An abbreviated and heavily sanitized one-volume version was published in 1962.
40. Child to Butler, 1 Apr. 1971, Butler to Miss Bowker, 18 Nov. 1971, FCO12/114/LRR8/6.
41. R. Hooper, head of PUS's dept., n.d., SC(58) 20, FO371/135611/ZP2/15G.
42. SC (59) 7, 12 Feb. 1959, FO371/143694/ZP15/2.
43. Butler, 15 Feb. 1963, p. 2, FO370/2694/LS18/3.
44. Butler, Sept. 1962, p. 2, R.W. Mason, 23 Nov. 1962, FO370/2694/LS18/3.

45. Selwyn Lloyd to Hoyer Millar, 3 Nov. 1958, FO371/135615/ZP2/40G.
46. SC (59) 7, 12 Feb. 1959, FO371/143694/ZP15/2.
47. Butler, Sept. 1962, FO370/2694/LS18/3.
48. Butler, Sept. 1962, 15 Feb. 1963, pp. 2–3, FO370/2694/LS18/3.
49. Butler, Sept. 1962, p. 3, FO370/2694/LS18/3. See Woodward to Eden, 1 May 1962, AP24/74/10A.
50. Butler, Sept. 1962, p. 3, FO370/2694/LS18/3. In 1966 Butler, claiming that its benefits were 'overrated', described the use of oral testimony as 'a difficult and dangerous exercise': Butler, 18 Oct. 1966, FO370/2906/LS13. During the early 1960s oral history represented an emerging form of historical evidence, or, as noted by Paul Thompson, was still being re-discovered by historians: Paul Thompson, *The Voice of the Past: Oral History*, 2nd. edn (Oxford: Oxford University Press, 1988), pp. 72–81.
51. Butler, Sept. 1962, p. 3, FO370/2694/LS18/3.
52. His brief mention of the 1953 coup is referenced by a press article: Andrew Tully, 'CIA – the Inside Story', *Sunday Times*, 25 Feb. 1962; Butler, Sept. 1962, pp. 303–4, FO370/2694/LS18/3.
53. The AIOC's files, housed in the BP Archive at the University of Warwick, are open only until the year 1954. Although the files remain closed still for the years when he was writing his Abadan history, Rohan Butler claimed that he made no attempt to consult the AIOC's archives. For readers wishing to study the AIOC's view of developments, see files 4338, 8511, 9932, 24366, 28341, 43859, 46596, 59161, 59799, 66105, 66248, 66900, 66955, 67239, 70556, 72126, 72166, 72224, 72226, 72366, 78160, 91032, 100387, 100570–71, 129288.
54. Butler, Sept. 1962, pp. 304, 309, FO370/2694/LS18/3.
55. Butler, Sept. 1962, p. 313, FO370/2694/LS18/3.
56. *Hansard (Commons)*, 30 July 1951, vol. 491, col. 1072.
57. *Hansard (Lords)*, 31 July 1951, vol. 173, col. 63.
58. Attlee to Strang, 7 Sept. 1951, FO800/653/54; *Hansard (Commons)*, 30 July 1951, vol. 491, cols 1072; Attlee, *As it Happened*, pp. 175–6.
59. Attlee, Cabinet 60(51), 27 Sept. 1951, CAB128/20, fols 55–7; Hugh Dalton, 2 July 1951, B. Pimlott (ed.), *The Political Diary of Hugh Dalton, 1918–40, 1945–60* (London: Jonathan Cape/LSE, 1986), pp. 548–9.
60. Lord Morrison of Lambeth, *Herbert Morrison: An Autobiography* (London: Odhams, 1960), pp. 282–3; Hugh Dalton's Diary, Pt 1/42, fols 20–21, 27 Sept. 1951. The Dalton Diaries are at the Archives, Library, LSE.
61. Butler, Sept. 1962, p. 309, FO370/2694/LS18/3. See Speller, 'Splutter of musketry'; James Cable, *Intervention at Abadan: Plan Buccaneer* (Basingstoke: Macmillan, 1991), pp. 95–123; Ian Speller, *The Role of Amphibious Warfare in British Defence Policy, 1945–56* (Basingstoke: Palgrave Macmillan, 2001), pp. 101, 119–25.
62. Butler, Sept. 1962, p. 309, FO370/2694/LS18/3.
63. Dalton's Diary, Pt 1/42, fol. 21, 27 Sept. 1951.
64. Butler, Sept. 1962, p. 318, FO370/2694/LS18/3.
65. Ibid., p. 309, FO370/2694/LS18/3.
66. Eden's Diary, 17 Dec. 1954, AP20/1/30.
67. Bertjan Verbeek, *Decision-Making in Great Britain during the Suez Crisis: Small Groups and a Persistent Leader* (Aldershot: Ashgate, 2003), pp. 53–8.

68. Butler, Sept. 1962, p. 309, FO370/2694/LS18/3.
69. Ibid., pp. 291, 307, FO370/2694/LS18/3; Eden, *Full Circle*, p. 195; Michael T. Thornhill, 'Britain and the Egyptian question, 1950–2' (D.Phil. thesis, Oxford, 1995), pp. 39–41, 136.
70. *The Times*, 9 Oct. 1951.
71. Butler, Sept. 1962, p. 289, FO370/2694/LS18/3.
72. *The Times*, 25 May 1951.
73. Butler, Sept. 1962, p. 309, FO370/2694/LS18/3.
74. Ibid., pp. 63–4, 312, FO370/2694/LS18/3.
75. Ibid., pp. 297, 307, 317, FO370/2694/LS18/3.
76. Ibid., p. 64, FO370/2694/LS18/3.
77. Ibid., pp. 22, 61, 310–12, FO370/2694/LS18/3.
78. Ibid., p. 319, FO370/2694/LS18/3.
79. Ibid., p. 314, FO370/2694/LS18/3.
80. Ibid., pp. 319–21, FO370/2694/LS18/3.
81. Quoted Butler, Sept. 1962, p. 322, FO370/2694/LS18/3.
82. Butler, Sept. 1962, p. 321, FO370/2694/LS18/3.
83. Quoted, 'The fog of war: eleven lessons from the life of Robert S. McNamara', *BBC Two Television*, 15 May 2005.
84. Morrison, *Herbert Morrison*, p. 281.
85. Woodward to Cadogan, 26 May 1956, ACAD 4/6.
86. Ibid., 13 June 1956, ACAD 4/6.

11 Using Butler's Abadan history to reappraise British Foreign policy

1. Quoted, Butler, 24 May 1963, para 36iv, FO370/2694/LS18/3.
2. Ibid., para 18, FO370/2694/LS18/3.
3. R.W. Mason, 6 Apr. 1962, 23 Nov. 1962, FO370/2694/LS18/3.
4. Butler, Sept. 1962, p. 308, FO370/2694/LS18/3.
5. F.C. Mason, 24 Apr. 1962, FO370/2694/LS18/3.
6. Stevens, 22 Apr. 1962, FO370/2694/LS18/3.
7. F.C. Mason, 24 Apr. 1962, FO370/2694/LS18/3.
8. In turn, the 1979 Iranian revolution is often interpreted as an anti-American event ushering in a difficult period of US–Iran relations: Stephen Kinzer, *All the Shah's Men: An American Coup and the Roots of Middle East Terror* (Hoboken, NJ: John Wiley, 2003), p. x; Mark J. Gasiorowski, 'Why did Mosaddeq fall?', in M.J. Gasiorowski and M. Byrne (eds), *Mohammad Mosaddeq*, p. 261.
9. Strang, n.d. (4 Feb. 1963), para 3, STRN2/10. This commentary is also in FO370/2694/LS18/3.
10. A. Samuel to Lord Home, 4 Dec. 1962, Home, 4 Jan. 1963, FO370/2694/LS18/3; Thorpe, *Douglas-Home*, pp. 245–9.
11. Caccia, 17 Dec. 1962, 7 Jan. 1963; Home, n.d., FO370/2694/LS18/3.
12. Caccia, 1 Jan. 1963, FO370/2694/LS18/3.
13. *The Times*, 5 Dec. 1963; T.A.B. Corley, *A History of the Burmah Oil Company, vol. 2: 1924–66* (London: Heinemann, 1988), pp. 255–70. In 1954 Attlee praised the example of Burma: Attlee, *As it Happened*, p. 176.

286 Notes

14. Caccia, 1 Jan. 1963, Caccia to Lord Plowden, 9 Jan. 1963, FO370/2694/LS18/3.
15. Strang, 28 Jan. 1963, STRN2/11.
16. Strang, n.d. (4 Feb. 1963), STRN2/10. 'Personal' comments in paragraphs 14–23, formerly extracted from FO370/2694/LS18/3 but subsequently re-inserted separately, are in STRN2/10. Nor did Strang mention Britain's role in the 1953 coup: Louis, *Britain and the Overthrow of Mosaddeq*', p. 176.
17. Strang, n.d., para 1; STRN2/10.
18. Ibid., paras 20–2, STRN2/10.
19. Ibid., para 70, STRN2/10. In October 1960, the Cuban government nationalized banks and large industrial and commercial enterprises. This move was followed by the imposition of a US trade embargo (October 1960), the Bay of Pigs incident (April 1961) and growing Soviet involvement in Cuban affairs culminating in the 1962 missiles crisis.
20. Ibid., p. 41, STRN2/10.
21. Ibid., pp. 3, 51, STRN2/10.
22. Ibid., p. 38, STRN2/10.
23. Ibid., paras 6–9, 65, STRN2/10; Michael F. Hopkins, *Oliver Franks and the Truman Administration: Anglo-American Relations, 1948–1952* (London: Frank Cass, 2003), p. 199. Like Attlee, Dalton proved highly critical of Morrison's performance as Foreign Secretary, as evidenced by his 'pseudo-Pam' [Lord Palmerston] descriptor. Dalton complained that Morrison's 'ignorance' was 'shocking': 'He had no background and knew no history': Dalton's diary, 16 Sept. 1951, Pt 1/42, fols 7–8.
24. Strang, n.d., para 10, STRN2/10.
25. Butler, Sept. 1962, p. 295, FO370/2694/LS18/3.
26. Strang, n.d., paras 11–13, STRN2/10.
27. *The Times*, 3 Oct. 1951.
28. Dean Acheson, *Present at the Creation: My Years in the State Department* (London: Hamish Hamilton, 1970), p. 599.
29. Strang, n.d., paras 7, 13, STRN2/10.
30. Ibid., para 4, STRN2/10.
31. Ibid., para 13, STRN2/10.
32. Ibid., para 75, STRN2/10.
33. Lord Strang, *Britain in World Affairs: A Survey of Fluctuations in British Power and Influence, Henry VIII to Elizabeth II* (London: Faber & Faber and Andre Deutsch, 1961), pp. 38, 108–110, 304; Strang, 28 Jan. 1963, STRN2/11.
34. Strang, n.d., para 75, STRN2/10.
35. Ibid., para 26, STRN2/10.
36. Ibid., para 53, STRN2/10.
37. Ibid., para 42, STRN2/10.
38. Quoted, Caccia to Strang, 7 Feb. 1963, STRN2/10.
39. Caccia, 1 Feb. 1963, FO370/2694/LS18/3.
40. Ibid., 1 Mar. 1963, FO370/2694/LS18/3. See Lord Caccia, *The Roots of British Foreign Policy, 1929–1960* (Enstone: The Ditchley Foundation, 1965), pp. 7, 14–15.
41. Gore-Booth to Caccia, 30 Apr. 1963, FO371/173334/WP30/4n; Butler, para 4, 24 May 1963, FO370/2694/LS18/3.
42. Butler, paras 3, 6, 51(i), 24 May 1963, FO370/2694/LS18/3; Gore-Booth to Caccia, 30 Apr. 1963, FO371/173334/WP30/4n.

43. Hankey to Caccia, 8 Feb. 1963, FO371/173334/WP30/2/i; Gore-Booth to Caccia, 30 Apr. 1963, FO371/173334/WP30/4n; Dean to Caccia, 16 Mar. 1963, FO371/173334/WP30/4j.
44. Wallinger to Caccia, 22 Mar. 1963, FO371/173334/WP30/4k.
45. Gore-Booth to Caccia, 30 Apr. 1963, FO371/173334/WP30/4n.
46. Maud to Caccia, 8 Feb. 1963, FO371/173334/WP30/2h; Parkes to Caccia, 22 Feb. 1963, FO371/173334/WP30/3k; Sir Saville Garner (Commonwealth Relations Office) to Caccia, 5 Mar. 1963, FO371/173334/WP30/4l.
47. Dean to Caccia, 16 Mar. 1963, FO371/173334/WP30/4j.
48. J. Maud to Caccia, 8 Feb. 1963, FO371/173334/WP30/2h; Hankey to Caccia, 8 Feb. 1963, FO371/173334/WP30/2/i.
49. Butler, 24 May 1963, para 17, FO370/2694/LS18/3.
50. Wallinger to Caccia, 22 Mar. 1963, FO371/173334/WP30/4k; Peden, *Treasury and Public Policy*, pp. 530–1.
51. Hankey to Caccia, 8 Feb. 1963, FO371/173334/WP30/2i.
52. George Vaughan, Panama, to Caccia, 14 Feb. 1963, FO371/173334/WP30/3d. Subsequently, lingering anti-British sentiment qualified initial impressions of success: Nigel Ashton, 'Britain and the Kuwaiti crisis, 1961', *Diplomacy and Statecraft*, 9 (1998), 163–81; Wm. Roger Louis, 'The British withdrawal from the Gulf, 1967–71', *The Journal of Imperial and Commonwealth History*, 31 (2003), 91; Simon Smith, *Britain's Revival and Fall in the Gulf: Kuwait, Bahrain, Qatar and the Trucial States, 1950–1971* (London: RoutledgeCurzon, 2004), pp. 119–28.
53. Maud to Caccia, 8 Feb. 1963, FO371/173334/WP30/2h.
54. Saki Dockrill, *Britain's Retreat from East of Suez: The Choice between Europe and the World?* (Basingstoke: Palgrave Macmillan, 2002), pp. 24–42; Peter Mangold, *Success and Failure in British Foreign Policy: Evaluating the Record, 1900–2000* (Basingstoke: Palgrave Macmillan, 2001), pp. 13, 121–4; Peden, *Treasury and Public Policy*, pp. 445–8. Pointing to its 'folly' and 'persistent stupidity', Acheson, the US Secretary of State (1949–53), proved highly critical of British policy over Abadan: Acheson, *Present at the Creation*, pp. 501, 506.
55. Caccia, 1 Mar. 1963, FO370/2694/LS18/3.
56. Butler, 24 May 1963, paras 25–7, 33–4, 39, 51, FO370/2694/LS18/3.
57. Wallace, *Foreign Policy*, p. 78.
58. Butler, 24 May 1963, para 52, FO370/2694/LS18/3.
59. Caccia, 29 May 1963, FO371/173334/WP30/1; Woodfield, 13 May 1964, PREM11/4808. See David Thomson, 'Gaullism's point of reappraisal', *The Times*, 22 Aug. 1963.
60. Minutes, 39th, 41st meetings of Steering Committee, 30 July 1963, 23 Aug. 1963, FO371/173334/WP30/8.
61. Butler, 24 May 1963, paras 51–2, FO370/2694/LS18/3; Ernest Barnes, 4 Oct. 1963, FO371/173334/WP30/8; Office Circular, no. 27: Reorganisation of planning work in the Foreign Office, 30 Dec. 1963, FO371/178812/PLA1/1; *Plowden Report on Representational Services Overseas*, pp. 55–8; James Cable, 'Foreign policy-making: planning or reflex?', in C.R. Hill and P. Beshoff, *Two Worlds*, pp. 95–115.
62. K. Scott, 24 July 1963, FO371/173334/WP30/1.
63. B. Burrows, 10 Oct. 1963, Nicholls, 14 Oct. 1963, FO371/173334/WP30/8.
64. Palliser to John Peck, 6 Feb. 1964, FO371/178812/PLA1/4; J. Nicholls, 9 Nov. 1966, FO953/2452.

65. Wilson, *Hansard (Commons)*, 16 Jan. 1968, vol. 756, cols 1577–85; Dockrill, *Britain's Retreat*, pp. 209–26; Louis, *British Withdrawal*, pp. 83–102; Smith, *Britain's Revival*, pp. 1–6, 151–6.
66. Heath, 15 Oct. 1963, FO371/173334/WP30/8.
67. Stewart to Gore-Booth, 5 July 1965, FO370/2807/LS13/4.
68. N. Henderson, n.d. (July 1965), FO370/2807/LS13/4.
69. Gore-Booth, 13 July 1965, FO370/2807/LS13/4; Gore-Booth, Oct. 1966, quoted, Cairncross, *The Wilson Years*, p. 165; Cairncross, *Robert Hall Diaries, 1954–61*, p. 84; Paul Gore-Booth, *With Great Truth and Respect* (London: Constable, 1974), pp. 230–1.
70. This claim should be viewed alongside reports that relevant material, including the British copy of the Treaty of Sèvres, was shredded: Avi Shlaim, 'The Protocol of Sèvres, 1956: Anatomy of a war plot', *International Affairs*, 73 (1997), 509–30.
71. Encl. F. Bishop to D. Laskey, 28 Dec. 1956, PREM11/1138.
72. Millard, Aug. 1957, pp. 1–2, 29, FO800/728.
73. Ibid., p. 2, FO800/728.
74. Ibid., p. 29, FO800/728.
75. Nicholls, 19 Sept. 1966, Gore-Booth, 19 Sept. 1966, FO370/2906/LS13.
76. 'Talking Points', n.d. (Oct. 1966), FO370/2906/LS13.
77. Gore-Booth, 31 Oct. 1966, Butler, 2 Nov. 1966, FO370/2906/LS13.
78. FCO Questionnaire for Public Records Committee, pp. 5–7, encl. M. Palliser to Aylett, 7 Mar. 1979, LCO27/21.
79. Butler to J. Bullard, 4 Sept. 1972, FCO28/1946/ENP10/1; Butler, 'The Katyn Massacre and reactions in the Foreign Office', Apr. 1973, FCO28/2309/ENP10/2.
80. J. Bullard to T. Brimelow, 16 Oct. 1972, FCO28/1946/ENP10/1; Brimelow, 14 Apr. 1973, M. Goulding to Bullard, 29 May 1973, FCO28/2308/ ENP10/2.
81. In 2003 Butler's history was updated by the FCO to mark the 60th anniversary of the discovery of the mass graves at Katyn in 1943, 'British reactions to the Katyn Massacre, 1943–2003': see 'Historical Papers' at http://www.fco.gov.uk.
82. Hannay, *Britain's Entry*, pp. ix–xv.
83. Douglas-Home to O'Neill, 9 Sept. 1972, FCO26/1156/PMW8/3.
84. Con O'Neill to Douglas-Home, 27 July 1972, FCO26/1156/PMW8/3.
85. M. Morland to B. Thornley, 8 Aug. 1972, FCO26/1156/PMW8/3.
86. Geoffrey Rippon, *Hansard (Commons)*, 6 Mar. 1972, vol. 832, cols 215–6.
87. 'World at One', *BBC Radio Four*, 4 July 2004.
88. Butler, 18 Oct. 1966, FO370/2906/LS13.
89. 'Talking points', n.d. (Oct. 1966), FO370/2906/LS13.
90. R. Mason, 10 Apr. 1961, FO366/3201/XS03; Caccia, Office Circular 7, 1 May 1963, LCO27/21.

12 Using history in the Foreign Office

1. Strang, 'Diplomacy', 25 Aug. 1958, STRN3/7.
2. Strang, n.d., paras 20–1, STRN2/10.

3. Butler, 15 Feb. 1963, FO370/2694/LS18/3.
4. David Parrott, 'European history from the inside looking out', *The Guardian*, 7 Nov. 1996; 'Obituary: Rohan Butler', *The Times*, 14 Nov. 1996.
5. Strang, n.d., p. 24, STRN2/10. Nevertheless, Strang agreed with Butler's decision to concentrate on documentary evidence rather than solicit oral testimony.
6. Strang, n.d., para 21, STRN2/10.
7. Ibid., para 24, STRN2/10.
8. Ibid., para 25, STRN2/10.
9. Ibid., para 29, STRN2/10.
10. Butler, 15 Feb. 1963, FO370/2694/LS18/3.
11. Butler, 18 Oct. 1966, FO370/2906/LS13.
12. Parrott to Caccia, 22 Feb. 1963, FO370/2694/LS18/3.
13. Vaughan to Caccia, 14 Feb. 1963, FO371/173334/WP30/3d.
14. *Plowden Report on Representational Services Overseas*, p. 79.
15. Butler, 24 May 1963, para 3, FO370/2694/LS18/3.
16. Butler to Mason, 9 Mar. 1962, Butler, 15 Feb. 1963, FO370/2694/LS18/3.
17. Butler, Sept. 1962, p. 308, FO370/2694/LS18/3.
18. *The Times*, 14 Nov. 1996.
19. Caccia, 1 May 1963, LCO/27/21.
20. F.C. Mason, 24 Apr. 1962, FO370/2694/LS18/3.
21. Butler, Sept. 1962, p. 308, FO370/2694/LS18/3.
22. Keith Kyle, *Suez: Britain's End of Empire in the Middle East* (London: I.B. Tauris, 2003), pp. 7–9.
23. Verbeek, *Decision-making*, p. 53.
24. Louis, *The British Empire*, p. 668.
25. Speller, 'Splutter of musketry', 40.
26. Annex, COS(51)86, 23 May 1951, DEFE4/43.
27. When Nasser informed ministers about the forthcoming decree nationalizing the Suez Canal Company, several drew analogies with Iran's action in 1951: 'More than one minister mentioned Mossadeq.' Reportedly, Nasser referred to the Western boycott thwarting Iranian marketing of its oil to demonstrate how he had learnt the importance of maintaining free passage through the canal to limit external opposition: Mohamedh Heikal, *Cutting the Lion's Tail: Suez through Egyptian Eyes* (London: Andre Deutsch, 1986), pp. 124–6, 133.
28. R. Makins, 11 Aug. 1951, Strang, 11 Aug. 1951, FO371/124968/ZP24/2.
29. D.C. Watt, 'Introduction', in J.T. Emmerson (ed.), *The Rhineland Crisis 7 March 1936: A Study in Multilateral Diplomacy* (London: Maurice Temple Smith, 1977), p. 13.
30. Steiner, 'The historian', p. 45; Steiner, 'On writing', 546; Neustadt and May, *Thinking in Time*, pp. 233–72.
31. Butler, Sept. 1962, p. 3, FO370/2694/LS18/3.
32. Strang, BBC Overseas Service, 'This day and age', 2 Mar. 1960, STRN3/8; Strang, *Diplomatic Career*, pp. 12, 71–4; John Young, 'Conclusion', in S. Kelly and A. Gorst (eds), *Whitehall and the Suez Crisis* (London: Frank Cass, 2000), p. 228. See Nailor, *Learning from Precedent*, pp. 25–29, 33–9; Khong, *Analogies at War*, pp. 3–18, 174–205; Record, *Making War*, pp. 11–18, 146–55.
33. A related issue concerns the implications of withholding from the historian certain 'top secret' Foreign Office papers.

34. The culture and mentality of post-1945 British diplomats is a topic in need of further research building upon studies on the interwar years: Donald C. Watt, *Personalities and Policies: Studies in the Formulation of British Foreign Policy in the Twentieth Century* (London: Longmans, 1965); Donald Lammers, 'From Whitehall after Munich: the Foreign Office and the future course of British policy', *The Historical Journal*, 16 (1973), 831–56; Raymond Smith, 'Introduction', in J. Zametica (ed.), *British Officials and British Foreign Policy, 1945–50* (Leicester: Leicester University Press, 1990), pp. 1–5; Michael J. Hughes, 'The peripatetic career structure of the British diplomatic establishment, 1919–39', *Diplomacy and Statecraft*, 14 (2003), 29–48; Kelly and Gorst, *Whitehall and the Suez Crisis*.
35. Donald N. Wilber, *Adventures in the Middle East: Excursions and Incursions* (Princeton, NJ: Darwin, 1986), pp. 155–71.
36. Wilber, *Clandestine Service History*, pp. 85–95; Wilber, *Adventures in the Middle East*, pp. 189–90.
37. Butler, 24 May 1963, para 41, FO370/2694/LS18/3.
38. Noble to Butler, 18 June 1963, FO371/173334/WP30/5.
39. Hannay, *Britain's Entry*, p. ix.
40. Douglas-Home to O'Neill, 9 Sept. 1972, FCO26/1156/PMW8/3.
41. *The Times*, 7 May 1977.
42. Millard, 17 June 1963, FO371/173334/WP30/1.

13 Making British policy, using and ignoring history

1. Nailor, *Learning from Precedent*, pp. 15, 21; Black, *Using History*, p. ix.
2. Marian Clay, 'Putting the records straight', *FCO Historical Branch Occasional Papers*, 1 (1987), 5; James E. Hoare, 'Present-day records: the prospects for future historians', *FCO Historical Branch Occasional Papers*, 1 (1987), 54.
3. Hancock, *Country and Calling*, p. 205.
4. Lord Alan Bullock, *Has History a Future?* (Aspen: Aspen Institute for Humanistic Studies, 1977), p. 4. See also Lord Alan Bullock, *Has the Past Ceased to be Relevant?* (Aspen: Aspen Institute for Humanistic Studies, 1986), pp. 20–2.
5. Bullock, *Has History a Future?*, p. 6.
6. Clarke to Brook, 30 July 1959, T199/664.
7. Rawlinson to Ogilvy-Webb, 1 July 1963, T311/202.
8. Richard Lavers, 'The role of research analysts in the FCO', *Foreign and Commonwealth Office, Research and Analytical Papers* (London: FCO, 2001), pp. 1–4.
9. Hoare, 'Present-day records', 55–6.
10. Vinter to Henley, Cairncross and Clarke, 29 Mar. 1965, T319/142.
11. Vinter to Collier, 7 Nov. 1966, T199/1240.
12. Steiner, 'The historian', p. 45; Steiner, 'On writing', 546; Neustadt and May, *Thinking in Time*, pp. 233–72.
13. Marshall, 25 Nov. 1958, T222/1029.
14. Clarke to Helsby, 1 May 1964, T311/202.
15. Stuart, 27 Nov. 1969, T227/3221.
16. Pliatzky, 27 Nov. 1964, T224/2235.
17. Henderson, 'Two costly British errors', 530.

18. Widdup to Anson and Jordan-Moss, 8 Mar. 1968, T227/2967.
19. Abbot to Collier, 4 May 1964, T311/202.
20. Reportedly, it regarded the rules as applying to the papers created by previous administration, not write-ups thereof: Gillian Bennett, the FCO's Chief Historian, to the author, 14 Sept. 2004.
21. Ogilvy-Webb to Wass, 31 Oct. 1975, EO25/85/01.
22. Hoare, 'Present-day records', 54.
23. Mason, 6 Apr. 1962, FO370/2694/LS18/3.
24. Collier to Sharp and Ogilvy-Webb, 5 June 1969, T199/1240.
25. G. Crane, 1 Aug. 1969, 8 Aug. 1969, T199/1240. Seen by Sharp, Vinter and Henley.
26. Ogilvy-Webb to Collier, 5 Aug. 1969, T199/1240.
27. Henley to Maude, 12 Jan. 1970, T199/1241; P. Lazarus, 'Historical note on Joint Steering Group for the railway review', Mar. 1968, MT124/1303.
28. Collier to Ogilvy-Webb, 29 Oct. 1965, Collier to King, 19 Oct. 1965, T199/987.
29. Symons to Owen, 7 Oct. 1968, Sharp, 24 Jan. 1969, T199/1241; THM 16, Jan. 1972, T267/29.
30. Collier to Ogilvy-Webb, 29 Oct. 1965, Collier to King, 19 Oct. 1965, T199/987.
31. Miss J. Court to Hancock, 24 June 1977, EO25/85/01.
32. Rampton to France, 31 Mar. 1967, T227/2522.
33. Gowing, 'Official histories', Mar. 1972, MG Cabinet Office War Histories.
34. Maude to Henley, 9 Jan. 1970, T199/1241.
35. Ogilvy-Webb to Vinter, 9 Dec. 1965, T199/987; Ogilvy-Webb to Sharp, (28) Feb. 1969, p. 9, T199/1240.
36. Gowing to Wass, 1 Aug. 1980, MG Corresp. Wass.
37. Sharp to Ryrie, 19 July 1974, T199/1305.
38. Alan Booth, 'Inflation expectations, and the political economy of Conservative Britain, 1951–1964', *The Historical Journal*, 43 (2000), 833–4, 840, 844. Pemberton, though citing them as sources, fails to develop the way in which THMs were intended to offer one way of codifying 'the lessons of negative policy feedback': Pemberton, *Policy Learning*, pp. 76, 113–4, 120, 129, 132–4.
39. L.S. Pressnell, *External Economic Policy since the War*, vol. 1 (London: HMSO, 1986), pp. xii, 370.
40. Ogilvy-Webb, 'Historical research', Feb. 1969, p. 7, T199/1240.
41. O'Neill to Douglas-Home, 27 July 1972, FCO26/1156/PMW8/3.
42. Hunt to Airey, 13 May 1965, T319/142; Lee, 'Public administration', 127–8.
43. Sharp to Henley, 1 Feb. 1972, T199/1240.
44. Lee, 'Public administration', 127–31.

Select Bibliography

Primary sources (unpublished)

Official documents
The National Archives, Kew, London (TNA): British government records – Admiralty (ADM); Air Ministry (AIR); Board of Trade (BT); Cabinet Office (CAB); Ministry of Defence (DEFE); Foreign Office (FO); Foreign and Commonwealth Office (FCO); Lord Chancellor's Office (LCO); Prime Minister's dept. (PREM); Ministry of Transport (MT); Treasury (T); War Office (WO).

The Treasury: Establishment Officer's branch files (EO), 1975–78.

Private papers
University of Birmingham, Special Collections dept., Library: Lord Avon (AP).
University of Cambridge, Churchill Archives Centre: C.B. Behrens (BEHR); Sir Alexander Cadogan (ACAD); Sir Richard Clarke (CLRK); Lord Strang (STRN).
London School of Economics, Archives, British Library of Political and Economic Science: Hugh Dalton; Michael Lee; Richard Titmuss.
University of Oxford, Bodleian Library: Lord Normanbrook.
University of Oxford, Library, Museum of the History of Science: Margaret Gowing (MG).
University of Warwick, BP Archive: Anglo-Iranian Oil Company archives.

Oral and written testimony
A.J. Collier; Sir David Hancock; Guy Hartcup; Sir Douglas Wass.

Primary sources (published)

Official documents
Hansard Parliamentary Debates: House of Commons, House of Lords.
House of Commons, Education, Science and Arts Committee, Public Records, Minutes, 4 May 1983;
Report of the Committee on Representational Services Overseas under the Chairmanship of Lord Plowden, 1962–63, Cmnd 2276 (Feb. 1964).
The Civil Service: Report of the Committee 1966–68, Chairman: Lord Fulton, Cmnd 3638: *Report*, vol. 1 (London: HMSO, 1968).

Newspapers

Newspapers, consulted at the British Library's Newspaper Library, Colindale, or on-line, are listed individually in the endnotes.

Memoirs and diaries

Acheson, D. *Present at the Creation: My Years in the State Department* (London: Hamish Hamilton, 1970).
Attlee, C.R. *As it Happened* (London: Heinemann, 1954).
Cairncross, Sir A. (ed.), *Sir Richard Clarke, Public Expenditure, Management and Control* (London: Macmillan, 1978).
—— *The Robert Hall Diaries: 1947–53*, vol. 1 (London: Unwin Hyman, 1989).
—— *The Robert Hall Diaries: 1954–61*, vol. 2 (London: Unwin Hyman, 1991).
—— *The Wilson Years: A Treasury Diary, 1964–1969* (London: The Historians' Press, 1997).
Cook, R. *The Point of Departure* (London: Simon & Schuster, 2003).
Eden, A. *The Memoirs of Sir Anthony Eden: Full Circle* (London: Cassell, 1960).
—— *The Eden Memoirs: The Reckoning* (London: Cassell, 1965).
Gore-Booth, P. *With Great Truth and Respect* (London: Constable, 1974).
Hancock, W.K. *Country and Calling* (London: Faber & Faber, 1954).
Heath, E. *The Course of My Life: My Autobiography* (London: Hodder & Stoughton, 1998).
Morgan, J. (ed.), *Richard Crossman: The Diaries of a Cabinet Minister, 1966–68*, vol. 2 (London: Hamish Hamilton and Jonathan Cape, 1976).
Morrison, Lord. *Herbert Morrison: An Autobiography* (London: Odhams, 1960).
Nutting, A. *No End of a Lesson: The Story of Suez* (London: Constable, 1967).
Parsons, A. *The Pride and the Fall: Iran, 1974–1979* (London: Jonathan Cape, 1984).
Pimlott, B. (ed.), *The Political Diary of Hugh Dalton, 1918–40, 1945–60* (London: Jonathan Cape/LSE, 1986).
Shuckburgh, E. *Descent to Suez: Diaries, 1951–56* (London: Weidenfeld & Nicolson, 1986).
Strang, Lord. *The Diplomatic Career* (London: Andre Deutsch, 1962).
Thatcher, M. *The Downing Street Years* (London: HarperCollins, 1993).
Wilson, H. *The Labour Government, 1964–1970: A Personal Record* (London: Weidenfeld & Nicolson and Michael Joseph, 1971).

Secondary sources

Aldrich, R. 'Policing the past: official history, secrecy and British intelligence since 1945', *English Historical Review*, CXIX (2004).
Arnold, L. 'A letter from Oxford: the history of nuclear history in Britain', *Minerva*, 38 (2000).
Ashton, N. 'Britain and the Kuwaiti crisis, 1961', *Diplomacy and Statecraft*, 9 (1998).
Balogh, T. 'The apotheosis of the dilettante: the establishment of mandarins', in H. Thomas, (ed.), *The Establishment* (London: Anthony Blond, 1959).
Bamberg, J.H. *The History of the British Petroleum Company: the Anglo-Iranian years 1928–1954*, vol. 2 (Cambridge: Cambridge University Press, 1994).
Beck, P. 'The Anglo-Persian Oil dispute, 1932–1933', *Journal of Contemporary History*, 9 (1974).

―― *The Falklands Islands as an International Problem* (London: Routledge, 1988).
―― 'The conflict potential of the "dots on the map"', *The International History Review*, 13 (1991).
―― 'History and policy-makers in Argentina and Britain', in C.R. Hill, and P. Beshoff (eds), *Two Worlds of International Relations: Academics, Practitioners and the Trade in Ideas* (London: Routledge/LSE, 1994).
―― 'Politicians versus historians: Lord Avon's "appeasement battle" against "lamentably, appeasement-minded" historians', *Twentieth Century British History*, 9 (1998).
―― 'The lessons of Abadan and Suez for British foreign policymakers in the 1960s', *Historical Journal*, 49 (2006).
Black, J. *Using History* (London: Hodder Arnold, 2005).
Booth, A. 'Inflation expectations, and the political economy of Conservative Britain, 1951–1964', *The Historical Journal*, 43 (2000).
―― 'New revisionists and the Keynesian era: an expanding consensus?', *Economic History Review*, 56 (2003).
Boyle, Sir E. 'Who are the policy makers? Minister or civil servant. 1. Minister', *Public Administration*, 43 (1964).
Bridges, Lord. *The Treasury* (London: George Allen & Unwin, 1964).
Bullock, A. *Has history a Future?* (Aspen: Aspen Institute for Humanistic Studies, 1977).
―― *Has the Past Ceased to be Relevant?* (Aspen: Aspen Institute for Humanistic Studies, 1986).
Burk, K. *Troublemaker: The Life and History of A.J.P. Taylor* (New Haven: Yale University Press, 2000).
Butler, J.R.M. 'Letter: Official war histories', *The Times*, 10 Oct. 1961.
Butler, Sir J.R.M. 'The British military histories of the war of 1939–45', in R. Higham (ed.), *Official Histories: Essays and Bibliographies from around the World* (Manhattan, Kansas: Kansas State University Library, 1970).
Butler, R. 'Sir Llewellyn Woodward, 1890-1971', *Proceedings of the British Academy*, LVII (1971).
Butterfield, H. *History and Human Relations* (London: Collins, 1951).
Cable, J. *Intervention at Abadan: Plan Buccaneer* (Basingstoke: Macmillan, 1991).
―― 'Foreign policy-making: planning or reflex?', in C.R. Hill, and P. Beshoff, (eds), *Two Worlds of International Relations: Academics, Practitioners and the Trade in Ideas* (London: Routledge/LSE, 1994).
Caccia, Lord. *The Roots of British Foreign Policy, 1929–1960* (Enstone: The Ditchley Foundation, 1965).
Carlton, D. *Anthony Eden: A Biography* (London: Allen Lane, 1981).
Chapman, R.A. *The Treasury in Public Policymaking* (London: Routledge, 1997).
Clarke, P. 'The Treasury's analytical model of the British economy between the wars', in M.O. Furner and B. Supple (eds), *The State and Economic Knowledge: The American and British Experiences* (Cambridge: Cambridge University Press/Woodrow Wilson International Center for Scholars, 1990).
Clay, M. 'Putting the records straight', *FCO Historical Branch Occasional Papers*, 1 (1987).
Conekin, B.E. *"The autobiography of a nation": The 1951 Festival of Britain* (Manchester: Manchester University Press, 2003).
Cook, R. 'The invasion of Iraq was Britain's worst foreign policy blunder since Suez', *The Independent*, 19 Mar. 2004.

Corley, T.A.B. *A History of the Burmah Oil Company vol.2: 1924–66* (London: Heinemann, 1988).
David, P.A. and Thomas, M. 'Introduction: thinking historically about challenging economic issues', in P.A. David and M. Thomas (eds), *The Economic Future in Historical Perspective* (Oxford: British Academy/OUP, 2003).
Day, J. 'A failure of foreign policy: the case of Rhodesia', in M. Leifer (ed.), *Constraints and Adjustments in British Foreign Policy* (London: George Allen & Unwin, 1972).
Dickie, J. *Inside the Foreign Office* (London: Chapmans, 1992).
Dockrill, S. *Britain's Retreat from East of Suez: The choice between Europe and the World?* (Basingstoke: Palgrave Macmillan, 2002).
Dorey, P. *Policy Making in Britain: An Introduction* (London: Sage, 2005).
Dutton, D. *Anthony Eden: A Life and Reputation* (London: Arnold, 1997).
Elton, G.R. 'Second thoughts on history at the universities', *History*, 54 (1969).
English, R. and Kenny, M. (eds), *Rethinking Decline* (Basingstoke: Macmillan, 2000).
Evans, R.J. *In Defence of History* (London: Granta, 1997).
Eversley, J. 'The history of NHS charges', *Contemporary British History*, 15 (2001).
Fabian Tract 355: The Administrators (London: The Fabian Society, 1964).
Ferro, M. *The Use and Abuse of History, or How the Past is Taught* (London: Routledge & Kegan Paul, 1984).
Fisk, R. 'New crisis, old lessons', *The Independent*, 15 Jan. 2003.
Fry, G.K. *The Administrative Revolution in Whitehall: A Study of the Politics of Administrative Change in British Central Government since the 1950s* (London: Croom Helm, 1981).
Fry, M. (ed.), *History, the White House and the Kremlin: Statesmen as Historians* (London: Pinter, 1991).
Furner, M.O. and Supple, B. (eds), 'Ideas, institutions, and state in the United States and Britain: an introduction', in M.O. Furner, and B. Supple (eds), *The State and Economic Knowledge: The American and British Experiences* (Cambridge: Cambridge University Press/Woodrow Wilson International Center for Scholars, 1990).
Gaddis, J.L. 'New conceptual approaches to the study of American foreign relations: interdisciplinary perspectives', *Diplomatic History*, 14 (1990).
Gasiorowski, M.J. 'Why did Mosaddeq fall?', in M.J. Gasiorowski and M. Byrne (eds), *Mohammad Mosaddeq and the 1953 Coup in Iran* (Syracuse: Syracuse University Press, 2004).
George, A.L. *Bridging the Gap: Theory and Practice in Foreign Policy* (Washington DC: United States Institute of Peace, 1993).
Goldsworthy, D. 'Keeping change within bounds: aspects of colonial policy during the Churchill and Eden Governments, 1951–57', *Journal of Imperial and Commonwealth History*, 18 (1990).
Gorst, A. and Johnman, L. (eds), *The Suez Crisis* (London: Routledge, 1997).
Goulter, C.J.M. 'British official histories of the Air War', in J. Grey (ed.), *The Last Word?: Essays on Official History in the United States and British Commonwealth* (Westport, CT: Praeger, 2003).
Gowing, M. *Britain and Atomic Energy, 1939–1945* (London: Macmillan, 1964).
—— 'Hancock: some reminiscences', *Historical Studies*, 13 (1968).
—— with Arnold, L. *Independence and Deterrence, Britain and Atomic Energy, 1945–1952*, vols 1–2 (London: Macmillan/UKAEA, 1974).

296 Select Bibliography

—— 'Peacetime official history', *SSRC Newsletter*, 21 Jan. 1974.
—— *Reflections on Atomic Energy History: The Rede Lecture 1978* (Cambridge: Cambridge University Press, 1978).
—— 'Modern public records: selection and access. The report of the "Wilson Committee"', *Social History*, 6 (1981).
Green, A. *Writing the Great War: Sir James Edmonds and the Official Histories, 1915–1948* (London: Frank Cass, 2003).
Grey, J. (ed.), *The Last Word?: Essays on Official History in the United States and British Commonwealth* (Westport, CT: Praeger, 2003).
Grieve, H. *The Great Tide: The Story of the 1953 Flood Disaster in Essex* (Chelmsford: Essex County Council, 1959).
Hamilton, K. 'Historical diplomacy: foreign ministries and the management of the past', in J. Kurbalija (ed.), *Knowledge and Diplomacy* (Malta: DiploProjects, 1999).
Hancock, Sir W.K. 'British civil histories of the Second World War', in R. Higham (ed.), *Official Histories: Essays and Bibliographies from around the World* (Manhattan, Kansas: Kansas State University Library, 1970).
Hancock, W.K. and Gowing, M.M. *British War Economy* (London: HMSO, 1949).
Hannah, L. 'Economic ideas and government policy on industrial organization in Britain since 1945', in M.O. Furner and B. Supple (eds), *The State and Economic Knowledge: The American and British Experiences* (Cambridge: Cambridge University Press/Woodrow Wilson International Center for Scholars, 1990).
Hannay, Sir D. (ed.), *Britain's Entry into the European Community: Report on the Negotiations of 1970–1972 by Sir Con O'Neill* (London: Frank Cass, 2000).
Harris, J. 'Economic knowledge and British social policy', in M.O. Furner and B. Supple (eds), *The State and Economic Knowledge: The American and British Experiences* (Cambridge: Cambridge University Press/Woodrow Wilson International Center for Scholars, 1990).
Hay, D. 'British historians and the beginnings of the civil history of the Second World War', in M.R.D. Foot (ed.), *War and Society: Historical Essays in Honour and Memory of J.R. Western, 1928–1971* (London: Paul Elek, 1973).
Heikal, M. *Cutting the Lion's Tail: Suez through Egyptian Eyes* (London: Andre Deutsch, 1986).
Heiss, M.A. 'The United States, Great Britain, and the creation of the Iranian oil consortium, 1953–1954', *International History Review*, 16 (1994).
Henderson, D. 'Two costly British errors', *The Listener*, 27 Oct. 1977.
—— 'Under the Whitehall blanket, *The Listener*, 17 Nov. 1977.
Hennessy, P. 'Civil Service accused of neglecting history', *The Times*, 28 Apr. 1978.
—— 'A crack appears in the door to Treasury documents', *The Times*, 18 July 1978.
—— 'Studies requested by The Times released', *The Times*, 6 Nov. 1978.
—— 'The pleasures and pains of contemporary history', *History Today*, 44 (Mar. 1994).
—— *Whitehall* (London: Pimlico, 2001).
Higham, R. 'Introduction', in R. Higham (ed.), *Official Histories: Essays and Bibliographies from around the World* (Manhattan, Kansas: Kansas State University Library, 1970).
Hill, C. 'Academic international relations: the siren song of policy relevance', in C.R. Hill and P. Beshoff (eds), *Two Worlds of International Relations: Academics, Practitioners and the Trade in Ideas* (London: Routledge/LSE, 1994).

Hoare, J.E. 'Present-day records: the prospects for future historians', *FCO Historical Branch Occasional Papers*, 1 (1987).
Hobsbawm, E. 'Introduction: inventing traditions', in E. Hobsbawm and T. Ranger (eds), *The Invention of Tradition* (Cambridge: Cambridge University Press, 1983).
—— *On History* (London: Abacus, 1998).
—— 'Spreading democracy', *Foreign Policy*, Sept./Oct.2004, http://www.foreignpolicy.com/story/files/story2666.php, accessed 14 Dec. 2004.
Holmes, C. 'Government files and privileged access', *Social History*, 6 (1981).
Hopkins, M.F. *Oliver Franks and the Truman Administration: Anglo-American Relations, 1948–1952* (London: Frank Cass, 2003).
Hoskyns, Sir J. 'Conservatism is not enough', *Political Quarterly*, 55 (1984).
Howard, M. *The Lessons of History* (Oxford: Clarendon Press, 1991).
Hughes, M.J. 'The peripatetic career structure of the British diplomatic establishment, 1919–39', *Diplomacy and Statecraft*, 14 (2003).
Jervis, R. *Perception and Misperception in International Politics* (Princeton, NJ: Princeton University Press, 1976).
Joll, J. *1914: The Unspoken Assumptions* (London: Weidenfeld & Nicolson, 1968).
Kelly, S. and Gorst, A. (eds), *Whitehall and the Suez Crisis* (London: Frank Cass, 2000).
Kemp, N. *Abadan: A First-hand Account of the Persian Oil Crisis* (London: Allan Wingate, 1953).
Kemp, P.K. 'War studies in the Royal Navy', *RUSI Journal*, 111 (1966).
Khong, Y.F. *Analogies at War: Korea, Munich, Dien Bien Phu, and the Vietnam Decisions of 1965* (Princeton, NJ: Princeton University Press, 1992).
Kinzer, S. *All the Shah's men: An American coup and the Roots of Middle East Terror* (Hoboken, NJ: John Wiley, 2003).
Kurzman, C. *The Unthinkable Revolution in Iran* (Cambridge, Mass.: Harvard University Press, 2004).
Kyle, K. *Suez: Britain's End of Empire in the Middle East* (London: I.B. Tauris, 2003).
Lammers, D. 'From Whitehall after Munich: the Foreign Office and the future course of British policy', *The Historical Journal*, 16 (1973).
Lamont, W. (ed.), *Historical Controversies and Historians* (London: Routledge, 1998).
Lavers, R. 'The role of research analysts in the FCO', *Foreign and Commonwealth Office, Research and Analytical Papers* (London: FCO, 2001).
Lee, J.M. 'Public administration and official history', *Public Administration*, 54 (1976).
Louis, W.R. *The British Empire in the Middle East, 1945–1951: Arab Nationalism, the United States and Postwar Imperialism* (Oxford: Clarendon Press, 1984).
—— 'Mussaddiq and the dilemmas of British imperialism', in J.A. Bill and W.R. Louis (eds), *Mussaddiq, Iranian Nationalism, and Oil* (London: I.B. Tauris, 1988).
—— 'The British withdrawal from the Gulf, 1967–71', *The Journal of Imperial and Commonwealth History*, 31 (2003).
—— 'Britain and the overthrow of the Mosaddeq government', in M.J. Gasiorowski and M. Byrne (eds), *Mohammad Mosaddeq and the 1953 Coup in Iran* (Syracuse: Syracuse University Press, 2004).
Lucas, W.S. *Divided we Stand: Britain, the US and the Suez Crisis* (London: Sceptre, 1996).

Macdonald, S. *Rolling the Iron Dice: Historical Analogies and Decisions to Use Military Force in Regional Contingencies* (Westport, CT: Greenwood, 2000).
Macleod, R. (ed.), *Government and Expertise: Specialists, Administrators and Professionals, 1860–1919* (Cambridge: Cambridge University Press, 1988).
Mandler, P. *History and National Life* (London: Profile Books, 2002).
Mangold, P. *Success and Failure in British Foreign Policy: Evaluating the Record, 1900–2000* (Basingstoke: Palgrave Macmillan, 2001).
Marsh, S. 'HMG, AIOC and the Anglo-Iranian oil crisis: in defence of Anglo-Iranian', *Diplomacy and Statecraft*, 12 (2001).
—— *Anglo-American Relations and Cold War Oil: Crisis in Iran* (Basingstoke: Palgrave Macmillan, 2003).
Marwick, A. *The New Nature of History: Knowledge, Evidence, Language* (Basingstoke: Palgrave Macmillan, 2001).
May, E.R. *"Lessons" of the Past: The Use and Misuse of History in American Foreign Policy* (New York: Oxford University Press, 1973).
Nailor, P. *Learning from Precedent in Whitehall* (London: ICBH/RIPA, 1991).
Neustadt, R.E. and May, E.R. *Thinking in Time: The Uses of History for Decision Makers* (New York: The Free Press, 1986).
Nicholas, H.G. 'Foreign historians get first say', *The Times*, 19 June 1962.
Onslow, S. ' "Battlelines for Suez": The Abadan Crisis of 1951 and the formation of the Suez Group', *Contemporary British History*, 17 (2003).
Palmer, W. *Engagement with the Past: The Lives and Works of the World War II Generation of Historians* (Lexington, Ky.: The University Press of Kentucky, 2001).
Parrott, D. 'European History from the Inside Looking out', *The Guardian*, 7 Nov. 1996.
Peden, G.C. 'Old dogs and new tricks: the British Treasury and Keynesian economics in the 1940s and 1950s', in M.O. Furner and B. Supple (eds) *The State and Economic Knowledge: The American and British Experiences* (Cambridge: Cambridge University Press/Woodrow Wilson International Center for Scholars, 1990).
—— *The Treasury and British Public Policy, 1906–1959* (Oxford: Oxford University Press, 2000).
Pemberton, H. *Policy Learning and British Governance in the 1960s* (Basingstoke: Palgrave Macmillan, 2004).
Playfair, Sir E. 'Who are the policy makers? Minister or civil servant. 2. Civil servant', *Public Administration*, 43 (1964).
Pressnell, L.S. *External Economic Policy since the War*, vol. 1 (London: HMSO, 1986).
Record, J. *Making War, Thinking History: Munich, Vietnam and Presidential Uses of Force from Korea to Kosovo* (Annapolis: Naval Institute Press, 2002).
Roberts, A. 'An inadvertent history lesson', *Evening Standard*, 29 Oct. 1994.
—— 'Betrayal of the brave at Suez', *Sunday Times*, 20 Oct. 1996.
Rock, S.R. *Appeasement in International Politics* (Lexington, Ky.: The University Press of Kentucky, 2000).
Roseveare, H. *The Treasury: The Evolution of a British Institution* (London: Allen Lane, The Penguin Press, 1969).
Roskill, S.W. 'Some reasons for official history', in R. Higham (ed.), *Official Histories: Essays and Bibliographies from around the World* (Manhattan, Kansas: Kansas State University Library, 1970).

Select Bibliography 299

Savage, C.I. *Inland Transport* (London: HMSO, 1957).
Seldon, A. *Blair* (London: Free Press, 2004).
Shlaim, A. 'The protocol of Sèvres, 1956: anatomy of a war plot', *International Affairs*, 73 (1997).
Skinner, Q. and Price, R. (eds), *Machiavelli, the Prince* (Cambridge: Cambridge University Press, 1988).
Smith, A. 'Tony Blair, the Iraq War and a sense of history', *The Historian*, 79 (2003).
Smith, R. 'Introduction', in J. Zametica (ed.), *British Officials and British Foreign Policy, 1945–50* (Leicester: Leicester University Press, 1990).
Smith, S. *Britain's Revival and Fall in the Gulf: Kuwait, Bahrain, Qatar and the Trucial States, 1950–1971* (London: RoutledgeCurzon, 2004).
Speller, I. *The role of Amphibious Warfare in British Defence policy, 1945–56* (Basingstoke: Palgrave Macmillan, 2001).
—— ' "A splutter of musketry?": the British military response to the Anglo-Iranian oil dispute, 1951', *Contemporary British History*, 17 (2003).
Staples, A.L.S. 'Seeing diplomacy through bankers' eyes: the World Bank, the Anglo-Iranian Oil crisis, and the Aswan High Dam', *Diplomatic History*, 26 (2002).
Steiner, Z. 'On writing international history: chaps, maps and much more', *International Affairs*, 73 (1997).
Steiner, Z. 'The historian and the Foreign Office', in C.R. Hill and P. Beshoff (eds), *Two Worlds of International Relations: Academics, Practitioners and the Trade in Ideas* (London: Routledge/LSE, 1994).
Stevens, Sir R. *Middle East Oil in International Relations* (Leeds: Leeds University Press, 1973).
Strang, Lord. *Britain in World Affairs: A Survey of Fluctuations in British Power and Influence, Henry VIII to Elizabeth II* (London: Faber & Faber and Andre Deutsch, 1961).
Taylor, A.J.P. 'Men of 1862: Napoleon III', in C. Wrigley (ed.), *A.J.P. Taylor, From Napoleon to the Second International: Essays on Nineteenth-century Europe* (London: Hamish Hamilton, 1993).
Theakston, K. *Leadership in Whitehall* (Basingstoke: Macmillan, 1999).
Thompson, P. *The Voice of the Past: Oral History*, 2nd edn (Oxford: Oxford University Press, 1988).
Thorpe, D.R. *Alec Douglas-Home* (London: Sinclair-Stevenson, 1996).
Tosh, J. *The Pursuit of History: Aims, Methods and New Directions in the Study of Modern History*, 3rd edn (Harlow: Longman, 1999).
—— (ed.), *Historians on History* (Harlow: Longman, 2000).
Tusa, J. 'A deep and continuing use of history', in D. Cannadine (ed.), *History and the Media* (Basingstoke: Palgrave Macmillan, 2004).
Venn, F. *Oil Diplomacy in the Twentieth Century* (Basingstoke: Macmillan, 1986).
Verbeek, B. *Decision-making in Great Britain during the Suez Crisis: Small Groups and a Persistent Leader* (Aldershot: Ashgate, 2003).
Wallace, W. *The Foreign Policy Process in Britain* (London: Royal Institute of International Affairs, 1975).
Wass, D. *Government and the Governed: BBC Reith Lectures 1983* (London: Routledge & Kegan Paul, 1983).
Watt, D.C. *Personalities and Policies: Studies in the Formulation of British Foreign Policy in the Twentieth Century* (London: Longmans, 1965).

—— 'Restrictions on research: the fifty-year rule and British foreign policy', *International Affairs*, 41 (1965).
—— 'Contemporary history: problems and perspectives', *Journal of the Society of Archivists*, III (1965–69).
—— 'The political misuse of history', *Trends in Historical Revisionism: History as a Political Device* (London: Centre for Contemporary Studies, 1985).
Webster, C. *The Health Services since the War: Problems of Health Care, the National Health Service before 1957*, vol. I (London: HMSO, 1988).
—— *The Health Services Since the War: Government and Health Care, The National Health Service, 1958–1979*, vol. II (London: HMSO, 1996).
White, S. 'Nuclear historian', *New Scientist*, 28 Nov. 1974.
Wilber, D.N. *Clandestine Service History: Overthrow of Premier Mossadegh of Iran, November 1952–August 1953* (Washington DC: CIA, Mar. 1954): http://www.nytimes.com/library/world/mideast/041600iran-cia-index.html, accessed 24 Apr. 2004.
—— *Adventures in the Middle East: Excursions and Incursions* (Princeton, NJ: Darwin, 1986).
Woodward, L. 'The study of contemporary history', *Journal of Contemporary History*, 1 (1966).
Woodward, Sir L. *British Foreign Policy in the Second World War* (London: HMSO, 1962).
—— *British Foreign Policy in the Second World War*, vols. I–V (London: HMSO, 1970–76).
Wrigley, C. (ed.), *A.J.P. Taylor: British Prime Ministers and Other Essays* (London: Penguin, 1999).
Young, J.W. *Britain and the World in the Twentieth Century* (London: Arnold, 1997).
—— *The Labour Governments, 1964–1970: International Policy*, vol. 2 (Manchester: Manchester University Press, 2003).
Young, J. 'Conclusion', in S. Kelly and A. Gorst (eds), *Whitehall and the Suez Crisis* (London: Frank Cass, 2000).

Theses

Thornhill, M.T. 'Britain and the Egyptian question, 1950–2' (D.Phil. thesis, Oxford, 1995).

Other

'Document: A very British coup', *BBC Radio Four*, 22 Aug. 2005.
Goldman, S. 'Clarke, Sir Richard William Barnes (1910–1975)', *Oxford Dictionary of National Biography* (Oxford: Oxford University Press, 2004): http://www.oxforddnb.com/view/article/30938, accessed 26 Oct. 2004.
Gowing, M. *Interviews with Historians: Margaret Gowing with Charles Webster* (London: Institute of Historical Research, 1988).
'The fog of war: eleven lessons from the life of Robert S. McNamara', *BBC Two Television*, 15 May 2005.

Index

Note: References to boxes and tables are in bold.

Abadan crisis history, 84, 193–7, 200–10, 211–19, 222, 224–6, 228, 229–35, 237–8, 244, 246, 268n54
Abbot, Elsie (1907–1983), 48, 53, 54, 60, 63, 81, 83, 94–6, 100, 115, 137, 139, 144, 189, 245
Acheson, Dean (1893–1971), 222, 237, 287n54
Acts of God history (1957), 56–7, 70, 83, 171, 175
administrators writing histories, 31, 32–3, 59, 62, 78–9, 82, 84, 90, 249–50
  see also Ogilvy-Webb, Arthur Keith (James) (1915–1988); retired civil servants
Advisory Council on Public Records (ACPR), 12, 38, 39, 41
Afghanistan, 7
aircraft purchasing history (1965), 101, 102–10, 140, 146, **175**, 184
Airey, Lawrence (1926–2001), 156–7
Allen, Philip, 138
Allen, Sir Douglas, later Lord Croham, 67, 97, 151
aluminium smelter history (1969), 156–7, 172, 277n64
Amery, Julian (1919–1996), 227
Anglo-Iranian Oil Company (AIOC, later British Petroleum), 84–5, 195–6, 202, 207–8, 212, 214, 216
appeasement, 7–11, 194, 196, 206, 217–18, 219, 221
Arab–Israeli War (1967), 44
Aramco, 207
Armstrong, Sir William (1915–1980), 53, 81, 93, 95, 118, 137, 139, 143–4, 151–2, 179
Ashworth, William, 25
Atkinson, F.J., 121

atomic energy histories, 3, 12, 46, 73, 110–11, 156, 279n4
Attlee, Lord Clement (1883–1967), 17, 30, 44, 98, 197, 200, 204, 206, 212, 215, 282n17, 286n23
Avon, Lord, *see* Eden, Anthony (1897–1977), Lord Avon (1961)

Baldwin, F.R., 121
Balogh, Thomas (1905–1985), 143
Bancroft, Sir Ian (1922–1996), 13, 38, 53, 139
Banks, Terri, 122, **123**, 273n13
Barratt, F. Russell, 121, 128–9, 164, 273n39
BBC (British Broadcasting Corporation), 197, 228
BEA (British European Airways), 103, 106
Behrens, Catherine Betty (1904–1989), 25, 31
Bell, G., 60, 84
Bevin, Ernest (1881–1951), 207, 212, 215, 216, 242
Black, Jeremy, 4, 5
Blair, Tony, 10, 11
BOAC (British Overseas Airways Corporation), 103, 105, 106
Booth, Alan, 249
Bretherton, Russell (1906–1991), 92, 122, 129, 153–4, 161, 167
Bretton Woods history (1976), 190
Bridges, Lord Edward (1892–1969), 20, 25, 26, 30, 182
Britain
  decline, 9, 18, 110, 133, 143, 194, 203–4, 205, 211, 217, 220, 225–6
  role in the world, 18, 19, 237–8
  "special relationship" with USA, 9, 12, 204–8, 225–6, 233

301

302 Index

Britain – *continued*
see also government departments;
Suez
British Petroleum Company (BP), *see*
Anglo-Iranian Oil Company
(AIOC, later British Petroleum)
Brook, Sir Norman, later Lord
Normanbrook (1902–1967), 12,
14, 17, 18, 23–36, 47, 53, 55–6,
60–4, 68, 69–70, 71, 74, 81,
86–9, 90, 92, 93, 102, 118,
144, 164, 165, 169, 180, 183,
186, 188–9, 190, 197, 198,
200, 201, 228, 231, 234,
241–6, 251, 263n125
Brown, George (1914–1985), 44
Bullock, Lord Alan (1914–2004),
37, 242–3
Burgess, Guy (1911–1963), 215, 231
Burma (Myanmar), 214
Burmah Oil Company, 214, 285n13
Butler, Rohan (1917–1996), 43, 47,
112, 139, 196, 197–210, 211–28,
229–34, 235–7, 244, 246,
248, 284n50
Butler, Sir James R.M. (1889–1975), 25
Butterfield, Sir Herbert (1900–1979),
28, 39

Cabinet Future Planning Working
Group, 214
Cabinet Office, including Historical
Section, 11, 17, 18, 19, 22, 23,
25, 29, 32–4, 35, 36, 37, 38, 39,
40, 41–2, 43, 45, 46, 60, 64, 69,
122, 137, 138, 155, 171, 173,
188, 190, 202, 246
Caccia, Harold (1905–1990), 213–14,
218–20, 222, 224
Cairncross, Alec (1911–1998), 77, 104,
138, 182, 277n64
Carey, Roger, 255n49
Carlton, David, 9
Cary, Michael (1917–1976), 37, 38
"Cassandra" (William Connor,
1909–1967), 34
Central Intelligence Agency (CIA),
195, 196, 202, 205, 236
Central Statistical Office, 145

Centre for Contemporary British
History, 5
Chamberlain, Neville (1869–1940),
8–10
Chapman, Richard, 20
Cherry, Gordon, 44, 46
Chester, D. Norman, 44, 46, 61
Chiefs of Staff, 30
Child, Clifton, 39, 43
China, 221
Choiseul, Duke of, 230
Churchill, Sir Winston (1874–1965),
9, 30, 195, 197, 216, 233
Civil Service
College, 13, 17
superannuation history (1960),
86, 171
see also Fulton Report (1968);
government departments;
retired civil servants;
staffing, staff development and
training
Clarke, Sir Richard (1910–1975), 59,
61–3, 69, 70, 71, 72–84, 87–8,
89–90, 93, 97–8, 99, 100, 101,
104, 106–7, 109, 115, 116, 119,
120, 123, 125, 138, 139, 140, 153,
160, 169, 172, 177, 178–9, 188–9,
243, 244, 275n80
Cold War, 204, 206, 207, 215, 227
Collier, A. James, 54, 116, 118–19,
121, 122–3, **124**, 127–8, 130–1,
138–42, 144–5, 146–52, 153, 158,
160, 162, 183, 185, 186, 247
colonial aid history (1959), 59, 61,
64–8, 69–70, 71, 74, 189
Comet aircraft crashes, 103
Common Market, *see* European
Economic Community histories
(1966 and 1972)
Commonwealth Institute History
(1968), 111, 129, **129**,
131, 133–4
contemporary history, 23, 36
convertibility history (1962), 74, 86–7
Cook, Robin (1946–2005), 11
Copeman, H.A., 121
counterfactual history, 87, 236
Couzens, Kenneth, 121, 187

Crane, G., 246
Cuban missiles crisis (1962), 213, 215, 236, 286n19
Cullingworth, J.B., 44, 46

Daily Mirror, 34
Daily Telegraph, 196
Dalton, Hugh (1887–1962), 204, 286n23
Day, John, 137
de Gaulle, General Charles (1890–1970), 113, 114, 115, 200, 217, 218, 219, 223, 238
Dean, Sir Patrick (1909–1994), 220, 221
debt situations history (1973), 128, 160, 164
decline, *see* Britain, decline
defence expenditure history (1976), 164
Dennis, Catherine, 122, **123**, 127–8, 131, 134–7, 155, 158, 167–8, 190, 273n15
devaluation crisis (1967), 146, **147–8**
Dickie, John, 193–4
Dixon, Sir Pierson (1904–1965), 113
Dockrill, Saki, 223
Documents on British Foreign Policy, 22, 39, 41, 42–3, 137, 138, **171**, 197, 198–9, 201, 226, 228
Douglas-Home, Sir Alec, Lord Home (1903–1995), 36, 38, 39, 43, 211, 213, 217–18, 220, 223–4, 227, 232, 237, 250, 262n113
Dow, J.C.R., 272n116
Downing Street rebuilding history (1968), 111, 120, **129**, 129, 131–3, 134, 158n175
Duncan report (1969), 19
Dunnett, Sir James (1914–1997), 93, 98

East Coast floods (1953, 1978), 55, 56–7, 63, 70–1
Eccles, Sir David (1904–1999), 113
economic planning history (1964), 75, 81, 83, 97–100, 106, 123, 139, **175**

economists and policy, *see* expertise in government
Eden, Anthony (1897–1977), Lord Avon (1961), 8–9, 11, 36, 45, 113, 194, 195, 200, 205–6, 207, 215, 216, 225, 233, 234, 254–5n35, 262n125
Egypt, 8–9, 135, 194, 205–6, 212, 222, 224–6, 233–4, 235
Ellis-Rees, Sir Hugh, 86–7, 90
Elton, Sir Geoffrey (1921–1994), 5
European Economic Community histories (1966 and 1972), 9, 73, 92, 97, 99, 112–15, 177, 211, 218, 219, 227, 236–7, 246, 250
Evans, Richard, 20
exchange control histories, 85, 131, 134–7, 138, 161, 183
expertise in government, 3, 13, 17, 18, 27, 78, 80, 86, 116, 143, 153, 155, 174, 182, 183, 190
external economic policy histories, 138, 161, 249, 275n80

Fabian Society, 143
Fairfields shipyards history (1966), 127, 128, 129, **129**
Falklands War (1982), 9–10
Ferguson, Niall, 4
Festival Gardens history (1957), 33, 55, 56, 57–8, 70, 88
Figgures, Frank (1910–1990), 73
financial rescues history (1976), 167–8
Foot, Michael, 43
Foreign and Commonwealth Office, *see* Foreign Office (later Foreign and Commonwealth Office)
Foreign Office (later Foreign and Commonwealth Office), 18, 19, 23, 35, 36, 42–3, 47, 84, 112–15, 135, 193–238, 245, 246, 248
circulation of histories, 212, 227, 244–5
planning, 208, 222–3, 225
publications, 42–3, 198–200, 209–10, 226–8, 246, 248; *see also Documents on British Foreign Policy*

Foreign Office – *continued*
  Research department, 39, 197, 198
  Steering Committee, 197, 200–2, 209, 222–3
  using history, 197–8, 209–10, 211–38, 250–1
Forsyth, Miss J., 182
Forward, N., 152, 153, 184
France, 9, 113, 114, 199–200, 212, 217, 218–19, 221, 222, 225, 238
France, Arnold (1911–1998), 146
France, Chris, 70
Franks, Susan, **123**, 125, 140, 145, **147–8**
Fulton Report (1968), 19, 143–4, 151, 153, 155, 172, 174, 183, 246
functional history, 6, 24, 45, 75, 84, 100, 124, 140–1, 163, 170, 172, 186, 201, 217, 232, 249
"funding experience", 17, 23–4, 25, 26, 32, 33, 35, 36, 53–4, 61, 62, 63, 65, 68, 69, 72, 75, 79, 81–2, 84, 87, 88–91, 92–3, 94–6, 100, 102, 108, 110–11, 115–17, 118, 121, 122, 124, 127, 130, 131, 137–42, 144, 146, 153, 155, 156, 158, 159, 160, 161, 163, 165, 169, 170–90, **171**, **175–6**, 197, 200–1, 208, 209, 226, 228, 241, 243–4, 245–7, 248, 250

Gaddis, John Lewis, 16
Gaitskell, Hugh (1906–1963), 204
Gardiner, Lord (1900–1990), 40
German support costs, 63, 73, 178
Glasgow Herald, 34
Glover, A., 134–5
Goldsworthy, David, 194–5
Gordon Walker, Patrick (1907–1980), 43
Gore-Booth, Sir Paul (1909–1984), 43, 220, 221, 224, 226
government departments
  Admiralty, 92–3, 243
  Agriculture, Fisheries and Food (MAFF), 112, 113
  Air, 122, 244, 273n14
  Aviation, 103–4, 105, 119
  Board of Trade, 11, 36, 92, 98, 106, 112, 113, 135, 224, 246
  Civil Service Department (CSD), 19, 143–4, 151–3, 154, 155, 162, 177, 251
  Colonial Office, 27, 64, 112
  Commonwealth Relations Office, 19, 112
  Economic Affairs (DEA), 19, 105, 106, 123, 128, 135
  Economic Warfare, 27
  Education and Science (DES), 246
  Environment, 71
  Fuel and Power, 202, 207
  Health, 35, 145, 146, **147–8**, 150, 151
  Housing and Local Government (MHLG), 35–6, 57, 63–4, 204, 246
  Labour, 76, 77–8, 98
  Overseas Development, 135, 246
  Pensions and National Insurance (MPNI), 35, 36
  Power, 35, 107, 109
  Production, 27
  Technology, 106, 153, 155
  Transport, 36, 93, 170, 246–7
  War Office, 35, 36
  Works/Public Building and Works, 35, 58, 132
  see also Cabinet Office, including Historical Section; Foreign Office (later Foreign and Commonwealth Office); Service departments and history; Treasury
Gowing, Margaret (1921–1998), 3, 11–15, 25–6, 27, 30–1, 32–3, 34, 36, 39, 40, 46, 47, 48, 55–71, 72, 74–5, 83, 86, 90, 171, 180, 188–9, 226, 241–2, 248, 249, 251
  Rede lecture (1978), 3, 11, 13, 20, 70, 241–2
Granger-Taylor, Barbara, 100, 102–11, 116, 122, **123**, 125, 126, 127–8, 140, 155, 156, 158, 160
Greenhill, Lord Denis (1913–2000), 237
Grey, Jeffrey, 23

Index

Grigg Committee (1952–1954), 12, 33
Grimond, Jo (1913–1993), 41, 262n96

Hall, Sir Robert (1901–1988), 59, 77, 272n116
Hammond, R.J., 260n52
Hancock, Sir David, 165–8, 181, 188, 189–90, 258n9
Hancock, W. Keith (1898–1988), 11, 25–33, 48–9, 61, 88, 138, 242, 258n9
Hankey, Lord Robert, 220, 221
Hannay, David, 227, 236
Hansford, J., 89
Harris, Jose, 17
Hartcup, Guy, 111, 116, 120, 122, **123**, 125, 126, 127–8, 131–4, 150, 154, 157–8, 161, 164, 167–8, 176–7, 188, 249, 273n14
Hay, Denys (1915–1994), 45
Heath, Edward (1916–2005), 41, 42, 46, 112, 114, 223, 224, 262n96, 272n103
Helsby, Sir Laurence (1908–1978), 53, 77–8, 93, 95, 98, 104, 118, 120–1, 137, 139, 143
Henderson, David, 47, 103–4, 143, 245, 270n50, 280n55
Henley, Douglas, 70, 103, 104, 106, **124**, 155, 156, 158, 162–4, 247, 250
Hennessy, Peter, 3, 9, 11, 17, 20, 67, 169
Hinsley, Francis H. (1918–1998), 37, 259n25
Hirsch, Fred, 162, 166
History and Policy website, 5, 20
Hitler, Adolf (1889–1945), 8, 194, 233
Hobsbawm, Eric, 7–8
Holmans, Alan, 116, 145, 148, 162, 272n116
Home, Lord, *see* Douglas-Home, Sir Alec, Lord Home (1903–1995)
Hooper, Robin, 200, 201
Hopkin, Sir Bryan, 77, 166, 169
Hoskyns, Sir John, 47
Howard, Michael, 37, 260n49

Hoyer Millar, Sir Frederick, later Lord Inchyra (1900–1989), 197, 201, 213
Hunt, Sir John, 47, 102, 104, 105, 106, 109–10, 121, 140, 163–4, 181, 188–9, 250
Hurstfield, Joel (1911–1980), 27

incomes policy histories, 136, 138, 139
see also wages policy histories
indexing, 62, 95, 116, 120, 125, 126, 129, 130, 140, 144, 158, 160, 185, 244
India, 23, 44, 129, 203, 204, 262n115
intelligence services, 195, 196, 202, 205, 206, 208
see also Central Intelligence Agency (CIA)
Iran, 193–7, 200–10, **203**, 211–21, 225, 228, 233, 235–6, 246, 281n1, 285n8
coup (1953), 195, 196, 202, 205, 228, 236, 286n16
Shah, 193–4, 195, 200, 228
Iraq, 7, 205
war (2003), 7, 10–11, 20, 228

Jebb, Gladwyn (1900–1996), 200
Johnson, President Lyndon B. (1908–1973), 209
Johnston, M.E., 84
Johnston, Sir Alexander (1905–1994), 55–6, 60, 61, 67, 69
Joll, James (1918–1994), 108
Jolley, J.L., 158
Jordan-Moss, Nicholas, 144, 148–50, 159, 169, 185–6
Jowitt, Lord (1885–1957), 204

Katyn massacre history (1973), 226–7, 228, 246, 288n81
Keeling, C., 98, 177
Kelley, Miss J., 157
Kemp, P.K., 19, 260n59
Kennedy, President John F.K. (1917–1963), 38, 209
Khomeini, Ayatollah (1902–1989), 194
King, K.T., **124**, 130

Kirkpatrick, Sir Ivone
(1897–1964), 218
Korean War (1950–1953), 201,
204, 215, 231
Kosovo, 10
Kuwait, 212, 222, 287n52
Kyle, Keith, 233

Lamont, William, 6
Lee, J. Michael, 48, 250
Lee, Sir Frank (1903–1971), 80, 81,
90, 93
"lessons of history", 3, 5, 6, 7–11, 12,
15–16, 17, 20–1, 24, 26, 35, 36,
45, 54, 56–8, 60, 62–3, 68, 73, 76,
79–82, 91, 93, 96, 99, 103–5,
107–8, 109–10, 112–15, 119–20,
121, 127–9, 131–4, 136–7, 140,
144–6, 149–51, 157, 162, 163,
168, 171, 173–7, 179, 183, 184,
187–9, 193–4, 196, 200, 202–8,
203, 209–10, 212–28, 229, 233–5,
236–7, 241–5, 247–51
see also memory, collective and
departmental
Littler, J.G., 135
Littler, Shirley, 65–7, 69, 189
Lloyd, Selwyn (1904–1978), 76, 201
London weighting history (1969),
128–9, **129**, **176**, 273n39
Lord Croham, *see* Allen, Sir Douglas,
later Lord Croham
Louis, William Roger, 194, 196,
197, 233
Lucas, Christopher, 112–14, 272n103
Lucas, J.E., 84–5

Machiavelli, Niccolo (1469–1527), 6
McIndoe, W., 41, 43
Maclean, Donald (1913–1983),
215, 231
Macmillan, Harold, Lord Stockton
(1894–1986), 38, 39, 113, 204,
264n18
MacNalty, Sir Arthur S.
(1880–1969), 25
McNamara, Robert, 209
Makins, Sir Roger, later Lord Sherfield
(1904–1996), 233–4, 265n54

Mansergh, P. Nicholas
(1910–1991), 44
Mantaro hydroelectric history (1966),
126, **129**, 160
Marwick, Arthur, 20
Mason, Frederick, 212–13, 233
Maud, John (1906–1982), 221, 222
Maude, E., 77, 82, 155, 158, 248
May, Ernest, 15, 234, 244
media and history, 3, 4, 22, 33, 34,
46, 259n24
Medlicott, William N. (1900–1987),
25, 27, 258n13, 259n34,
260n52
memoirs, 8, 22, 23, 36, 39, 46,
205, 234
memory, collective and departmental,
3, 5, 7, 14, 18, 48, 54, 62, 63,
64, 69–71, 73, 75, 79–80, 85,
86, 90, 92, 94, 101, 107, 110,
112, 114, 115, 135–6, 138,
149, 170, 172, 174–5, 185,
190, 201, 212, 227, 231,
235, 241, 243–4, 248
see also "lessons of history"
MI6, *see* intelligence services
Middleton, Peter, 174
Military, *see* Chiefs of Staff;
government departments;
Service departments and history
Millard, Guy, 225, 237–8
Milne, Sir David (1896–1972), 88
Milosevic, Slobodan (1941–2006), 10
Mitchell, Derek, 87, 89, 178–9
monetary histories, 56, 59, 138, 264n10
Morgan, David J., 44, 68
Morrison, Herbert (1888–1965),
204, 207, 208, 209, 215, 216,
233, 286n23
Mossadegh, Mohammad (1882–1967),
195, 205, 206, 207, 213, 215, 233,
236, 237, 289n27
Munich analogy, 8–11, 20, 195,
196, 234–5
Mussolini, Benito (1883–1945), 8, 233

Nailor, Peter (1928–1996), 20, 241
Napoleon III, Emperor
(1808–1873), 221

Index 307

Nasser, Gamal Abdel (1918–1970), 8–9, 194, 225, 233, 289n27
National Economic Development Council ("Neddy"), 18, 98
National Land Fund history, 111, **129**, 131, 134, 274n57
National Research and Development Corporation history (1966), 126, **129**
nationalized industries histories, 56, 73, 100, 101, 102, 106–10, 125, 138, 156, **176**
  see also Chester, D. Norman
Neustadt, Richard (1919–2003), 15, 234, 244
Nicholas, Herbert G., 33, 38, 39
Nicholls, P., 64, 67, 74
Nicholls, Sir John, 47, 223
Noble, Sir Andrew, 236
Northedge, F.S., 255n49
Nunn, Jean (1916–1982), 17
Nutting, Anthony (1920–1999), 9, 45

official histories, 11–12, 13–14, 22, 23, 24, 28–34, 36, 38, 45–6, 47–9, 56, 69, 76, 80, 138, 170–1, **171**, 173, 190, 198–9, 229, 245, 248, 279n29
  intelligence histories, 46, 259n25
  peacetime histories, 12, 24, 32, 37–42, 43–6, 48, 53–4, 68, 86, 88, 137–9, 171, **171**, 226, 227, 228, 245, 251, 276n33
  wartime histories, 11, 23–4, 25–35, 41, 43, 45, 46, 87, 88, 97, 137, 171, 199, 209–10, 268n66
official secrecy, 12, 30, 47–8, 81, 109, 119, 249, 263n138, 289n33
Ogilvy-Webb, Arthur Keith (James) (1915–1988), 48, 69, 72, 76–81, 82–4, 88, 90, 97–100, 105, 114, 115, 116–17, 119, 120, 122–3, 125, 127–8, 131, 140–1, 143–6, **147–8**, 150, 152, 153, 154–6, 158, 161, 162, 164–7, 169, 171, 172–3, 174–87, 244, 246, 247, 249, 250, 278n13
  see also administrators writing histories

Ogmore, Lord (1903–1976), 43
O'Neill, Sir Con (1912–1988), 114–15, 227–8, 236, 237, 250
Oppenheimer, Robert, 260n60
oral testimony, 11, 26, 29, 37, 41, 71, 77, 82, 89, 106, 107–8, 173, 175, 190, 202, 216, 230, 231, 235, 248, 284n50, 289n5
Owen, J., 161, 167, 190

Padmore, Sir Thomas (1909–1996), 106, 108, 109
Pakistan, 44, **129**
Palliser, Sir Michael, 193, 223
Palmer, William, 7
Parkes, Sir Roderick, 221
Parliamentary Select Committee on Estimates (1957), 34, 93
Parrott, Cecil, 198, 200, 201, 232
Parsons, Sir Anthony (1922–1996), 193–4, 197, 223
Payton-Smith, D.J., 260n52
Peck, A., 65–7, 189
Peden, George, 20
Pemberton, Hugh, 20, 190, 291n38
Permanent Secretaries Conferences, 22, 92, 93
Persia, *see* Iran
Phelps, A.J., 134
Philby, Kim (1912–1988), 46
planning, *see* economic planning history (1964); Foreign Office (later Foreign and Commonwealth Office), planning
Playfair, Sir Edward (1909–1999), 36, 88
Pliatzky, Leo (1919–1999), 116, 185, 245
Plowden, Lord (1907–2001), 177, 214, 232
  aircraft industry report (1965), 103, 105
  public expenditure report (1961), 19, 72, 93
  representational services overseas report (1964), 19, 197, 214, 216, 222, 223, 232
political vocabulary, 9–11, 20

Postan, Michael, 26, 27, 30
postmodernism, 7
Powell, Sir Richard, 98
prescription charges history (1967), 126, 130, 131, 140, 144–51, **147–8**, 175–6, 181, 273n30, 276n33
Pressnell, Leslie, 167, 249, 275n80
Price, Christopher, 14
Privy Counsellors Group on official peacetime histories, 40, 42, 43, 45
public expenditure histories (1971), 157
Public Expenditure Survey Committee (PESC), 71, 73, 150
public history, 4
Public Record Office (now called The National Archives), 12, 32, 48
public records, 12, 14–15, 22, 23, 26, 29, 30, 33, 36–41, 44, 46, 47–8, 53, 73, 76, 78, 80, 89, 190, 194, 200, 202, 226, 227, 231, 237, 248, 249, 279n29
see also Grigg Committee (1952–1954); Thirty Year Rule; Wilson Committee (1978–1981), chaired by Sir Duncan Wilson

Radcliffe Committee, 56, 59, 264n10
Rampton, Jack (1920–1994), 111, 140, 144–5, 248
Rawlinson, Anthony, 98, 134–5, 136–7, 183, 243
refugees, 55
retired civil servants, 35–6, 86–8, 90, 116, 229
Rhodesian sanctions history (1972), 128, 131, 134–7
Rickett, Sir Denis (1907–1997), 88, 178, 268n66
Roberts, Andrew, 7
Roseveare, Henry, 20
Russell-Edmunds, Colonel William, 64, 65, 68, 122, **123**, 127, 160, 162, 164, 265n57

Saudi Arabia, 207
Savage, Christopher, 26, 31
Sayers, Richard (1908–1989), 29, 138, 171, 275n80
Schama, Simon, 4
Service departments and history, 18–19, 35, 42, 260n59
see also Chiefs of Staff; government departments
Sharp, Richard L., 151, 153, 154, 156, 162, 164, 165, 172, 180, 185, 186, 248–9, 250
Shinwell, Emanuel (1884–1986), 233
Shuckburgh, Sir John (1877–1953), 27
Smith, W., 159
Social Science Research Council (now called the ESRC), 48
Soviet Union, 116, 199, 203, 213, 215, 220, 227, 238, 286n19
Speller, Ian, 233
staffing, staff development and training, 14, 17, 35, 36, 60, 63, 65, 74, 83, 86–8, 89–90, 94, 96, 111, 116, 122, 143–4, 150–1, 152, 159, 162, 165, 169, 170, 172, 175, 181, 183, 186, 201, 245
see also Civil Service; retired civil servants
Starkey, David, 4
Steiner, Zara, 16, 194, 234, 244
sterling balances history (1972), 247
Stevens, Sir Roger (1906–1980), 195, 212
Stevenson, Sir Matthew (1910–1981), 77, 82, 106–8, 109
Stewart, Michael (1906–1990), 47, 224, 232
Strang, Lord (1893–1978), 15, 206–7, 214–19, 221, 229–32, 285n16
Straw, Jack, 10, 228
Stuart, M., 159, 245
Suez
crisis (1956), 8–9, 11, 20, 36, 44–5, 47, 55, 84, 113, 135, 194–5, 201, 203, 205, 206, 211, 213, 219, 221–2, 224–6, 233–4, 254–5n35, 288n70
East of Suez, 146, 223

Index   309

Sugars, R.C., 86, 90
Symons, Ronald, 85, 123, 161, 162, 167, 247

Taylor, A.J.P. (1906–1990), 199, 253n16
Taylor, A.W., 85
Taylor, L.J., 94
terrorism 9/11 attack in USA, 10
Thatcher, Margaret, 9
Thirty Year Rule, 20, 23, 38, 39–40, 42, 43, 46, 47–8, 137–8, 261n93, 262n113
   historians's campaign to reduce the closed period, 23, 37–8, 39–40, 41, 45
Thomson, David (1912–1970), 223
Thucydides, 6
Times, The, 3, 11, 20, 196, 232
Titmuss, Richard (1907–1973), 26, 29, 30, 31, 259n27
Tosh, John, 5, **6**, 20
town and country planning history, 138
Treasury, 12, 18–19, 36, 196, 202, 207, 216, 217, 243–51
   divisions: Agriculture, Towns and Transport division (AT), 125, 127, **129**, 129, 130, 154, 185, 187; Civil Pay division (CP), 128–9, **129**; Defence policy and Materiel division (DM), 103, 125; Finance divisions, 112, 125, **129**, 131, 134–7; General Expenditure division (GE), 157; HOPS (Home and Overseas Planning Staff), 59, 61–3, 72, 73–4, 75, 83, 88, 90, 178–9; Imperial and Finance division (IF), 59, 64–8, 69, 74; Industry and Agriculture division (IA), 167; Organisation and Methods division, 89, 171; Overseas Finance division (OF), 84–5, 88, 160, 167; Public Enterprises division (PE), 100–11, 115, 116, 156–8, 170; Social Services division (SS), 89, 94, 111, 122, 125, 126, 128, **129**, 130, 131–4, 140, 144–50, **147–8**, 159, 185–6, 245; Trade and Industry division (TI), 183
   historical activities: circulation of histories, 56, 61, 69, 76, 79, 81, 85, 90, 98, 102, 103–4, 106, 107, 112, 113–14, 116, 119, 127, 134, 141, 145, 146, **147–8**, 150–1, 177–8, 185, 244, 245; divisional notes, 72, 74, 89, 94, 95, 101, 102, 116, 124, 139, 150, 156–8, 159, 170–2, **171**, 174, 190; Historians's Sub-Committee (HSC), 121, **124**, 125–6, 128–9, 131, 139, 152, 153, 155, 160; "seeded files", 62–3, 72, 73–4, 75, 84, 89, 90, 94, 95, 101, 102, 111, 116, 124, 139, 150, 159, 170–2, **171**, 178–9, 185, 190, 243; Treasury Historical Committee (THC), 53, 111, 118–31, **124**, 137, 139–42, 144–5, 146, 151–2, 155, 158, 160, 161–3, 168–9, 170, 180, 181, 185, 189; Treasury Historical Memoranda (THMs), 20, 33, 56–8, 60–1, 62, 67–8, 69–71, 75, 76, 83–4, 85, 86, 88, 91, 94–5, 98, 101, 102, 104–5, 109, 110–12, 113–15, 119, 125, 136, 144, **147–8**, 161, 164, 167, 168–9, 170–1, **171**, 173–8, **175–6**, 180, 181–6, 189–90, 244–5, 247–51, 252, 291n38; Treasury Historical Section (THS), 12, 13, 20, 23, 48, 53, 90, 118, 121, 122–3, 143, 152, 154, 155–6, 157, 160, 161–9, 170–1, 172, 180–1, 185–90, 245, 249–51; using history, 12, 14–15, 20, 33, 35, 36, 47–8, 53–4, 68–71, 75–6, 77–8, 79, 82, 84–5, 88–9, 90–1, 95, 104–5, 108, 116–17, 118–20, 124, 128, 130–1, 136, 139, 144–52, **147–8**, 154, 158, 159, 163–5, 168–9, 172–3, 174, 179–81, 182–4, 187–90, 245, 247–51; *see also* indexing

Treasury – *continued*
  Management Review (1974–1975), 165, 166, 188
  reorganization, 19, 93–6, 115, 143–4, 155, 165
Trend, Burke (1914–1987), 22, 25, 28, 32, 33, 36–41, 46, 47, 69, 93, 98, 163, 188–9, 260n55
Trevor-Roper, Hugh, later Lord Dacre (1914–2003), 13
Troutbeck, Sir John (1894–1971), 205
Truman Doctrine (1947), 205
Truman, D., 162–3
TSR2 aircraft history, 128, 189
Tusa, John, 20–1

United Kingdom Atomic Energy Authority (UKAEA), 12, 33, 39, 40, 64–5, 72, 157, 242
United Nations (UN), 196, 212, 218, 221
unspoken assumptions, 77, 87, 97, 99, 100, 108–9, 174, 190, 249
USA, 8, 9, 13, 19, 27, 28, 38, 40, 57, 86–7, 103, 113, 138, 194–6, 199, 203–5, **203**, 212–13, 215, 217, 218, 219, 220, 223, 225–6, 234, 235, 281n3, 285n8, 286n19
  see also Britain, "special relationship" with USA
'usable past', 4, 5, 15–16, 54, 76, 231–2, 242–3

van der Post, Laurens (1906–1996), 9
Vaughan, George, 232
Verbeek, Bertjan, 233
Vinter, Peter (1914–2002), 59–60, 61, 69, 71, 77, 81, 100–7, 108–10, 115, 118, 119, 121, 123, **124**, 125–8, 130–1, 139–41, 145–6, 150, 152, 157, 160, 162, 169, 170, 172, 178, 184, 187–9, 244, 245
von Ranke, Leopold (1795–1886), 6

wages policy histories, 14, 75–81, 90–1, 97, 103, 115, 123, 162, **175**, 182, 187, 189
  see also Hirsch, Fred; incomes policy histories
Wallace, William, 198
Wallinger, Sir Geoffrey (1903–1979), 220, 221
Wass, Sir Douglas, 11, 20, 67, 116, 165–6, 169, 181, 185, 188, 278n13
Watt, Donald Cameron, 6, 38, 39, 234
Watts, R., 167
Way, Sir Richard (1914–1998), 103–4
Weston, K., 116
Widdup, Malcolm, 148, 245
Wilber, Donald, 236, 282n10
Wilson Committee (1978–1981), chaired by Sir Duncan Wilson, 12, 226
Wilson, Harold (1916–1995), 39–42, 43–5, 47, 48, 53, 114, 126, 146, **147–8**, 262n115, 273n30
Woods, A., 246
Woodward, Sir Llewellyn (1890–1971), 25, 42, 43, 45, 47, 199–200, 202, 209–10, 263n125, 283n32, 283n39
World Bank, 196

Yeo, E., **124**
Young, John, 9